IN SEARCH OF R.B. BENNETT

In Search of R.B. Bennett

P.B. WAITE

McGill-Queen's University Press
Montreal & Kingston • London • Ithaca

© McGill-Queen's University Press 2012

ISBN 978-0-7735-3908-2

Legal deposit second quarter 2012
Bibliothèque nationale du Québec

Printed in Canada on acid-free paper that is 100% ancient forest free
(100% post-consumer recycled), processed chlorine free

This book has been published with the help of a grant from the
Canadian Federation for the Humanities and Social Sciences, through
the Aid to Scholarly Publications Program, using funds provided by the
Social Sciences and Humanities Research Council of Canada.

McGill-Queen's University Press acknowledges the support of the
Canada Council for the Arts for our publishing program. We also
acknowledge the financial support of the Government of Canada
through the Canada Book Fund for our publishing activities.

Library and Archives Canada Cataloguing in Publication

Waite, P. B. (Peter Busby), 1922–
    In search of R.B. Bennett / P.B. Waite.

Includes bibliographical references and index.

ISBN 978-0-7735-3908-2

    1. Bennett, R. B. (Richard Bedford), 1870–1947. 2. Canada –
Politics and government – 1930–1935. 3. Prime ministers – Canada –
Biography. 4. Politicians – Alberta – Biography. I. Title.

FC576.B45W33 2012   971.062'3092   C2011-908453-8

Typeset by Jay Tee Graphics Ltd. in 10.5/13 Sabon

Every effort has been made to identify, credit, and obtain publication
rights from copyright holders of illustrations in this book. Notice of
any errors or omissions in this regard will be gratefully received and
corrections will be made in any subsequent editions.

To Lorraine who has done much to help with this book, and whose elegance and beauty has so much enriched this author

Contents

Acknowledgments

First of all, I want to thank Michael Day, who has been responsible for taking the original manuscript through to its publication. He has read and corrected an error-laced text. He became my chief liaison officer with McGill-Queen's while I was out of action with two medical operations. His tenacity, skill with computers, perception, and reverence for the English language have been a wonderful tonic.

A 2010 trip to Mickleham with Michael Day and his wife, Suzanne, who is an artist and photographer, sought out an elderly, retired sexton of St Michael's ninth century church who still remembered RB. The villagers were fond of Bennett. He in turn was good to them. Seeing Suzanne's wonderful photographs of Mickleham helps one to understand RB's delight in living in such serenity.

My research was given a delicious early fillip when Pamela Miller, now the Sir William Osler historian at the McGill Archives, told me about the Hazel Colville Papers. It is the one great love affair of RB's life of which we have any record. RB would have been appalled to know that they have seen the light of day, for he was secretive about his personal life. Hazel Colville kept his letters; he did not keep hers. She willed the Bennett letters to her daughter, Frances Ballantyne, to keep or destroy. Fortunately, Frances chose to keep them. She agreed to meet me, and we talked personally and by letter about her mother and her mother's famous caller. Frances had her own perceptions of RB and a near view of her mother's side of things.

I owe many thanks to Prof. Peter Toner at the history department of the University of New Brunswick, who told me about his aunt, Alice Toner Tompkins. She was secretary to R.B. Hanson, RB's minister of fisheries, and knew both Hazel Colville and RB.

My gratitude also goes to the Library and Archives of Canada whose facilities I have used over the years, especially for their having Mackenzie King's diary online. That I learned this from an Irish colleague, Dr Ged Martin, and my companion, Lorraine, shows how pervasive the readers of our archives can be. To be able to read King's diary from my study in Halifax has been a tremendous advantage.

Finally, I thank all the staff at McGill-Queen's University Press for their tremendous work in bringing this work to fruition.

P.B. Waite
Halifax, Nova Scotia

Preface

R.B. Bennett still inhabits a fairly rugged reputation. He had a brilliant mind and a huge appetite for work, but conjoined to those great strengths was a volatile and sometimes irascible nature. If he set high standards for himself, he tended to apply them to others. Generous to his personal staff, he could be abrupt or bad tempered with colleagues.

Marriage might have softened those sharp edges, but he never married. He was not a misogynist. Medical problems complicate and explain his early relations with women. In 1905 when he was thirty-five, he told his friend Max Aitken, the future Lord Beaverbrook, that he might never marry. But twenty-seven years later, in 1932, he fell in love with a twice-widowed, handsome Montreal lady, Hazel Kemp Colville, some twenty years his junior. A late love affair can be dangerous, delightful; it can be demoralizing. For RB, it was all three. He would probably have married Hazel Colville, had she been willing, but by the summer of 1933 she had backed away. She was rich and comfortable: why should she give up her cocktails, cigarettes, and bridge for RB, who thoroughly deplored every one of those things – and who was never chary about saying so? She was really looking for a husband like her second, Arthur Colville, who died of lung cancer in 1931. Arthur smoked, drank, and did the things a wealthy man about town in Montreal was wont to do. RB's 1933 breakup with Hazel Colville hurt him badly. It was said in Ottawa that she broke his heart. RB's heart was not broken easily. He said in 1935, "I do not deal in regrets," but he did not sound like that in May 1933.

By 1933 he knew his own political regime was not going well either. The Depression was savaging him and his party. Nevertheless, he would do whatever he thought had to be done to keep the Canadian vessel afloat and on course amid brutal gales and rough seas. His achievements were considerable, and they were long lasting. They included the establishment of the CBC and the Bank of Canada, and the beginning of unemployment insurance. He trusted that, when elections came, Canadians would appreciate what he had done. In July 1935 a majority of Canadians did not. That hurt, too.

Historians since have not been all that kind. RB had little tact and less patience with academics or newspapermen. Academics were long-haired idealists, out of touch with reality. As for newspapermen, they should report facts, not fantasies; they should publish truth, not exaggerations. RB had not the slightest qualm about raking editors over the coals for what he conceived were misrepresentations or errors. As a result, his press coverage was not generous. A long and bitter feud with the *Winnipeg Free Press* seriously affected his reputation, not least because of the devastating, clever lampoons by its cartoonist, Arch Dale.

RB had always thrived on politics. In 1892, as a senior law student at Dalhousie University, he was elected premier of the student parliament. His "government" then proceeded to unite the three Maritime provinces and followed up by bringing Newfoundland into Confederation – half a century before it actually happened. However, the Bennett student government was defeated when it tried to give women the vote. Just six years later, in 1898, eighteen months after his arrival in Calgary, RB was elected to the Assembly of the North-West Territories for Calgary.

An intensely private man, RB covered his tracks. After his mother died in 1914, he destroyed all their letters. All the correspondence between him and Jennie Shirreff Eddy also disappeared sometime after her death in 1921; they had been closely associated for over a decade in the E.B. Eddy Company. When in August 1930 RB took over the government of Canada from Mackenzie King, he told King that he kept very little private correspondence. King replied that he kept almost everything. The Bennett Papers and the King Papers are as different as the two men.

Yet the Bennett Papers at the University of New Brunswick are substantial: some 627,000 items, and that does not include reel after microfilm reel of newspaper clippings. That huge collection was mostly due to Max Aitken, Lord Beaverbrook. Aitken was a boy of fifteen when he met Bennett; he learned from him and admired him, and on Bennett's death in 1947 set about gathering up his old friend's papers. Beaverbrook did it the way he did everything else, with assiduity and ruthlessness. He put researchers to work, starting where Bennett died, in Mickleham, Surrey, and his reach kept going, extending to Bennett's parliamentary papers in Ottawa, to Eddy's in Hull, to Calgary. He had everything shipped to the University of New Brunswick in Fredericton.

Bennett's long-serving secretary, Alice Millar, had worked for him since 1914 and was devoted to his memory – too much so. As the Bennett papers came in to Fredericton in 1947–48, she wreaked some havoc, burning in the University of New Brunswick incinerator letters she deemed "unhistorical." A.G. Bailey, a history professor at UNB, rescued some that he found floating among the trees on a windy day. One was a letter from Beaverbrook to Bennett. Beaverbrook himself, an expert at collecting letters, wondered how much of the real Bennett would survive once Alice Millar had pitched out all the "unhistorical" ones.

On the other hand, I have had some luck. My most startling discovery was that of Bennett's 1932 letters to Hazel Colville. It is the one love affair of his that has come to light; it may well have been the supreme one. The Colville letters in Bennett's own hand (and not easy to read) are from an RB in love at sixty-two, an RB unguarded and utterly vulnerable. In November 1932 Hazel deposited the letters under seal at the Royal Trust Montreal for her daughter, Frances Ballantyne. Frances was to destroy them or keep them. Happily, she kept them. Those thirty letters and telegrams are a rare and important glimpse of the inner Bennett.

In 1986 I met James Gray, a great Western historian, who was working on Bennett's Calgary career. Jim and I liked and trusted each other from the start. We shared ideas and research, and Jim wanted us to do a Bennett biography together. But he was a newspaperman at heart; research to him was only a way to develop and fill out a story. Good research, he used to say, ought not to be left to go cold and unpublished. I was an academic working to more distant horizons, wanting to master as much research as possible before putting pen to paper. So each of us went at Bennett in our own way. In 1991 Jim published *R.B. Bennett, The Calgary Years*; that same year I gave an overview of Bennett's life in the Joanne Goodman Lectures at the University of Western Ontario, published in 1992 in a little book titled *The Loner*.

This present work is a larger search for the character and ideas of R.B. Bennett. I cannot pretend to have mastered everything about him, least of all the massive Bennett Papers. These chapters might be called *essais*, in the sense that Montaigne first used the word in the late sixteenth century. Bennett has had to be sought out, a little obliquely at times, and the seeking has gone on across articles and books by authors who seemed at times readier to denounce his failings than to measure his strengths. An exception is a valuable book that appeared in 1992, Larry Glassford's *Reaction and Reform: The Politics of the Conservative Party under R.B. Bennett, 1927–1938*. It underpins not a little of what I have written here.

This book is an attempt to get at R.B. Bennett, to try to assess him. If he often lived like a saint, he was also a mercurial and sometimes a bad-tempered one, not much given to praise, apologies, or forgiveness. But he had a tremendous mind, and he gave prodigally of his energy and his fortune to Canada at a most difficult time. It was the judgment of the great economist Harold Innis that no one in Canada could better have pulled our country through the Depression. By and large, however, RB has received little credit for it.

The German historian Leopold von Ranke (1795–1886) used to say that what he aimed at was history as it really was: *Geschichte wie es eigentlich gewesen war*. It really can't be done, as von Ranke himself admitted, but perhaps that aim is its own justification.

P.B. Waite,
September 2009

Dick Bennett, aged about ten, at Hopewell Cape, New Brunswick. (Library and Archives Canada, C-003867)

Bennett in 1912: Calgary corporation lawyer and rising politician. (Glenbow Archives, NA-166-1)

R.B. Bennett, ca. 1916. (Library and Archives Canada, c-006909)

Leader of the Opposition, 1927–1930

On the campaign trail with Mildred. (Library and Archives Canada, C-021528)

Being sworn in as prime minister, with Mildred, 7 August 1930. (University of New Brunswick, Harriet Irving Library, Box 897, #561804)

RB with future brother-in-law William Herridge, Washington, ca. 1931.

Hazel Colville, the glamorous widow who came into RB's life in 1932, pictured here in a studio portrait of 1924. (Courtesy of Mrs Frances Ballantyne)

RB after his heart trouble in 1935, a weary but still determined prime minister. (Jules A. Castonguay / Library and Archives Canada, PA-037914)

"I am aware that the age is not what we all wish, but I am sure that the only means to check its degeneracy is heartily to concur in whatever is best in our time"

Perhaps these words of Burke are worthy of consideration in these "degenerate days" —

Oct 12/1938

RB quoting Burke on the "degenerate age" of the 1930s. (Courtesy of the author)

Viscount Bennett walking at Juniper Hill, his ninety-six-acre country estate in Surrey adjacent to Lord Beaverbrook's Cherkley. (Beaverbrook / Library and Archives Canada, PA-117652)

A thinner Bennett in a portrait taken in 1945, two years before his death. (Beaverbrook / Library and Archives Canada, PA-117659)

Sketches of RB by cartoonist Jack Boothe, 1941. (Source: *Vancouver Daily Province* obituary, 30 June 1947)

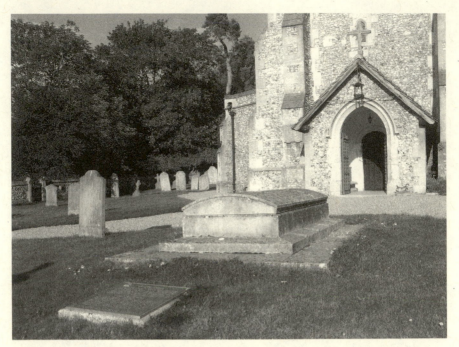

St Michael's Church, Mickleham, Surrey, with memorial plaque and RB's tomb in foreground. (Courtesy of Suzanne Day)

IN SEARCH OF R.B. BENNETT

Introducing "RB," 1870–1927

In 1987, forty years after R.B. Bennett's death, the Canadian journalist Jeffrey Simpson stopped at The Running Horses, an eighteenth-century pub in Mickleham, a small village nestled in the Surrey hills not far from Epsom Downs. Simpson's accent caught the ear of the publican, and they fell into conversation. The publican revealed that when he was a boy growing up in the 1940s, he had met and liked R.B. Bennett, who lived at Juniper Hill half a mile away. "What on earth did you Canadians do to him?" the publican asked. "You seem to have forced him out, as if you wanted to drive him into exile. Why? He was the nicest man imaginable."[1]

"RB," Richard Bedford Bennett's friends and associates called him. His sisters, brothers, old New Brunswick friends, and fellow students at Dalhousie called him "Dick." When he became Conservative leader in 1927, he was fifty-seven years old, six feet tall, and impeccably turned out. With a taste for chocolates and maple sugar creams, he had by this time also developed a "corporation" – a stomach substantial enough to pass muster in a society that still equated girth and well-being. He always wore a wing collar; so did many other men, though few so invariably as RB. Mackenzie King, the prime minister in 1927, wore wing collars too, but mostly on formal occasions – of which, in that time, in that milieu, there were many. By the late 1920s, RB's suits, shirts, collars, handkerchiefs, and hats came mostly from London.

For some years he had been living in a suite in the Palliser Hotel, at that time Calgary's most imposing building. He had acquired a big house in southwest Calgary by liquidation of a debt, on what was by then called Mount Royal, but he never lived there, preferring to be downtown close to work and clients. He worked at all hours, every day but Sunday. And what better place to be anchored than on the seventh floor of the

Palliser Hotel, a block or two from his office, with the long bar of the Alberta Hotel in between, to meet cronies, friends, and clients? It was there that he met up with Bob Edwards, the editor, proprietor, and factotum of a slightly scurrilous Calgary paper, *The Eye-Opener*. Edwards and RB disliked each other almost immediately. Edwards loved to report on CPR train wrecks; with four lines of CPR track running through the centre of Calgary and a dozen level crossings, there was no dearth of wrecks. RB was the main CPR lawyer in Calgary – another CPR wreck, Edwards once remarked.

Bennett and Edwards were very different animals. Edwards was a drinker; RB never drank liquor. Edwards had a rich vocabulary of bad language: RB's vocabulary was rich too, but of the other kind. Both had lively senses of humour, Edwards's rather lusty. (A notice in the *Eye-Opener* of 11 November 1916 read: "A bouncing ten-pound boy arrived at the home of Mr. & Mrs. P.T. Gilpen of Fifteenth Avenue West last Tuesday. Mr. Gilpen has fired the hired man.") RB and Edwards settled their differences when Bennett was elected to the House of Commons in 1911. Edwards then observed, "R.B.'s been 'it' long enough!!!"[2] They not only became friends but Bennett drafted Edwards's will and was executor of his estate when he died in 1922.

Like most Calgarians, RB had come from the East – a long way east, Hopewell Cape on the far southeastern corner of New Brunswick. The village is on the broadening estuary of the Petitcodiac River as it turns down into Shepody Bay at the northeastern end of the Bay of Fundy. The Petitcodiac is a fiercely tidal river. Tides run forty-seven feet between high and low water at certain times of the month. Those huge tides were watched and feared. The ferry at Hopewell Cape that crossed to Westmorland County (Hopewell Cape is in Albert County) ran by tide time; everyone did. The poet Charles G.D. Roberts, ten years older than Dick Bennett, grew up a few miles away in Westmorland County. He never forgot the dykes and distances of that tidal world:

Ah, how well I remember those wide red flats, above tide-mark
Pale with scurf of the salt, seamed and baked in the sun!
Well I remember the piles of blocks and ropes, and the net-reels
Wound with the beaded nets, dripping and dark from the sea!
...
Now at this season the reels are empty and idle; I see them
Over the lines of the dykes, over the gossiping grass.

Now at this season they swing in the long strong wind, thro' the
lonesome
Golden afternoon, shunned by the foraging gulls
...
Ah, the old-time stir, how once it stung me with rapture,
Old-time sweetness, the winds freighted with honey and salt!

Half a century later, RB recalled those lines from "Tantramar Revisited,"
published in 1886 when he was sixteen. He was always good at committing verse to memory.

Hopewell Cape was a shipbuilding and fishing village, nourished by
the sea and small farms. The Bennetts had come there via Nova Scotia
out of Connecticut a decade before the American Revolution. In the
1760s American migration westward was blocked by the Appalachians
and by British policy of preserving the trans-mountain lands for Indian
tribes. So in 1761 Zadok Bennett took his family east to lands in Nova
Scotia left empty when the Acadians were expelled six years before. He
was more interested in shipbuilding than farming and later moved across
the Bay of Fundy to Hopewell Cape. RB's grandfather, Nathan Bennett,
was a shipbuilder and a good one. Henry Bennett, Nathan's son and
RB's father, born in 1842, was apprenticed to a Captain Read who ran
schooners, shipping New Brunswick grindstones down the American
seaboard and to the West Indies. After four or five years Henry Bennett
went into his father's business, grew up in the firm, and was a partner
by 1868. A year later he married Henrietta Stiles, a schoolteacher in
Hopewell Village eight miles to the west. Richard Bedford Bennett was
born there on 3 July 1870. The "Bedford" was for one of the Read seafaring uncles. Six other children followed over the next nineteen years.

In the 1870s the wooden shipbuilding business began a long decline.
Wooden ships continued to be built, but they were apt to be schooners
and other small vessels for the coastal trade rather than the big three-
masted full-rigged ships. Schooners were the jacks-of-all-trades up and
down the Bay of Fundy then and for many a year to come – they were
still plying the coast in the 1930s. But the big square-rigged, wooden
sailing ships, like the 800-ton *Favourite* that Nathan Bennett built, were
being outpaced and replaced by the tougher iron-hulled sailing ships
built elsewhere.

The world depression of 1873–78 exacerbated these changes in the
industry. Henry Bennett had to turn himself into a country general
merchant and blacksmith. Unfortunately, the well-being of the family

was grievously affected by his lack of business sense. Gregarious, reckless, and feckless, Henry Bennett could sail through money. One rumour had it that RB's father was a drunken blacksmith and his mother a teetotal schoolteacher.[3]

Several Canadian prime ministers had mothers who were the backbone of their families: Sir John A. Macdonald, Sir Robert Borden, Mackenzie King, R.B. Bennett. Their fathers were easygoing and often charming but weak; it may well be that those women were attracted to genial and gregarious men. Certainly such men needed strong women. Henrietta Stiles Bennett was a strong woman. She had to be. A serious, intelligent Methodist schoolteacher, she had imbibed deeply, perhaps from her sea-captain father or her mother, the lessons of John Wesley. His was a gospel of work; Wesley wrote in 1763, "Gain all you can by honest industry; use all possible diligence in your calling. Lose no time ... Every business will afford some employment sufficient for every day and every hour ... [it] will leave you no leisure for silly unprofitable diversions. You always have something better to do ... Do it as soon as possible ... And do it as well as possible. Do not sleep or yawn over it ... Put your whole strength to the work. Let nothing in your business be left undone if it can be done by labour and patience."[4] In some religions, sloth might have been considered the most amiable of the deadly sins, but not in the Methodism of John Wesley. Sloth was indulgence, bad stewardship of oneself. Labour was not just a virtue but ought also to be a pleasure. *Labor ipse voluptas*. The same idea dominated Victorian England, as Gilbert and Sullivan expressed it in song in *The Gondoliers* (1889): "And the culminating pleasure / That we treasure beyond measure / Is the satisfying feeling that our duty has been done."

Central to Methodism was its view of money. Although possession of money was not a sin, love of it certainly was. The trilogy of the Methodist ethic was: Earn all you can, save all you can, give away all you can. This doctrine was neither revolutionary nor reactionary. It was ascetic. It was bourgeois. Generous to the world outside, it was exacting to the inner self: discipline of the self! Holiness was marked by personal discipline over the wickedness inherent in the human animal. It also embodied certain duties to society – to quote one of Wesley's sermons, "feeding the hungry, clothing the naked, comforting the sick, assisting the stranger, relieving the afflicted."

Dick Bennett learned these doctrines at his mother's knee and lived with them all his life. Several thousand letters (and replies) in the Bennett

Papers, mostly from the 1930s, show how faithfully he tried to do his duty to society.[5]

Yet Methodism was also tolerant. In this respect it came close to the Quakers. One of RB's favourite poets, one who marked the beginning of his long love of poetry, was John Greenleaf Whittier (1809–1892), a New England Quaker. In "Mary Garvin" Whittier wrote, "Creed and rite perchance may differ / Yet our faith and hope be one." As Wesley put the same idea, "We think and let think."[6]

What of all this Henrietta Stiles Bennett conveyed to her eldest son can only be guessed at; after her death on 1 October 1914, RB destroyed their correspondence. He adored his mother. She was "the very mainspring" of his life. Mothers usually have more time for the firstborn child; often that relationship can be more intense and enduring than with other children. Dick recalled her reciting Longfellow's "The Wreck of the Hesperus," a poem that must have evoked sea-going life at Hopewell Cape. Soon there was Tennyson, and later Byron and Milton. She taught him the history of empires old and new and the beauties of higher mathematics. She was, he told his old friend Alma Russell in November 1914, "teacher, guide, counsellor, companion, friend," and, he added, "above all an impartial and candid critic."[7] His devotion to her lasted all her life, and he followed her precepts for all of his. Don't smoke, don't drink, she said. *Work*!

Every Christmas until her death, RB came home to Hopewell Cape – from Douglastown, from Halifax, from Chatham, New Brunswick, and after 1897, from 2,500-mile distant Calgary. There was something else she fired in him: ambition. *You can do anything if you work at it.* She got him to memorize Longfellow's "Ladder of St Augustine":

The heights by great men reached and kept
Were not attained by sudden flight,
But they, while their companions slept,
Were toiling upward in the night.

Perhaps Henrietta Bennett's ambition for her eldest son was vitalized by the increasing failure of her husband to provide for his family. Four children were born between 1870 and 1876, and two more would come after that. Henry Bennett had delightful ways with friends but not with money. Certainly Dick grew up learning to account for every penny. A debt he owed was just not $7, but $7.18. He was just as exigent the other way. In his early years in Chatham, a cobbler had repaired the Bennett boots. The cobbler asked for $1, which RB thought was high and wanted it itemized. The cobbler, a wag and a poet, replied,

> For planning and conniving,
> For making pegs and driving,
> For workmanship and leather,
> One dollar altogether.[8]

When RB was sixteen, his mother received a small legacy that allowed him to attend the Provincial Normal School at Fredericton. Most of the students were very young like Dick Bennett, sixteen to eighteen years of age. There were 180 students in his group, 40 men and 140 women. That proportion suggested the future: clever young men were already heading toward the professions, particularly law and medicine. Clever women were going into teaching and nursing. RB couldn't afford law or medicine; his family had no money.

Qualifying after three months for a second-class teaching licence, in January 1887, aged sixteen, he began teaching at a country school near Moncton at $160 a year. With a brimming intelligence, a love of learning, and a delight in language, he was a natural teacher. He raised his licence to first class in 1888; at age eighteen he was then made principal of a four-room school in Douglastown, on the north bank of the Miramichi three miles downriver from Newcastle. The school is still there. He had charge of 159 students and three lady teachers. He taught the upper grades, 6, 7, and 8, a total of nineteen students. Early on he established a reputation for firmness and fairness. He believed in having students memorize poetry, not just as an academic exercise but lines "to refresh us with spring flowers ... to win us by pure delight from the tyranny of foolish castle building, self congratulations and mean anxieties. They may be with us in the work-shop ... on pleasant hillsides or by sounding shores ... Never intrusive, ever at hand, coming at our call." His examinations were exacting. His grade 8 geography paper asked: What and where are Esquimalt, Digby, Mistassini, Simcoe, Nipissing? The 1889 grade 8 spelling examination was not easy either, and might well tax students now: "disembarkation," "penuriously," "sequestered," "vehemence," "analogies." He was as exigent with parents as with examinations, and the school trustees in Newcastle did not escape, either. He reported them to Fredericton for not once having visited his school in 1889–90.[9]

Over that winter he met Lemuel Tweedie, lawyer and MLA, across the river in Chatham. After the young man helped him in the provincial election of February 1890, Tweedie asked him to assist in his law office on Saturdays. So began RB's acquaintance with law, crossing the Miramichi in winter from Douglastown to Chatham on snowshoes, the ice several feet thick. Tweedie asked him to stay on in June 1890 when the Douglastown school closed for the summer.

RB was now faced with the question of a career change. Working for Tweedie, he would have enough money by summer's end to contemplate going to Dalhousie University Law School. Fees and room and board in Halifax would run to $150 a year. He opted for Dalhousie over schoolteaching, and as it turned out, gave up teaching for good. But the didactic habits already acquired would remain with him forever.

That first autumn in Halifax he met a triumvirate of powerful Ottawa Conservatives who were in Nova Scotia to do some political fencemending: Sir John Thompson, Sir Charles Tupper, Sir John A. Macdonald. At Dalhousie, he worked and studied to the exclusion of almost everything else. He was seldom to be found cheering on sidelines at rugby matches or being bounced against boards in a hockey game, but he did like long walks, and one fine winter evening, 27 January 1891, he records going tobogganing on Gorsebrook Hill with a couple of girls. Fundamentally, though, his sense of fun and games was more of mind than body.

His work habits stood him in good stead. Though he had never underestimated his talents, his first-year law results surprised even him. He stood head of his year in two subjects and second in others. The next year he continued this record, despite the determination of some fellow students to bring him down to size, each concentrating on certain subjects. Their strategy worked better in 1892–93 when RB was elected premier of the mock parliament and transferred some of his effort there.

With a Dalhousie law degree in hand, he returned in April 1893 to the Chatham law office, now called Tweedie and Bennett. The pay was $600 a year plus free room and board at Tweedie's home. RB's career as a small-town lawyer was underway. In 1896 he was elected alderman of the newly incorporated Town of Chatham. He did so with the help of an admiring but mischievous seventeen-year old from Newcastle, Maxwell Aitken, the son of the Presbyterian minister of the church of St John and St James.

That summer RB attended a picnic at a beach out on Miramichi Bay where people often took out-of-town visitors or just went to swim in the sea. Jimmy Dunn, a twenty-two-year-old Dalhousie law student from nearby Bathurst, was also there; so was the irrepressible Max. Max and a friend were made beasts of burden collecting driftwood for the fire.

Jimmy pumped an Ottawa visitor for news, while RB sat on the sand "keeping the others in roars of laughter as they got supper ready – he was always a brilliant conversationalist." Thus were brought together on a summer beach that afternoon three New Brunswickers who were all later to be wealthy and famous.[10]

That same year, Senator James Lougheed, looking for a new junior for his Calgary law office, heard about RB through Dean Richard Weldon of the Dalhousie Law School. Weldon was then also MP for Albert County. Lougheed offered young Bennett a partnership in the Lougheed firm, with 20 per cent of the firm's earnings (up to $3,750) for the first year and 30 per cent after that.

It was a good offer – but was it a good move? Bennett knew little about the West. At that time Calgary was at least 10 per cent smaller than Chatham. Lougheed no doubt stressed the potential: the firm acted as the CPR's solicitors; population growth was coming. But then all prairie communities talked up growth like that; it had been constantly expected for years. RB weighed his options for a month or so and accepted. His decision was more intuitive than rational. He believed in challenges; they expanded one's mind and capacities. Among his favourite lines were those from Browning's "Andrea del Sarto": "Ah, but a man's reach should exceed his grasp, / Or what's a heaven for?"

RB left Chatham by train on Saturday, 16 January 1897, going first to Hopewell Cape, thence to Saint John, to Montreal and so westward. When he arrived in Calgary later in the month, the weather was bitterly cold, windy and unforgiving, and, as was usual in winter, the train was hours late. Low temperatures made it difficult to keep up steam pressure, and that morning the thermometer was at −40° (the temperature at which Fahrenheit and Celsius meet), with a wind that scurfed grey dust over the thin snow.

He inquired about getting a cab. "We don't have them things here, stranger," he was told. He bundled up as best he could and walked the frozen blocks to the Alberta Hotel.[11] Thus his Calgary career began.

For two years the Lougheed practice brought RB no more than $1,000 a year. The Calgary cost of living was about 25 per cent higher than in New Brunswick. Then things improved. The population indeed increased, rapidly after 1900. In the 1901 Census, Calgary had 4,392 people (Chatham had 4,868), but by the 1911 Census, Calgary had shot up to 43,704, whereas Chatham actually declined to 4,506. RB's business took off with Calgary's growth, as his practice included the buying and selling of real estate and arranging mortgages – the usual way that frontier lawyers made money. As a lawyer for the CPR, he was also able to make judicious purchases of CPR land on his own account, buying by instalments over five to seven years at, say, $4.50 an acre, and selling later at $6. An ambitious lawyer in Nanaimo asked him about possibilities in Alberta. RB told him in March 1903, "For law mixed with speculation real estate etc. there are most excellent openings. Edmonton seems to be the most promising point ... but every member of the profession on the main line [of the CPR] east of here is making money. Most of them buy and sell real estate in a small way and are agents for insurance companies etc ... The climate is everything that could be desired ... The next five years will be years of unexampled progress in the Territories and I am quite certain that good money could be made by a capable and honest solicitor."[12] It is an apt description of RB's own technique. And Calgary was indeed expanding rapidly. Two months after that letter was written, some four hundred houses were reported to be under construction.

The Lougheed-Bennett practice developed rapidly too. The firm came to represent a number of national companies – the CPR, Bell Telephone, Canadian Bank of Commerce, Hudson's Bay Company, Royal Bank, and London Life Insurance, together with local enterprises. Most of RB's practice was with defendants: a local business defended against government regulations, the CPR against a local business, CPR against negligence. He did not win all his cases by any means; in the nature of things he was more likely to be on the losing side. Basically he believed in avoiding litigation by settling out of court. But if he lost in the initial trial, he often appealed, much more so than most of his colleagues. Sometimes the threat of appeal would suggest to opposing lawyers the virtue of persuading their clients to settle out of court.[13]

He was dedicated to his clients, large and small. Once he accepted a case, he would take it through to the end, all the way to Edmonton, to Ottawa, or even to the Judicial Committee of the Privy Council in England. He was especially tenacious if he saw real injustice. *In re Lewis* (1918) is one example. When the Canadian Parliament brought in conscription in 1917, it specifically exempted active farmers from military service. In April 1918, however, the government changed the law by order-in-council. Young Norman Lewis on a farm near Calgary was called up under this new rule. Bennett believed the order-in-council was *ultra vires*, that only Parliament could change the effect of that law. He applied to the Supreme Court of Alberta for a writ of *habeas corpus* to get Lewis released. The full bench of the Supreme Court of Alberta heard the application. It backed Bennett 4–1. Thirty or more similar applications followed in the wake of that decision. The Ottawa government soon passed a further order-in-council reiterating its stand. A confrontation ensued in Calgary over which was right: Ottawa or Bennett. The case then went to the Supreme Court of Canada where it was set against an analogous Ontario case, *In re Gray*, in which Gray had lost. Bennett took the flack, as the Ottawa and Calgary newspapers thought pettifogging lawyers should not be impeding the war effort. The Supreme Court threw out the Gray case by 4–2 and heard argument about the Lewis one. The case was never concluded, as the war finished first.[14]

Other Calgary lawyers did not mind RB being defeated. Many thought he needed to be taken down a peg or two, finding him too cheeky by half; New Brunswickers were not famous for being shy and retiring. Bennett was aware of his reputation, but he believed that integrity and duty to clients were of supreme importance. He also liked to get his own way. His complete lack of what can be called "Western style" also helped to make him a target. Although he seemed to be armed at all points, it might have been better for his popularity if he could have developed the art of concealing the skills he was bringing to bear. But with RB, modesty was never a pre-eminent virtue, and in western courtrooms it was an impossible one. So there he came with his citations from English law, eastern law, sometimes of a quite arcane kind. Western judges, many of them Laurier Liberal appointees, did not always take kindly to being presented with bully precedents from eastern Canada or British law by an aggressive young eastern Conservative lawyer who seemed to know too much for his own good.

Then, of course, there was the way he dressed – as he thought a gentleman and a lawyer should, whether in Chatham or Calgary. No chaps and cowboy boots for him, nor a Stetson either, though from time to time he may have opened the Calgary Stampede wearing one. His style of dress probably began when he was the very young eighteen-year-old principal of the Douglastown school. He had to look the part. It may not have been all vanity either; as Thomas Mann remarked in *Buddenbrooks* (1901), a professional man had to "radiate confidence" to the world around him, and that certainly began with dress and appearance.[15]

By 1908 Calgary needed more residential space. The CPR owned most of the land; some of the hill southwest of the town centre had already been sold to Americans, and the area had acquired the name "American Hill." Neither Bennett nor the Bennett table at the Alberta Hotel liked that; Bennett's connections with the CPR land commissioner in Winnipeg were invoked, and out went "American Hill" and in came "Mount Royal." With Mount Royal came street names out of Canadian history: Wolfe, Durham, Quebec, Sydenham, Vaudreuil, all probably thought up by Bennett. He even acquired a large house at the top of the hill through failure of a mortgage, although he never seems to have lived there. It was rented out over the years and sold in 1939 while Bennett lived downtown in his suite at the Palliser Hotel.[16]

By 1910 he was well on his way to being a corporation lawyer and businessman. He was astute, tenacious, and talented, with a growing reputation for honesty and integrity. He had learned to read balance sheets like an open book and ask pointed questions about what might lie behind the sometimes misleading figures. He was part of the driving force, and sometimes the moral control, behind some big enterprises: Calgary Power (1909), Max Aitken's Canada Cement (1910), Alberta Pacific Grain Company (1912), and by 1914, a Turner Valley oil firm called Royalite, later sold to Imperial Oil.

One of RB's particular concerns as a lawyer was conflict of interest. He was into many different lines of endeavour but was scrupulous to avoid suspicion that the information from one concern might be used for or against another. Aitken was particularly interested in such information, but Bennett would almost invariably tell him that what he was asking for was impossible to give. Yet it was an era when few businessmen bothered about conflict of interest; worrying about that was being too nice by half. It was not too nice for RB. In December 1909 he wrote to Aitken, "I have learned to be extremely careful in the statements I make in any way dealing with financial matters ... when you are acting as its [a company's] solicitor ... [you] must not divulge private information that you receive in the transaction of its business."[17] On the other hand, if business information were being sent to someone else outside the closed circle of the company directors, RB then felt free to disclose it to Aitken.

By this time RB was very much involved in politics. He was first elected to the North-West Territories Assembly in 1898 for West Calgary, the year he turned twenty-eight. He ran unsuccessfully in the federal election of 1900, returning to the Territorial Assembly. He was already being listened to by Robert Borden, the Conservative leader in Ottawa. What was most needed, he told Borden in 1903, was provincial status for Alberta. Laurier conceded that in 1905. The next most important matter was to have freight rates "absolutely under the control of the [Dominion] government." It cost farmers too much to get their wheat to seaboard, east or west. Nor would a government railway help unless it was better managed than the Intercolonial, the government railway that ran between Montreal and Halifax. "As long as a Government railroad is run as a political institution," RB wrote to Borden, "its benefits are imaginary."[18] If there were to be another western railway to compete with the CPR, its administration should be placed "in the hands of a strong commission and absolutely beyond political control."

Borden listened; Bennett was a coming star, and his ideas were not far from Borden's own. Neither man was afraid of government enterprises, but there was a big proviso in Bennett's mind: any government enterprise must be run free from political interference. That was a tall order in the Canada of 1903. (In Stephen Leacock's *Sunshine Sketches of a Little Town*, the independent candidate in the 1911 election, Edward Drone, is told that "what Mariposa needed was a straight, clean, non-partisan post office, built on a piece of ground of a strictly non-partisan character, and constructed under contracts that were not tainted and besmirched with party affiliation. Two or three men were willing to show Drone just where a piece of ground of this character could be bought."[19])

This non-partisan view of administration is early Bennett, but it gets his long-term position right. He was not far from what is called a "Red Tory" – that is, a Conservative who believes in active government, active social legislation, and a thoroughly non-partisan civil service. A high-minded Civil Service Act was passed by Laurier in 1909. Some civil service reforms were then effected, and later more were undertaken by Borden. The trouble was that governments – Laurier's, Borden's, and Mackenzie King's – found it impossible to live up to those austere principles, especially for the Outside Service (the civil service outside Ottawa). Bennett was not pleased. He told the Civil Servants Association in Calgary in 1928, "I am unalterably opposed to any departure from the principle of the Civil Service Act."[20]

A Red Tory could also be pro-labour. When the Calgary carpenters went on strike in 1902 for more wages, the employers resisted. The union brought in Bennett. He gave a rousing speech on their behalf at a public meeting. Workers should have wages sufficient to afford decent homes for their families. Reasonable men, he said, were trying to resolve a dispute in a reasonable way. There was nothing wrong with union recognition. Everyone had that right. "So long as I live, I will give my best efforts to uphold right causes, make better homes for people and help to build a strong and reliant race." Note the qualifications: "right causes," "better homes," "a strong and reliant race." The Tory in Bennett was not just socially progressive but Methodist and bourgeois as well.[21]

RB believed in the British Empire. To his mind, the Anglo-Saxon race had given to the modern world the supreme example of law, order, and parliaments. If the British Empire had been won by war, its present hegemony was justified by its traditions of discipline and democracy. But by 1910 the empire needed reform. Bennett's imperial ideas, poetic and inchoate in the 1890s, had begun to accommodate his Canadian nationalism. Canada would not, could not, go on within the empire as it presently stood. He regretted British resistance to Max Aitken's ideas of imperial federation based upon imperial free trade. He wrote to Aitken on 13 November 1910, "I am convinced that the real crisis in the life of our Empire is upon us. If the Empire is to endure[,] the self-governing nations which compose it must in some way be federated. Unless there is a recognition of common interests common traditions & above all common responsibilities and obligations and that too within the lifetime of this generation[,] independence is inevitable not of Canada alone but of all the nations that now make up the empire. In Canada the situation is really acute. We have gone and made commercial treaties with the nations of the world and are now thinking of reciprocity with the U.S."

With Americans moving into the Canadian West, reciprocity would be dangerous, for the ties of sentiment with eastern Canada were "daily becoming weaker. St Paul, Chicago and New York mean more to most of our people [out West] than Montreal, Toronto, St John and Halifax." Despite the Canadian preference on British goods, despite the Canadian tariff, the West was still buying carloads of American manufactures. If Canada negotiated a reciprocity treaty with the United States, "within a few short years half of the factories of Eastern Canada will be closed. The West is the market of the East." Trade had to be kept Canadian if Canada were to survive.[22]

Americans took considerable interest in the 1911 Canadian election, as well they might. On the hustings, Bennett delighted in retailing wildly irrational American comments about Canada. And with his compelling oratory and considerable clutch of ideas, he won the only federal Conservative seat in Alberta, MP Calgary.

In Ottawa RB proved to be something of a maverick member, all too frequently giving his own views and readily criticizing party policy if he did not agree with it. Never one to hold to a position when it no longer seemed tenable, he once quoted Cardinal Manning, "To live is to change and to live nobly is to change often." Some years later, someone sent him New Year's wishes with hopes for "a quiet mind." Bennett sent back his own good wishes but added, "Just why you should contemplate such a disaster I cannot understand." His was not a quiet mind but an intensely restless one, translated into action by a huge capacity for work and enormous energy, delivered on the hustings and in Parliament with hortatory enthusiasm for what he believed in and vigorous criticisms for what he did not.[23]

These qualities did not make him an easy colleague. He had come to Ottawa feeling that Borden and the party owed him more than he was being offered. True, he had been given the honour of making the Address in Reply to the Speech from the Throne, but that did not get him very much attention. RB thought he should have been in the cabinet. Perhaps he would have been, had not his senior colleague, Sir James Lougheed, been there already as government leader in the Senate. Two cabinet colleagues from the same province, the same city, the same law office, was asking a lot of Borden. Nevertheless Bennett had given up his CPR retainer of $10,000 a year the day after he was elected MP for Calgary, and there were precious few compensations for it. Now he was in Ottawa uselessly cooling his heels. Within three weeks of coming East, he wrote to Aitken impatiently, "I am sick of it here. There is little or nothing to do & what there is to do is that of a party hack or departmental clerk or messenger. I will probably leave here. There must be more doing than is at present apparent. I really cannot tell you what I think of the Government. I will do that later when I have more adequately sized up the situation."[24]

He was not really one of Borden's Conservative team. Of independent means and independent mind, he would go wherever his loyalties, penchants, and principles took him, amplifying with enthusiasm whatever he believed in. He believed in Borden's Naval Aid Bill of 1912–13 and made a four-hour speech in support of it, ending with a ringing declaration about the British Empire and Union Jack accompanied by law, justice, and freedom. But it was a special empire he had in mind, run by an empire parliament where Australians, New Zealanders, South Africans, and Canadians sat with English and Scottish and Welsh to legislate empire policies. And in the long run, that empire could well become Canada's, a Canada writ large: "I hold out to this house the vision of a wider hope, the hope that one day this Dominion will be the dominant factor in that great [Empire] federation."[25] The Naval Aid bill got through the House of Commons only by Borden and Meighen bringing in closure; it foundered in the Liberal-dominated Senate.

RB's independence showed in his 1914 denunciation of the government's Canadian Northern Railway bill. His speech against his government's support of the Canadian Northern was based on his wide knowledge and experience of western railways, including the Canadian Northern. He knew what he was talking about, and Parliament listened. His target was not just the Canadian Northern and its principals, Sir William Mackenzie and Donald Mann, but Solicitor-General Arthur Meighen, to whom Borden had given the task of shepherding the bill through the Commons. Meighen with consummate self-assurance kept interrupting Bennett. Exasperated, Bennett told the House that Meighen was simply "the gramophone of Mackenzie and Mann."[26]

Borden did not seem to mind Bennett's independence, nor in the long run did Meighen. Both recognized that in Bennett's long denunciation of the Canadian Northern he was condemning in detail one of Laurier's more dubious railway adventures. That speech won headlines in the Calgary papers on 15 May 1914, but it had to share space with the blowing in of the A.W. Dingman oil well in the Turner Valley. In the summer of 1912 in the Highwood River valley, some fifty miles west of High River, RB and Dingman had watched in amazement while a rancher friend put a match to a fissure in the ground and cooked a pot of coffee over the flame. Turner Valley was six miles to the north. RB invested in Dingman's Calgary Petroleum Company, of which he became a director and solicitor. The company eventually became Royalite, then Imperial Oil. By 1929 Bennett's $25 shares were worth $200.[27]

When the war came late that summer of 1914, RB tried to enlist. He had been connected with the militia in New Brunswick, but now was a year over the age limit of forty-three. And there was something else: he was not apparently medically fit. The reasons he did not divulge, but he told Mackenzie King in 1930 that he was missing two toes owing to some childhood accident.[28]

Then the sudden death of his mother on 1 October 1914 supervened everything. Henry Bennett had died in 1905, probably without much insurance, and it is almost certain that RB supported his mother and helped his youngest sister, Mildred, when she went to Mount Allison Academy in Sackville. His brother Ronald was by now a sea captain; his brother George had been a bank clerk and now enlisted in the Canadian Army and was at Valcartier on his way overseas. His sister Evelyn was teaching school at Hopewell Cape, about to be married to H.W. Coates, a Methodist minister in Fredericton. Coates soon had a call to Vancouver and thither the couple went, where RB bought them a modest house. Mildred followed them there. RB's Christmases between 1915 and 1927 were spent in Vancouver.

He was now fairly well off. His income, in 1917, the first year of federal income tax, was $73,000, of which over 60 per cent came from dividends of the stock he held as president of Alberta Pacific Grain. To get a rough present-day equivalent of RB's 1917 income, multiply by 15, viz. $1.09 million.

In July 1915 Borden invited RB to accompany him as his assistant on a reconnaissance trip to London. The purpose was to see how Canada could help meet British military and civilian needs. Neither Borden nor Bennett was impressed with how the British were running the war. In their view, the besetting sin of the British was their slowness, their unwillingness to change the way things had always been done. The result was muddle, relieved only by infrequent flashes of brilliance like tanks and convoys and even then accepted grudgingly and half-heartedly.

The war seriously affected Bennett's office in Calgary. In August 1916 the 137th Battalion left Calgary for overseas, taking with it RB's political organizer and campaign manager, George Robinson, as well as several other political assistants. The 137th also took William Robinson, RB's personal secretary since 1912. He felt the loss of these associates keenly; many linchpins gave way at once. "The departure of these men," he wrote to Max Aitken (now Lord Beaverbrook) in London, "leaves me absolutely without assistance and heartbroken." He added a qualification: "so far as it is possible for a man of my type & temperment [sic] to be heartbroken about anything."[29]

What was that type, that temperament? He had been a devoted son, was a dutiful brother; he was conscientious almost to obsession about charity, giving away money to young and deserving students, needy widows, and a host of charities, to the tune of about 10 per cent of his total income. His generosity was already considerable, driven by his sense of Methodist duty, perhaps by tenderness for the less fortunate. Where and what were the real springs of his nature? First of all, he revelled in hard work, not just for itself but also for the sheer satisfaction of mastery of finance, taxation, and law. He was a positive wizard with precedents and uncanny at pointing out the flaws in a balance sheet. Even Sir James Dunn, no slouch at finance himself, envied that ability. After a 1934 visit to RB in Ottawa, Dunn thanked him for a most profitable visit "and your lesson in balance sheets." With that mastery of course came rewards, triumphs – in short, the winning.

RB could also hold grudges. Forgiveness was one of the great Christian virtues he found difficult to practise. Injuries to the ego were particulaly hard to forgive. He was a sublime egotist, clever, irascible, unsparing of himself or of others; wound up in the coils of his own nature, he seemed only rarely to consider the effects of his words and actions upon others. Joined to all of that was a quick temper, evanescent as a rule but stormy while it lasted. These characteristics are summed up in a jingle from Fredericton Normal School days: "Next comes Dick Bennett, conceited and young, / Who never knew quite when to hold his quick tongue."[30]

RB's limited receiving capacity was often the source of his strength and his courage. Mackenzie King's sensitive antennae tended to make him timid and hypocritical, more devious as he got older. RB scorned hypocrisy. He had the dangerous habit of saying what he really thought. What drove him was his own mind, not what others might think of him. At the core of his being was a fundamental aloneness. He had never been one for the give and take of games. He was not a lonely man, but he was what one might call a loner. A poem, "The Crossing Paths," that he set down in 1890 and quite possibly wrote himself when he first came to Dalhousie Law School in Halifax, conveys this:

> Our far diverging lines of life,
> Have for a moment crossed,
> To touch and wind away again and be
> In the dim distance lost
> As passing ships whose wide-flung sails
> Are for an instant furled
> We hail, and banter words of cheer,
> Brought from the other world,
> With eager question, quick reply
> Across the deck we lean,
> Then part and put the silences
> Of ocean wastes between.
> We turn and watch the fading sail
> Until our eyes grow dim
> And the blue billows melt away
> On the horizon's rim
> How sad it seems! a few brief words
> A kiss a handclasp given

Then paths that cross on land or sea
No more this side of Heaven![31]

The poem seems to express the expansion of the young man's self, as if
he were coming to enjoy his own singular resources within the panoply
of a growing and busy externality.

In the fall of 1916 Borden appointed RB as director of the Canadian
National Service Board to effect an inventory of Canada's population
and what their functions might be. He was to calculate how to get
enough manpower and womanpower to allow Borden to make good on
his promise of half a million soldiers in Canada's army while keeping
farmers farming and workers in the mills and munitions factories, and
bringing women into the labour force at pay equal to men's wherever
they could do men's work. At Vimy Ridge in April 1917, Canada had
10,000 casualties, with 3,600 dead. Voluntary enlistment could not sustain such losses, and Bennett supported the Military Service Act of July
1917, which brought in conscription. His work was now turned over to
other hands.

Nevertheless RB opposed Borden's idea of a Union Government. He
thought Union between Conservatives and Liberals, even for purposes
patriotic like the war, would end in disaster for the Conservative Party.
Borden sought coalition to secure Canada's military honour and his own
political future, but in the long run it was a disaster for his party, exactly
as RB had predicted.

In December 1917 RB campaigned for the Conservatives but did not
run in the election. In February 1918 he was further alienated from
Borden by Borden's failure to honour a promise Bennett believed the
prime minister had made: to appoint him to the Senate. Instead, Borden
appointed an obscure Alberta Liberal. It was done to satisfy coalition arrangements with the Liberals, but the appointment was so bad
that Calgary papers saw it as a deliberate attempt to make the Senate
look ridiculous. Bennett was furious. He wrote Borden a twenty-page
letter rehearsing the history of Borden's promise. As for being a senator,
Bennett said, he needed neither the money nor the position; his object
was to put his knowledge and experience at the service of Canada. His
letter was also intended to mark "the formal termination of our friendship." His parting shot was from Matthew Arnold: "Life still / Leaves
human effort scope. / But since life teems with ill, / Muse no extravagant
hope. / Because thou must not dream thou needst not then despair."
Borden did not reply.[32]

RB had other Ottawa interests and responsibilities. The most import-
ant of these was his growing commitment to the E.B. Eddy Company, of
Hull, Quebec. That relationship developed from his acquaintance with
Jennie Shirreff Eddy (1863–1921), whom he had met in Chatham in
1890 when he was working in the long, Dalhousie-free summers (30
April to September 30) as clerk for Lemuel Tweedie. Born in Chatham,
Jennie Shirreff trained as a nurse in Boston and went to work in the
Halifax General Hospital. She married E.B. Eddy in Halifax in 1894.
When he died in February 1906, Eddy left a substantial business, arran-
ging a ten-year trust to keep it and the Eddy name intact. But almost at
once his widow encountered a serious hurdle: the Quebec Succession
Duty Act.

   E.B. Eddy had been Hull's richest citizen, more than once mayor of the
town, and while he gave some gifts to Catholic institutions in Hull, he
left the great bulk of his estate to Protestant charities across the river in
Ottawa. Most of the rest was tied up in the Eddy trust. The three thousand privately held shares of the Eddy Company were held by Jennie
Shirreff Eddy, a grandson, and four senior Eddy officials. Quebec government officials were not disposed to be generous. A few months after
Eddy's death, the province presented the estate with a bill for $700,000
in succession duties. That properly floored Jennie Eddy. The company
was asset rich and cash poor, so she called on her old friend R.B. Bennett
to help her. He managed to work out an agreement with the Quebec
government for the company to pay the money by instalments.

   The ten-year Eddy trust ran out in 1916, at which time, on Bennett's
advice, Jennie Eddy bought out her grandson's 250 shares. That gave her
1,509 shares out of 3,000, with clear majority control riding on them.
There had been talk and negotiations from time to time about the sale of
the firm, but she had always resisted, and now such resistance was fully
effective. Then, in April 1921, she went to the Ottawa General Hospital
for an operation; peritonitis set in and she died at her home in Hull on
9 August 1921.[33]

   Her will left 500 of her shares to Bennett, and the other 1,009 to her
brother, Joseph Thompson Shirreff (for some reason known as Harry),
vice-president of the firm. The Quebec government came at Eddy's
again, this time on a greatly increased assessment of the value of those
3,000 Eddy shares: $1,600 each. Bennett found that valuation "little
short of iniquitous." He protested vigorously, even reaching Premier
Taschereau, and succeded in having the valuation reduced to $1,000.
He had a wry appreciation of J.-A. Bégin, treasurer of Quebec, "who has
treated us with the utmost respect ... but whose grim determination to

extract revenue from the estate [of Mrs. Eddy] has compelled my reluctant admiration, although it has filled me with dismay." All of this took several years, and Mrs Eddy's estate would not be wound up until 1927. Harry Shirreff would die suddenly in May 1926, leaving all his shares to RB, and there were more long discussions with Quebec over that estate.

RB then became majority shareholder of a very big concern. By this time, Eddy's shares were being assessed at $1,500 each. At that valuation RBs holdings were worth $2,263,500.[34] He was thus the principal director of the firm. He never chose to become managing director, preferring to leave the running of Eddy's to the small clutch of senior Eddy personnel and the management team they hired. He kept a close watch on the firm but rarely seems to have interfered.

His relationship with Jennie Shirreff Eddy ought to be mentioned here. There were rumours, especially after Jennie left five hundred of her Eddy shares to RB in her will, that there had been a romance between them. Some even said that Bennett's sister Mildred, born in 1889, was really his daughter with Jennie. Bennett would have prosecuted for slander if he could have, but such prosecutions were notoriously difficult to bring off, and he was wise to leave the allegation alone. He replied in 1935 to such a suggestion: in 1889, when Mildred was born, he had not even met Jennie Shirreff. Moreover, Jennie was seven years older than he was. As to whether there had ever been any romance between them, Beaverbrook, in some position to know, thought not. There is no evidence, and any Bennett-Shirreff correspondence has disappeared.[35]

Politics were once again on RB's horizon. Worn out with war and politics and Versailles, Sir Robert Borden had resigned as prime minister on 1 July 1920. The Unionist caucus selected Arthur Meighen as his successor and renamed itself the National Liberal and Conservative Party. Meighen disliked the name and wanted to revert to Liberal-Conservative. The Liberals began to drift back to the Liberal fold. Laurier had died in February 1919, and the party now had as its leader the young forty-five-year old Mackenzie King.

The Meighen government lost three important by-elections in 1921. Liberals were being pulled away by the tug of ancient loyalties. With his majority crumbling, Meighen would not sail any longer under the false colours of Borden's war coalition. On 1 September 1921 he called a general election for 6 December. Now that Borden had retired, Bennett decided he would run again. Meighen also wanted RB in his government as minister of justice before the country went to the polls. Although at first Bennett resisted Meighen's call, he began to feel that Canada was in disarray socially and politically and decided to put his influence "on the side of law, order and constituted authority."

Appointed minister of justice on 21 September 1921, after his swearing in he called his new staff together. He made a short speech, closing with a couple of lines of poetry. E.L. Newcombe, the deputy minister (from Nova Scotia) spoke up: "Pardon, but that last line isn't quite correct." "No?" bristled the new minister. "Then quote it correctly." Newcombe did. "Since you're so clever," RB then challenged him, "perhaps you'd quote the next six lines." Newcombe did that too, and said to RB, "Perhaps you'd quote the next six!" Bennett did. Laughter with warm compliments were bestowed all round.

Notwithstanding that happy beginning, RB soon realized that there was little hope for the Meighen government in the upcoming election. It was doomed by anti-Meighen votes in Quebec and the Maritime provinces, to say nothing of the party's precarious hold on the West. Bennett and his friends were too confident of Calgary West; it was a dead heat between him and a Labour candidate, so close that the outcome of a judicial recount depended on the way the "x" on the ballots had been made. Bennett lost by sixteen votes and was rather aggrieved at his Calgary constituents.[36]

By March 1922, out of politics once again, RB was spending much time with Eddy's in Ottawa. Western crop prospects were not good just then, and he wrote to Beaverbrook from Calgary that his plans did not include "my making this part of the country my home much longer." He was thinking of giving up his law partnership with Senator Sir James Lougheed. Lougheed was sixty-eight years old now, did little of the firm's work, and had been hiring juniors whose quality Bennett doubted. In Ottawa on a Supreme Court appeal – his election recount – he was seeing Lougheed about dissolving the partnership when a Privy Council appeal forced him to leave for England immediately. The arrangements with Lougheed were left pending until his return, or so he believed. A junior in the firm, W.H. McLaws, had a different view of what had been concluded, believing that the way was now clear for the firm to break up. Divorce arrangements were set in motion unilaterally.

After a flurry of irascible cables between Ottawa and London, Bennett bounced back from England to Calgary in a high state of indignation. He had been stabbed in the back; the man with whom he had been in partnership for twenty-five years was trying to seize the whole of the law practice they had built up together.[37] The result was a massive and messy litigation. The old Lougheed-Bennett firm split three ways:

Lougheed, McLaws, Sinclair & Redman stayed in the old offices in the Clarence Block; Bennett, Hannah, and Sanford moved to the Lancaster building one block away; Brokovski became Brokovski, Green & Co. The clients of the old Lougheed-Bennett firm made individual choices, the Bennett firm retaining the great majority, Pat Burns, A.E. Cross, John T. McFarland not least. One old client that Bennett would not touch was the Bank of Montreal. It had been Lougheed's when Bennett came in 1897, and it would remain Lougheed's.

There was one late attempt at reconciliation, perhaps early in 1925. Lougheed sent word he would like to see Bennett and they met and talked in Bennett's office. Bennett asked Alice Millar, his secretary, to leave the door open and sit near enough to hear. She remembers Lougheed's quiet voice saying, "If that's how you see it, RB ..." However, RB was still adamant that a great wrong had been done him, and there was no reconciliation. But it was typical of him that he was unhappy to learn later that the seventy-year-old Lougheed had to walk down the six flights of stairs in the Lancaster Building because the elevator man had gone off duty.

Lougheed was in Ottawa at the time of the 29 October 1925 general election and by then was not well. He asked his secretary how Bennett was doing in Calgary West. Bennett had been elected, his opponent having conceded, the secretary said. "Isn't that fine," Sir James replied. A few days later he was dead.

If RB could hold grudges, he never forgot kindness. After Sir James's death, Lady Lougheed fell upon hard times, especially in the Depression years before her death in 1936. RB knew her well; she had been extremely kind to him when he first joined the Lougheed practice in 1897. "I want you to assure your mother," he wrote to her daughter, Dorothy Lougheed, "that whatever happens I will see that she is looked after. I will never forget her kindnesses to me in days that are past."[38] He kept his word.

The secretary whom Bennett relied on to verify his conversation with Lougheed in 1925 was Alice Elizabeth Millar, at that time thirty-seven years of age. Her father was Scottish, her mother English; she was born in Galt, Ontario, on 4 June 1888 and came west with her parents. She joined Bennett's office as stenographer about 1914, and when his male private secretary, William Robinson, left in 1916 to join the army, she assumed that role. Tall, shrewd, and amiable, she had a wry, whimsical sense of humour. She was clever, quick, sensible, good at finance, and completely trustworthy. She could also fend off unwanted visitors and in that respect could be something of a dragon.

Alice Millar and Mildred Bennett were the two women of RB's mature life who understood him well. One day in the early 1930s, Mildred came into RB's suite at the Château Laurier proudly sporting a new hat. When he asked how much it cost, something he often did, her announcement of the price provoked an outburst of the RB temper. Mildred bore it patiently. After he left she turned to Alice and remarked, "Millar, don't ever walk out on Dick. We're the bumpers on his car. We save him a lot of damage." Alice never did leave him; she became a buffer between him and the world outside. RB was grateful; when there were interesting stock options, he often arranged a block for her.[39]

By 1924 he had come to be extremely well off. His total 1924 income was $76,897, in present-day terms well over $1 million. Only 25 per cent of that income came from his legal practice. His 1924 director's fees, mostly Alberta Pacific Grain and Eddy's, contributed another 7 per cent of his total income. The bulk of it, 62 per cent, came from dividends. Almost half of his 1924 dividend income was from Alberta Pacific Grain of which he was president; two others, Eddy's and Canada Cement, made up 16 per cent and 13 per cent, respectively. By 1927 his total income was $152,261, of which 65 per cent was from dividends. The proportion of dividends kept growing. In 1930 his income had reached $262,176, of which 85 per cent was dividends. That represented the high point of his income until that of 1937 slightly exceeded it.[40]

Ever since 1922 he had been little involved in his Calgary law practice, the Bennett name carrying the firm. Eddy's took up much of his attention until 1925. RB and Harry Shirreff, Jennie Eddy's brother and the company vice-president, had decided to spend $3 million on plant improvements, in particular a new newsprint mill. The new machinery seemed to require a good deal of breaking in. By 1924 Eddy's was a large operation with 1,400 employees. It held some 1,931 square miles of woodland in the Gatineau and Ottawa valleys.[41] Bennett avoided having much to do with the actual day-to-day business operations, but if he was not the managing director, he was close to being so. He held 1,509 of the 3,000 Eddy shares; it would have been unlike him not to be concerned with the overall direction and policies of the company.

By this time Bennett had divested himself of Alberta Pacific Grain, which he sold to Spillers Milling of England in 1924, exchanging shares and continuing as a director. After the 1923 bumper Alberta grain harvest, it was a good time to sell. Then, on 14 October 1924, Royalite No. 4 in the Turner Valley blew in, with such force that the wellhead valve came through the top of the seventy-foot derrick. It took weeks to bring the oil and gas under control. Bennett's Royalite shares went from $25 to $300. A subsidiary he had devised, the Dalhousie Oil Company, went from 50 cents to $5 a share. Bennett was also a director of Metropolitan Life Insurance Co. of New York and was soon to be on the board of the Royal Bank of Canada.[42]

In the meantime Arthur Meighen was trying to persuade him back into politics. Politics with Bennett was not so much an avocation as a cause; although he was highly successful in most of his business ventures, they were not satisfying as ends in themselves. He was already rich enough. Politics with RB was a higher calling, a challenge, adventure, and not least, duty.

When Meighen offered him the Ministry of Justice, if and when there was to be a Meighen government, RB was interested. The King government of 1922 to 1925 had made a lacklustre impression, and Bennett threw himself into the federal campaign of October 1925 with great vigour. He scorned the Progressives' theme of Western alienation. Easterners were the same as Westerners, he maintained. They had as much interest in the future of Canada as did people in the West – more, indeed, since Ontario paid 44 per cent of federal taxes and Alberta under 3 per cent.[43]

This time Bennett won Calgary West with a comfortable majority of over 4,300 votes. The Conservative party had received 20 per cent of the Alberta popular vote in 1921 and won no seats; in 1925 it got 32 per cent and three seats. Overall, the Conservatives took 115 seats, the Liberals 100. King was personally defeated in York North. It looked very much like a Liberal defeat. Still, King did not resign; he believed that with the support of twenty-four Progressives (twenty-two of them from the Prairie provinces), he could carry on. In the meantime, as he awaited the verdict of Parliament when it met in January 1926, he would find a new seat. The governor-general, Lord Byng, agreed to that on condition that, should King be defeated in the course of the session, the governor general would feel free to call on Arthur Meighen to form a new government. King may or may not have accepted that proposition; at least he put his own peculiar gloss on it.

Parliament met on 7 January 1926, without the prime minister. King managed to get a seat in Prince Albert, Saskatchewan, at a by-election on 15 February. In the meantime a serious Customs scandal had broken out, the motion of censure being launched in Parliament on 2 February by H.H. Stevens, MP for Vancouver Centre. Bennett and Stevens knew each other well; they had shared the same office in 1911 as new MPs. The government had no option but to appoint a select committee to investigate the charges: four Conservatives (including Bennett and Stevens); four Liberals; and a Progressive, Donald Kennedy, MP for Peace River, as chairman. The investigation went on for four months. King managed a nine-seat majority on the conclusion of the Throne Speech debate, and survived fifteen other non-confidence motions. The committee's report became public on 18 June, with a strong condemnation of the minister of Customs, Jacques Bureau, now in the Senate. The action did not satisfy the Conservatives. Stevens moved an amendment that specifically censured Mackenzie King and his government. That fairly put the government's back to the wall. They could be saved – they could only be saved – by coalition. Labour MP J.S. Woodsworth, a Methodist minister of great integrity and a squeaky voice, and fellow Labour Party MP A.A. Heaps guaranteed King a coalition government in return for the creation of Canada's old-age pension plan. Woodsworth, however, was torn by the awful revelations of the Customs scandal, rum runners, and bribery, a reeking mixture of money, liquor, and wickedness.

It was in the midst of this that Harry Shirreff died unexpectedly on 20 May 1926. He was only sixty years old. He was not strong or energetic but had seemed to be sound in heart and lungs. Over the years he had developed a drinking problem, and his sudden collapse was probably owing to liver failure. Harry had married Lena Troop of Dartmouth, Nova Scotia, in 1895; she died in 1916. Harry remarried, probably in March 1925, to Gulielma Patching, who was many years younger. There were stories that this marriage got off to a rocky start. Bennett, who used to visit the couple often at Dunara, their home in Hull (once Jennie Eddy's), observed that there was some truth in that, but Harry's marriage had much improved in recent months. Harry and RB got on well together; in fact Harry depended on RB.

Bennett was upset by Harry's death. "Nothing that has happened to me in recent years was quite such a shock as the passing of poor old Harry," he wrote a Shirreff family friend in Boston. He was also concerned about the young widow, for whom he and Harry had set up a $250,000 trust fund. Edith Shirreff Richardson, Harry's sister in California, who already received $20,000 a year from Jennie Eddy's estate, was sure her brother had been imposed upon by a conspiracy between an unscrupulous young wife and a greedy lawyer – R.B. Bennett. Edith Richardson wanted a quarter million to keep quiet. RB was outraged and refused to communicate with her. As he told a friend, "I am a rich man and have no need of any of the legacies left me by either Mrs Eddy or Harry." But he was in a vulnerable position: he was both executor of Harry's estate and its principal beneficiary. That was unusual, and it created problems. For the will to succeed, as T.P. Foran, the family lawyer put it, it had to be made "fireproof." It was. The aim was to preserve Eddy's as Jennie Shirreff Eddy had striven for in her lifetime, to keep the firm intact and keep the shares under close control. Foran wrote on 24 August 1926, "A consolidation in one or two hands of the majority of the shares obviated any danger that Mr Eddy's life work should become obsolete and his name disappear from the ranks of the builders of Canada." That was what Jennie Shirreff Eddy's will aimed at and what her brother's did too. Foran had done at least four wills for Harry, with the legacy to Bennett in all four of them. He had become the guarantor of the integrity of Eddy's and the guardian of its historical importance.[44]

Meanwhile he was also busy in Parliament. The Customs Committee had been going since February 1926 and Bennett had been a vital member. The report and what it might contain kept the Liberal government of Mackenzie King on pins and needles. The government depended absolutely on the support of Labour, and while Labour preferred Liberals to Conservatives, it was not at any price, and they found the reeking revelations of corruption nauseating. Montreal was the centre of the scandals, with Quebec officials accepting bribes and kickbacks to wink at smuggling.[45] Corruption reached right up to the ministerial level. The Customs Committee Report was tabled in Parliament on 18 June; the chairman, D.M. Kennedy, a Progressive, was skilful in avoiding any direct censure, noting merely that the minister's actions were "unjustifiable." He took care to assuage the susceptibilities of French Canadians who were not going to see one of their own pilloried by Anglos. That did not satisfy H.H. Stevens, who had been the leader, with Bennett, in the four-month investigation. Stevens moved an amendment that was a direct motion of censure. The debate began on 22 June and went on for four days and nights, the King government's life hanging by a thread. On Friday, 25 June, King was not able to adjourn the House until 5 AM on the Saturday morning and then got his weekend adjournment by only one vote. The House of Commons was exhausted. King decided that he could not go on any longer and decided to ask Lord Byng for a dissolution.[46]

At that point Bennett reluctantly left for Calgary. A provincial election was underway in Alberta, and he had promised to help. He tried to get out of the obligation, but Alberta Conservatives held him to it. He found himself a "pair" – a member of the opposing party who agreed to abstain from voting – and went. (There were, incidentally, twenty-two other pairs in the Commons that riven and tense week.) By the time of his return on 6 July, the Byng-King-Meighen crisis had drastically changed the landscape. King was out, Meighen was in. Meighen had, however, just been defeated early on 2 July by one vote in the Commons. The Liberal motion was the result of King's spurious attack on Meighen's "acting ministers."

RB declared that if he had been there, he could have prevented King from ever being heard on such an arcane subject. Any competent House of Commons man, he said, would have roared out denunciations on the Customs scandal. The one vote that brought the Meighen government down was from Rev. T.W. Bird, a Progressive from Manitoba. He protested that when he voted, he was dozing and forgot he was paired. Not many believed him; Bird was adept at parliamentary footwork and probably knew exactly what he was doing. In any case the speaker declined to change Bird's vote.[47]

Meighen now got the dissolution that King had been refused, with the election set for 14 September 1926. Meanwhile, Bennett was sworn in on 7 July to a clutch of portfolios: minister of finance, acting minister of the interior, minister of mines, and superintendent general of Indian affairs. Meighen expected to win the election on the strength of the Customs scandal; King hoped to win it with the constitutional issue – that is, by focusing on the wickedness of a British governor general refusing his Canadian prime minister a dissolution of Parliament when asked.

In the September election the Liberals took 116 seats out of 245, the Conservatives 91, Progressives 11, others 27. Meighen lost his own seat in Portage la Prairie, as did his Quebec colleague E.L. Patenaude. Meighen was devastated. Grant Dexter of the *Winnipeg Free Press* wrote, "Poor Meighen is heartbroken. 'I am 52 years old,' Meighen said 'and without a job.'" For Meighen the worst of it was the ignominy of being defeated by Mackenzie King, whom he regarded as slippery, duplicitous, and capable of almost any act to stay in power. "He is not to be trusted," Lady Byng had told her husband in November 1925. "Did you get his promises in writing?" "No," said Lord Byng, "I believe he is honourable." "Don't you believe it," she said. "I took King's measure from the first time that I shook hands with him."[48]

Although the Conservative Party did not want Meighen to resign, he insisted. In his view, there were two possible successors, Bennett or H.H. Stevens. Among other opinions, some thought it should be a French-speaking Roman Catholic like Robert Manion. The party called a special caucus of Conservative MPs and defeated candidates in Ottawa on 11 October 1926. They named a temporary party leader, Hugh Guthrie, MP from Guelph, Ontario, a former Liberal MP under Laurier who had gone over to the Union government in 1917, then stayed Conservative. More surprising, the caucus recommended a party convention in 1927 to select a new leader as the Liberals had done in selecting Mackenzie King in 1919.

By early 1927 most of the party had concluded that Meighen, for all his forensic talent and his ineffable poise and mastery in Parliament, was not the man to bring the Conservatives back to power. His was hardness burnished and sometimes repellent. He had been the bully boy for Borden, whose generosity, even softness, sometimes needed a warrior with a sword. Meighen had been Borden's knight errant. He had brought in closure in 1913, conscription in 1917, had gone to Winnipeg in 1919 to help put down the General Strike and nationalized the Canadian Northern and the Grand Trunk between 1917 and 1920. Besides, it was now clear that Quebec would not have Meighen in any role, at any price.

The party, moreover, had been too interested in power and not nearly enough in policy. Meighen's tariff program was too shapeless and shop-worn; the party needed more progressive policies to attract the young, the new immigrants, and especially the West, the growing edge of the country.[49]

A burden and a problem for both parties in Parliament was the Montreal, Ottawa, and Georgian Bay Canal project. Around for years, it had been recently taken up by Sir Clifford Sifton. It had started as a shipping route from Montreal to Lake Superior, saving some three hundred miles of distance by using the Ottawa River and the French River, to reach Georgian Bay. It needed twenty-seven locks to connect the Ottawa with Georgian Bay, and by 1927 it was an anachronism as a shipping route, although its power sites, the Carillon in particular, were growing more valuable all the time. However, it was beset with a tangle of jurisdictions between Quebec, Ontario, and the federal government. The project was pushed hard by Sifton and his sons, and in the Commons by E.R.E. Chevrier, Liberal MP for Ottawa. Mackenzie King did not mind a quarrel with Ontario; Howard Ferguson, the Conservative premier, had been "offensively political" over the past year; but to fight Taschereau, the Liberal premier of Quebec, upon whose support King so much depended, was unthinkable. Then there was Sir Clifford Sifton pushing hard for the project. King picked his way through this thicket with some dexterity, arranging that the renewal of the charter get to second reading in the Commons and then be sunk in the Railway and Canals Committee. RB spoke against this old Liberal warhorse, a metaphor he would cheerfully have applied to Sifton, whom he had always disliked. That dislike could extend to other Siftons.[50]

RB took up other ideas in 1927 that eastern Conservatives could well be uneasy with. One was a suggestion, he said, from Sir Edmund Walker (1848–1924), president of the Canadian Bank of Commerce, that the best tax for Canada to adopt would be a universal turnover tax – what we now would call a sales tax. "It is simple, it is universal, it is equal, it is easily collected – it has all the qualifications that were mentioned by the late Adam Smith."[51] The suggestion was an interesting one, well ahead of its time. It eventually disappeared. More immediately relevant were old age pensions.

In the 1920s government pensions usually meant those given to wounded or disabled soldiers and their dependants. The Pension Act dealt with the results of the Great War, and it was a mighty expense, under a whole government department, Pensions and National Health. Then there was Soldiers' Civil Re-establishment, which was running eight military hospitals across Canada. Together those two departments in 1926 ate up 14 per cent of the government's whole current expenditure. Only interest on the national debt was more expensive. The Department of Public Works, long famous for its appetite for money, cost only half as much as Pensions and Soldiers' Civil Re-establishment. The hesitation of the King government before the idea of old age pensions was partly owing to its fear of this formidable and expensive engine that war and the Borden government had created.

Bennett had laid out his ideas about pensions for old age the year before in the March 1926 debate on King's proposed old age pension legislation. Britain had had old age pensions since 1909, and Bennett had studied them first hand. These were non-contributory until 1925 when Neville Chamberlain brought in a contributory system. In 1926, fifteen countries in the world had contributory systems, and twenty-five had non-contributory ones.

The system proposed in 1926 by Mackenzie King had flaws, the most serious being that it was a fifty-fifty arrangement with the provinces.

The provinces could sign up one by one, but until a province did, no one in it could get a federal old age pension. The system thus required provincial cooperation. To many provinces it looked like federal coercion. But it passed the Commons on 26 March 1926 without a division, Conservatives offering comments and criticisms but not opposing it. It was killed in the Senate, 45–21 on 8 June 1926, most but not all the Senate Conservatives voting against it. Not all Liberal senators voted for it either. In the 1926 election the Liberals accused the Conservatives of killing old age pensions. That was untrue for the House of Commons, but it could be alleged against the Senate, heavy with eastern Conservatives.[52]

In 1927 the King government brought the proposal for old age pensions in again, somewhat revised but still with weaknesses that Bennett thought unfortunate. It was still to be fifty-fifty with the provinces; "we are imposing our will upon the provincial legislatures," RB said. He thought old age pensions should be fully Canadian, that is, funded wholly by Ottawa. "I believe in an old age pension scheme," he said. "But I do not believe in an old age pension scheme based on mere granting of money to a provincial authority." Moreover, it should be contributory. Thrift, he argued, in the form of pension fund contributions, would earn its corresponding reward. Those who could not afford contributions would have them paid by Ottawa.[53]

King was profoundly uneasy over old age pensions and within two years was regretting he had ever had a part in the legislation. But it was a bargain with Labour and the Progressive members; it passed the Commons in February 1927 and went to the Senate in March. On 15 March, when Senator Dandurand, the Liberal Senate leader, moved second reading, there were only a few Liberal senators in the House; Senator Curry (Nova Scotia) remarked that it might allow the Liberals to say that the "wicked Tory Senators were the murderers." But few Conservative senators were wicked, division bells called Liberal Senators back, and old age pensions passed the Senate 61–14 on 24 March 1927 and became law.

An old age pension gave $20 a month to the pensioner, maximum $240 per year. If the pensioner's total income were more than $365 a year, the pension income was reduced accordingly. The individual had to be seventy years of age and have lived in Canada as a British subject for five years.[54] One must say a word about what these figures represent, for they are meaningless in present-day context. They are more generous than they would seem now. In the 1920s and 1930s milk cost about 10 to 11 cents an imperial quart (1.14 litres). A loaf of bread was about 10 cents. Movies were 10 cents for children, 35 cents for adults. In 1928 one could not live on $20 a month, even single; but on $40 one could begin to. A young clerk starting in an office or a bank could expect $35 a month.

In less than five months, British Columbia adopted old age pensions; Saskatchewan and Manitoba followed in 1928, Alberta and Ontario in 1929. Nova Scotia, New Brunswick, and Prince Edward Island could not afford even their half share, and their inhabitants had to await easier terms brought in by RB in 1932. Quebec joined in 1936.

The old age pension was not the only social issue brought to the fore in 1927. On 15 March, A.A. Heaps, Labour member for North Winnipeg, raised the issue of unemployment insurance. He goaded the Mackenzie King government by quoting from its 1919 platform, asking for an inquiry into insurance against "unemployment, sickness and invalidity." RB supported this idea but with certain conditions. His basic premise was that all men and women should have at least enough income to be able to look their fellow Canadians confidently in the face, with the inner knowledge that they were not recipients of the country's charity and that they had helped to produce what they were receiving. Similarly, unemployment insurance was to be *insurance*, as was disability insurance. Like any insurance, it was funded by premiums, in this case paid by the government and by the person concerned. "Compensation and payments," RB told the House on 16 March 1927, "are corollaries of one another." That subscription principle would, he said, encourage thrift, initiative, and industry.[55]

In a number of ways, then, RB was more progressive than many in his party. He shared with Borden the same Maritime penchant for reasonable, responsible social legislation. He was a Methodist businessman with a strong social conscience; his mind was also well stocked with experience and precedents from Britain, where social legislation was a generation ahead of Canada. A major debate late in the 1927 session arose over the administration of Soldiers' Civil Re-establishment, especially veterans' pensions and the narrow way they were being interpreted by the Pensions Board. Every MP on Parliament Hill had been getting letters about it. Thomas Cantley, MP for Pictou, said that over half the letters he was receiving from his constituents were about the current hard-headedness of the Pensions Bureau. The Canadian Legion was up in arms.

Bennett was well aware of the difficulty of administering that Pensions Act, but he agreed it was being administered too harshly, too much like a criminal statute, the board placing on the applicant the onus of proving the case beyond reasonable doubt. On 7 April 1927, Bennett, with Guthrie seconding, moved amendments to the Pensions Act to the effect that, unless there were malfeasance, the act be construed as remedial legislation and the applicant be given the benefit of the doubt. RB's amendment won Progressive and Labour support. The government had to defeat it, of course, which it did 95–78, but it promised that the act would be revised over the next year.

Bennett's contribution to the 1927 session had been considerable, with new ideas and new policies seeming to arise almost spontaneously. In urging changes to the Pensions Act, he asked, "Shall we be statesmen or politicians?" His quotation of James Russell Lowell seemed to suggest the forward thrust of his mind: "New occasions teach new duties; / Time makes ancient good uncouth; / They must upward still, and onward, / Who would keep abreast of Truth."[56]

Meanwhile, keeping abreast of Eddy's was getting to be a formidable challenge. Harry Shirreff's death had placed heavy responsibilities on his shoulders as the majority shareholder of the firm. True, Eddy's had a president and a general manager, but RB was the senior director, and to him the balance sheet did not look right. Compared with the size of Eddy's plant and its annual expenditure, profits were not large enough. From his suite on the first floor of the Château Laurier, he could see Eddy's property across the river, taking up two whole miles of the north side of the Ottawa from the Chaudière Falls to the Gatineau River. It was an immense enterprise, turning out 4,000 tons of newsprint a month, 1,000 tons of specialty papers, 21,000 cases of matches. Behind all that was a huge back-up operation: bush camps to cut lumber, logging drives, stockpiles of raw material. With plant and equipment valued at $6 million, the annual net profit should have been 6 per cent. In 1926 it was more like 2 per cent. When he was in Ottawa, RB spent much of his spare time across the river in Hull. The newsprint side of the firm was not run to his satisfaction. C.V. Caesar, Eddy's general manager, told him on 3 January 1926 that his New Year's Eve telegram had been passed round the office and shown to important operating chiefs.[57] Another telegram of 17 May 1927, from Bennett to George R. Millen, president of Eddy's, reveals Bennett's hand: "Apparently publishers wearying of inability to secure anything but promises at Hull think by appealing to me will secure redress and are threatening immediate cancellations of contracts amounting to eight hundred tons per month owing to inferior quality of newsprint now produced. We cannot afford this loss of tonnage ... Situation serious and causes me great anxiety." He could be blunt too with Caesar: "I know you were busy early in July," he wrote, "but I am sure you'll agree, on mature reflection, that that cannot be an excuse for failing to manufacture matches when we were advised they would be required."[58]

There were opportunities that summer for him to bail out of Eddy's, or at least to get rid of parts of it. In May 1927 he received an offer for his Eddy shares at $1,800 each. A richer offer came in August at $2,050, although that one, he gradually realized, was not bona fide, perhaps intended to block the sale of minority shares to Victor Drury of Montreal at $1,700. The sale did go through, and Drury became an Eddy's director. Bennett had offers to sell Eddy's match business, including one from Ivar Kreuger, the Swedish match monopolist. It was broken off by Kreuger on 10 October 1927; Bennett's terms were too stiff. That side of the business was, however, sold in December 1927 to Bryant and May, the English firm, and the match factory moved out of Hull to Pembroke, Ontario. The Eddy name was kept. In 1939 RB still had 4,900 shares of Eddy Matches, some common and some preferred. The rest of Eddy's still remained his to control.[59]

This flurry of offers to buy all or part of Eddy's was brought on by late 1920s prosperity and doubtless too by rumours that RB might be a candidate for the leadership of the Conservative Party; it was assumed that he would not want to run Eddy's and the party too. The Conservative convention was set to meet in Winnipeg in the autumn of 1927. But even as late as August 1927, six weeks before the Winnipeg convention, RB had not made up his mind to stand for the leadership. A younger friend in Toronto, Mark Irish, an MLA in the Ontario legislature, urged him against it – he might win it.

Irish was a public-spirited insurance agent in Toronto, involved in the building of the Toronto General Hospital in 1911; during the war he became an arbitrator with the Labour section of the Imperial Munitions Board. Irish had a way with words and negotiations. In settling a 1917 labour disagreement, he remarked that the workers conceded his point "with a grace that did them proud. The manufacturer kept his bristles up until the last moment."[60] Irish was a hard worker, drawn to father figures, first to Canadian business leader Sir Joseph Flavelle, then to RB. He wrote to RB on 31 August 1927:

My dear R.B.,
When I think of the sacrifice you must make it staggers me. Perhaps the sacrifice bulks larger to me than to some men because what you

would let go is, from my training and environment, a far greater prize than you could possibly attain in the other sphere. Prestige, liberty, ease, hobbies, delights, leisure all thrown to the winds, and an existence surrounded by abuse, ingratitude, selfishness and slavish work substituted. Am I presuming if I say to my friend R.B. Bennett, "Don't do it – and I pray you to find some other way out."

Again I say, Don't do it.

RB listened, but in August 1927 he was fifty-seven years of age, brimming with energy, good health and, not least, ambition. He had no hobbies, no sports, though he does seem to have known something of bridge. His leisure life was reading. Thus for him there might be a new world of action opening up. Eddy's two miles of factories along the Ottawa were all very well, but Canada was bigger than Eddy's. And there were those lines of Browning's that he was fond of quoting, "A man's reach should exceed his grasp, / Or what's a heaven for?"

Besides, he told Irish, there were such things as duty and public spirit. Someone had to take these things on. Canada had been good to him: should he not do his duty by Canada? He was not concerned, he later said, about ease or delights or even prestige. And, he told Mackenzie King in January 1928, "I didn't seek the leadership. It had come about suddenly."[61]

RB's Canada and Canada's RB,

1927–1930

The Canada in which RB considered taking on the leadership of the Conservative Party in 1927 was dramatically different from the nation we know today. Nine million Canadians lived in a vast country of forest, prairie, mountains, and lakes bordered by three great oceans. Canada was beginning to develop a sense of itself, an identity nourished by the South African War (1899–1902) and the Great War, the victory at Vimy Ridge. Rudyard Kipling's poem of 1897–98 honoured this beginning: "'I am first in the battle,' / Said our Lady of the Snows." If Canada's was an identity still inchoate, a bloom of pride was burgeoning within it. The ethos of the Group of Seven revealed to Canadians, a little unexpectedly, an almost instinctive aesthetic direction of woods, water, land, bigness.

What was a Canadian? J.S. Woodsworth (Labour) and R.B. Bennett (Conservative), both Methodists, discussed the issue in the House of Commons in 1929. The two men, Bennett in New Brunswick and Woodsworth in Ontario, had grown up in the 1870s and 1880s with unclear perceptions of what Canadians might even call themselves. Woodsworth told the House of Commons in February 1929, "I can remember as a child feeling almost ashamed of myself because while my schoolmates, when asked what nationality they were, could say English, Scotch or German, poor I could only say that I did not belong to any nationality, that I was only born in this country." It was time, Woodsworth said, to get rid of the designation "British subject domiciled in Canada." RB agreed: if we are British subjects, he said, we are also Canadian citizens. It should be possible for people born in this country to describe themselves as Canadian. When Bennett was in Germany and Austria in 1928, he said, "I had no hesitation in describing myself as a Canadian. I did so with much pride, and I am bound to say that I received ... a courtesy and consideration which would not have been accorded me had I described myself as a resident of another part of the American continent."[1]

In 1925, Sir Joseph Flavelle offered this realistic perception of the nation: "We are a long narrow strip, stretching from the Atlantic to the Pacific, each section divided by great physical barriers, denying a continuity of population." There was no easy way to go by road from Saint John to Montreal or from Fort William to Winnipeg or from Calgary to Vancouver and stay within Canada. Agnes Macphail underlined that point when she and RB tried to persuade the King government to construct a national highway. Canadians east and west, said Macphail, "disliked having to go out of their own country to cross their own country."[2]

A large part of it, the province of Quebec, was a mysterious and not easily understood world. English Canadians rarely grasped the ambiguity at the heart of French Canada. It is neatly suggested in Fréchette's 1888 poem, "Le Drapeau Anglais." As a father shows his son downtown Montreal, the son asks about the Union Jack flying above a building:

– Regarde, me disait mon père,
Ce drapeau vaillament porté,
Il a fait ton pays prospère,
Et respect ta liberté ...

– Mais, père, pardonnez si j'ose,
N'en est-il pas un autre, à nous?
– Ah, celui-là, c'est autre chose
Il faut le baiser à genoux!

That flag, the father says, you can respect: it has given us freedom and prosperity. But the son rejoins politely, "Don't we have another of our own?" "Ah," says the father, "that flag is something else altogether. We kiss that flag on bended knee." The significance of that juxtaposition escaped most anglophone Canadians, RB included. In most of English Canada, one never heard French – so much so that an English-Canadian child could be surprised to discover that telephones would actually transmit French. Most high schools taught French, but focused on learning vocabulary and grammar, with no sense that it would be used in real life. "Bilingual" was something Canadians thought francophone Canadians should be; it did not usually work both ways.

In 1927, however, when Canada celebrated the Diamond Jubilee of Confederation, its postage stamps for the first time intimated that this was a country of two official languages. On a celebratory issue of five stamps, on each stamp opposite "Postage" was "Postes." That surprise was the initiative of P.J. Veniot, the Acadian New Brunswicker who became Mackenzie King's new postmaster general after the 1926 election. The twelve-cent stamp had a geo-political map of Canada, showing how Canada had been put together. What was also remarkable about that stamp, aside from the "Postes," was its inclusion of the Privy Council's Labrador boundary decision of March 1927, showing the vast gouge out of Quebec awarded by the British Privy Council to the Colony of Newfoundland. Schoolchildren were used to the old boundary in the big Mercator maps showing the British Empire, and Canada, hugely in red. To some it seemed that a huge chunk of Quebec had been torn away from the very body of Canada. Large that chunk was, indeed, some 113,000 square miles.

The Privy Council, on an agreed reference between Canada and Newfoundland, had decided that the coast of Labrador meant the watershed of all the rivers flowing down to that coast. Drastic though the decision was, it did not create much stir in the Canadian Parliament. There were distant suggestions that Canada might one day buy Labrador back; the Taschereau government of Quebec was occasionally blamed for the loss. But Newfoundland and Labrador was still a distant world, master of its own sometimes rancorous politics and its own precarious economy. With so little arable land, Newfoundlanders depended largely on the sea, and life there was a hard struggle in the face of often severe odds, as in E.J. Pratt's "Erosion":

It took the sea a thousand years
A thousand years to trace
The granite features of this cliff,
In crag and scarp and base.

It took the sea an hour one night,
An hour of storm to place
The sculpture of these granite seams
Upon a woman's face.

According to the 1921 Canadian census, Canada's rural and urban populations were roughly equal, at 50.5 per cent rural and 49.5 per cent urban. But different provinces defined urban differently. If "urban" were defined as an aggregation larger than a thousand, then Canada was still 55 per cent rural and 45 per cent urban. In character and outlook it was substantially rural, and for some provinces that was preponderantly the case. Something of that old rural world comes through in Thomas H. Raddall's 1938 short story, "Before Snow Flies": "Ah, Fall. A wonderful time of year, boy. Trees an' shrubs handsome as a picture, crops in ... There's work too; storm doors an' windas to put on, an' sods to bank around the house, an' a big pile o' cordwood to saw an' split an' pile in the woodshed ... Doin' them Fall chores gives a man a queer kind of cosy feelin'..."

But there were less cosy consequences. Farmers were still the largest employers of unskilled labour; this pool, much needed at planting and at harvest, was not so much needed at other seasons and stood virtually idle in winter. Industry paid better and could offer wages year-round. That was one major attraction of towns and cities. But industries could be cyclical too; they were more unpredictable than farm seasons and more drastic in fluctuations and effects. In the 1920s unemployment in Canada ranged from 9 per cent of the labour force in 1921 to 3 per cent in 1927. Skilled workers made up only 12 per cent of Canada's labour force as against 21 per cent in Britain, and 17 per cent in the United States.[3]

The distinction between rural and urban was beginning to be blurred by the advent of the automobile. In 1908 there were three thousand cars registered in Canada. They crouched spider-like on their high, narrow wheels on mostly still unpaved streets. The Model T Ford appeared in 1909 and was still something of the people's car when the Model A Ford arrived in 1927. By then there were 940,000 cars across the country, half of them in Ontario. The new Model A Ford came at about $525. Up-market cars were usually American, like the Essex Super Six (roughly equivalent to a present-day Buick), which could be got for $1,010, f.o.b. Detroit.

If the automobile was the way of future, many people still tended to live within the template of their pasts – in a world of railways and trains. Railways had stitched Canada together; and in the 1920s the CPR and CNR were still doing it, on an expansionist scale. On winter nights the lonely demonic shriek of those monsters' whistles echoed out of the cold and darkness and distance. If one were close enough, one could see their monocular headlights driving into the darkness, as in E.J. Pratt's 1931 poem "The 6000":

His body black as Erebus
Accorded with the hue of night;

His central eye self-luminous
Threw out a cone of noon-day light,
Which split the gloom and then flashed back
The diamond levels of the track ...
Out to the spaces – there to toss
The blizzard from his path across
The prairies of Saskatchewan.

In daytime children stood to watch the big black engines going by, fascinated by the elemental force of ruthless driving wheels and hissing pistons. Sometimes they would test that force by putting one of the big Canadian 1927 pennies on the track to see how the train would flatten it.

In 1927 Canada had about 3,300,000 horses, most of them on farms, but every community in Canada had them and used them. Horses were still used heavily for transport: milk wagons, bread wagons, ice wagons, coal wagons. In winter the wagons would be converted to sleighs, the snow on the street packed down with the horse manure to an icy tractable base. An obliging bread man would sometimes allow children to hitch their sleighs to the back of his big one. Villages and towns still had hitching posts, but horses and buggies were gradually being given up for cars. Cars did not need to be harnessed before use; they did not have to be groomed, fed, and stabled. In the countryside, blacksmith shops slowly gave way to gasoline stations.

A 1933 by-election in Restigouche-Madawaska in northeast New Brunswick provided an interesting example of the contrast between the old and the new modes. Rumour had it that the date would be set for early spring. "Whatever you do," a local organizer wrote to RB, "do not have the election in March." Roads were breaking up; in the afternoon and evening they were impassable. With several feet of snow on the country roads, horses "slumping through them, you have to lead the horses and you'll do well to make 3 miles an hour." Wait, he advised, "until we can get over the roads in automobiles."[4]

Every household was a chore centre. Every house had to have a source of heat, and for several decades fireplaces were steadily replaced by a combination of kitchen stoves and furnaces as the main source of heat. It was not until the 1930s that oil furnaces controlled with thermostats provided welcome relief from interminable furnace tending. Coal furnaces had to be watched and fed, sometimes coaxed and pampered. That was usually a man's job, but often delegated to wives and children. When the Liberal cabinet minister C.D. Howe was away from home, which in the 1920s was often, his wife, Alice, commanded their monster Port Arthur furnace, as she did the rest of the house. Sons and daughters laboured to keep furnaces going on winter nights. It was a great joy to go down to the basement on a frigid winter morning and find the embers of last night's fire still alive. One would pull out the clinkers (coal impurities fused together), stir the fire with a long poker, and put on fresh coal. A winter's supply of coal ran to tons. A good-sized house might take four tons a winter, to be stored in several bins in the cellar – either that or have the supply renewed in mid-winter, the coal sliding down long chutes from the wagon outside. A popular subject of dinnertime debate was which coal was the best, Welsh anthracite being preferred but Pennsylvania anthracite not far behind. Nova Scotian soft coal was nearly universal in the Maritimes, but it was messy to use and did not give as hot a fire; the smoke was much dirtier. All Maritime towns had layers of coal dust on the houses, unsuccessfully concealed by painting them an unlovely chocolate brown. With railway subventions, the price of Cape Breton coal made it competitive as far west as Montreal.

Children and chores went hand in hand, as every household entailed manifold duties. Not least of these was bringing coal up from the cellar for the kitchen stove – although by 1927, the new electric stoves were already becoming popular, made in Canada and selling for $99. Stoves of both kinds were presided over by the mother, the maid, or both. Most middle-class families, and some not so middle, had maids because there was so much to do. The workload was alleviated somewhat when washing machines began appearing at the end of the 1920s. But refrigeration was still done mostly in ice boxes; ice cutting was a winter task in the majority of communities. Ice came in great seventy-five to eighty pound cubes, handled with special tongs that allowed the ice man to sling the block into the refrigerator. Electric refrigerators began to appear early in the 1930s.

Many households had gardens for berries and fresh vegetables in summer, along with a chicken run and hen house to keep the eggs coming. Even in town, many a property had a hen house. The birds did not lay well in winter, so eggs would be preserved in large crocks for the cold season. A chicken dinner was a luxury. Cooking tended to be homespun: things like pastas, yoghurts, sour cream, and salami were what foreigners or immigrants ate. Canadians' appreciation of such things was at least a generation in the future. Roasts, stews, potatoes, turnips, cabbage all winter, and heavy solid desserts were general fare. Fresh fruit or vegetables out of season were luxuries. One lived on root vegetables and apples from the cold cellar. Apples were bought by the barrel and stored as far away from heat and frost as possible. Four barrels of Northern Spys could last a family three to four months. Macintosh apples were three pounds for 25 cents; potatoes, 13 cents for eight pounds; sugar, ten pounds for 72 cents; prime rib of beef, 19 cents a pound. A can of pork and beans was 9 cents. Woollen overcoats were brought out of moth-balls in early October; a new made-in-England one could be bought for $27.

Movie theatres were supplanting touring vaudeville and theatre companies, but communities also made their own entertainment. In 1928, the Ontario town of Napanee, population three thousand, put on Gilbert and Sullivan's 1882 comic opera *Iolanthe*. Gilbert and Sullivan operas would be popular for many a year to come, surviving into the 1950s and beyond among high school, university, and civic groups.

Perhaps what one remembers most from that time is the singing, the visceral thrill that came with elegant close harmony or the glorious descants on the top of some Christmas carol. Around campfires in summer, pianos in winter, there always seemed to be songs, spirituals out of the American South, "Sewanee River," "Ol' Black Joe," "Swing Low, Sweet Chariot," or the odd Civil War song like "John Brown's Body." There were the Great War songs too: "It's a Long Way to Tipperary," a 1912 song made popular by British and Canadian troops, and "There's a Long, Long Trail A-Winding," about love past, present, and future.

Churches were nourished by singing; most had choirs. In the small Protestant ones the choirmaster and organist was usually an unpaid volunteer who played the organ Sunday mornings and evenings. One enterprising organist in small-town Ontario, looking for a postlude more sprightly than the usual tumpy hymns, sent his Anglican congregation home to their midday Sunday dinner with "Walking My Baby Back Home."[5] Some of its lyrics catch fleeting echoes of the way life was:

Gee, but it's great after being out late,
Walking my baby back home.
Arm in arm over meadow and farm,
Walking my baby back home.

We go along harmonizing a song,
Or I'm reciting a poem.
Owls go by and they give me the eye,
Walking my baby back home.

The song's words were familiar because of radio broadcasting, which had begun early in the 1920s. Receiving sets required a two-dollar licence. In 1927, there were only 140,000 radios in Canada, but numbers were rising steeply. By 1930, over half a million sets were licensed. At first, more attention was paid to wavelengths and licences than to content, but Britain and the United States, each in very different ways, established the main rules for the future. In Britain the BBC was given substantial autonomy, along with the task of controlling radio's primary duty, seen by the BBC as education, with entertainment as secondary. After two years and more of radio chaos, the US Congress in 1927 established the Federal Radio Commission, which allowed American stations to concentrate on entertainment, with education as incidental. This entertainment was sponsored by commerce – manufacturers of brand-name products like Jell-O and Johnson's Wax, their virtues paraded at intervals, usually decorously at the beginning and end of programs.

In Canada, communications policy drifted. Canada's, as with most of its policies that drift, gravitated toward American practice. The first broadcasting station in Canada was CFCF (Canada's First, Canada's Finest) in Montreal in 1920. By 1929 there were over sixty Canadian stations, most of them with low power, limited range, and wobbly signals. In the early 1920s under the imaginative drive of Sir Henry Thornton, president of Canadian National Railways, the CNR developed the beginnings of a radio network. But American stations rapidly increased their power and their obtrusiveness, the uncertainty of wavelength control aggravating the problem. Canada was flooded with American radio, and although the programs were often good listening, many Canadians were concerned about being subjected so relentlessly to American styles, manners, and advertising. In that respect, francophone Quebecers were automatically insulated.

Commerce had long since filled the newspapers. The advent of cheap pulp paper at the turn of the century had allowed newspapers to greatly expand their advertising and their size. They exploited their double faces of news and advertising: murder and mayhem helped to sell makeup and manicures. Over the 1920s the changes in advertising style were dramatic. In 1919 an unadorned rectangle promoted Listerine as a safe antiseptic. By the end of the 1920s it was full-page of a bridesmaid weeping over being "always a bridesmaid but never a bride," the halitosis that could have been cured by Listerine still dooming her to single life.

Comic strips had started in the 1920s. "Bringing Up Father" and "Mutt and Jeff" were early favourites. Mackenzie King was reputed to prefer "Tillie the Toiler," the adventures, domestic and office, of a young secretary. Bennett may have enjoyed "Bringing Up Father," a standing daily comment on female dominance – daily except on Sunday, that is. On Sundays, newspapers did not publish.

Visitors to Canada could find the Canadian Sunday a distinct trial. In Protestant Canada at least, the world simply shut down. In Toronto a generation before, there had been a ferocious debate on the morality of allowing streetcars to operate on Sunday. Streetcars won. However, in places where no streetcars ran (that is, in most of the country), when church was over, people retired behind closed curtains. Playing outside was frowned on; children were supposed to be in Sunday school on Sunday afternoon; there they would be told stories (with pictures) of baby Moses in the bulrushes along the Nile, God creating the cleft in the Red Sea for the Israelites to cross, the frightening scene of Abraham about to sacrifice Isaac and being stopped by God in the nick of time. A Catholic church after Sunday mass in Quebec presented a quite different scene; people talked and gossiped, children played, and in the afternoon one could even go to the movies. Protestant Canada thought that was evidence of the insidious wickedness of the Roman Catholicism.

In those days everyone dressed formally for church. "En dimanche" was Sunday best both in French and English Canada. But then there was a good deal of formality every day and particularly for funerals, weddings, dinners, and parties. Clerks in banks wore suits and ties, and when outside, hats. Most men wore hats; bowlers were still common, and silk hats with white tie and tails were de rigueur for formal occasions with ladies present. Felt hats were becoming more common, usually in the homburg style. Snap brims tended to be favoured more by salesmen and reporters or those who did not know better. Caps with a peak usually marked the wearer as a workman or farmer. Sartorial differences were not so distinctive in Canada as in England, where someone stood in society could often still be judged on the basis of what they wore. That was one reason why Bennett advised the young juniors in his Calgary law office to "dress well." When a junior from the Calgary law office, J.J. Saucier, was invited to come to Ottawa for a year to help out, he asked Alice Millar, RB's secretary, what he would require in the way of clothes. She told him he would need both morning clothes and evening clothes; "A dinner jacket [tuxedo] will not do down here, although it will be useful on a few occasions." He would also need a silk hat.

Women were now wearing skirts cut just below the knee, their sack-like shape emphasized if they were made of silk or crêpe de Chine. The editor of the *Dalhousie Gazette* praised these short skirts; an old Dalhousie alumnus, a school principal, complained about them. The student editor suggested the principal acquire a special pair of glasses that allowed him to see only the top half of every woman he met.[6]

The *Manitoba Free Press* of Saturday, 8 October 1927 and the week following reflect many of the details above. Monday, 10 October, marked the opening of the Liberal-Conservative Party Leadership Convention in Winnipeg. Great were the preparations. The Royal Alexandra Hotel was filled to overflowing. The delegates gathered in the Amphitheatre, a hockey and skating rink in winter, a horse show palace in summer, its atmosphere redolent of both. It was also used for concerts. The building was about one hundred metres south of the Manitoba legislature, toward the Assiniboine River. It could seat seven thousand in the tiered hockey seats and on folding metal chairs on the floor in the middle. One imaginative reporter thought he heard, up among the rafters, faint echoes of a Mackenzie King speech from the 1926 election, and even of the divine singing of Amelita Gallicurci. Now those rafters were emblazoned with banners carrying mottoes and party legends: "What Canada Makes, Makes Canada," and "Build Up Imperial Trade," with not a blush at any contradiction. An ample platform flanked with two large Union Jacks was for selected party notables: former prime ministers Sir Robert Borden and Arthur Meighen, the provincial premiers, Conservative leaders in the provinces, and privy councillors past and present.

The weather had not been altogether propitious. The previous week the main road from Regina to Winnipeg had heavy ruts in several places. Gangs of harvesters were moving back east because the fields were too wet for work. Marketing of wheat was down. By the weekend before the convention, harvesting had started up again in Alberta, but in Winnipeg the weather was still unsettled, the temperature 3 degrees Celcius with a few showers. The city was bulging at the seams. More than a hundred reporters from newspapers across Canada were there to report proceedings and doings of some sixteen hundred delegates plus visitors and onlookers. Winnipeg had seen nothing like it in years.

The big question was the Conservative leadership. Two favourites had been mooted for some time. One was Howard Ferguson, the premier of Ontario, who had pulled the Ontario Conservative Party out of defeat and defeatism to victory in 1923. In 1927 he had repealed the thorny Regulation 17 that had severely limited French-speaking education in Ottawa and eastern Ontario. That action brought him great plaudits from Quebec. He had also dealt adroitly with prohibition, bringing in the ingeniously titled Liquor Control Board of Ontario. He could probably have had the Conservative leadership without lifting a finger. Of course he said he didn't want it; all respectable candidates said that. He claimed that he would rather be premier of Ontario than leader of the Opposition in Ottawa. That could well have been true, for he was a political animal to his bones. Not for him high-minded views about a non-partisan civil service; he not only revelled in political patronage but believed in it. Party workers worked better if they had hope of rewards, so rewards they should have. That was the way of the world.

Arthur Meighen, out of politics only a year, was another strong possibility. He said he did not want to succeed himself, but he was being encouraged from several quarters. Arthur Ford, editor of the *London Free Press*, told him there was "overwhelming desire" for his return. Meighen was still vigorous, still young; indeed, he was the youngest but one of all the possibilities. That he could have had the leadership was the judgment of John Dafoe of the *Manitoba Free Press*, George Smith of the *Toronto Globe*, and not least, of the young, thirty-two-year-old John Diefenbaker of Saskatchewan. On the Saturday before the convention, a *Free Press* reporter asked Meighen if he would accept nomination. Meighen's reply was massively oblique: "I was very interested in noting the seating arrangements ... I think everything has been splendidly arranged."

On the first afternoon the two undeclared candidates clashed bitterly. Meighen as courtesy had been asked to give a short address. He made a brilliant forensic defence of his controversial speech in December 1925 in Hamilton, when he had taken the position that in any future war, his government would not send troops overseas without electoral endorsement. Ferguson was furious. All through Meighen's speech he whispered angrily to Rhodes and Bennett. Amid resounding cheers for Meighen, Ferguson took over the microphone. "I never could see the wisdom of digging up a corpse that had been buried for two years just for the purpose of receiving a smell," he said. Meighen went white with anger. Ferguson said Meighen had come to him in November 1925 for an opinion of the speech and he had advised against it. It would do little good in Quebec, he told Meighen, and make plenty of trouble in Ontario.

But after Meighen's lithe and spirited performance that Monday afternoon, the convention was not having pudgy Ferguson. The mutterings swelled the longer Ferguson spoke. Saskatchewan delegates called out at him, "Shut up and sit down!" Ferguson held on, but it did him no good.

Any prospect of his being leader vanished that afternoon.[7] The next day both men were nominated; both refused to stand.

Two provincial premiers were nominated, E.N. Rhodes of Nova Scotia, and J.B.M. Baxter of New Brunswick. Both had been MPs, but both thought it wiser to stay as premiers for the time being and support the party from power bases in Halifax and Fredericton. H.H. Stevens, only forty-eight years old, slim, short, and in good health, was nominated too, but because of parlous financial circumstances he decided he could not stand.

Six did agree to stand. In alphabetical order, they were: Bennett of Calgary, aged fifty-seven; C.H. Cahan of Montreal, aged sixty-six; Sir Henry Drayton of Ontario, aged fifty-eight; Hugh Guthrie of Guelph, aged sixty-one; R.J. Manion of Fort William (now Thunder Bay), aged forty-six; Robert Rogers of Winnipeg, aged sixty-three. Except for Manion, Bennett was the youngest. To a reporter from the *Manitoba Free Press* the platform party looked tired, like "roses of yesteryear." It seemed ironic that the stout, "massive, slow-gaited youth" of nearly sixty years of age, J.B.M. Baxter of New Brunswick, should be making a plea for youth. The six nominees each had three speeches associated with their nomination: nominator, seconder, and the candidate himself. There were time constraints on each; but the speeches came in three languages, English, French, and Oratory. By midnight on the Tuesday, delegates had all the speeches they could stand.[8]

By this time the party platform had been hammered together and showed evidence of some skilful joinery. The aim was to make it "fool-proof and Grit-proof." Resolutions of every variety had come to the Resolutions Committee, and many disappeared into wastebaskets. The gap between "What Canada Makes, Makes Canada" and "Build Up Imperial Trade" had been bridged by saying that there should be preferential tariffs throughout the empire but not at the expense of Canadian farmers or workmen. The party supported social legislation to relieve distress of unemployment, sickness, or old age "so far as is practicable." The present old age pension law was unworkable and inadequate; old age pensions should be under the jurisdiction of the dominion government. As for immigration, British settlers were to be encouraged, and "such races be excluded as are not capable of ready assimilation." That was the West Coast speaking, the phrasing included at H.H. Stevens's insistence.[9]

RB demonstrated his nationalism at a noon Winnipeg Rotary Club speech on Wednesday, 12 October. "The first thing we must do in this country," he said, "is to build up a strong national consciousness – a virile Canadianism – we have suffered from an inferiority complex long enough." That was the day of balloting for the leader. On the first round that afternoon 1,564 ballots were cast. Bennett received 594, Guthrie 345, Cahan 310, Manion 170, Rogers 114, and Drayton 31. Bennett did not have a majority and so a second round was held. This time 1,554 votes were cast, and the leader would have to poll 778. On this ballot Cahan lost some Quebec support to Bennett, as did Guthrie; Rogers's support largely went in the same direction. Bennett emerged with 780 votes. Nearly everyone was taken by surprise at this early victory, including RB, who seemed overwhelmed by the suddenness of his triumph. There was wild enthusiasm on the floor of the Amphitheatre as the election was made unanimous.[10]

Bennett's acceptance speech was full of sincerity and sentiment. He admitted being rich. He'd made it from his own work. Now that he was elected leader, he would resign his directorships, for, he said, "no man may serve you as he should, if he has over his shoulder always the shadow of pecuniary obligations and liabilities." No man could serve two masters, or two mistresses either. Service! – that would be his motto. He took his sentiment from St Mark (9:35): "If any man desire to be first, the same shall be the last of all and servant of all." Henceforth he would give his time, his talent, his fortune to his country. "Such as I am, such as I have, I consecrate to the service in which I am." It was a fair promise, fairly meant. That night the *Winnipeg Evening Tribune* commented, "The party cannot ask more of its leader. The country cannot ask more of its sons."

Once Bennett had been elected, train reservations that had been suspended in anticipation of a late night were reactivated, and by midnight four trains full of delegates were heading east and west. The amphitheatre shorn of delegates reminded a reporter of these lines from the Irish poet Thomas Moore:

I feel like one
Who treads alone
Some banquet-hall deserted,
Whose lights are fled,
Whose garlands dead,
And all but he departed![11]

By the time the news reached Ontario, it was evening. Newspapers came out with late editions. "Bennett Chosen Leader!" newsboys cried in the streets of downtown Toronto. RB's acceptance speech was admired by many Conservatives, especially the lean, pensive financier at National Trust, Toronto, J.M. Macdonell. The Conservative Party, he said to RB, had to take "its courage in both hands" and stand for principles. So, "as they used to say in the Army, 'Up you go and the best of luck.'" The metaphor was from the trenches on the Western Front. Indeed, the party in electing RB as leader had "declared for war," said the *Montreal Daily Star*. "In the parlance of war he is a cavalry leader rather than a Fabian." If he was polished and shining and glittering, he was also ready for attack. The *Star* drew him as Lochinvar on horseback: "From out of the West there rode a knight."[12]

Almost at once Bennett left Winnipeg for New York, accompanied by his sister Mildred, for discussions about the sale of Eddy's. Part of it was already concluded; the match side had been sold that autumn to Bryant and May in England. Bennett undoubtedly insisted that the Eddy name be kept; the Eddy Match factory would be established at Pembroke, Ontario. The pulp and paper side of the company was another story. Bennett's New York negotiations were unsatisfactory. He would not get a buyer or a price for Eddy's for a few years yet.

In late November he came back West to a fat Calgary reception. The city was proud of him, proud of his success, proud indeed of the fact that he still wanted to live there. He was the best-dressed man in town, and that had been true ever since 1897, even when he had not "two half-dollars to rub together." He was known by more than that, however. Every fifteen minutes, day and night, the chimes of Central United Church rang across downtown Calgary – it was RB's memorial to his mother, but it could well have been to honour him. He had been a Calgary MP since 1911, except for a close defeat in 1921. From 1925 onward he was MP for Calgary West as long as he chose to be. His charities to schools, to good students, were everywhere. And it was in Calgary too where he acquired his strong dislike of American encroachment upon Canada. "My boy," he said to a young man in his office after the First World War, "I have lived in this town for more than twenty years, and whenever I have seen signs of degeneration or corruption in business morals, they have always been due to American influence. Canada's future depends utterly upon maintaining its freedom from all that is worst in American life."[13]

He received a flood of letters congratulating him, Calgary, and Canada on his new role. Among them was one from Isabella ("Daisy")

Macdonald Gainsford (1877–1960), the granddaughter of Sir John A. Macdonald and the daughter of Sir Hugh John Macdonald. She saluted RB as "the right man in the right place." Lord and Lady Byng each wrote, for RB had been solicitous and generous to them when they were forced out of Canada in 1926. "Bless you dear R.B.," Lady Byng wrote. She was longing to come back, especially to see the West, trying not to dwell on the hurt she still felt after five wonderful Canadian years. She did not want even to think about Mackenzie King, that "one unspeakable cad!!" Agnes Macphail remarked that long before the Winnipeg convention, "we in Ottawa decided we quite liked Bennett." She would always have a soft spot for him.[14]

A cable of congratulations came from Gladys Drury Beaverbrook, one of the most beautiful women of Bennett's acquaintance. She was the sister of his Eddy colleague, Victor Drury, of Montreal. The Drurys were a well-established family, originally from Halifax, where Max Aitken and Gladys met and married in 1906. The Drurys were a cut above the Aitkens, and Gladys was a lovely creature with green eyes and auburn hair. In a photograph of her taken in the early 1920s, her eyes are full of infinite patience and sadness. Aitken's adventures had brought her to both. Sadly, seven weeks after her cable to Bennett, she was dead of a brain tumour at age thirty-nine. She left three young children and Aitken distraught with grief and a very bad conscience.[15]

Bennett now had to face the task of bailing out of his many directorships – at the Royal Bank, General Electric, International Paper Co., Metropolitan Life of New York. His stock holdings (except for CPR shares) he would keep and manage as any other investments, but he felt he had to give up the direction of company policy in the several enterprises of which he was a director. He resigned from the board of directors of Metropolitan Life on 30 December 1927. His letter filled the company's president, Haley Fiske, with dismay. It seemed to him so unnecessary; were Bennett already prime minister, perhaps the case might be different – though even there, Fiske noted, Premier Taschereau of Quebec seemed to be able to function both as premier and a director of Metropolitan Life Insurance. "Do you really think it is necessary for you to resign when you are not an office-holder? ... Please withhold the resignation if you possibly can." Bennett regretted that he had to insist: "As the subject of insurance is dealt with by Parliament I feel I must divest myself of any connection with an insurance company, as it might be regarded by my opponents as influencing any criticism I might offer."[16] That would be the way with all the other directorships, except for Eddy's. His Eddy shares, and that controlling interest in Eddy's, were not going to be sold at bargain-basement price because of his being Conservative leader. Nevertheless, with Eddy's he was careful to keep an arm's-length relationship, saying frequently to inquiries that he had nothing to do with the actual running of the company. That was true more or less. His important job now was pulling the Conservative Party together into a working and fighting machine.

It badly needed an overhaul. One Manitoba Conservative, Dr F.L. Schaffner, originally from Nova Scotia, congratulated Hugh Guthrie on February 1927 on becoming the pro-tem leader of the party, adding, "What there is left of it. Never since Confederation has the Party been so stranded." Rebuilding it, said Schaffner, would take courage and patience. Guthrie seemed to think, as many eastern Conservatives did, that the future hope of the party lay in the West. That was the hope behind Conservative support for Bennett. But Guthrie shouldn't count on it, Schaffner said. One Conservative from Toronto wrote to RB saying the position of leader would not be "a bed of roses for a time at least." In Parliament the front bench was short of "fighting men," of whom there were only RB, C.H. Cahan, Robert Manion, Stevens, and Guthrie.[17]

Of 245 seats in the House of Commons in mid-1927, the Conservatives held 89; the Liberals and their allies, the Liberal-Progressives, 127; the Progressives including the United Farmers of Alberta and Ontario, 23; others, 6. Conservatives were strong in British Columbia, holding twelve of the province's fourteen parliamentary seats, but locally they were fractured into competing factions. The *Vancouver Sun* was Liberal and the *Province* was uncertain. No one east of the Rockies seemed quite to master the intricacies of BC politics; like BC geography, it was riven into mountains and valleys. East of the Rockies, RB was the only Conservative elected in the three Prairie provinces. Quebec was passionately anti-Meighen, Conservatives holding only four of Quebec's sixty-five seats. Nova Scotia and New Brunswick still had Conservative majorities. Prince Edward Island was the exception. Of the twenty-nine Maritime province seats in Parliament, the Conservatives held twenty. The popular vote there was much closer, around 53 per cent; that was the result of single-member constituencies and old, inherited Maritime political loyalties. The key to Conservative strength in 1927 was Ontario – Ferguson's Ontario – with fifty-three (of eighty-two) House of Commons seats. Even there ancient loyalties gave Conservatives only 54 per cent of the popular vote in the 1926 federal election.

So RB would have work to do. In 1927 the future of the party did not look all that promising. Ahead of him lay years in opposition, of letters and speeches to rally his party, and none of that with the responsibility of office in which he obviously delighted and which was the real outlet for his abundant energy. In Ottawa the Conservative party's national office was in the back rooms of a few Conservative MPs; the party had no funds and, around Ontario, uncertain newspaper support.

Indeed, across Canada there were only eleven dailies that could be called Conservative, and not all of these were reliable. In Quebec, which fifty years before had been the heartland of Conservative support, Conservative papers had been devastated financially and morally by the war and by the hard determination of the Borden and Meighen governments in fighting it. Bennett was soon receiving a stream of appeals to do something – usually financial – to rescue Conservative newspapers inside and out of Quebec: *L'Evénément*, in Quebec City, *La Presse in* Montreal, the *Star* in Regina. Several less important papers also clamoured for attention. W.H. Price, the attorney general of Ontario, Premier Ferguson, and Bennett were all involved in a long correspondence about the *Port Hope Times*, the only Conservative daily between Belleville and Toronto. Its loss would threaten Conservative loyalties in the three counties of Northumberland, Durham, and Ontario (county town, Whitby). E.B. Ryckman, MP for Toronto East, owned the paper; after pleas from Price and Ferguson, and promises of Ontario government support, Ryckman reluctantly kept it going until 1929. Some of the losses of Conservative papers were owing to the gradual process of newspaper consolidation in what had once been two-newspaper towns. Still, it was a worrying trend. A cartoon summarizes it: Mackenzie King has a huge microphone with "90 per cent of Canada's press" inscribed on it; RB has a much smaller microphone. King says, "I don't care how good an orator or leader he may be, I get the broadcast." Bennett says, "Yes, but wait!"[18]

One of RB's considerations as leader of the Opposition was where he was going to live. As an MP he had stayed at the Rideau Club. He and others assumed that he would now need more ample quarters. He could have bought Earnscliffe, once the residence of Sir John A. Macdonald. He also considered buying a house in Hull. He knew Hull well, and there he could avoid Ontario income tax. But Hull was not that accessible. Montebello, the estate of Louis-Joseph Papineau, seven hundred acres and a chateau, was also available. The owners were asking $100,000 but would probably have accepted less than $70,000. By mid-December

1927 Bennett had decided he would not buy a house. He was used to hotel living; he'd been well satisfied with his life on the seventh floor of the Palliser in Calgary. Now the Château Laurier beckoned. At least twenty MPs and their families stayed there during the session. Opened in 1912, it had been a Grand Trunk Railway hotel and was now owned and run by the CNR. RB took a suite on the second floor on the side facing the Rideau Canal. Earnscliffe was bought by the British government early in 1930 for their high commissioner.[19]

Eleven days before Parliament opened in January 1928, Mackenzie King called on Bennett to wish him the best of the season and to congratulate him on the leadership. King was anxious to create a senior group from both parties to work toward the beautification of Ottawa. Bennett talked of buying buildings on Wellington Street; King thought also of Hull across the river. They then talked about Meighen. King said Meighen was contemptuous of him, that Meighen could not get it into of his head that he was no longer prime minister. Bennett thought Meighen's attitude was wrong. Altogether it was an amiable and friendly talk. King went away thinking Bennett would be a refreshing change. No doubt he would sometimes get irritated and he did have a bumptious manner, but if taken the right way, "he will be a more agreeable opponent than Meighen." Bennett told the governor general later that the Conservative Party thought he was being too friendly, too generous to King and to King's government. As the session went on, King reflected, "He is in many ways a big boy, rather speaks his thought. I am beginning to have a real liking for him."[20]

Parliament opened on 26 January 1928, and some civilized amenities were demonstrated on the occasion. Mackenzie King gracefully congratulated Bennett on being elected leader of the Conservatives. Bennett's own view, then and later, was that "courageous criticism must always be tempered with constructive suggestions." The Throne Speech, he said, had reasoned that if Canada was getting along so well without its government doing anything, perhaps that happy state of inaction ought to continue. But the front bench of the Opposition was not in very robust condition. Sir Henry Drayton was in the West Indies; H.H. Stevens was in England; so was W.A. Black, MP for Halifax. Those who were left had to do the committee work – some of them, according to RB, neither adept nor knowledgeable. But as the new leader, he wanted to avoid being too obtrusive. When the budget was brought down in mid-February, he asked C.H. Cahan to reply. Cahan was duly answered by J.H. King, MP for Kootenay West and minister of national health.

No government, RB said, "is ever defeated because it is extravagant ... people may be debauched with their own revenues." Despite Liberal claims of debt reduction, Canada's funded debt was still formidable. In 1914 before the outbreak of war it had been $303,559,938. As of March 1922 it was $2,420,791,260. In March 1927 it was $2,435,395,197, on which Canada was paying $100 million a year in interest. The vaunted Liberal debt reduction of $6 million had been on further debt accumulated between 1922 and 1927. The worst part of the Canadian debt was that there was no sinking fund for repaying it, and some $2 billion of it would mature between 1933 and 1937. RB dismissed J.H. King's financial expertise with a wry quote from Tennyson: "An infant crying in the night, / An infant crying for the light, / And with no language but a cry."[21]

An important, indeed, historic debate turned around the government's amendment of Section 98 of the Criminal Code, which defined and punished sedition and seditious utterances. Labour unions had been pressing every year to have the section abolished altogether. Ernest Lapointe, minister of justice, brought in an amendment reducing the maximum imprisonment from ten years to two. He said Section 98 was hasty legislation, passed at a time of crisis in June 1919 during the Winnipeg General Strike, that it had got through all stages in the Commons in twenty minutes and emerged from the Senate an hour later. Bennett had believed the story too – he was not in Parliament then – but thought it sensible to send for the 1919 Hansard and get the facts. The Immigration Act amendment, allowing deportation of British subjects who were not Canadian, had indeed been passed in just such a headlong manner on 6 June 1919. But the government, with Sir Robert Borden back from Versailles, had serious doubts about the legality of the Criminal Code amendment, so the legislation, drafted by Meighen, was considered by the House of Commons and the Senate in the usual way, with a committee appointed. It had gone through the normal parliamentary procedure, taking two months from 1 May until Royal Assent was given on 7 July 1919. Bennett reflected ruefully on the insidious power of rumour: "Had it not been that I sent to the library for Hansard, the statement [of Lapointe's] would have gone on record that this bill [Sec. 98], supposedly a panic measure, was passed in twenty minutes by parliament because it was believed there was red revolution in the streets of Winnipeg. That was not the fact ... I resent any effort to mislead the people."[22] Thus surfaced one of RB's most enduring penchants, love of accuracy, hatred of distortion, of misrepresentation – the lawyer's need to get the facts right.

He and J.S. Woodsworth disagreed, of course, on Section 98, but they did not always disagree. Half an hour earlier they joined together in supporting Woodsworth's amendment to a Senate divorce bill; the amendment would allow divorce or marriage annulment in the Province of Ontario. It was defeated by the Liberals, 51–21. The twenty-one supporters included Conservatives, Progressives, and Labour, among them Bennett, R.B. Hanson, the two Blacks (Halifax and Yukon), Stevens, William Irvine, and Woodsworth.[23]

Henri Bourassa (1868–1952), MP for Labelle, whose mind seemed to follow a logic not dissimilar to Bennett's, wanted a debate on the implications of the Balfour Declaration of 1926. First proposed by Mackenzie King and South Africa's prime minister, it recognized the growing autonomy of the dominions following the First World War.[24] The declaration had been the subject of a brief debate in the House in 1927. It was to RB the principle of separation from Britain brought in by the back door, "the evidence in many minds of the end of our connection with the empire. For that is what it means ... if we are a sovereign state we cannot belong to the British Empire." While he did not say so in Parliament, he believed the declaration had been brought on too suddenly, with no preparation made to deal with questions that would flow from it. So too thought King George V.[25]

In 1928, on motion to go into Committee of Supply for External Affairs, Bourassa moved regret that Canada had not given full effect to the Declaration of 1926. That brought Bennett out. Equality of status was, he said, a false use of words. Canada was not an independent state, and ought not to be; instead it should discharge fully its responsibility "as a member of the commonwealth of nations called the British Empire." Did Canadians want to be living at "the grace and favour of powerful neighbours"? Without the empire, how could Canada survive next door to the United States? Bourassa withdrew his motion; it had produced exactly the debate he had intended.[26]

Much as RB loved the Crown and the panoply of British governance, he could not now tolerate the Privy Council. He was indignant over the decision in *Nadan v. The King* (1926) in which a Canadian rule in criminal law that had been standing since 1885 was overturned since it was in conflict with a British statute of 1865, the Colonial Laws Validity Act. In *Riel v. Regina* the Privy Council had declared in 1885 that in the North-West Territories, the peace, order, and good government clause of Section 91 of the British North America Act authorized "the utmost discretion of enactment." Then, in 1927, the Privy Council decision in the Labrador Boundary case only made things worse.

Bennett's view of changing imperial relations included the ending of appeals to the Privy Council and allowing Canada to control its own tariff structure. He cited with approval a Canadian statesman's remark that "a woollen factory in Canada was as great an asset to the British Empire as a woollen factory in Yorkshire." That got Bennett's imperial perspective about right. The trouble had been, he said, that negotiations with Britain on tariff questions were apt to be pleasant but fruitless. No Canadian had ever been heard on the tariff before a British House of Commons committee, he said. Canada would get a hearing in their offices, "and a highly intelligent conversation will ensue" – but that would be that.[27]

Still, apart from Canada's independence on the tariff, Bennett believed the British Empire ought to aim at a common foreign policy, a common agreement on action. He would have agreed with King George V's remark to Neville Chamberlain in 1930 that "old Balfour has disintegrated my empire." King George V on those empire stamps looked outward to imperial distances, as he did on the stamps of Fiji and Mauritius. Symbolically, Fiji and Mauritius were equidistant from London, part of the net of the king's empire. Like Australia, Canada, and the other dominions, all were there to help with imperial problems, to help shoulder imperial burdens. One day Britain might run out of coal, Beaverbrook told Bennett in November 1927; then the centre of empire might have to shift westwards to Canada.[28] In that sense Canada was not only a junior partner but a senior legatee.[29]

Bennett and Mackenzie King were at opposite poles regarding Canada's role within the empire. Bennett did want true equality – equality of function and action, not mere "equality of status" as proposed in the Balfour Declaration. (Bennett made much of this juxtaposition between appearance and reality.) However, for King, the imperial federation was dead. As he mentioned, "the way to maintain the British Empire in its foreign relations is not by monopoly of control." In 1923, he had pressed hard for as much autonomy as possible, and in November 1926, after his victory over Lord Byng in the "Byng-King Affair" when the governor general refused King's request to dissolve Parliament, King was amiable and purring like a cat. It was South Africa and the Irish Free State that made the running in the1926 Imperial Conference.

King was open to having British Empire representatives meet to work out common policies, but he did not want Canada to foot the bill. Across the House he asked Sir George Perley, who had been secretary of state in the short-lived 1926 Conservative government, if he would be agreeable to having "all our foreign business conducted at the expense of Great

Britain?" Sir George Perley: "No." Mackenzie King: "Then what is the alternative? It is to tax the Canadian people to pay part of the expenses of British officials to look after our affairs?" Sir George Perley: "Certainly not." Perley's solution was that each part of the empire would have a say in Foreign Office diplomatic appointments, that it would no longer be the sole authority for them. On that argument King poured ridicule. "My honourable friend will strive from now till doomsday but will never succeed in working out a plan of that kind." King had the best of the exchange.[30]

Bennett felt there had to be a common imperial foreign policy. How could Australia have one, New Zealand another, and Canada a third? The British Foreign Office did not like King's Canadian initiatives, taking the same position as Bennett that the diplomatic unity of the empire would be put into question. King George V thoroughly disliked the idea of Mackenzie King setting up three Canadian legations in Washington, Tokyo, and Paris, and at a luncheon at Buckingham Palace, 7 October 1928, he questioned Mackenzie King about them. When the Canadian Legation opened in Paris on 29 September 1928, Mackenzie King proudly in attendance, the British Embassy maintained a polite diplomatic distance and was not represented. However, the foreign secretary, Sir Austen Chamberlain (Neville's half-brother), took a different position, and by 1929 the Foreign Office had reluctantly accepted the principle that Canada could make its own diplomatic appointments but that there would be consultation with the British ambassador whenever there were need of common imperial policy. It was not exactly to Bennett's way of thinking.[31]

Bennett would have liked to have upset the King Government in Parliament by unhinging the loyalty of the Progressives. He initiated three want-of-confidence motions in May, but lost them by majorities of 51, 55, and 58. He had also to remind his followers to be more dutiful in attendance. On one occasion in May there were only twenty Conservative MPs in the House, while the prime minister, RB noted, was there the whole afternoon. At the third confidence motion on 23 May, King sent RB a note across the House suggesting that, from the way such motions were going, it would be best to leave them alone and let the session finish as soon as possible. Bennett laughed and nodded assent.[32]

King welcomed Bennett as relief from the unremitting shafts from Arthur Meighen. However, J.A. Robb, King's minister of finance, found Bennett a trial. Bennett knew banking and finance in ways that made Robb, formerly a merchant from Valleyfield, feel like a country grocer.

And if Bennett failed to dislodge the Progressives altogether, 1928 was not a session that did the government much credit. The Newfoundland and Labrador boundary was debated only in the Senate. Supply could sometimes explode in rancorous debates. One such exchange was on refurbishing Rideau Hall and the Quebec Citadel for the governor general (the Byngs had never cared much about such things); another was on the delights of firing and hiring Nova Scotia postmasters.

A debate near the end of the session in June, during Estimates for Immigration, concerned the Doukhobors, particularly a radical splinter group called Sons of Freedom. Most of the Doukhobors had come to Saskatchewan between 1898 and 1902. Milton Campbell, a Prince Edward Islander who was now Progressive MP for Mackenzie, Saskatchewan, remarked that he had never seen better examples of truly Christian communities of "meticulously clean habits; they were moral to the extreme." It was the fanatics, said Woodsworth, who were feared, often by the Doukhobor communities themselves. William Esling, MP for Kootenay West, originally from Philadelphia, was much offended by the Sons of Freedom and their naked protests in southeastern British Columbia over the issues of land registration and compulsory schooling. There were daughters of freedom too. What would the prime minister do, asked Esling, if he went into his garden one fine morning to pick violets or pansies and was confronted there with six naked Doukhobor ladies? Mackenzie King was quick off the mark. "I would send for my honourable friends, the leader of the opposition and the leader of the Progressive party." The House rocked with laughter: all three men were bachelors. RB put in, "There would be a riot if you overlooked your own followers." J.S. Woodsworth sensibly kept silent on the question of naked Doukobor ladies.[33]

Prorogation was to take place on Saturday, 9 June 1928. The governor general, Viscount Willingdon, duly came in from the country club, Lady Willingdon and friends were in the gallery, and all was ready. But to Mackenzie King's chagrin, the Commons got into a wrangle on Estimates and the ceremony had to be put off until Monday. Sir Robert Borden wrote to RB congratulating him on his work. "During the Session we thought it merciful not to inflict on you any social invitation, but now there is a respite ... would you and your sister come to dinner?" RB said he was at his desk every evening dictating letters, trying to catch up on arrears of work, and had been refusing invitations left and right. However, he and Mildred would try to arrange a visit in the fall. Meanwhile, "I hope I shall always be able to avail myself of your wise counsel.

I certainly needed it at one time this year, but unfortunately you were in the South."[34]

Borden's inclusion of Mildred Bennett in the invitation reflected the degree to which she was now part of RB's public life. Since 1927 she had been accompanying him on many of his political and other travels. In 1928 she was thirty-nine years of age, tall, slim, not pretty, perhaps, but a handsome woman, charming to men, intelligent, vigorous, and with an acute political sensibility. She was born in 1889 when RB was nineteen and had already gone off teaching up on the Miramichi. Mildred's birth came as a shock to RB; "Great Thunder!" he is said to have exclaimed, "I'd as soon have thought of Queen Victoria having a baby!" The birth was also a surprise to Henrietta Bennett, who at age forty-four believed she was well into menopause.[35] RB saw Mildred occasionally, certainly at Christmas almost every year, and he paid for her education at Mount Allison. After Henry Bennett, their father, died in 1905, RB took sixteen-year-old Mildred to London on her first trip overseas. She lived with her mother at Hopewell Cape until Henrietta's death in 1914, and then moved to Vancouver to live with her elder married sister, Mrs Evelyn Bennett Coates, at 12th Avenue West.

Mildred adored her brother. There was nothing improper about her living with him en suite at the Palliser in Calgary or the Château Laurier in Ottawa, but there was an indefinable something between them. She said she would marry the day he did and not before. Borden once said to RB that, just as the sister of the former British prime minister Arthur James Balfour was said to be the only one who could handle Arthur James, "I wonder whether Mildred is the only one who can handle Richard Bedford?" There were three people in Bennett's life who could manage him. All were women. One was his mother, another was Mildred; the third was his secretary, Alice Millar.[36]

It was sometimes said that RB was afraid of women and that explained his being still a bachelor at age fifty-eight. Some suggested he liked only submissive women. There is not much substance in either explanation. RB liked women, depended upon them, enjoyed them; at the Government House reception for MPs on 6 February 1928, he was "rather coquettish" with Joan Patteson, as Mackenzie King wryly observed. A misogynist RB never was.

At the heart of this mystery is the awkward question of RB's sexuality. It can be said at once that there are no clear answers; the evidence is all oblique, second or third hand, but it is impossible not to consider it.

In 1904 when Max Aitken in Halifax got engaged to Gladys Drury, he wrote to RB about it. RB did not know Gladys but was sure that Aitken with his good Scotch sense would not marry a young woman with nothing in her head but clothes and a good time. Then he went on reflectively, "I am now almost an old man. I will not marry. I guess I have made a mistake but it can't be remedied."[37] At that time he was all of thirty-four years old. Answers to his state of mind are not easy to find, but perhaps the explanation is not so much psychological as medical. The Conservative Party Archives has a biographical file on Bennett, remarkably accurate in other respects, that asserts that from youth onward he had a penile problem known as phimosis, a tight foreskin that at erection could be extremely painful.[38] This could be corrected by surgery and may have been done in London in 1905. A more intractable difficulty may have developed by 1914, when he was forty-four. He tried to join the Canadian Army in 1914 but was rejected on medical grounds. He would never say what these were. He was a year over age, a perfectly acceptable reason, so why the secrecy? For one thing, as he told King in 1930, he was missing two toes. The army could well have rejected him on that ground. Another possible answer, suggested by an acquaintance of RB, is Peyronié's disease, characterized by a fibrous thickening of the penile shaft creating a distinct bend with erection pain. It is a chronic condition, sometimes a side effect of incipient diabetes, with poor response to surgery.[39]

The effect of such physical conditions on RB personally would be ambiguous and uncertain. His approach to women was usually bold and confident; he was tall and well turned out, by no means unattractive to women; but love's deeper progress for him could be a road to pain. So there would be hesitation, even retreat. In such circumstances Mildred would be for him the perfect companion and hostess. She had wonderful social skills; she could dance; she was good at a party; she was excellent company. Sometimes, to her brother's dismay, she liked a glass of champagne.

In the summer of 1928 Mildred accompanied RB on many of his tours aimed at making himself familiar with ridings and the party stalwarts in them. They began 23–30 June in the Eastern Townships in Laprairie-Napierville, south of Montreal. It was ancient Liberal territory; indeed, some of the events of 1837–38 took place there. Bennett knew some French, having once taught it as a teacher; but that was a long way from reading it comfortably. He did not always trust his comprehension and would often ask for translations. There is no evidence that he could or would speak French nor of how well he understood it. But in the 1920s, bilingualism was not expected of national politicians. Francophone Quebecers had long been used to English-Canadians' incompetence in French. On public occasions they seemed to prefer a word or two as gesture to having someone murder their language by trying to speak it. They lived with the English-Canadian assumption that they could learn to speak English.

The old équipe of the Conservative party in Quebec had been savaged by political fallout from the Borden-Meighen conduct of the war. Many Conservative newspapers in the province lay wounded or dying, their readers fleeing or fled. Postwar Quebec Conservatives were reduced to what the political journal *L'Action canadienne française* called "*la plus complète impuissance.*" Perhaps that sentiment was exaggerated, but adding to the damage caused by Conscription was the bitter struggle over Ottawa bilingual schools that had ended only in 1927. The feeling in Quebec was that the Conservative Party was increasingly dominated by Toronto.[40] The situation had been helped a little by Meighen's Hamilton speech of 1925 renouncing participation in any overseas war without Canadian approval, though at the time it was much resented by Ontario Conservatives.

Bennett's meetings in Quebec were well attended, and he himself was warmly received. His message about protection for Canadian producers was also pleasing. The farming communities in the Eastern Townships counted on the Montreal market; they feared the carload lots of American produce being turned out on Montreal markets. So they liked his anti-dumping stance. His enthusiasm for the St Lawrence Waterway, as yet unbuilt, made him doubly welcome.[41]

RB and Mildred went to Calgary for the Stampede, returning back east late in July for his major party effort in 1928: the Maritimes. The first stop was Nova Scotia. Conservatives had won a landslide victory in the provincial election in 1925, taking forty of forty-three seats and throwing out a Liberal regime that had been in power since 1882. The hunger of Conservatives for the sweets of office after four long decades in the desert was consuming, but Edgar Rhodes, the new high-minded premier, hated the old Nova Scotian patronage habits. He resisted, and many an old Liberal stalwart retained his government job. What Rhodes did do was finally extinguish the old Legislative Council. Fighting off death as long as possible, it died 31 May 1928.[42]

Arriving by train in Halifax on 26 July, on the way to their hotel, RB pointed out to Mildred the house on Hollis Street (at Morris) where he had lived as a Dalhousie law student between 1890 and 1893. That night he made a major speech at the arena on Pepperell Street, with three thousand in attendance, stressing Canadian national responsibilities, a national duty to support Halifax's harbour, a national duty to develop Canadian industry. Why should the United States import Canadian pulpwood? Canadian wood was being taken across the border, made into paper in the mill towns of New England (often by Quebec immigrants), and then re-exported to Canada as newsprint. That seemed to RB like poor national economy. Voters should ask Mackenzie King, "What port are you bound for, helmsman? What is your course?"[43]

Bennett's course for the next three weeks lay in rural Nova Scotia, much of it by car. It was strenuous going, even if Sundays were set aside for rest. He was kept going from early morning until late at night. He usually managed three meetings a day with driving in between, about a hundred miles a day over roads that were often in poor shape. His route was Halifax, southwest to Yarmouth, and back through the Annapolis Valley to New Glasgow in Pictou County. After that it was Cape Breton. He relaxed for a few days on the return with Thomas Cantley, a steelmaker in New Glasgow and a salty Pictou MP. Bennett's secretary, Arthur Merriam, teased Cantley about his continuing to be Presbyterian when most Presbyterians in 1925 had joined with Methodists to form the United Church. "My dear Cantley," Merriam wrote, "don't you regard Methodists as 'poor white trash'"? Cantley replied that he had never had any quarrel with Methodists – "indeed, have slept with one for forty years."[44]

From Pictou, RB and Mildred crossed to Prince Edward Island by ferry, spending a busy two days there before crossing back to New Brunswick. They got a rapturous welcome in a Moncton heatwave, made a pilgrimage to Hopewell Cape, and then came on to Saint John where they took the train to Montreal, the old CPR route through Maine. Their Maritime trip was declared a proper Roman triumph, and Bennett was delighted.

He was in Toronto in September, the main speaker at the Maritime Provinces Association. He was not talking politics at all, but doing what many commentators thought he did best, simply being entertaining. The editor and critic Hector Charlesworth, hearing Bennett for the first time, was struck by the beauty of his language. "A singular faculty of his is apt quotation from poems usually unfamiliar." As MP for Calgary, he was often called on to preside at talks of visiting speakers; in May 1927 he chaired a crowded Grand Theatre when Roald Amundsen came to town, telling of his adventures at the South Pole and the North. RB was struck by Amundsen's modesty in recounting his explorations, especially since modesty was not something he himself was famous for. A year later Amundsen would die trying to rescue an Italian explorer stranded in the Canadian Arctic.[45]

In late November 1928, RB turned his attention to British Columbia. There was a critical federal by-election to be held in Victoria on 6 December, and politics in British Columbia were not always clear sailing. Mountains seem to make for riven politics, and both parties found in-fighting a congenial occupation. Conservatives provincially had had a good run under Sir Richard McBride, premier from 1903 to 1915. W.J. Bowser (1867–1933), a New Brunswicker and fellow Dalhousian, succeeded McBride as premier in 1915–16 and was leader of the Opposition 1916–24. But when "Bovril Bill" stepped down as leader, he left the BC Conservatives badly divided. Their convention in November 1926, virtually deadlocked, turned to Simon Fraser Tolmie, the sitting federal MP for Victoria, to accept the leadership.

In the meantime the BC Liberal government badly wanted to complete the Pacific Great Eastern (PGE) railway to Prince George, there to connect with the Grand Trunk Pacific, Edmonton to Prince Rupert. The bankruptcy and nationalization of the Grand Trunk in 1920 stopped the PGE at Quesnel, with the BC government left holding the mortgage. After unsuccessful appeals to the King government, the province sent their lawyer, Gerry McGeer, to England with Frank Sutton, a British railway entrepreneur, to find $45 million to finish the PGE. They came back after three months of wining and dining with not a nickel. The railway would remain for some time yet as the "Please Go Easy." But on BC provincial accounts, it was anything but easy. RB never thought much of the PGE, which seemed to him "a hopeless undertaking, starting from nowhere and ending nowhere."[46]

Tolmie, the new Conservative provincial leader, a Victoria-born veterinarian, was MP for Victoria, 1917–28. He was well liked, expert in returning soft answers, unscarred by Conservative infighting. Bennett was pessimistic about Conservative chances in a BC provincial election, urging Tolmie to go home from Ottawa as soon as possible and take charge. Be sure to send him, BC Conservatives told Bennett, "with his pockets full." Of course RB told them that to get eastern money for a BC provincial election was "quite impossible." Tolmie did not share Bennett's pessimism and was confident he would win. He resigned as MP only in June 1928 and came home, and on 18 July 1928 he and his Conservatives swept the BC Liberals out of power, taking thirty-five seats as against the Liberals' twelve.[47]

The federal by-election in Victoria to replace Tolmie as federal MP brought RB and Mildred to Victoria. The date was set for 6 December 1928. The federal Liberals dearly wanted to win the seat back and nominated the former BC Liberal leader, J.D. MacLean. The Conservatives won it but it was a squeaker; Bennett thought it was a miracle and told the new MP, D'Arcy Plunkett, that it was the women of Victoria who had elected him. He might have added that it was Mildred as well. Lottie Bowron, formerly secretary to Sir Richard McBride while he was premier of the province and now the province's first rural schools welfare officer, wrote to RB about how grateful Victoria was to both RB and Mildred. Bowron had heard "many comments on your remarks to the women – by the women – you heartened them by your belief in them – do keep up this splendid work – for the Conservative Party is slow in this respect and how much you can now do – but don't only believe in them – show them recognition when possible."[48]

RB and Mildred went to Europe for Christmas 1928 and New Year's. Neither of them seem to have been bothered by mid-winter crossings of the North Atlantic. Not much is known of that trip; they went on to the continent via Harwich; they surfaced in Prague, Bennett's Canadian passport being stamped with a Czecho-Slovak border exit on 24 December 1928. It was more than six hours by express train to Vienna. There they stayed at the Bristol Hotel on the Kärtner Ringstrasse and were at the Stefanskirche for Christmas Eve mass. On Christmas evening they followed a Viennese tradition by going to the opera. It had been Wagner's *Tannhäuser* until 1924, when it was changed to Richard Strauss's enchanting *Der Rosenkavalier*. That night it was conducted by Strauss himself. RB thought the opera remarkably fine; it was doubtless the staging and the singing that caught him, for he knew little German. That was a pity, for he was enough of a poet himself to have appreciated Hofmannsthal's lines. Toward the end of act 1 the Marschallin reflects about time passing between her and her young lover, Octavian: "I can hear it passing in the night; it's passing between you and me now, silently, like an hour-glass."[49]

RB and Mildred were travelling with a friend, Adeline Solest, who had a troublesome knack for doggerel poetry, and something of the tenor of their visit to Vienna comes from that curious source. On Christmas morning RB came at 9 AM to wake the ladies but could rouse neither of them. He came again at noon, and Mildred ordered orange juice for breakfast. The waiter arrived, saying that it was too late for breakfast but that lunch was on: fried fish and brussel sprouts. That did sound just like a hotel with an English name! Adeline Solest's lines about their Vienna stay were rough and ready:

> The opera Rosenkavalier
> With Strauss conducting crystal clear
> I fear our friend Arbee has made
> In these three hours, his great tirade
> 'Gainst Government ...
> Affaires de coeur of Richard B.
> Were dragged to light quite brutally ...[50]

RB was in London in January 1929 when the Prince of Wales invited him to visit. RB found the Prince of Wales "a very changed and older man." Edward had not yet encountered Wallis Warfield Simpson; that was two years in the future. RB and Mildred departed on the *Majestic* for New York on 12 January 1929.[51]

Parliament opened again on 7 February 1929 with Mackenzie King in an expansive mood. A European trip to Geneva, Venice, and Paris had developed his already considerable sense of his own worth. One lovely October morning in Paris, being chauffeured to a sculptor's, his delight was such that he burst out singing in the car. The song was "The Light of the Lonely Pilgrim's Heart." As he wrote in his diary, "I seem to have come into my own in *everything*." There had been a fierce wrangle in King's cabinet in November over Arthur Cardin's insistence on having two new Canadian destroyers built in Canada. King wanted no part of it; he was not going to have a war industry started in Canada, in Montreal or anywhere else. He threatened to resign; cabinet backed off. King then essayed one more triumph. Meeting Sir Robert Borden at a Canadian Club luncheon at the Château Laurier on 11 January 1929, he asked Sir Robert if he would like a Senate seat; he could lead the Conservative Party in the Senate. If Bennett had been consulted on this curious proposal, there is no evidence of it. Borden sensibly said he did not think he would be interested.

The 1929 Speech from the Throne reflected King's triumphs and Canadian prosperity. "Never in the history of Canada has there been such industrial and commercial expansion," he said, referring to the previous year. The Hudson's Bay Railway was within thirty-seven miles of

Churchill; Manitoba, Saskatchewan, and Alberta would (at long last) get control of their natural resources. There was a great deal to be thankful for.[52]

Bennett accepted that speech of "glittering generalities." He would not divide the House on it. His complaint was that the government had "been content to rest supinely" on its laurels, as if to demonstrate that no further improvement was possible. RB was too good a financier not to know that things like that do not go on forever. What was the government doing to prepare for the day "which must come when, with contracted trade and lessening opportunities we must meet conditions of a different kind?" He had warned with great prescience the year before, "It is all right to rejoice in these days of seeming prosperity and say we have ample moneys and let us spend them. But there comes a day of reckoning, and that day you can almost see in the distance now." It was time to shorten sail: "This great speculative era we now have on the American continent is one fraught with possibilities of the greatest disaster ... In this country speculation is rampant. Some people imagine that trading in pieces of paper upon which there are engraved words and figures constitutes new wealth. It is not so. The new wealth of the country is being created by labour and capital to the natural resources of the country." He proposed that "since England can no longer take the lead," Canada should call "a great ... economic conference of the British Empire" to meet in Ottawa to consider the two pressing problems, settlement and development. "We are running the risk of losing overnight through hostile tariffs, namely, our markets." The Smoot-Hawley tariff was already being debated in the American Congress.

However, the King government would do nothing about an imperial conference. It did announce that a royal commission on radio broadcasting had been appointed. All very well, said RB, but why had it taken so long?[53] In 1926 the British had established the British Broadcasting Corporation under royal charter to commence its existence on 1 February 1927. The Americans in 1927 had set up the Federal Radio Commission to regulate the confusion and cacophony that was American radio. The two systems were quite different. The BBC had a monopoly and complete control, while the American system was mainly a regulating body. In Canada no one yet knew which way policy would go. With Canada's forty-four radio stations mostly in private hands, one might have expected it to imitate the American system. But was radio for entertainment or education? What ought to be the focus of public policy? That entertainment was radio's main purpose was the view prevailing in the

United States. In Canada there was support, mainly latent, for radio as a public service.

The King government appointed the Aird Commission by order-in-council on 6 December 1928. It was bipartisan: Sir Charles Aird, president of the Canadian Bank of Commerce, was Conservative; the second member of the commission was Dr Augustin Frigon of Montreal, a French-Canadian electrical engineer, neutral politically; the third member was Charles Bowman of the *Ottawa Citizen*, sympathetic to the Liberals. He had given King in May 1928 a glowing accolade for his work at the Imperial Conference of 1926, which King much appreciated. It may have turned King's mind to the possibility of a role for himself in international affairs. More important, Bowman had run a series of editorials in the *Ottawa Citizen* in March and April 1928, reprinted widely, pointing to the absence of radio policy. Bowman maintained that Canadian drift was the height of folly; Canada surely did not want to imitate the chaos in the United States. The huge success of comedies like *Amos 'n' Andy* (which started in March 1928) only pointed up the necessity of finding some Canadian system that might, if not rival that of the United States, at least offer some intelligent alternative.[54]

The Aird Commission went first to New York, where Aird was disconcerted by the bland assumption of American broadcasters that Canada was simply part of their territory. In England, Sir John Reith put the whole of the BBC at the Canadian commission's disposal. The commission also went to Europe; Frigon was especially interested in the German system with its combination of federal and Land broadcasts. In Canada, station owners and radio dealers were already strong for private ownership of stations. The New York State governor, Franklin Roosevelt, watched the Canadian commission with some interest. He told Vincent Massey, Canadian minister to Washington, that he hoped Canada would not let radio grow up every which way as it had in the United States. Radio should be organized, Roosevelt believed, on the principle of public service. Arthur Meighen told a meeting of the National Council of Education in Vancouver attended by the Aird Commission that as long as the selection of broadcast material was in commercial hands, it could never be aught but "mere pabulum."

Bennett thought it was long past time to have a working system in place. Canadians, he said in Parliament on 6 June 1929, were being made apprehensive by the overwhelming obtrusiveness of American radio.[55] He recognized the importance of radio, especially coming from the West as he did. Many farmers in the West and elsewhere had radios;

most early radios depended upon battery power and did not need out-side power lines. He was being told that the next election might be won through radio. He was good at broadcasts and knew it. He had a deep resonant voice that carried well; King's, at a higher pitch, sometimes had a shrill or plaintive tone. (Radio also had a strange effect on King: it seemed to confirm his belief in a world beyond the material one, intro-ducing him, as he put it in his diary, "to an understanding of the reality of the invisible." It allowed him to believe that out there in the ether lay access to his mother, his siblings, and Laurier.)[56]

By 1929 there was the beginning of a national radio network under the auspices of the Canadian National Railways, inaugurated by Sir Henry Thornton, since 1922 CNR's president. The CNR transcontinental radio network had begun operation in December 1923. *Hockey Night in Canada* was first broadcast in March 1924. In 1927, at the time of the Diamond Jubilee of Confederation, the network presented a pro-gram marking the centenary of Beethoven's death. In the fall of 1929 it inaugurated the Canadian National Symphony Hour, at 5 PM every Sun-day with the Toronto Symphony. Each week the program opened with "O Canada."

Bennett had some objections to CNR Radio, on the basis not of its cul-tural programs but its politics. The system, he said, gave open and free access to the whole Liberal government, while it offered the same oppor-tunity only to the leader of the Conservative Party: "The radio broad-casting system of the Railway Company is being used by the Government for the advancement of its fortunes and against that I protest." There was some truth in Bennett's suspicions. King believed that national radio would wean Canadian voters away from their long-held local loyalties, where lay, King thought, the basis of Conservative strength.[57]

CNR's Sir Henry Thornton was a large, generous, hearty man with talent to burn. Like many outgoing people, however, he often concealed a more reflective self. In 1929 he told King, "Three-quarters of life is made up of disappointments; best not to think of them but go on." He was a genius at adapting his style to his audience, whether railwaymen or royalty. He met King in Paris in October 1928 – Thornton could be met with in Paris, London, or New York – and told him that the CNR would clear $60 million profit in 1928. It was their best year yet. It meant that the CNR's 1928 earnings would cover interest on its bonds and on some government loans. King was overjoyed. By this time the CNR had acquired a certain esprit de corps, a pride in what the railway had become and what it was doing. Sir Henry thrived on competition with the CPR. The CPR was subsidizing the building of the Lord Nelson Hotel in Halifax? Was not Halifax the Atlantic terminus of the Canadian National? Excavation for CNR's Nova Scotian Hotel was started on 21 October 1927, the same day the first sod was turned for the Lord Nelson. The sheer bravura of it took one's breath. But was it wise? That was Bennett's sobering reflection in Parliament.[58]

In 1929 the CNR badly needed a new major railway terminal in Montreal. The old Bonaventure station was, as Bennett put it in Parliament, "grossly inadequate." He was a well-worn veteran at railway travel and he thought union stations, as in Toronto, were the way of the future. Did Canada need two railway terminals in Montreal? Could not the CPR's Windsor Station be broadened to include the CNR? Thornton told the Railway Committee of Parliament that a new $50 million terminal was the only possible scheme. But was it? Should Parliament not have an independent report by the Board of Railway Commissioners? A great deal of money was at stake. Bennett did not want to be alarmist, but "we are talking today in much the same way as the country used to talk before 1914, when we had such a collapse in our railway undertakings ... we cavalierly wave our hands and talk about $40,000,000 or $50,000,000 as though it were a mere bagatelle." He moved that the Montreal Terminal bill not be not read a third time but be sent to the Board of Railway Commissioners for their opinion.

Montreal MPs, Liberal and Conservative, resisted. C.H. Cahan, the well-established Montreal Conservative warhorse, did not want any such delay: the Board of Railway Commissioners could not give any better opinion than Parliament had already. Arthur Denis, Liberal MP for St Denis, set out a position characteristic of MPs defending their turf: "This bill proves to the citizens of Montreal that the government acknowledges its responsibilities and is ready to grant their legitimate claims." Bennett's motion went down to defeat without recorded division. It would have been embarrassing to record Conservatives voting with the government.[59]

Bennett's best speech of the 1929 session was about the way that banks and banking worked. He began with a story. A man from Macleod, Alberta, came to his Calgary office complaining that the banks would not give him a loan. RB asked him, "Where does the money come from?" The man said, "It is those rich men in Montreal and Toronto, and they will not lend it out here." Bennett then proceeded to read him, and the House, a short pithy lecture on money and banking. A bank's capital, he said, was never available for loans. Banks lent out depositors' money.

"The science of banking is the maintenance of an equilibrium between time loans and time deposits, on the one hand, and demand loans and demand deposits on the other." Banks in Macleod, Alberta, were perfectly ready to lend money to people who would be willing and able to pay it back – that is, people with what RB called "character." Bank managers knew they were lending someone else's money and had to be cautious. "Ah, Mr Speaker," he concluded, "somebody else's money! Will the House please keep that in mind? Somebody else's money."[60]

Mackenzie King thought it was the best speech he had heard from Bennett. "I have heard nothing clearer in the House of Commons," he said. The influential Toronto weekly *Saturday Night* noted on 23 February 1929 that "if Mr. Bennett could become as impassioned on other subjects of greater appeal to the people as he invariably is on the sacred subject of money he would be a very effective leader in the House of Commons."

Ten days later, just as the budget debate was coming on, RB and Mildred had to leave by train for Vancouver. Their sister Evelyn was dying of cancer. RB returned in two weeks, impressed with Evelyn's complete indifference to dying. It was as though, he said, "she was taking a journey to a not distant country." Her religion, he told Mackenzie King, is "a real thing." Evelyn died on 1 May 1929; RB was unable to attend her funeral.[61]

At work in the House of Commons he pointed out the dangers threatening in the Smoot-Hawley tariff proposals, currently before the American Senate and possibly to come into effect in June 1929. Canadian action was needed, but the King government was holding back. Bennett made fun of King's timidity toward Americans. The prime minister was saying in effect, "Hush! Hush! Don't provoke them over there, they might do something to you; and don't you dare talk about preferences for the mother country for you will provoke them worse."[62] If this attitude worked in 1929, it did not survive for long in 1930. Senator Reed Smoot of Utah would push his proposals to raise US import tariffs to record levels through the American Senate in the session of 1930.

In the autumn of 1929 Bennett was elected president of the Canadian Bar Association. It was loaded onto much else that he was doing. By that time he was not sure that what he had taken on as leader of the Conservative Party was altogether wise. Was it a triumph of vanity disguised as duty to his country? Whatever it was, it was much harder work than he had imagined. He wrote to a Calgary friend on 26 November 1928, "More and more I realize I have taken on heavy responsibilities, but I am doing my best. Sometimes I wonder why I ever undertook this work at my time of life, after all my years of toil and effort, but it has some compensations, although they are at times difficult to discover." A year later he confided to Sir Robert Borden, "You ... can readily appreciate that, at times, I yearn greatly for the peace and happiness that I used to enjoy before I undertook the strenuous duties of my position." He now had ample opportunity to reflect on Mark Irish's advice of August 1927. It was also in his mind in replying to Senator G.P. Graham, a senior Liberal statesman and a leading candidate for the Liberal party leadership in 1919. Senator Graham had written him a friendly avuncular letter after the Winnipeg Convention: "You are young with dynamic energy, hence the greater necessity to be on guard constantly lest the wonderful energy be misdirected ... The populous [sic] is not always right, and one sometimes has to assume an attitude almost of isolation among his own friends in order to pursue the course he thinks is the proper one. History ... occasionally, but not always, does justice to the public man who fearlessly follows the dictates of his own conscience." Bennett cherished the letter and wrote a heartfelt reply, saying, "I shall never forget your kindness." Probably no letter had better pointed out his difficulties.

In the House in October 1928 he welcomed Mackenzie King back to Canada; King thanked him warmly and hoped he had given expression to "our united views" on imperial policy and international relations. (That was doubtful.) When Ramsay MacDonald, the new British prime minister, visited Canada in October 1929, King invited RB to join him in proposing MacDonald's health. Politics can sometimes be civil.[63]

Perhaps RB could have remembered that in some of his own political dealings. He could make judgments too quickly, his temper too soon translating his energy into action. In the tricky cross-currents of BC politics, this created difficulties. In July and August 1929 he made a summer tour of British Columbia, which seemed to him to go well. Returning to Calgary, however, he sharply criticized Premier Tolmie over the granting of a beer licence in Fernie, BC. The problem was created by an aggrieved faction of the party who wanted that big provincial Conservative victory of 1928 – thirty-five of forty-eight seats – matched by patronage rewards. Tolmie, like Rhodes of Nova Scotia in similar circumstances, was against a patronage free-for-all and would not sanction a housecleaning of old Liberal stalwarts in the BC civil service. A letter from Bennett to Tolmie was fairly brutal: "If the Liberal party were in power in the province, the fortunes of our Party federally would be brighter than they now are ... none would regret more than I that your place in the political history of Canada should be that of a Conservative Prime Minister [Premier] who destroyed his party in the most Conservative Province in Canada." Tolmie was taken aback and did not reply for two months. He had his own grievances, including the "pessimism you displayed before the provincial election [in July 1928] ... you pestered the life out of me at Ottawa to leave and go to B.C." As to the situation in Fernie, Bennett had simply listened too much to complaints from "irresponsible persons."[64]

Bennett's excuse for sharpness was worry generated by his BC supporters. He was being told that Tolmie was wrecking the party's chances in the next federal election. H.H. Stevens complained that the BC Conservatives were disillusioned with the Tolmie government mainly because its ministers had utterly failed to appreciate that their 1928 electoral success was owing to work done by party supporters. That was a code meaning a dearth of patronage. Others complained of Tolmie's subservience to the "machine" controlled by distillers and brewers. Bennett was reported to have told one Conservative MLA, "If I, as a Conservative member [of the Assembly] had been treated as you have been ... by the government, I would resign my seat and resign it quickly."[65]

In the midst of these cross-currents it was not surprising that Bennett's BC tour of July and August 1929 was, as he put it, "heavily chaperoned." He hoped it would produce good results. "I certainly worked hard enough," he confided to Cy Peck of Nanaimo, an old friend from Hopewell Cape. But reverberations from the Tolmie government continued even afterward. RB had written a personal letter to a BC lady in which he made unkind references to Tolmie and his attorney general, R.H. Pooley. Pooley saw the letter. The lady was a friend of Duff Pattullo, leader of the BC Liberal opposition, who was well capable of airing such an issue in the Assembly. If he does, wrote Pooley angrily to Bennett, "I'll be ready for him. Damn it all, man, have a heart!"[66]

Bennett did have a heart, but it was difficult for him to be generous when his sharp sense of what was right, politically or morally, was offended. In this respect Mildred could sometimes act as governor of his moral engine, controlling its excesses. RB was instinctively generous, provided his sense of fitness was not affronted.[67] Unlike King, he was appreciative to secretaries and assistants, and his charities were legion. In 1930, not an exceptional year for him, his charitable gifts amounted to 9.3 per cent of his gross income, which in 1930 was $262,176. The Christmas gift lists that he sent out to Calgary for Alice Millar to take care of were positively formidable: gifts to servants at the Ranchmen's Club in Calgary, at the Country Club in Ottawa; chocolates to staff

in the Palliser Hotel in Calgary, the Château Laurier in Ottawa; the
telephone girls in both hotels should get silk stockings. And old Mrs
Pinkham in Calgary should get half a dozen bottles of whisky – the doctor had prescribed it – George Robinson knew the brand she liked. It
would be like that every Christmas.[68]

His charity reached into strange places. William Irvine (1885–1962),
Labour MP, Calgary East (1921–25) and Wetaskiwin (1926–35), in
1927 wanted to buy a farm for his sons; Bennett guaranteed an $8,000
line of credit at the Bank of Montreal, Bentley, Alberta, about 50 kilo-
metres northwest of Red Deer. Irvine paid the interest (7 per cent, then
6 per cent) until June 1930, after which he could not pay anything. By
30 December 1935 the loan reached $8,579.67; Bennett paid off the
Bank of Montreal a little ruefully. Providence decreed that the sons
could not make a living on the farm, so "the Bank gets their money and
I got experience."[69]

Neither Bennett nor King seems to have commented on the stock market crash of October 1929. There was plenty of advance notice that
things could not go upward forever. *Saturday Night*'s financial page
of 18 May 1929 was titled, "Are Stocks Heading Downward?" King's
money, about $250,000, most of it from Peter Larkin, was invested in
solid government bonds, largely at the Old Colony Trust in Boston; he
was never one for ventures in the stock market and so rode through
the Depression with that steady confident cushion. Bennett's money was
widely and on the whole wisely invested. His current income was 85
per cent from dividends, of which four-fifths came from Eddy's. Eddy's
was his only directorship remaining after he resigned all the others late
in 1927, and after October 1929 Eddy's would not be easy to sell. Since
he was the majority shareholder, he was really responsible for the fate
of the firm. He and Eddy's would stay together for many a year yet. He
was too shrewd to be caught by the stock market bubble. He did not buy
stock on margin, and when he sold he liked to do it on a rising market.
He told Alice Millar on 12 December 1928, "I think the market will go
up and we should sell some McLeod shares ... Vulcan had better be sold
unless there are reasons for you thinking otherwise." That letter measures something of his confidence in Alice Millar and the responsibilities
he entrusted to her. In October 1929 he asked, if agreeable to her, could
she come to Ottawa for two to three weeks to look after his affairs?[70]
Then he would go to Calgary by early November so that he could get
a rest.

Citizens of Calgary of whatever persuasion swore by him, said *Saturday Night*; they liked him as a human being, that "he has never lost his appreciation of the value of the individual ... Humanity is not a brute fact with him because it is made up of his friends and neighbours." An old lady with a large farm, all alone, having lost her sons in the war, had so many problems they seemed to quite overwhelm her. A friend told her to go and see Bennett. "Don't take no from any of his office staff. His very efficient body-guard of secretaries will naturally try to sidetrack you, but just brush them aside and march right in to R.B.'s sanctum." She did. At the end of her recital, "R.B. got up and put his hands on her shoulders. 'Leave all your papers with me and come back in six weeks. You'll find everything then in shipshape order. 'But how can you do it?' she exclaimed ... 'Leave that to me,' he said, 'if men like me can't look after mothers like you this world would be a poor place to live in.'"[71]

The Conservative party fortunes were generally improving. Conservative Premier Howard Ferguson won a resounding mandate from Ontario in November 1929; Camillien Houde became leader of the Quebec Conservatives, replacing Arthur Sauvé, a seigneur of the old school, with a tough, able, outspoken man of the people. The Quebec Assembly, which met early in 1930, was warned to look out for squalls. Houde (with Bennett's agreement) decided not to risk contesting two 27 January 1930 federal by-elections in Chateauguay-Huntingdon and Bagot. That led some to wonder if the Conservatives were becoming pusillanimous, but with Houde and Bennett that was an unlikely conclusion; "optimistic inactivity" was better.

All this while King was debating whether to have elections in 1930. There were dangers in waiting too long; unemployment was a burgeoning problem. So was the western wheat surplus, and worse, the growing world wheat surplus bode ill for the wheat pool's big accumulation. Against that, King very much wanted to attend the Imperial Conference called for September 1930; what if he were to be defeated? But Mrs Bleaney, the medium, came on Saturday 9 February and told him he would win, so over that weekend he made up his mind. He told only Lapointe, his Quebec lieutenant, and Charles Dunning, his finance minister, who was directed to get a real pre-election budget ready.

Parliament opened on 20 February 1930. Bennett thought the King government celebrated too much of its past, adumbrated too little of the future. Given the range of unemployment that winter, what was the government prepared to do? "I have found," Bennett said, "more privation than I have seen in a quarter of a century, more bread lines and soup kitchens." King was sure that Bennett and his party were exaggerating. Winter had always been a season of unemployment. To King, unemployment was fundamentally a provincial responsibility; he had long believed that governments, provincial and federal, should raise and spend their own money in their own spheres. Why should Ottawa pay for provincial problems? In particular, why should Ottawa's well-husbanded money go to support Conservative Ontario's extravagance? Indeed, there were other Conservative provincial governments who would be watching such a precedent: British Columbia, Saskatchewan, New Brunswick, Nova Scotia, to say nothing of Progressive ones in Alberta and Manitoba. Quebec and Prince Edward Island, with Liberal governments, seemed to manage their affairs without turning to Ottawa. For help with unemployment, King told the Commons on 3 April 1930, he "would not give a single cent to any Tory government."

MR BENNETT: Shame! ...
MR KING: May I repeat what I have said? With respect to giving
moneys out of the federal treasury to any Tory government in this
country for these alleged unemployment purposes ... I would not give
them a five-cent piece.

It was a fighting speech, and King got the biggest ovation he had ever received in the House. But not all fighting speeches are wise. King said later in his diary that the "five-cent speech" was a slip made in anger; it would be all too easy to pull that remark far out of context. It was, moreover, inaccurate; none of the provincial governments had come into power on a fight-Ottawa platform. And it was a gift that the Conservatives would positively relish.[72]

When the budget came down a month later, it overturned some cherished policies. It was clear as early as March 1930 that the United States was going to raise duties substantially on Canadian agricultural products. The US Senate had already passed the upward revisions, and the House of Representatives was expected to agree. Up went Canadian countervailing duties against the United States; cut away were whole slices of protection against British goods. "We switch trade from the U.S. to Britain" was King's summary. Budgets are kept secret; King thought his 1930 budget came down on Bennett and his followers "like an avalanche." Liberals were delighted. Bennett suggested that the Liberal party had become Conservative. Where were the great Liberal policies of 1893, of 1919? "It is always a matter of satisfaction to see those who have erred converted to the light." But countervailing duties were a poor substitute for policies that Canada made herself. It meant that Canadian tariff policy vis-à-vis the United States was simply being made in Washington, an admission that the Canadian government was "so lacking in courage ... that it dare not stand up today and name the tariff it will impose against the United States ... I am in favour of every proposal that will make for the advancement of Canada as an independent economic entity."[73]

The real problem of the 1930 budget, Bennett said, was lack of forecasts. There were no statements of projected revenues to 31 December 1931. Supply ought to be granted on the basis of projections of future income. The new British preferences the King government was proposing would doubtless make favourable headlines in British papers when the Imperial Conference met in late September. Bennett's own credo was: "I can say now what I have said from my youth, that the future of Empire depends upon the development of the great resources of Canada. Any sacrifice that we may make of our position whereby we cease to be autonomous in the development of this great state is fraught with the greatest disaster not to us alone but to the Empire of which we form a part. To grant trade preferences to another state or empire without forming those preferences on a mutually helpful treaty is unsound business, profitless and filled with ill-will and misunderstanding." It is a good summary of his position on Canada's trade, then and later.

So, Bennett went on, the King government was trying to pass legislation it had previously opposed, and it had therefore lost the confidence of the country. It was now 5:50 PM on Tuesday, 6 May 1930. That left Mackenzie King ten minutes to announce that in view of the forthcoming Imperial Conference in September, the sooner general elections were held, the better. That produced schoolboy enthusiasm on both sides of the House, MPs looking forward to being released from Parliament.[74]

In the evening there was the Ontario Divorce Bill, which had been fought over for several years. Ontario divorce, championed by J.S. Woodsworth, now triumphed; a negative amendment that would have defeated it once more was put down 94–65, King voting with the losing 65. He believed in Ontario divorces, but he believed even more in supporting the Roman Catholic Quebec bishops, who had been very stern on the subject.

After that King and Bennett met to discuss winding up the session. Bennett agreed that it was wise now to expedite the business of the House, and so he would confirm arrangements with his colleagues. King spoke of three possibilities: Liberals winning the election, Conservatives winning, or a draw; but whatever the outcome, there would be an immediate need afterward of summoning Parliament to see who would go to England. (King himself was aching to go.) Bennett then said something odd but heartfelt: "I never thought of defeating you, it was all part of the day's work to go on." Indeed, he felt that he'd been "foolish to let himself in for the leadership."[75]

On 15 May the budget resolutions carried by a healthy Liberal majority of twenty-five, the House boisterous but good-natured. Bennett was a bit crestfallen over that majority but took it well. King rather admired Bennett at that point. "He is really very brave about it all, shows fine command of himself (for him). He is very much alone ... I felt a little sorry for him and a certain admiration. He has a fine sense of duty and is giving himself wholeheartedly to the party & its work." King actually crossed the floor to talk to him about certain budget votes.

It was Rodolphe Lemieux's last parliament. Speaker since 1922, he had tried steadily to be non-partisan. Every morning, he said, he would stop at the statue of Alexander Mackenzie on the west side of Parliament and read the French words at its base: "*Le devoir était sa loi et la conscience son maître.*" Bennett praised Lemieux for his fairness, "his urbanity, his courtesy, characteristic as it is of his race." Still, his Quebecois colleagues did not like him and would not agree to his continuing as speaker. It was useless, King reflected, to oppose them: "They know their problems."[76]

Bennett was praised for the dignity with which he had conducted Parliament's business during the past three sessions. The cheerfulness and charm with which the Parliament ended, said *Saturday Night* (7 June), owed much to him. His speeches were seldom marred – as Mitchell Hepburn's were – with partisan venom. They seemed indeed to disarm enmity rather than create it. This effect was symbolized on the last day, Friday, 30 May, by Liberal members flocking across the floor of the House to shake Bennett's hand and wish him well. King and he shook hands and shared a joke together. The galleries were full, though some of the MPs had already started for home. There were the songs, raucously, "Show Me the Way to Go Home," and more sentimentally from the war,

There's a long, long trail a-winding
Unto the land of my dreams,
Where the nightingale is singing,
And the white moon beams ...

So ended the Sixteenth Parliament.

3

Coming into Power and After: RB's First Year, 1930–1931

At 2:10 AM on Sunday morning, 8 June 1930, the CNR train, Bennett's railway car with it, left Ottawa heading westward along the great arch of the railway across northern Ontario through Cochrane for Winnipeg. RB was four weeks from his sixtieth birthday on 3 July 1930. He was an imposing figure, six feet tall, dressed impeccably, and with the solid girth almost de rigueur among successful businessmen in the 1920s and '30s. Photographs of him as early as 1910 when he was forty years old show the Bennett stomach being developed. He ate well (he loved chocolates and maple sugar), he slept well; he was indeed a picture of rotund good health.

RB was glad to get away from the confusion and pressures of Ottawa and of being leader of his party in the throes of beginning a general election. Mail had piled up inexorably. Local party officials (often called "the boys," by RB and Mildred as well) were wanting him to weigh in for or against some local worthy. RB was reluctant to interfere with local choices, however. He told one Manitoba supporter, "The essence of democracy is with the local organization, and the constituency shall determine who the candidate representing the party should be." But he was not averse to urging a good candidate to stand. David Beaubier, a First World War veteran, had been defeated in Brandon in 1925 and 1926, but RB urged him to stand again in 1930. (He did and won.)

Bennett's Centre Block office was constantly thronged with people with important exigencies, but they were not always the men he needed to see. He wrote to Senator P.-E. Blondin that he had dearly wanted to see him, "but the truth is I have been so driven I can neither find time to deal with my daily correspondence nor see as many people as I would otherwise like." Being confined to his railway car was almost a relief, his home on noisy and bumpy wheels for the next seven weeks. Travelling with him were Mildred, his office secretary, Arthur Merriam, a consultant named William Herridge, and some reporters.

Political campaigning was done mostly by train, supplemented now by automobile for shorter trips. RB paid for his own rental of a railway car. He had only one; his rival Mackenzie King often had two, and in later campaigns, three. They were paid for from the funds of the Liberal party. RB said he couldn't afford two railway cars, let alone three, and his party couldn't afford to help. There was another significant difference: the King train had an attentive steward who was unstinting with the gin and whisky stowed amply aboard. Ray Milner of Edmonton rode the King train from Edmonton to Vancouver in 1926; he reported to Bennett in May 1930 that press reports of King's Edmonton meetings were as generous as the drinks on the train. Not surprisingly, even reporters from Conservative papers drifted aboard the King train; reporting can often be a thirsty business. RB was an excellent host too, but he was not likely, he told Milner, "to seek advantages from a generous or other use of intoxicants."[1]

Mildred Bennett was by this time a power in her own right. When RB had been elected leader in Winnipeg in October 1927, she told him she would stay with him until he became prime minister; after that she would consider herself free to do what she liked. From 1927 onward Mildred was a marvellous asset to the Conservative party. She had a range of qualities her brother had not: she could dance, she liked champagne; she had tact, vivacity, a sense of humour, and a willingness to listen. She could talk to anyone about anything.

She could also rein in her brother. When in the heat of the 1930 campaign, RB said something about Judas Iscariot that could easily have been misconstrued by King (and was), she said to him, "Now, Dick, don't you say that again." With large reserves of pity and generosity, she had the moral sweep of Shaw's Candida. Peter McGibbon, MP for Muskoka, wrote to Bennett a few months after the election, "There is no position in the gift of the Conservative party that she has not earned." The photograph of Mildred and RB together at his swearing-in as prime minister on 7 August 1930 speaks volumes about their close relationship.[2]

Another occupant of the Bennett car was Arthur Merriam. Bennett had inherited him, as principal secretary to the leader of the Opposition, from Hugh Guthrie late in 1927. Merriam was quiet, skilled, and diplomatic, with a nice ironic turn of humour.

The third person helping Bennett was Major William Herridge (1888–1961). A military hero from the war (DSO and MC), now a well-to-do patent lawyer in Ottawa, he had easy social graces and a way with words. He had married Rose Fleck, the granddaughter of J.R. Booth, the Ottawa timber baron. Rose died in 1925, and Herridge seems to have inherited much of her wealth. There were no children from the marriage. Herridge had been a Liberal, but as an intimate of Lord Byng, he had broken with Mackenzie King over the 1926 King-Byng dispute. After being brought to RB's attention by Premier Rhodes of Nova Scotia, Herridge came to see RB in January 1930 and offered "helpful suggestions ... Just how far he can carry into effect his views, I cannot say ... But I'm glad he's ready to help the party and will if necessary take the platform." RB found Herridge's fluency with language and literature useful and rapidly brought him aboard the party train. The invitation aroused some jealousy; how could such a raw recruit rise so quickly from private to field marshal? But he could if RB liked him. Mildred liked him too.[3]

Bennett opened the 1930 campaign in Winnipeg on Monday, 9 June. His speech was broadcast far and wide. King listened from Kingsmere and confided cheerfully to his diary that it looked as if RB were going to be one of the Liberal party's greatest assets. The dangerous part, King suggested, was his emphasis then and later on national old age pensions and a national transcontinental highway; the rest – that is, Bennett's economic nationalism – was demagoguery.[4] RB insisted that the Canadian producer, farm or factory, was surely entitled to his home market. The rhetoric worked; by the time Bennett and others had finished in the Eastern Townships of Quebec, a pound of New Zealand butter (the bane of Canadian farmers) looked as big as a house. It was bigger: in 1925 Canada imported 163,000 pounds of it, in 1930 almost 40 million pounds![5] If existing tariff structures did not sufficiently protect the Canadian farmer, a new Bennett government would.

Bennett preached this with all the considerable powers at his command. It was as if the microphone were his pulpit; in full flight he had an almost biblical rhythm and resonance. Not only would he protect the Canadian market from the ferocious competition outside but he would use every tariff device possible to put Canadian goods into Commonwealth and foreign markets. He would, he said, "blast" his way into the markets of the world. That verb came from Herridge, who was beginning to write some of Bennett's speeches. RB had deleted it, but Herridge sneaked it back in. The rhetoric in general (this time in Vancouver) was pure Bennett: "So will I continue to blast a way through all our difficulties. What else would I be there for, to cringe to others with soft words, and to recoil from each rebuff?"[6] Those last rhetorical questions were a direct hit at what RB believed were King's pusillanimous responses to American tariff bullying.

Radio was now playing a significant role in political campaigning. But if it could spare RB quite so many public meetings, it took him and others time to discern the range and impact of the new medium, to learn to rein in the constant demands for the man and the speech in person. Rhodes made this point to him: "Don't let them wear you out with meetings." RB found it impossible to follow Rhodes's advice. From Monday, 9 June, until Saturday, 26 July, he reeled in some thirteen thousand miles by train and car, with speeches at whistle stops, railway divisional points, and innumerable school auditoriums, at the rate of as many as five meetings a day. Bruce Hutchison (1901–92), then a journalist at the *Victoria Times*, recalled his manner, "at once lofty and sympathetic. His radiant smile encouraged the weak and humble. As he lowered his massive head and glared over his glasses, the strong quailed. Before a vast audience or a small group he struck a pose of natural sublimity." Behind that radiance and sublimity lay the confidence of wealth. RB neither denied it nor flaunted it, but invariably he looked and dressed the part. He did not look like a man of the people; he was tailored, pressed, carrying his generous stomach like a badge of honour.[7]

He had put a good deal of his own money into the campaign and into party funds, even before the 1930 election activities began. He had given about half a million dollars to the party, helping, along with other senior Conservatives, to set up a Conservative headquarters in Ottawa at 140 Wellington Street, and to publish *The Canadian*, a monthly Conservative magazine. Its anti-King cartoons made the most of the prime minister's utterance of May 1930 that he would give "not a five-cent piece" to any provincial Tory government to help buffer the effects of unemployment. Bennett was also responsible for getting funds for fighting the election in Alberta and Saskatchewan ridings. The British Columbia and Manitoba ridings were supported by the financial worlds of Vancouver and Winnipeg, but there were no financial worlds in Alberta or Saskatchewan back then. The Maritimes and Quebec were looked after by the sweeping imperial grasp of Montreal's business community. In 1931, with a population of 820,000, Montreal was the largest city in Canada, one-third larger than Toronto. It was the commercial centre of the country and headquarters of two of the most important banks, the Bank of Montreal and the Royal Bank of Canada. In solidly Conservative Ontario, political financing was under the firm control of Premier Howard Ferguson

There were in fact five provinces and five premiers supporting RB's federal Conservatives: Rhodes of Nova Scotia, Baxter of New Brunswick, Ferguson of Ontario, Anderson of Saskatchewan, and Tolmie of British Columbia. (Quebec and Prince Edward Island had Liberal administrations; Manitoba's was Progressive but Liberal leaning, as was Alberta's United Farmers.) Despite Bennett's having the support of five provincial administrations, Mackenzie King was confident as late as 12 July that he would win – with an increased majority. "I really look for gains for the Government," he told his diary that day.

Both King and Bennett spoke about the need to have women elected to the House of Commons. Liberals put up a number of women candidates to attract the female vote but always in hopeless constituencies. Bennett tried hard for women candidates too, but thought it only fair to run them in safe seats. But neither Conservatives nor Liberals could manage to secure a safe seat for women candidates. The only female candidate, Agnes Macphail, was with United Farmers of Ontario, and she'd had to fight her way into the House of Commons, which she had been doing every election since 1921.[8]

The 1930 election was perhaps the first federal election where the personalities of the leaders were the dominant theme. Chubby Power, MP for Quebec South for many years and no mean authority, maintained that the modern cult of personality in Canadian political campaigning began with R.B. Bennett in the 1930 election. He was vigorous, confident, with a vast knowledge of men and affairs. His voice was strong, resilient; if it sometimes had a strident edge, that was part of his blazing force. His high character, his standards, his eloquence and force in a time of growing uncertainty and unease, were spellbinding. "Mr King promises you conferences. I promise you action," he thundered. "He promises consideration of the problem of unemployment; I promise to end unemployment. Which plan do you like best?" Canadians voted in record numbers: 75 per cent of registered voters. On the night of Monday, 28 July 1930, as the returns came in, it was clear that Bennett and the Conservative Party had won a clear and convincing victory. The final tally was Conservatives and Progressive Conservatives, 135 seats, Liberals and Liberal-Progressives, 93, Progressive and United Farmers of Alberta, 12, and others, 5.

Quebec was the surprise. With the fearsome spectre of the dreaded Meighen gone and a new Westerner promising to end the depression or perish, Quebec responded: the Conservatives had four seats in Quebec before the election; they now had twenty-four. Much of the credit can go to the work of General A.D. McRae, the Conservative organizing genius who set in motion the party headquarters on Wellington Street, to the excellent publicity it generated, and to the mistakes of Mackenzie King. But fundamentally the election of 1930 was won by Bennett, his drive, his knowledge, and not least his stainless reputation. Four days before the election, one follower wrote to him that, whether he won or not, "If old Sir John himself were alive he would be proud of the way you conducted the campaign." Perhaps the greatest tribute came from the veteran Liberal Chubby Power, who had fought every election from 1917 up to and including 1953; he knew personally every prime minister from Laurier to Diefenbaker. He observed that Bennett's character and force had more to do with his 1930 victory than did the principles of the Conservative party. "There is no question that Bennett *was* the Conservative party."[9]

The afternoon after the election, on Tuesday, 29 July, RB and King met in the prime minister's office to discuss arrangements for the change of government. They shook hands and began a long and fairly amiable talk. RB said he thought that during the campaign they had preserved civility and not attacked each other too harshly. King said a little waspishly that *he* had been most careful, but he was not so sure Bennett had, that he should not have brought in references to King and the war that re-aroused prejudices and were most unfair. Bennett explained that those references were in reply to King's in Hansard to personal circumstances that had kept him at home. Bennett admitted that he had not been in the war either, but it was on medical grounds of two missing toes, and because Borden needed him for war work in Canada and abroad. They then talked about the campaign, King suggesting that RB must have been rather pleased at the result. RB said he had expected to win but that he had done better than expected in Quebec. It was New Zealand butter, he said, that had done the trick.

King said he was ready to resign at once if that would suit Bennett; or, if he needed time to get his government together, King could wait. He knew that putting together a cabinet was not easy – as a rule one had to take what the electorate provided. RB thought it might be a week or ten days before he would be ready to take over the government.

King explained that he was not going to allow any appointments other than a couple of minor judicial ones, which Bennett agreed to. As to Vincent Massey's appointment as Canadian high commissioner to London, King had had that passed by order-in-council just before the election. RB had his own ideas about the appointment, but for the moment he said nothing. King also had a favour to ask: he wanted a car and chauffeur. The leader of the Opposition should have one – it should be a perquisite attached to the office, in the same way that cabinet ministers had a car and chauffeur. Bennett opined that in the past that privilege had been much abused, but King made the sensible rejoinder that it was not right that wives and daughters of government ministers should have to drive husbands or fathers around on government business. Bennett made no promise but said he would consult his colleagues. In the end the Bennett cabinet severely restricted cars for its ministers; King did *not* get his car and chauffeur. Giving it up, he said, was the hardest blow of all, and the expense of a car became a chronic grievance with him. (A year or so later, General Motors of Oshawa offered him a new Cadillac, which he cheerfully accepted.) The two men also talked about the expense of their campaign trains, Bennett having paid for his out of his own pocket, while King's campaign train cars were paid for by the Liberal party. King said he saw no reason why Bennett should give either CPR or CNR even "a five cent piece." Both laughed at the sally.[10]

A week later on Tuesday, 5 August, Bennett saw King at a luncheon and talked about the accession of the new government, now set for two days later. King duly handed the governor general his resignation as prime minister as of 2:30 PM that Thursday. He added a strange caveat: would the governor general please not accept his resignation until Bennett was actually sworn in? There was the possibility that in the meantime Bennett might have a stroke or apoplexy. How hard it was for King to surrender power![11]

"I will not give you much of a government," RB had told King two days earlier, but nevertheless he would be ready to begin. While he had as many ministers as King had had, he did not think much of their quality. He himself took the finance position, almost certainly because there was no one in Parliament who could do it better. Indeed, he was one of the most sophisticated financiers in the country. Some wondered why he had not chosen Arthur Meighen for that role, but though Meighen was a skilful, even ruthless, parliamentarian, he did not have RB's superb grasp of finance. After Meighen's defeat and retirement from politics in 1926, Bennett had written generously to him. However, after the 1927 convention when Meighen defended his anti-war speech at Hamilton in November 1925, that generosity chilled somewhat. The defence created more stir than the original speech. Still, in 1929 Bennett told Dr J.C. Webster of New Brunswick, a fellow board member of Dalhousie University, that

Meighen had the finest mind in Canada. In 1930 Meighen had not been an MP for four years, and when offered the Conservative nomination for Long Lake, Saskatchewan, declined to run. However, he supported RB's high tariff against American farm products. Their relations can be described as cordial though cool; Meighen's 1930 letter is addressed "My dear R.B."[12]

Another possibility for finance had been Edgar Rhodes, premier of Nova Scotia since 1925 and one of the ablest. He needed to be. His provincial Conservative party had been out of power since 1882 and, once elected, they were ravenous. Over those four decades Liberal stalwarts had honeycombed the civil service, but Rhodes hated patronage and did his best to combat Nova Scotians' century-old passion for it. He left many Liberals where they were and said no right and left to his followers, and they did not like it. That Conservative dissatisfaction mostly explains his narrow victory on 1 October 1928, the closest provincial election in Nova Scotian history up to that time. The death in a car accident in September 1929 of a Halifax member of cabinet, John Mahony (a notorious party-goer) created the necessity of a federal by-election. With a majority of only two seats in the Assembly, the by-election was a fearsome prospect, and Bennett persuaded Rhodes to run. The whole force of the Liberal party, federal and provincial, was brought to bear; the Halifax Harbour Commission was stuffed with federal Liberal appointees. There were so many people sweeping floors, said Rhodes, that they couldn't keep out of each other's way. It was, he said, "quite the bonniest fight I have ever been engaged in." In that bitter winter election, he arranged to have each of his followers equipped with Stanfield's unshrinkable long underwear and enjoined them every night to have a hot water bottle and a nurse put in their bed! He might have looked like a stiff-necked Conservative, austere pince-nez perched on a prominent nose; he had the visage of a bank inspector. But behind all that lay a disciplined intelligence, great capacity, and a keen sense of humour.

Rhodes won the January 1930 by-election handsomely. RB told him, "You've little idea of the great effect of your victory in Halifax on the rank and file of the Conservative Party throughout Canada." Ardent fisherman that he was, Rhodes sometimes longed for a less strenuous life. When first approached, he did not want to enter a Bennett cabinet at all, fearing its life would not be long. Perhaps that was one reason he was content with the less arduous portfolio of fisheries.[13]

In RB's cabinet there were of course the party stalwarts, including another Nova Scotian, Charles Cahan, nine years Bennett's senior, with wide business experience in Halifax, Brazil, Mexico, and Montreal. In 1902 Cahan and B.F. Pearson of Halifax created the Mexican Light and Power Company on the basis of substantial concessions by the Mexican government at the Necaxa River falls. It was a mighty enterprise: in a horizontal run of less than 500 metres, the river fell some 750 metres. Early in 1903 Cahan and Pearson transferred the firm to Montreal, with Cahan as its senior attorney. Max Aitken was its brash and clever promoter. He too moved to Montreal from Halifax after his marriage to Gladys Drury in 1905. Cahan was called to the Quebec bar in 1907, and in 1910 Aitken sent him west to examine Sandford Fleming's Exshaw property west of Calgary for possible inclusion in the future Canada Cement. Cahan produced a damning report, so much so that Aitken changed tactics and brought in enough other cement companies to swamp the Fleming interests. From 1915 to 1917, Cahan acted as British-Canadian agent buying munitions in the United States, after which he became Borden's director of public safety. In 1925, at the age of sixty-four, he was elected to the House of Commons for a Montreal constituency. Tall, rich, and experienced, he had a high opinion of his accomplishments. RB thought his presence and command of French would make him a good speaker of the House, but Cahan wasn't having it. In the end he grudgingly accepted the quasi-diplomatic post of secretary of state. Almost at once Bennett sent him to Berlin in October 1930 as Canadian representative regarding the settlement of German war debts.

Sir George Perley, the other Quebec anglophone in RB's cabinet, was born in New Hampshire and educated at Harvard; he made his money in lumber on the north side of the Ottawa in Argenteuil County. He represented that constituency in the House of Commons continuously from 1904 until his death in 1938, except for a few years after the war when he lived in England. RB made him minister without portfolio; he was seventy-three, his age, experience, savoir faire and good standing with French-Canadians valuable. He was, as John English remarked in an elegant little sketch, "an exquisite period-piece ... sporting an Edwardian goatee and Victorian opinions; and suspicious of levity, modern opinions." As the senior member of the government, it was he who would take over as acting prime minister when Bennett was away.[14]

In 1930 financiers on Montreal's St James Street had expected King to be returned with a smaller majority. The Mount Royal Club crowd now felt RB was ignoring them; he was playing too much to the West. RB's view of French Quebec was that of a New Brunswicker become Albertan, his ideas and presuppositions those of an English-Canadian nationalist: "This is my country, and yours," he would have said to a French-Canadian. "It came to us English-Canadians in 1763 by the spoils of war. We try to be generous to you French-Canadians; Quebec has its own civil law, but all provinces constitutionally are the same. So we all live under the same national rules." In 1928 Armand Lavergne, editor, journalist and lawyer and member for Montmagny, suggested that RB adopt a bold policy: it was time to stop talking of Catholic and Protestant, English and French, and take up "Canadianism." RB listened; he could do so if his own principles were not affronted. Indeed, on 10 August 1930 he made Lavergne deputy speaker of the House of Commons. What RB really never did seem to grasp, however, was Quebec's isolation, surrounded by a vast ocean of English, both Canadian and American. As one Quebec historian remarked two decades later, "*Survivre n'est pas vivre.*"[15]

RB was able to read French, but perhaps not comfortably. He had French correspondence translated; he was lawyer enough to need to be certain of meanings. What his spoken French was like is simply not known. He made a speech in Montreal at the Quebec provincial Conservative convention in 1928; it was well received but was mostly in English. Unlike Mackenzie King, who was embarrassed about his lack of facility in spoken French, RB seemed not much concerned. Behind his shiny carapace of confidence was an ego sublimely content, though easily bruised. Fundamentally, he was willing to accept the realities of French Canada and not repine. The Roman Catholic Church still functioned effectively; it seemed indeed to bear out Napoleon's dictum, "religion is a wonderful policeman." That suited RB; his Methodist religion had policed him well.

Few of the French-Canadian Conservative MPs were of promising cabinet timber. Almost all were new to Parliament. None of Bennett's three French-speaking ministers, Arthur Sauvé, Alfred Duranleau, and Maurice Dupré, had been in Parliament before. Sauvé had been leader of the Quebec provincial Conservatives and had warmly supported Bennett's convention speech in Montreal in October 1928; but in July 1929 he had lost the leadership to Camillien Houde, a more charismatic but rougher man of the people, an engaging rogue who looked like and sometimes acted like an all-in wrestler. Bennett had tried fruitlessly to head off Houde's selection, which naturally did his relations with "*le petit gars de St Marie*" no good. Sauvé asked for and got the position of postmaster-general, a traditional French-Canadian portfolio. Duranleau, another Montrealer, was given the marine portfolio. Maurice Dupré, educated at Laval and at Oxford, got the minor portfolio of solicitor general. Bennett thus had no experienced Quebec lieutenant; that was because any experience among the Quebec Conservatives had vanished during the war years under Borden and Meighen.[16]

As a rule Bennett was reluctant to interfere with local riding decisions; the choice of a candidate was up to the local nominating committee, RB told one Manitoba supporter in May 1930: "The essence of democracy is with the local organization and the constituency shall determine who the candidate representing the Party should be."[17] However, the tangles and infighting of politics in British Columbia could make him impatient. His most important political asset in helping to sort that out was Harry Stevens.

Stevens was born in Bristol, England, in 1878 and came to Canada with his parents nine years later, settling in Peterborough, Ontario. By 1900 he was in Vancouver, a grocer and later an accountant and real estate dealer. He and RB were both first elected in 1911 in the Conservative sweep under Borden, two fledgling western MPs, Stevens for Vancouver City, RB for Calgary. Stevens continued as MP for Vancouver from 1911 until 1930. Short, energetic, outspoken, he was a good swordsman in the House of Commons. It was said in 1928 that, had he been two inches taller, he might have been a prime minister. In Vancouver he had some successes in business and a failure or two to encourage caution. A tee-totalling Methodist, he had a close-knit family of five children and a wife who had learned to accept his long absences in Ottawa. Bennett liked him. Stevens recalled Bennett saying, after the 1927 Winnipeg convention, "Harry, I owe this entirely to you. You are the one who put me here." In 1929, when business problems were beginning to bite, Stevens told Bennett in October that he wanted to retire from politics as he needed to look after his business and his family. RB reacted with horror. Nothing that had happened since his becoming leader, he wrote, "has given me greater concern than your desire to resign during the present Parliament ... I feel certain ... that you will not leave me in the lurch." A by-election now in Vancouver Centre would be too awful to contemplate. RB was told it could mean the loss of three to four other seats. He was coming west to make a tour of the province late in the fall, and they would discuss the whole problem then. At least don't resign until the session of 1930 is over, he said.

In Vancouver doing the tour that December, RB and Stevens discussed the situation at length. RB was sympathetic: Stevens was taking "the only course he could take if he was to make any provision for the future of his family." But he certainly did not want Stevens to give up public life; behind the scenes he arranged with friends to provide an annuity so that Stevens could continue, as RB put it, "to give your service to your country." But Stevens was a proud man and would not accept the annuity. He did not want to be bailed out by anyone, least of all by the rich men in the party. Nevertheless he stayed on, ran in the 1930 election for Vancouver Centre, and was defeated. He attributed it to too much campaigning outside his constituency and too much confidence on the part of his friends. RB, however, still wanted Stevens in his government. He appointed Stevens as minister of trade and commerce with the rest of the cabinet on 7 August 1930, and a seat was vacated in East Kootenay for him. A month later he was with RB in England at the Imperial Conference of 1930.[18]

One colleague in the party, whose occasional scorn Stevens found it hard to tolerate, was E.B. Ryckman, MP for Toronto East from 1921 onward, a wealthy Toronto lawyer and vice-president of the Russell Car Co. Ryckman moved easily between Ferguson's Conservative regime in Ontario and the federal Conservatives. Both looked to him for support, especially for Conservative newspapers east of Toronto. By the late 1920s there was only one Conservative daily between Kingston and Toronto, the *Port Hope Times*, and it was struggling to stay afloat. This attrition of Conservative papers in smaller centres right across Canada, was one result of eight years of Liberal rule, especially after the Conservative defeat in 1926. Ryckman financed the Port Hope deficit at $500 a week, but in 1927 he had wanted to bail out. Ferguson and his attorney general, W.H. Price, persuaded him to keep it going for one more year. Then it landed in RB's lap. He did not like the idea of surrendering three whole Ontario counties "to the enemy," as Ryckman put it, and produced some help, but by April 1929 the paper had suspended publication. In 1928 RB had been seriously contemplating buying as an investment the National Press, a clutch of German, Ukrainian, and Hungarian newspapers around Winnipeg, but he broke off that deal when the auditors reported to him. It was typical of RB that he wanted "thorough statements about everything" and he did not like what he saw: "Anyone who knows me should realize I would not be interested in buying a 'pig in a poke.'"[19]

Bennet and his cabinet were sworn in on 7 August 1930. The by-elections confirming the appointments – a requirement then, and one that RB had already determined to end – were on 25 August. He drove his cabinet hard, the way he drove everything. Ryckman was almost seventy; so was Dr Murray MacLaren, longtime MP for RB's old county of Albert in New Brunswick. He'd had a distinguished medical career, once president of the Canadian Medical Association, then head of Canadian hospitals overseas in the war and on innumerable medical commissions. But as minister of pensions and national health, in effect what we would now call veterans affairs, he was soon showing signs of fatigue.

Parliament was called to meet on 8 September. RB had promised to end unemployment and conquer the Depression. His energy and application were unprecedented. The country had in effect voted for his purposefulness rather than for the Conservative party. The country was at his feet, waiting. Action was what the country wanted and action was what it was going to get. Chubby Power, MP for Quebec South and an Irish Catholic Liberal, was impressed: "There is no doubt that Bennett's high character, his great reputation, his forceful utterances, and his eloquence on the hustings had more to do with the victory achieved in 1930 than ... the principles and policies of the Conservative Party." Bennett's power, talent, and momentum were felt everywhere. He overawed his cabinet; he would overawe Parliament. Even veteran Liberals seemed to become mute. The country needed a saviour. Here he was: let him save us.[20]

He would do three things. First, he would hit unemployment straight on with a grant of $20 million. Unemployment was a provincial matter, but never mind: the provinces would be glad to accept the money. Second, he would deal with the dumping of foreign products into Canada that was wrecking Canadian business. Third, he would revise the tariff steeply upwards – in effect, let Canadians buy Canadian as far as tariff arrangements could manage it.

In the session that followed, when chided that the provinces and municipalities would use the $20 million in partisan ways, RB hit that pitch out of the park: "It is not a question of politics ... Surely the suffering of humanity transcends that. The safeguards are that the province or municipality are the judges. It is our duty to support their efforts. As for the tariff increases, we want to arrange as far as we can that the lives of the 10 million Canadians on the northern half of this continent be provided for by Canadian producers. Shall we, for example, develop a glass industry or not? Shall a Belgium cartel direct what Canadians shall pay for glass?"

At the same time, shoes were being imported from Northampton, England. The English machines were not as good as the Canadian equivalents, and English operators were no better, but English shoes were being dumped on the Canadian market at a price aimed "at one thing only; and that was to destroy Canadian business."

The main motion on the principle of tariff changes was agreed to, 121–87. The great tribute of the session came from Agnes Macphail (Labour MP for Grey South East); she was always fond of RB, sending him maple sugar and maple fudge. Her faith in humanity, she said, had been restored by "the Prime Minister himself ... he has apparently the courage of his convictions and I like people who have decision and act with despatch."

He would need all of that, for the King government had left the cupboard bare. The government lacked funding for even projected expenses for 1931. It was very soon clear that an immediate loan of $100 million was needed just to cover immediate expenses; there was talk of $150 million, though eventually they settled for $100 million. The New York reception of the loan was, as Watson Sellar told RB, "fair to good." But the syndicate that had taken the loan went under in mid-December 1930, and the Canadian bond issue was thrown on the market. It opened at 91.5 but within two hours dropped to 90.75 Perhaps to make RB feel more comfortable, Sellar noted that Australian 4.5 per cents were at 70, New South Wales 5 per cents were at 68. By Christmas of 1930, Canadian 4 per cents were up slightly at 91.5 to 92.[21]

From December 1921, external affairs had been in Liberal hands. Since then Mackenzie King delighted in periodic triumphs over the British: slapping down British assumptions in 1922 over a possible war with Turkey; signing the 1923 Halibut Treaty with the United States without the British ambassador; and even more, coming off triumphant in his 1926 quarrel with the governor general, Lord Byng. With Arthur Meighen's fleeting three-month summer government in ruins, a majority government in his pocket, King had gone to the Imperial Conference in October 1926 in a euphoric mood. The only question in his mind had been bringing British governors general to order, and he had done that. It was the South Africans and the Irish who pushed the British into the Balfour Declaration, although King did tone down the South African draft, in effect changing the dominions from "independent" communities within the empire to "autonomous" ones. "Independent" would have alarmed Canadians; it had too much of an American smack to it.

Canadians tolerated this policy direction, but many did not like it. Bennett did not. Neither did he much like Vincent Massey, the first "Canadian Envoy Extraordinary and Minister Plenipotentiary to the United States for His Majesty's Government in Canada." Massey was a King Liberal who had been appointed to cabinet in September 1925 but later failed to get elected and resigned his post. Still, RB would not have taken him out of Washington right away, but Massey had resigned his post there in order for King to appoint him as Canadian high commissioner to London. King had done that, a little wickedly, on 24 July 1930, four days before the election. Massey called on Bennett on 13 August 1930. Bennett told him that he regarded the London high commissionership as a political post, and asked Massey if he could unequivocally support the Bennett government. Massey was forced to demur and, clearly with reluctance, tendered his resignation. He had dearly wanted London and would have been ready to return to Washington, but neither option was open. He left RB's office venomous.[22]

Many of the departures in the field of external affairs that were made in the 1920s came from King's own instincts; Britishers' assumptions, their style and manners, often rubbed King the wrong way. In May 1929 he blew up at Sir William Clark, the British high commissioner, who complained of some protocol missing at the opening of the Canadian legation in Japan, "We do not intend," King said, "to be told [off] by the British Foreign Office ... I told him this 'tranquil consciousness of effortless superiority' on the part of Englishmen was intolerable."[23]

King's instincts were one thing; the translation of them into a sensitive, sinewy, effective policy was quite another. That was the work of O.D. Skelton, deputy minister of external affairs. Skelton had been a professor of political science and economics at Queen's University. His was an exceptional mind, profound, ductile, shrewd; his magisterial biography of Sir Wilfrid Laurier, published in 1921, brought him to King's attention and is still readable and relevant today. Skelton was invited to accompany King to the Imperial Conference of 1923 and to the League of Nations General Assembly in 1924. In 1925 King appointed him deputy minister of external affairs. King could be a very difficult man to work for, but there is no doubt that he soon came to trust Skelton and used his advice more than any other single civil servant in Ottawa. As C.P. Stacey put it, deputy heads of other departments had to *get* in to see King: Skelton *was* in already. King found his own ideas reflected in Skelton's memoranda but set down with a skill and pungency that King himself could not match.[24]

About 1929 Skelton was approached by Queen's University to see if he would accept the principalship. He was interested but liked his position in external affairs where so many of his ideas could be translated into action. Expecting King to be re-elected in 1930 or 1931, whenever King chose to go to the polls, Skelton was rather dismayed at Bennett's victory. He told King the next day that, had he known what the result would be, he would have gone to Queen's.

At one early meeting after the election it seemed the Conservative caucus was prepared to throw the Department of External Affairs to the wolves, as they believed External Affairs was the perview of the British government in the empire. Caucus was unanimous. Unanimous, that is, except for one vote: Bennett's. Besides being prime minister and minister of finance, RB was also minister of external affairs. He told them they could certainly abolish the portfolio if they wanted, but they would have to find a new prime minister.[25] He was nevertheless uneasy about his deputy minister. He thought then, and a few times afterward, that he might have to fire Skelton; his ideas and Skelton's jarred. The first meeting with Skelton after the election was not all that amiable. When Skelton came to see RB about the Canadian delegation to the Imperial Conference, planned to open at the end of September, RB was firm. "I'm not going to have you monkeying with this business. It is for the Prime Minister's office and not for External Affairs to run these conferences." In vain Skelton argued that that was not the way it had been done by Borden or by King. Finally RB compromised; he would take John Read, External's legal adviser and former Dalhousie dean of law, with him to London. (RB was then on the Dalhousie board of governors.) Skelton would remain in Ottawa.

It was just as well that Read was seconded. Not long afterward, Herridge, now RB's official assistant, came to Read and said, "We're rather in a mess. We don't understand how these Conferences are run ... Can you do anything to help us?" Read could and did explain the mechanisms. Later on, according to Read, when a question of procedure came up, RB would ask him, "What would Mr King have done?"[26]

Premier Anderson of Saskatchewan suggested to RB that there be a representative of each province at the conference "as speculators." To which RB replied, keeping a straight face, that he had thought about provincial representatives "as spectators" and would advise later. In the end he did not accept the idea, but consulted all three Prairie premiers and others about whom best to send as experts with the Canadian delegation. A spate of telegrams went out from Ottawa on 17 September to wheat officials in the West: could they on short notice come to the Imperial Conference in London on 30 September?

Parliament prorogued on 22 September. That day illustrates RB's energy. He was at the Finance Department at 8:30 AM; he dealt with correspondence, saw ministers, and was at the Commons by 11. Lunch was at 1 PM, Commons again at 2:15. He was in his state uniform for prorogation at 4:30. Cabinet met at 5 and continued after dinner, confirming what he would do at the Imperial Conference. He was in the prime minister's office dictating letters on and on into the evening. At 3 AM he stopped temporarily. A male secretary had thrown himself down on the sofa for a break and was asleep; two female secretaries, their notebooks crammed to the gills with dictation, had fallen asleep in the outside office, heads on each other's shoulders, oblivious to the world. RB nudged them awake, cheered them up with a story or two about the old Calgary days, and went on. At 4:00 AM Mildred arrived and said it was time to get going. RB had yet to pack; he said there was work still to do, and the train for Quebec City did not leave until 5:30 AM. He and the Canadian delegation sailed from Quebec on the *Empress of Australia* late that day, 23 September 1930, for Liverpool.

The *Empress* was a big luxurious three-stacker, some 20,000 tons. Formerly the *Tirpitz*, built in Germany before the war, owned by Hamburg-Amerika, after the war she was handed over to the British as part of German reparations. Bought by Canadian Pacific in 1921, she was newly refitted in 1927 and given four knots extra speed. As long as radio contact existed with Louisburg on Cape Breton, the *Empress* was pursued with radio messages for RB from (and back to) Sir George Perley, RB's second-in-command in Ottawa.[27]

The pattern of the three postwar Imperial Conferences in 1923, 1926, and 1930, at least on tariff issues, was basically Canadian and Australian importunity and UK intransigence. Canada and Australia wanted Britain to impose tariffs on all foreign foodstuffs entering its ports, while at the same time admitting empire products free of duty. That was roughly what had been proposed by Joseph Chamberlain's Tariff Reform in 1903, with the untoward result that it split Britain's ruling Conservative Party and did much to contribute to the sweeping Liberal victory of 1906. By the 1920s with Canada's and Australia's industries growing apace, and South Africa's not far behind, tariff concessions from Britain were needed and expected. Thus the tariff discussions in 1923 and 1926 were always one sided, the dominion ministers attacking especially Britain's free trade in agricultural products, while protecting their own domestic manufactures. This situation worried the British, for in the 1920s the pound was overvalued, exports were slow, and unemployment was fairly high. The Canadian tariff preferences offered by Laurier in 1897 and after were not all that preferential. Canadians were not above exaggerating their generosity to the mother country.

In the 1929 general election, the British electorate split three ways, perhaps the only three-cornered election in British history, with Labour winning 288 seats, Conservatives 260, and Liberals 59. Stanley Baldwin, the Conservative leader, resigned, and in came Ramsay MacDonald, the Scottish miner who headed the Labour party. The Labour party were resolutely opposed to what were called "food taxes," and indeed the "untaxed breakfast table" had a following in the Conservative party.

Thus the *Empress of Australia* steamed across the Atlantic with what was for the British a boatload of trouble. She carried the whole official Canadian delegation to the 1930 conference, some twenty-six in all: Bennett and three of his cabinet: Harry Stevens, Hugh Guthrie, and Maurice Dupré, who all brought their wives; William Herridge; John Read from External, H.M. Tory of National Research Council, R.H. Coats, head of Dominion Bureau of Statistics, wheat officials from the West, General McNaughton, chief of general staff, Sir Robert Borden, and not least Alice Millar, RB's Calgary secretary. RB was paying for Mildred's travel, despite a generous offer from the British government's Hospitality Fund to pay her hotel bill. Howard Ferguson, premier of Ontario, came with his wife, Ella, to open a new Province of Ontario building on the Strand. The Canadians stayed at Bennett's favourite London hotel, the Mayfair on Berkeley Square, arriving Tuesday, 30 September, The conference started 1 October, having been postponed a day to meet Canadian exigencies.[28]

At an initial meeting of heads of delegations with Ramsay MacDonald at 10 Downing Street, a point arose that RB couldn't answer. Read had a looseleaf notebook and gave him the page, saying "This is the view of the Canadian government on this point." RB looked it over quickly, took in its import, and proceeded to make a quick, sensible speech on the subject. "RB," said Read, "was brilliant at this sort of thing." RB soon found he was becoming the most important person present. He was also strengthened by Leo Amery, a British Conservative Party politician and journalist who wrote to him 1 October, "Remember you hold the key position in this whole business and your action may mean the whole turning point between the unity and the break up of the Empire."

Bennett's opening statement on 8 October shook up the whole conference: the policy of the Canadian government was, he said, "Canada first." He went on to explain. If the conference were to get anywhere in meeting the problems, "my attitude towards my own country will be the attitude of you all toward yours. On no other basis can we hope to effect an enduring agreement of benefit to each one of us ... I offer to the Mother country, and to all other parts of the Empire, a preference in the Canadian market in exchange for a like preference in theirs." That proposition fairly put the cat among the pigeons, as RB knew it would. His speech lasted seventeen minutes and the next day was published verbatim in the London papers and reverberated from London to Glasgow to Bristol and back. The chancellor of the exchequer, Philip Snowden, had come the next day, Thursday, 9 October, denouncing Bennett's proposition as impossible. Britain's existence depended on her external trade, and it could be no part of British policy to make any change that would jeopardize a large part of it.

The papers were full of Bennett's bombshell. It was, said the *Spectator* of 18 October, "the engrossing political topic of the week." "Empire or not?" was the headline in the *Observer*. Duff Cooper in the *Sunday Times* said the same. Bennett's speech had created such a stir that he had to ask the dominion statistician, R.H. Coats, to act as what was in effect a press secretary, answering newspaper correspondents' questions about Canada and Canada's position. Coats's answers should of course be non-partisan, so RB instructed him through Herridge.[29]

In an early meeting of the constitutional committee of the conference's secretary-general, Maurice Hankey, what Read called "a dreadful jam" developed. Hankey said that at their next meeting they would discuss the issue of self-governance of the dominions of the Commonwealth – which would result the following year in the passage of the Statute of Westminster. At that Maurice Dupré got up and said that Canada could not possibly deal with that issue at this conference. "That's definite," he said. "I think in these circumstances, we'd better adjourn this meeting." The London press got hold of the story and the news was off and running that Canada was pulling out.

RB wanted to know what had happened. Read told him. "Well," said RB, "I am going to fire Dupré off that committee for making such an ass

of himself." Read objected. "Mr Bennett, I want to raise two objections
to that course. The first is, in defence of Mr. Dupré, it's not his fault. We
never got proper instructions from you as to what ... should be done. So
it's our fault not his ... The second objection was that you'd throw the
whole Quebec vote overboard."

What followed was a marvellous example of RB's way of dealing with
objections and objectors:

> "He got hot under the collar," said Read, "and got hotter and
> hotter."
> "Who are you to talk like that?" said RB in a temper.
> "Well," said Read, "It's my job to give the advice that I can. You
> can fire me [off the delegation] if you like, that's your privilege. I've
> got to tell you what I think of these things or else I wouldn't be any
> good to you."
> So he said, "What would you advise me to do?"
> I said, "Suggest Dupré follow my advice and I'll make arrange-
> ments with Hankey ... I'll tell Hankey *not* to ask questions of Dupré.
> Ask me."

One can almost see RB in this talk, eyebrows bristling like quills as
he became angrier and angrier and then, hearing Read's cool, unintimi-
dated reply, simmering down and asking for advice. This was one reason why civil servants liked Bennett: after he calmed down, he listened
to what they had to say. Of course it was easy for them as permanent civil servants, and for Read especially; just the year before RB
had told Parliament how lucky External Affairs was to get Read from
Dalhousie. But RB could intimidate, even frighten, his political and
parliamentary colleagues.[30]

RB had largely accepted the constitutional changes that flowed from
the Balfour Declaration of 1926. However, the hated *Nadan v. the King*
(1926) Privy Council ruling had done much to change his mind. He
accepted – welcomed – that Canada could go her own way constitutionally, once the Colonial Laws Validity Act of 1865 was repealed
(as it would be the following year by the Statute of Westminster). The
remaining ties to the British Parliament would be those of Canada's own
choosing. That was the main thing that concerned him in the constitutional discussions in London. The provincial premiers, Ferguson and
Taschereau, wanted to safeguard provincial rights in respect to any constitutional changes.

In economic matters Bennett was a Canadian nationalist first and an imperialist second. He had told the House of Commons five months earlier, "I am in favour of every proposal that will make for the advancement of Canada as an independent economic entity." Not only that, but in his mind the future of Britain's empire depended on the development of Canada. Canadians, he said, could not risk any economic departure "whereby we cease to be autonomous in the development of this great state." He explained his position to the *Manchester Guardian* in a parable about cotton printed on 24 November 1930: Cotton didn't grow in Lancashire or in Canada. Lancashire had cotton mills and so did Canada. Both had good machinery, good workers. Lancashire made some cottons that Canada didn't. But in the same type of goods, he said, "we can't allow Lancashire to drive out our industry. I'm putting it brutally but as frankly as I can." Canada had to "look after itself and to maintain a standard of life for its own people."[31]

In External Affairs back in Ottawa, Skelton quite liked what Bennett was doing in London and said so. "I was much pleased to see you adhered so firmly to your policy of reciprocal preferential tariffs ... There has been criticism in some quarters of your frankness ... but the dominant feeling has been that frankness and definiteness are necessary."[32]

Bennett's blunt proposal was not so well received by Ramsay MacDonald's Labour government, as it put them in a terrible quandary. They would not have been unhappy if the Canadians had packed their bags, with Bennett's ideas in them, and gone home. The issue split the Labour government, and MacDonald and his colleagues spent the next weeks backing-filling and debating. The economic apsects were complex enough: quotas, government purchase (an idea left over from the war), bulk purchase, each with a set of supporters and detractors from each of six dominions. Each commodity had its own set of problems. For Canadians, wheat was the most important. The figures for British sources of wheat (with flour imports converted back into wheat) show Canada as the leading supplier.

One major problem for the British was British millers, who wanted no Canadian flour at all imported, yet half of Canada's wheat was imported into Britain as flour. So the conference ran into slow going on that point from the start, and it soon became highly technical. A burgeoning cloud for Canada was Russian hard wheat, which RB said was as good as Canadian and could be delivered in Liverpool at 60 cents a bushel. The second

British Wheat Sources by Country of Origin	Bushels (million)
Britain	55
Canada	78
Australia	26
India	10
Total Empire (grown outside Britain)	114
United States	61
Argentine	36

day after RB's speech, Herridge was asking for briefs from his Canadian experts on anti-dumping duties, bulk purchase of commodities, and import boards. RB would tell a Conservative party worker, Mary Waagen, in Vancouver on 18 October that half of the British government agreed with the Canadians and the other half was opposed. "The result is," he said, "nothing is being done. Mr Baldwin has accepted our position, but that does not count."[33]

One reason that Baldwin's acceptance did not count was that the British Conservative party was in Opposition; the other reason was that the Conservatives themselves were divided. They had a maverick in their midst with a powerful propaganda engine at his disposal: Max Aitken, now First Baron Beaverbrook, and his London *Daily Express*. He had embarked in July 1929 on a campaign he called Empire Free Trade – that is, free entry into all British and Commonwealth countries of all British and Commonwealth products, with tariffs against the rest of the world. Beaverbrook was sincere about the object, cynical about the slogan. Britons would accept it, he believed, so long as it had "free trade" somewhere in it.

There was also a strong whiff of old New Brunswick United Empire loyalism in Aitken's Empire Free Trade. RB was from New Brunswick too, but his family were pre-Loyalist. He and Aitken had talked about the British Empire for thirty years, but on the issue of Empire Free Trade they were on somewhat different paths. Both wanted the greater glory of the British Empire and agreed that the most promising future was some form of economic union. But as RB told an Edinburgh friend, "Free Trade within the Empire is, of course, impossible … we [in Canada] cannot develop our resources under a system of Free Trade, and to develop our resources is essential." Free trade, whether of the empire kind or any other, would have wiped out almost every manufacturing industry in Canada. Beaverbrook's position suggested, as Churchill speculated, that he had taken up Empire Free Trade either from vanity or boredom. More likely, he wanted to dish Stanley Baldwin, whom he hated. The Beaver had few compelling hates but Baldwin was among them.[34]

Lady Diana Cooper described Aitken as "this strange magnetic gnome with an odour of genius about him." He courted women and men freely with money, champagne, rare cheese, fine claret and plenty of well-turned flattery in rich King James I language. He could call even academics to his side, A.J.P. Taylor being one. "Of course, I loved him," said Taylor. RB's bond with Aitken went back to the days when he had shepherded young Max out into the world in 1893. Since then, Max had taken off on his own bent. They had consulted each other constantly on politics and finance. They soon had the common aim of the greater glory of the British Empire. A year earlier, as RB left England in December 1929, he had written to his old friend from the ship, "I have never left G.B. since you went to live there with greater pride in you & your work ... Your old friend Dick."[35]

But in 1930 there had been a row between them. Both were at fault; though Aitken blamed himself, the situation was exacerbated by RB's hard, unforgiving temper. In May 1930 Aitken had given an interview to the *Toronto Globe* praising Mackenzie King's budget that had just given improved tariff preferences to Britain. The *Globe* did not publish the interview at once but chose to hold it until just before the 28 July election. *Globe* readers could thus conclude that Beaverbrook and the *Daily Express* were supporting King and opposing Bennett.

RB was furious. Aitken sent a personal envoy over to explain and make peace; RB wouldn't see him. Aitken tried to make peace via letters. There was dead silence from RB. When Bennett arrived in London on 30 September 1930, that silence continued. In his 8 October speech RB told the Imperial Conference that Empire Free Trade was "neither desirable nor possible." The anti-Beaverbrook pro-Baldwin Conservatives made hay with that. Ten days later RB phoned Aitken and said, "I suppose my picture is turned to the wall!" It was not; Aitken was willing to make up. RB, however, was still cooling off. On the night of the South Paddington by-election on 30 October, which Aitken's candidate won, RB came to call at Stornaway House, Aitken's London home. The two sat in front of the fire and agreed to let bygones be bygones. When RB asked for a chocolate, Aitken knew the quarrel was over.[36]

By early November the conference was beginning to wind down. Heads of delegations met on 4 November at Downing Street, and the final curtain was rung down a week later, the economic issues still unresolved. On the last day RB issued an invitation to all the delegates to come to Ottawa in 1931 and complete what he hoped would be the economic coping stone of the empire. It would be needed if each dominion were to have its constitutional independence. Much was going to be expected and much was at stake. Even as the 1930 conference was ending, there was a crisis in Canada over the imminent arrival of large shipments of Australian butter, with cables from Vancouver eastward about the demoralization of the domestic butter market.[37]

Throughout the six weeks' meeting in London, the conference delegates had been showered with invitations. The City of Edinburgh offered them the Freedom of the City, which Bennett went to take up in October. The Prince of Wales offered a dinner to the Canadian ministers (white tie and decorations, of course) on 17 October, Bennett seated on the prince's right, J.H. Thomas, British secretary for the dominions, on the prince's left. RB turned down an invitation to go to Howard Hughes's new movie, *Hell's Angels*, but he did accept an invitation from the Wyndham Theatre to attend a play by Edgar Wallace. RB had probably read some Edgar Wallace, perhaps one or more of his eleven *Sanders of the River* novels in which a selfless, dedicated British colonial administrator serves king and empire in the depths of Africa. Walter Allward, the designer of the Vimy Memorial, asked RB if he could come and discuss progress. "Very willing," said RB. Six years later the memorial was unveiled by Edward VIII.[38]

After the conference RB left on 16 November for a tightly scheduled tour of Dublin, Belfast, Glasgow, and Edinburgh. He received an honorary degree from Queen's University in Belfast. The timing that day was detailed and close: address by Lord Mayor and Corporation of Belfast, 12:15 PM; degree granting, 1:30, then luncheon by both houses of the Stormont Parliament and a tour; then dinner before catching the boat for Glasgow. Returning to London on the morning of 21 November, RB went on to Paris with Mildred and Bill Herridge for dinner with the French government and lunch the following day with Philippe Roy, the Canadian minister to France, who, though appointed by King in 1928, had been Canada's commissaire general in France since 1911.

On their return to London, now joined by Alice Millar, the Bennett party went to Oxford on Sunday, 30 November, to meet three Canadian

Rhodes Scholars, including the young G.F.G. Stanley from Calgary, reading history at Keble College, and Burton Kierstead from the University of New Brunswick, reading economics at Exeter. They met at the Mitre Hotel, where RB gave an informal talk on his favourite theme, the evils of strong drink. When they were seated in the dining room, RB asked, "What would you boys like to drink?" He was a generous host, and it is possible he meant the question innocently. However, Stanley remarked later, "Cowards we were. All three of us." They muttered something about ginger ale, and ginger ale was what they got. Young Stanley took the party on a tour of Keble College; in the dining hall was a portrait of Charles I, labelled "Charles the Martyr." Stanley's mother was with the group and mischievously pointed out the portrait. A Cavalier sympathizer, she knew RB was not. RB launched into a lecture on Oliver Cromwell, a man of strength, a man of action, one of his heroes. It seemed to young Stanley that the two men had resemblances. One of RB's early maxims was "Make things happen."[39]

During the time in Britain, RB made an offer of the position of London high commissioner to Premier Howard Ferguson, of Ontario. RB had originally intended the appointment for General McRae, his campaign manager in the recent election. McRae had been defeated in Vancouver North, and the London appointment seemed eminently suitable. But McRae's wife had become unwell, and McRae was now reluctant to move so far from Vancouver. On the other hand, what about Washington? But RB had already in mind a candidate for Washington: William Herridge. RB's second choice for the London high commissionership was Ferguson. The story that Ferguson gave to his caucus in Toronto was that he refused RB's offer but that King George V pleaded with him to reconsider: perhaps he could save the British Empire from going to pot. Of course in those circumstances, said Fergie, he had to accept. This tale was followed by a string of egregious comments on British politics.

RB ostensibly treated Fergie's breakouts coolly but almost certainly chewed him out in private. Later in 1931 when Fergie had been spending far too much time in Toronto when he should have been in England, RB gave him a dressing down. Charles Murphy, minister of the interior, was ushered into RB's office one day in October 1931 to find Ferguson there. Murphy apologized, "I thought the high commissioner was through." RB smiled wickedly. "Howard has been through for fifteen minutes but doesn't realize it yet."[40]

On 27 November 1930, a few days before RB left England, J.H. Thomas, secretary of state for the dominions, commented in the British

House of Commons on RB's conference proposal. Thomas was nothing if not blunt: "There never was such humbug as this proposal." RB waited for some disavowal from the Labour government. What came was a letter of apology from Thomas that same day, saying that in the excitement of the debate he'd used the word "humbug," but it wasn't meant to refer to Bennett himself. That was almost worse. RB drafted a reply, contrasting the conference agreement to have its economic section meet again in Ottawa within a year against Thomas's inflammatory remarks – "language which will be deeply resented by the Government of Canada ... [which] is honestly working for economic association. But, if her proposal is to be thus contemptuously rejected, Canadians can only accept and act ... by embracing the other means at hand of further strengthening her economic position in the world." The draft well represents RB's feelings; that it was ever despatched is doubtful. When the Canadians left London for the ship at Portishead on 4 December, Thomas was at the station to shake hands and say goodbye. RB's last words to him were "See you at Ottawa!"[41]

RB sailed from Portishead on the Bristol Channel on the *Duchess of Athol*. She was a two-year old, 20,119 ton Canadian Pacific steamship, built on the Clyde, sailing to and from Saint John in the winter. One would see the CP Duchess ships with their twin buff-coloured funnels every fortnight, berthed across the harbour in west Saint John.

Saint John was a city familiar to RB. He'd left from there in January 1897 for Calgary. Grimy with a century of coal smoke, its frame houses painted the usual brooding Maritime brown, it had an friendly ebullience quite at odds with its looks. The CPR train to Montreal via the "Short Line" left from there at noon and travelled through Maine to arrive in Montreal for breakfast the next morning. RB, Mildred, Herridge, and probably Harry Stevens and others caught it on 12 December. When they got to Ottawa the following day, RB arranged to have Stevens take the train car on, stopping in the East Kooteney riding on the way to Vancouver to touch some constituency bases.

That's where Stevens put his foot in it. He sent RB an uncoded telegram that it would be useful if the Crow's Nest rates were extended to include BC coal, instead of, as it was, just grain. But that issue was delicate in the extreme. In the Crow's Nest rates, originally established in 1897, the CPR had taken a 15 per cent reduction on freight rates in return for a federal subsidy on railway construction through the Crow's Nest Pass. The rates were suspended during the war, and their revival had been fought over in Parliament and only settled in 1927, and then for grain only. Stevens knew all that, of course, but as often happened, he was carried away by his sympathies for his constituents and their arguments.

Though RB had great respect for Stevens in general, he was not pleased when his ministers made policy statements on their own. His telegram in response to the Crow Rate comments was terse. "You have placed us all in a difficult and embarrassing position. Please leave Vancouver Christmas night ... Cabinet greatly distressed." Stevens got the telegram on his arrival in Vancouver on December 24. He sent two telegrams back. One was to RB at his brother's home in Sackville, New Brunswick, where RB was spending the holiday, wishing him a happy Christmas. The irony of it was in the second telegram of 25 December: "Leaving tonight. Arrive Ottawa Tues. Morning [30 Dec.]." It was not a happy Christmas in Port Coquitlam, Stevens's home. Stevens's close-knit and religious family bitterly resented having him recalled to Ottawa on Christmas Day. Stevens appeared philosophical, but then he had not been blameless.[42]

RB did not stay in New Brunswick for long either. He was in Regina to give a major speech about the time that Stevens reached Ottawa. The Regina Armouries was filled to overflowing with eight thousand people. RB's basic argument was how important it was, "in the midst of the greatest depression the world has ever seen," to save Canada's national credit. There were big projects afoot: the Hudson's Bay Railway, the St Lawrence Seaway, national old age pensions. Important as they were, still more important was Canada's credit standing in the London and New York financial worlds. It was not just a conservative businessman's prejudice. There were hard reasons for it. Canada's net debt in 1914 was $336 million, about three-quarters of it held in London; in 1930 it was $2,178,000,000, most of that 700 per cent increase owing to Victory loans, war debt, and paying for soldiers' rehabilitation and soldiers' and widows' pensions. And much of the debt was now held in the United States. In May 1931, $639 million of it would be converted. A stable credit rating was essential for such conversions.[43]

In Regina, RB was also dealing with the premier of British Columbia, Simon Fraser Tolmie, MP for Victoria, 1917–28, and premier of British Columbia since. Tolmie telegraphed RB in Regina: "Australia lumber preference vital to BC. Let nothing stand in the way." That nettled RB: why that telegram now? For the past two months Canada had been negotiating with Australians and others in London. Why would Tolmie think the Government of Canada incapable of looking after Canadian interests? RB added in a second telegram the next day, "I think the present Government can be relied on to look after the business of Can-ada quite as well" as those who seemed to be advising Tolmie. Where was Tolmie getting the rumours from, anyway? Nevertheless, from Calgary RB got his Ottawa secretary to report on the current state of affairs with Australia.

Two weeks later Tolmie apologized for his outburst. The telegram from Victoria had been drafted and sent in a hurry. Victoria is a long way from Ottawa, four days and nights by train; it was not difficult for BC officials to imagine that the province was being shafted by politicians or civil servants back East. The trade negotiations with Australia were neither simple nor easy, but the text was out by mid-July 1931 and was given an enthusiastic welcome in British Columbia. "Hearty congratulations," Tolmie wrote, making generous amends for past criticism. "British Columbians very much elated." RB warned him that the treaty might meet opposition in Parliament. Indeed, wine producers in Niagara threatened retaliation if free entry of Australian wine went through as planned. But the treaty would pass on 22 July and was signed 3 August 1931.[44]

RB was back in Ottawa for a dinner on 13 January 1931 at the Château Laurier in honour of the retiring governor general, Viscount Willingdon. There were two hundred guests, the Château's dining room decorated in spring green, silver vases filled with spring flowers. RB made a short speech of thanks that the governor general replied to graciously enough, but underneath there were tensions. Willingdon was a Liberal, appointed on King's recommendation in 1926 after Lord Byng's departure. Willingdon was not pleased with Bennett's role at the Imperial Conference, and he seems to have chatted readily about it to King. On the other hand, he told King that talking to Bennett informally was pleasant; it was only when Bennett got onto business preoccupations that he could become arrogant.

RB left for Washington on 29 January 1931, Herridge going with him, for informal talks with President Herbert Hoover, in office since March 1929. There was a protocol even for a one-day informal visit. RB was to call at the State Department to speak with Secretary of State Henry Stimson at 3:30 PM, then on to the president (4:30 PM), followed by tea at the Canadian Legation. At a small informal dinner that evening at the White House with Hoover, Stimson, and Hume Wrong, the Canadian chargé d'affaires, the talk was about what was now being called the St

Lawrence Deep Waterway. The St Lawrence route and its power potential was the kind of public works project that appealed to Hoover, an
engineer by training.

The White House was a leaky place even then, and news of Bennett's
visit got out. The Associated Press put a reporter on the Canadians' tail,
and a car followed them, parking outside the Canadian Legation until
the lights were turned out. The reporter was sure that he was onto something important, and his AP reports were in that tenor. RB and Wrong
were furious and protested to F.R. Noyes, president of Associated Press.
The Americans were perplexed at the Canadian fuss. Noyes concluded
that the contretemps was owing to the fundamental difference between
Canadian and American standards in press behaviour.[45]

Work on the St Lawrence waterway had already started in the Canadian section of the river. Lord Willingdon had presided at a ceremon-
ial dynamiting of a large rock near Valleyfield, Quebec, on 12 October
1929, to mark the beginning of construction on the Canadian side. It
was suitably dramatic; the band played "O Canada" and as the rock
blew up, an old lady fainted. This was the start of the Beauharnois section, between Lake St Francis upstream and Lake St Louis down (the
"lakes" were really large widenings in the river). The power potential in
the Beauharnois section alone was huge: the whole of the Great Lakes
emptied down through the St Lawrence, and in that section, roughly
eighteen miles between Cornwall and Montreal, the drop was over one
hundred feet. The power potential was two million horsepower. A stretch
of forty-eight miles from above Cornwall to Prescott came to be called
the International Rapids, its ninety-two foot drop offering a further two
million horsepower. That section would be shared with the Americans,
an arrangement that Hoover and RB discussed.

The project created great difficulties with Ontario, which needed the
power but was firmly committed to public power. Beauharnois was a
private corporation. R.O. Sweezey, the brilliant Quebec-born engineer
who drove the whole Beauharnois enterprise, pointed out to the Ontario
officials that hydro power could be divided into separate though inter-
related parts: its generation, transmission, and distribution. The divisions were worked out after lengthy, indeed tortuous negotiations in
Toronto by the end of October 1929. So RB's visit to Washington was
kept low key; there were three sets of sensitivities to be thought of and
cosseted, Ontario's, Quebec's and New York State's, although Franklin
Roosevelt, governor of New York State, was supportive.[46]

RB was soon back at his Ottawa desk in the East Block. It was a large office, most of its fittings seemingly dating back to 1867. There was not a bank president in Canada who would have tolerated such primitive facilities. A washstand was curtained off in one corner. Deputations were greeted by an office boy and then had to wait around while Arthur Merriam attended to the demands of senators, would-be senators, MPs, and other personages of all sorts and descriptions, most of whom knew not the meaning of the eight-hour day, assuming rightly that the prime minister didn't either.

RB's large desk was piled high with work, too much of which he was doing himself. No British prime minister would have been expected to deal with so many petty details of administration. RB was a phenomenon. "His knowledge, his memory and his resourcefulness were unfailing," said the *Ottawa Journal*. Everyone marvelled at it; a few were dismayed at the huge drafts he made on his own health and strength. He had shouldered a gigantic burden: prime minister, minister of external affairs, acting minister of finance, and, for a time in 1931, acting minister of labour. John Stevenson, chief Canadian correspondent of the *London Times* for fourteen years (1926–40), wrote in the *Queen's Quarterly* in 1931, "One thing is certain, that no Canadian Premier since Sir John Macdonald has been so completely master in his own house or more entitled to say at the present moment, 'L'état c'est moi.' Throughout all his adult life he has scorned delights and lived laborious days and his powers of industry are little short of prodigious." He would have early breakfast in his Château Laurier rooms and get to the Finance Department while many others were still in their bathtubs. The *Mail and Empire* noted that RB could easily have escaped all of that and lived a life of comfort and leisure. That he didn't, that he preferred days of toil and nights of worry, was a tremendous "revelation that there is such a thing as patriotism, as the desire and instinct for public service."[47]

The public service that occupied RB most in his first year was as minister of finance. On his return from London in December 1930 he had his officials work on the financial reporting across the whole of Canada's civil service. Public funds were already sufficiently protected against defalcations, and Parliament was sufficiently well informed, but the accounting system was not designed to safeguard against departments overspending their appropriations. The government needed "timely information throughout the fiscal year." The new system was far ranging in its effects, and it had to override real opposition from within the civil service. However, RB had the good sense to lay his legislation privately before Mackenzie King prior to bringing it to Parliament. It went through without difficulty in June 1931 to come into effect with the new fiscal year, 1 April 1932. Watson Sellar was the new key official, the comptroller of the Treasury. In effect he was deputy minister of finance until the appointment of W.C. Clark in autumn 1932.[48]

The second major change that Bennett effected as minister of finance was the reimposition and energizing of the power of the Treasury Board. Something of an arcane mystery to outsiders, often blamed for everything by insiders, the Treasury Board had been set up in 1867 by Sir John A. Macdonald as a virile committee of cabinet to oversee and approve accounts and to authorize appointments. By the late 1920s it had been shorn of several duties but was still an active if slightly corpulent agency within the executive arm of government. RB saw the Treasury Board as the engine that he needed to maintain and develop strict control over expenditures. The pressures to increase them came from all sides, and they were growing. As the Depression took deeper hold, there were ever greater demands for the comfort and permanence of a civil service position. But RB "rode the economy horse hard"; he went to Treasury Board meetings personally to make sure nothing got through that he did not approve of.[49]

His demeanour during the 1931 session of the House of Commons was similar. Parliament opened 12 March 1931, with RB boldly defending what he had done so far: "Conditions in Canada, bad as they are, are not comparable to what they would have been if we had not taken the action we did ... The burden is heavy, of course it is. The difficulties are many, of course they are," Then, a little later in the debates:

MR BENNETT: "I came into power."
SOME HON. MEMBERS: "Oh, oh."
MR BENNETT: "Our government came into being."

It was a slip of the tongue but revealing. J.A. Stevenson had a savage alliterative comment: "In the Commons Ministers sit like a serried lot of silent sphinxes while Mr. Bennett defends their estimates." RB perhaps did not intend to leave the impression that his ministers were a set of unimportant non-entities, but King, who had a sensitive seismograph, noted that effect. Truth be told, it was not a great ministry. John Read judged them harshly, excepting Guthrie and Stevens. Of the nineteen ministers, eleven were new to cabinet rank, while six had never before sat in the Commons. RB may have felt he had reason to be the school-master, lecturing, hectoring, trying to keep them up to the mark, and being impatient when some were simply not capable of it. He could at times bully his colleagues and some were afraid of him. King reported on 18 February 1931 that Bennett had reduced C.H. Cahan, the secretary of state and nine years his senior, to "crying like a child." This might have been true; still, Cahan stayed with Bennett to the end.[50]

RB chided the Opposition for its doom and gloom scenarios, for its "Jeremiah wall of despair." Was it not time, he asked, that the House of Commons should be thinking "not of our weaknesses but of our strength; not that we are caught in a great world depression, but that we have the courage and the enterprise and the skill to get out of it?" World conditions were, he admitted, "difficult to ascertain the reasons for." He was not seeking to escape responsibility: "This government seeks no quarter so far as criticism of its actions is concerned. This government realizes that it has come to power at a very serious moment ... unswerved from their course by abuse, undeterred by vilification or misrepresentation from any quarter, they will go forward to discharge their duties that the people have placed upon them."[51]

As to remedies, Labour MP A.A. Heaps moved in April for insurance against unemployment, sickness, and invalidity. RB had long believed in unemployment insurance but had always insisted it was *insurance* – that is, to be paid for by a premium like any insurance, the premium in this case to be shared by the state and the person concerned. The question was ringed with problems: who was to be insured, agricultural labourers, casual ones, industrial ones? What was the nature of the risk to be insured against? Britain had established unemployment insurance in 1911, and the British public was now in debt to the state for for some 100 million pounds. Furthermore, Heaps's motion had the words "federal" and "immediate" in it. Neither of those words could stand. The 1931 Census was soon going to be taken; they would then have specific numbers to go on. And they would require the agreement of the provinces. Before his government's term of office was over, RB assured the House, there would be legislation on unemployment insurance for Parliament. However, he said, "I have never had any illusions as to what was involved; I have none now." Such legislation had to be based "upon knowledge, not upon guess work."

That was RB: clear, firm, unsparing. He had been accused, he said, "of coercive methods. Well, if to state the facts frankly, to set down one's ideas without malice, to believe that words should be used to express thought and not to disguise it" – a jibe across the floor at King – "if that is of value, then I can say that this is all the coercion that has been practised."[52]

RB brought down his first (and only) budget as minister of finance on 1 June 1931. In the Liberal budget of 1930, Dunning and King had assiduously avoided a forecast of revenue and expenditures; they did not want a potential deficit, certain to be large, hanging over their heads going into a general election. It was large; RB rightly chided them for the omission, for it came to $75 million.

It is useful to note here how important customs duties still were for federal government revenues. Total taxes collected for 1930–31 (the fiscal year being 1 April to 31 March) were $296 million; of that, 44 per cent were custom duties, 24 per cent Income War Tax. (It was still being called that.) In 1929–30 the total taxes collected had been $399 million, 48 per cent coming from customs and 18 per cent from income tax. From 1931–32 onward, the proportions continued to narrow until by 1935–36 it was 23 per cent customs and 26 per cent income tax.[53]

RB's 1931–32 budget included three increases: a rise in the federal share of the old age pension, from 50 per cent to 75 per cent; a higher subvention for coal freight rates (a consolation prize for Harry Stevens); and a subsidy for wheat of 5 cents a bushel. Bennett omitted any forecast for farm relief and unemployment, remedied later when he asked for and got virtually a blank cheque from Parliament. The budget as a whole was passed 18 June, 102 to 72. King denounced vigorously, and with some effect, a change in the income tax to ease its application at the very upper end of the scale. Bennett may not perhaps have been fully aware of this proposal, for it had come from his departmental advisors; he was embarrassed, and on 16 July asked for and got leave to withdraw it. There was substantial support in the House for his arguing that he had no personal motives in having proposed the income tax changes that would have affected him and other Canadian millionaires.[54]

His aim was to get a budget with as little deficit as possible and to dislocate business as little as could be managed. Deficit there would be, however, for 1931–32: some $114 million, about equal to one-quarter of total expenditures. But RB was nourished by the great success of the conversion loan of May 1931, when a huge chunk of Canadian national debt, most of it from the war, was converted, most of it from 5.5 per cent to 4 per cent. Altogether he won praise even from King: "He had everything worked out most skilfully" – though King confined that remark to his diary. Agnes Macphail told the House that she thought the prime minister had done miracles with the budget, although Canada could stand some inflation. Why not print a little more money? In a deflationary time this was by no means bad advice. But it came up against RB's horror of depreciating Canada's national credit, especially with so much debt coming up for renewal, set against hard current thinking for economy and retrenchment when so much seemed in dissolution.[55]

During these tumultuous times, RB's own life was undergoing a dramatic transformation. Mildred was leaving him to get married. In 1927 she had promised to stay with him until he was elected prime minister, after which she would do what she pleased. She had had at least two suitors; however, by the early summer of 1930, before the general election, it was being whispered that she was engaged to William Herridge. J.D. Chaplin, Conservative MP for Lincoln, in the Niagara Peninsula, went to RB to insist that nothing be said about any engagement until the election was over. Mildred was too important to the party; her pending marriage, if that was what it was, could seriously weaken her and her brother's electoral appeal. So any prospective engagement was hushed up. When the announcement was made early in 1931, there was a *cri de coeur* from the party ranks. Peter McGibbon, MP for Muskoka-Ontario, wrote to RB, "There is no position in the gift of the Conservative party that she has not earned ... Her departure will be an irreparable loss." Edna Chaplin, J.D.'s wife, told King that the party did not know what they would do without Mildred. She was invaluable.[56]

A fortune-teller read Mildred's hand in mid-February, telling her that she had had two or three love affairs, and that the next one would bring her position but would be for convenience, not for love. Mildred became annoyed. "Why should I have such a marriage? I have everything that I want." Her fiancé was her brother's senior adviser, who had now been close to both Bennetts for some time.

Several months earlier when RB had broached the possibility of Herridge being Canadian minister in Washington, Herridge had apparently been taken aback by the offer. His own wishes, as Grant Dexter remarked, had more to do with the Gatineau Hills than with Foggy Bottom. But he thought about it; perhaps Mildred had a hand in persuading him. The morning papers on 9 March 1931 gave out the news that he was to be Canada's new minister to the United States. "Young Canada goes to Washington" was the headline in the *Canadian Magazine*. The appointment upset many in the party, and there were rumours of trouble. But Herridge was well received in Washington, and ultimately those clouds drifted away on the strength of his skills with the Americans.[57]

Herridge and Mildred were married in Chalmers United Church in Ottawa on 14 April. It was a beautiful day. RB accompanied his sister down the aisle in her blue chiffon wedding gown as the choir sang the lovely old hymn, "Praise my Soul the King of Heaven." RB's brother, Ronald, and his wife, Elva, came from New Brunswick and Herridge's married sisters from around Ontario. The church was packed. There was a large reception at the Château Laurier. King, in his waspish way, noted that the champagne and the wedding cake both ran out, but Bennett was a good host and would not have stinted at his sister's wedding. The couple took the train for New York at 6:15 PM and sailed the next day for England on the Hamburg-Amerika liner *Europa*. When RB returned to his Château Laurier suite that evening, now bereft of Mildred's presence, he found a note from her. It says much about them both:

> Dick, my dear dear brother,
> I can't leave this address without a little note to you – If I could only say all that is in my heart but I can't – and I know that you realize that in the midst of my most sacred and divine love you have never for a moment been out of my mind – In fact, I sometimes wonder if I am not going to be very lonely for you. I've *not* changed and never will. I sometimes think that loving Bill as I do – I've loved and valued you even more – I can't write more my darling Dick, but always my adoration and devotion to the grandest and finest brother a sister ever had –
> Ever and *forever*,
>   Your devoted sister,
>   Mildred

She had been living with her brother for almost four years, and had been part of his working life; she cosseted him, coaxed him, advised him, on occasion upbraided him. He was not above bullying her about champagne and wine (and her expenses), but that was a losing battle, for Bill Herridge was not a teetotaller. If RB missed her badly now, it would not have been surprising. Frank Regan, manager of the Château Laurier, wrote, "I think of you and your loneliness." Mildred had what RB did not have enough of: delight in common touches. One Montreal correspondent wrote to RB of "her profound devotion to you and her unstinted love of democracy." To that RB replied, "She has been of inestimable assistance to me." Following the wedding trip the couple returned to Ottawa, and Herridge left for Washington on 18 June. In the days before air conditioning, Ottawa in summer was fierce enough, but Washington was worse. Mildred stayed in Ottawa until the autumn.[58]

Ottawa too was hot that summer. In eastern Canada and in the West, it was the hottest summer in years. RB visited King on 1 July to discuss some of his problems: the hard bargaining with the Australians over the proposed trade treaty was one, but he especially wanted to apprise King directly of conditions in the West. "King," RB said (calling him by his last name of course, first names being reserved for close friends), "you had your troubles, but I tell you they are as nothing." The drought had already destroyed crops over a huge area; the earth was as dry as dust, swept by wind into heaps like snowdrifts. Sixty thousand people were expected to be on the government's hands that coming winter for food. A week later RB told the House that 100,000 people in the West were facing starvation unless the federal government provided help. The copious rains of 29–30 June had come too late; there would be no grain harvested in Saskatchewan in 1931 across some five million acres. King confided to his diary, "Oh how grateful I am we went to the polls when we did & are not in office today."[59]

On that same scorching Dominion Day, the House of Commons Select Committee made an extensive and well-nourished excursion by railway flatcars the length of the Beauharnois excavations near Valleyfield. The *Toronto Telegram* reported they had made a wonderful picnic of it, though some whose railway cars had no canopy got broiled unmercifully. The Beauharnois Company had provided ample supplies of cold beer for those in need and even had ready-made newspaper copy for reporters who after three or four beers were in no shape to write anything.[60]

Most of the Beauharnois principals were acquaintances of RB's. He knew them well enough to measure how to keep his distance. But despite the miasma of political skulduggery that surrounds it, Beauharnois was, as T.D. Regehr puts it, a great project, brilliantly conceived and elegantly engineered by the daring, innovative, competent Quebec-born engineer, R.O. Sweezey (1883–1968). There was just one major problem: it had to work through three democratic governments in Quebec, Ontario, and Ottawa, and a fourth, if one added New York State. Democratic governments have often needed to be looked after, especially at election times. The King government approved the project by order-in-council P.C. 422

on 6 March 1929. That order-in-council was not achieved merely on the Beauharnois's intrinsic merits, great as those were.[61]

From the start RB believed that the project, however brilliant, should have been conducted in a less clandestine manner. "We are pussyfooting ... because men think that your friend or my friend may be associated ... and we have not the courage to stand up and talk about it." He would talk about it. As for threats, electoral or otherwise, "I snap my fingers, that is my answer." Even after he became prime minister, he held to the importance of having "clear-cut opinions and convictions." But his relationship with Beauharnois principals tested his convictions, for he had to keep them at arm's length. He held to that as long as possible. When in 1930 the election campaign was getting under way, his campaign manager, General A.D. McRae, was offered $200,000 by Beauharnois as a contribution toward Conservative campaign funds. The offer was spurned. McRae said, "Not a damned cent." RB had in fact vetoed it. The federal Liberal party were less fussy. Beauharnois expected them to win the election, and the offer was generous, some $700,000. Despite these large amounts and despite strenuous efforts by an anti-Beauharnois working group holed up in the Château Laurier, which was trying to get the story out onto the hustings, Beauharnois funding did not become an issue in the 1930 election. RB was not interested in washing Liberal dirty linen; he just wanted his own party's linen to be kept clean. The Ontario provincial Conservatives were not so scrupulous.[62]

Before going to England, RB asked both the Department of Public Works and the Department of Justice for confidential reports on where the Beauharnois application stood. They were ready when he returned in December 1930. It was just as well. Robert Gardiner, MP for Acadia (Alberta), raised it in the House on 19 May 1931. An Aberdeen Scot and a Progressive, he laid particular emphasis on the fact that Beauharnois had applied for and received from Quebec the right to divert additional water from the Soulanges section, yet there was no federal warrant for it. Sweezey always said that he wanted everything from the St Lawrence except the roar of the rapids – though in fact that he would take that too. The 19 May debate produced a nine-member Special Select Committee of five Conservatives, three Liberals, and Gardiner, the Progressive. The chairman was W.A. Gordon, MP for Temiskaming South, an able lawyer but new to the Commons.

Three senators, Donat Raymond, Andrew Haydon, and W.L. McDougald, all Liberals, had been deeply involved in the Beauharnois promotions. Now Haydon was in serious condition from a heart attack;

Raymond took refuge in the fact that the committee had no power to investigate fundraising for the government of Quebec; McDougald took the view that a House of Commons committee had no power to quiz senators. At that argument RB threatened a royal commission, which certainly did have power to subpoena senators. McDougald became more tractable. Newspapers carried delicious stories of suitcases full of cash being carried through the Château Laurier lobby. They were almost certainly untrue: registered bonds, not cash, were the way of such businessmen.[63]

The committee's work went on in the stifling heat until 13 July. On that day, C.H. Cahan, secretary of state, told RB about a bill turned up by the committee, submitted by McDougald to Beauharnois for repayment, of $852.32. It had been paid. The bill was for Mackenzie King's Bermuda hotel in April 1930. Cahan asked RB whether the voucher should be kept out of evidence. RB agreed. He already knew about it. Committee members knew, and Liberal members told King, who was appalled that McDougald had not paid for the hotel instead of charging it to Beauharnois. King was now in a very uncomfortable position. He sent a note to RB on Sunday, 12 July, asking to meet, and subsequently pleaded that the voucher be withdrawn, on the argument that it "would be unfair to me and to the high office of Prime Minister." RB and King agreed that, however much they might disagree on matters political, on the office of prime minister they should work together. RB said that King's remarks in the Commons about RB being a dictator had "hurt him greatly." King replied by way of excuse that RB had been rude. It ended by their shaking hands. The Bermuda hotel bill was put to rest and King walked back to Laurier House with relief in his heart. That relief was short-lived: Gardiner refused to have the hotel bill swept under the rug, so it was out in public.[64]

There were other revelations, not least $150,000 to Ontario Conservatives under Howard Ferguson, as gratitude for Ontario Hydro's accepting a contract for Beauharnois power. RB phoned Ferguson in London by transatlantic phone to ask about the $150,000. Ferguson asserted roundly that he was without stain or blemish, that the Select Committee "can dig to China and back, they'll never find anything on me." The suspicion was that his sins were well buried. But one Ontario Conservative, John Aird Jr, still had his 120 $1,000 bonds and could prove it. He did not quite remember what it was for.[65]

The Select Committee's reports were debated in the House on 30–31 July 1931. King had not appeared before the committee; perhaps it would have been wiser if he had, but he did not want to have to answer questions under oath. Instead he made a three-and-a half-hour Commons speech. He claimed it was no part of the leader's job to organize money campaigns or to possess an inventory of those who make contributions to party funds. "That is my view," King said. "Does my right honourable friend hold a different view?" Bennett's reply was hard. "I have always held that the receiver of stolen goods was a criminal." King's speech was replete with insinuations against Conservatives but it was also furnished with plenty of sackcloth and ashes for himself and his party. "The party is not disgraced but it is in the valley of humiliation. I tell the people of this country today that as its leader, I feel humiliated."

He did not get a lot of sympathy from RB. All King had to do, he said, was to appear before the committee. Instead of that, he inflicted an interminable self-pitying speech on the House. As for the whole Beauharnois episode, the worst thing, in RB's view, was the injury "done to parliament, to our institutions and the fuel it provided for Bolshevists from one end of the country to the other to deride our country and its institutions." The remarkable fact was that the Beauharnois committee's report was unanimous, for it was a subject about which "the most acute differences were possible."[66]

The Commons accepted the Beauharnois reports on division without recorded vote. Parliament prorogued 3 August and thus brought to an end all parliamentary committees and their doings. Beauharnois had created a vast summer diversion in the newspapers. *Saturday Night* consecrated a poem to it on 25 July 1931:

> The magnate has
> A lot of fun
> He splits up stocks
> At ten to one
> And think how he
> Is tickled when
> He sells them out
> At one to ten.
> ...
> The witness prides
> Himself a lot
> On what he did
> For what he got
> But on details

He will be frank –
He finds his mind
A perfect blank.

Beauharnois remained a brooding miasma over the business and political scene. Three senior Beauharnois executives were disclosed to be unfit to stay in their positions: R.O. Sweezey, the president; Senator McDougald, chairman of the board, and R.A.C. Henry, vice-president and general manager. The Commons committee had recommended, and by this time the public demanded, that the three executives and the three senators (McDougald being both) be removed. Sweezey wrote Bennett a rather sad letter that he had been blocked from seeing the prime minister. He had been truly caught in political swamps. The project was less than a year away from completion. Would RB let him, he asked, "remain on the Board of my company?" RB thought Sweezey "an engineer of vision" and probably believed him to have been more sinned against than sinning but amazingly naive. RB replied in as kindly a manner as he could that he'd given a month's careful thought to Sweezey's letter, but, "under all the circumstances ... it is perhaps better that you should retire from the Board. I dislike sending you a reply of this nature."[67]

Sweezey had much support from the financial press as an honest engineer and "above reproach." In the end he had to give up the presidency, but happily he remained within the orbit of the company, R.A.C. Henry was also an able engineer, in many ways as indispensable to the success of Beauharnois as Sweezey, but he was tarred with the same unsavoury brush as McDougald. RB tried earnestly to get Henry out, but it was not an easy undertaking. Henry was important to the company and threatened trouble if he were forced out. It seemed as if Beauharnois could not go ahead with him – he was too distrusted by St James Street – but it also could not proceed without him. Aimé Geofrion, a senior lawyer in Montreal, suggested to RB on 13 September 1931 that Henry be kept on at a reduced salary in a lower position, but be allowed to keep most of his Beauharnois shares. Henry balked at first, but he needed civil service approval for changes to railways and canals. RB leaned on the civil service; by that fairly rugged mode, he brought Henry to heel. As for the three offending senators, their retribution would have to await Senate action in the next session of Parliament.[68]

By now, September 1931, Bennett had been prime minister for a full year. It had been a difficult, even harrowing time for both government and people, and it was getting worse. Serious crop failure now hung over most of Saskatchewan and part of Alberta. RB described it as "perhaps the greatest national calamity which has ever befallen our country." It hit Regina with devastating impact. In June 1931, 23 per cent of male wage earners were out of work. Purchasing power in the Prairies was down 50 per cent from 1930, already a meagre year. Provincial and municipal treasuries across the West were bare. The crop failure in Saskatchewan involved something like 100,000 people. In the last days of that session, RB put through a new Farm and Unemployment Relief Act. They'd tried not to shock the constitutional niceties, he told the Commons, but one of two things had to happen. Either the government had to take on large obligations that were properly the provinces' – done by declaring it was for the peace, order, and good government of Canada – or they had to let the provinces fend for themselves. King's motion to derail the bill was defeated 51 to 16.[69]

The Bennett ministry had not been having an easy time. Too many of the 1930 recruits to cabinet showed a distinct lack of parliamentary skills. The best ministers that first year were Rhodes and Guthrie, but that meant RB had to take on much himself. He showed an amazing mastery of a great variety of problems that the Canadian public and its affairs had thrown at him; but in taking on so much, he drew upon himself the concentrated fire of the Opposition. They harried him with questions and criticism and seemed to "take a malicious delight in putting the temper of the Premier to a strain which it does not always survive." He could have used, as John Stevenson remarked in the *Queen's Quarterly*, a little more of the *suaviter in modo*.[70]

By the fall of 1931 RB and his government were facing what seemed to be an unending stream of baffling problems, bristling with difficulties and yet, as Beauharnois showed, requiring solutions that could not wait but were often complex and drawn out. RB was capable of dealing with most of them; his financial and business experience, his huge capacity for work, had served the country well. But by September 1931 he and his senior ministers were tired to the point of exhaustion. How long could RB go on at the rate of twelve to fourteen hours a day?

If ever a strong able hand was needed at the helm, it was in September 1931. And it would be needed for a while yet.

4

Canada's Imperial Conference and RB's Love Affair, 1932–1933

The searing summer of 1931 lingered east and west, but by the last half of September it was easing. Sunday, 20 September 1931, was a lovely day. RB's cabinet were off with their families, getting relief from the heat and the unending, corruscating problems. That afternoon RB was sitting in his Château Laurier suite after lunch, reading, thankful that for a few hours when he could put aside the cares and duties of state. Sunday, as always for him, was a day of rest. His reflections that day were, according to his secretary, "I am not interested in politics. I am here in Ottawa as Prime Minister today, and I may be gone tomorrow! ... I don't care! Life has given me about everything a man can desire. I am sixty-one, old enough to sit back and enjoy what I have. But what I have, I owe in a considerable degree to Canada, and if I can do anything for the people of Canada that is what I want to do. When the Canadian people are finished with my services, I am also content."

Suddenly he was called to the phone. A code message from London had come: "Tomorrow England will go off the gold standard." Immediate precautions had to be taken. A dozen currencies and more would be pulled in the wake of that momentous decision. RB at once knew, said the *Montreal Daily Star*, "what it all meant. He did not have to go, hat in hand, to the bankers and great financiers to find out what to do. He was one of them ... He acted for the nation; he acted the very night the news came – and he saved the country millions of dollars." He at once issued an announcement: "Canada will pay her obligations in gold – the terms of her agreements."[1]

The British government's abandoning the gold standard for the pound sterling was a shock. The gold standard – that is, paper money freely convertible into gold – was epitomized by the pound sterling. The gold sovereign had dominated Europe from 1870 to the First World War. It had been suspended in 1919 and restored in 1926. In Canada too the gold sovereign and the American eagle (a $20 gold coin) passed as legal tender. The shock of the 1931 British decision was felt everywhere. In Britain it had been preceded a month earlier by the formation of a new coalition government in London, replacing the Labour government of Ramsay MacDonald. Although MacDonald continued as prime minister, as of 24 August 1931 a new National government was in place with a cabinet consisting of four Conservatives, four Labour members, and two Liberals. The new government steadied the pound for a while, but the run on it soon continued. Strong Labour opposition to the new National government did not help, nor the refusal of sailors of the Royal Navy's Atlantic fleet to accept cuts in their wages. After 21 September the pound fell 25 per cent in a few days, from US$4.86 to $3.80, then to $3.23, eventually settling at around $3.40. A dozen or more currencies followed this flotation. Bennett said officially that Canada would maintain its gold standard; if he may not have grasped entirely what was involved with that, he soon did.

The abandonment of the gold standard sent shock waves right down into the main streets of little Canadian towns, wherever there was commerce and a bank. Some three thousand bank branches were scattered across Canada. There had not been a bank failure in Canada since 1923, nor would there be one now. One reason for the stability of Canadian banks was that they were not allowed to lend money secured by mortgage. Nevertheless, the new floating pound put all financial markets in disarray, including Canada's. At the end of the first week the Canadian dollar had steadied at 91 cents (US).[2]

The retrospective report about RB's philosophy by his secretary was laced with some illusion. By October RB was deeply troubled, especially by the Canadian bank crisis that followed Britain's gold standard announcement. King reported on 7 October 1931 that "Bennett is meeting with terrible difficulties. A rumour this morning that the Royal Bank has closed its doors." Depositors were said to be transferring their accounts to the Bank of Montreal. That kind of rumour was exactly what had brought down the Home Bank in Hamilton in 1923. Such rumours are easy to generate and in a crisis-ridden climate are almost impossible to smother. The worst part was that, however smothered, there was some truth in it. Macaulay Securities of Montreal, a subsidiary of Sun Life Assurance, owed $10 million in call loans that it couldn't pay; one-fifth of that was owed to the Royal Bank. And the Royal had too many other unpaid loans. RB knew most of it, and as both minister of finance and prime minister, he was extremely uneasy. Canada could not let the Royal Bank go down. It was the largest in the country with over seven hundred branches across Canada, 25 per cent more than its nearest rival, the Canadian Bank of Commerce. RB told the Royal's president in 1946 that the bank's fate "gave me more concern than any other single matter that I had to deal with during my term of office as Prime Minister."

But the Royal Bank was not the only major institution in difficulty. The CPR was also in trouble, its fixed charges a massive and cumbersome dead weight, its earnings down heavily, its bellwether 4 per cent debenture stock quoted at only 50. Paraphrasing a Bennett interview of Monday, 5 October, Grant Dexter, the *Winnipeg Free Press*'s able Ottawa correspondent, told his editor in Winnipeg, "the CPR is up against it real hard." Thus RB's letter to Beaverbrook in 1942: "Some day remind me to tell you of the 'chances' I had to take with a bank [the Royal] and the C.P. [Canadian Pacific]. In some ways more difficult than Sun Life." In 1928 RB told T.B. Macaulay, Sun Life's president, that Sun Life Assurance was "our greatest corporation." He certainly felt in 1932 that it could not be allowed to go under. King and Mitchell Hepburn, MP for West Elgin, met on 21 October 1932 over Sun Life; a crash in that quarter, King said, "wd. be far reaching indeed ... I tried to keep Hepburn from going too far, in precipitating a crisis thro' exposures in part." George Finlayson, superintendent of insurance, told RB that if Sun Life were to publish its annual report as the statutes required, it would reveal insolvency. RB passed an order-in-council under the 1931 Relief Act that allowed the company to reveal its condition only bit by bit. His financial knowledge and his willingness to take risks may well have staved off a major crisis in all three institutions. A run on the Royal was averted and its stability eventually restored. But it was 1935 before a positive tone began to creep into the institutions' annual reports. Sir Bobert Borden would write a letter of appreciation to RB on 3 October 1932 for "the ability, courage and resourcefulness" with which he was meeting the tremendous difficulties he was encountering." RB thanked him but added, "Sometimes I am very, very weary."[3]

By late October 1931 Canadians were being asked not to exchange their Dominion banknotes for gold; this position was confirmed by an order-in-council on 19 October 1931. Dominion bank notes were $1 and $2 bills, plus much larger denominations for inter-bank transactions. All other bills from $5 to $100 were issued by Canada's ten chartered banks, their prerogative under their federal government charter. Of those ten, two were French-Canadian, one was British, and the rest English-Canadian with headquarters in Montreal or Toronto. Their banknotes added a picturesque touch to Canadian wallets. The front of the bills had stern but reassuring portraits of bank presidents and general managers; the backs had engravings of beautiful goddesses of harvest, nymphs of forest, mermaids of sea, clothed in decorous but thin, clinging draperies. One had the illusion that the garments of the goddesses on the $100 bills were delightfully scantier than on the lowly $10 bill.

The sombre bank presidents looked in much better physical condition than did the Canadian cabinet. The "toll of public life," as the *Ottawa Journal* noted, had been ferocious. By November 1931 the cabinet were quite worn out from work and strain. Not more than two or three of them played any golf. Only Gordon, Rhodes, and Manion were fishermen. Stevens had been ailing, the candle being burned at both ends, *Saturday Night* said. Senator Gideon Robertson, minister of labour, was in Ottawa Civic Hospital from overwork. Cahan, crippled by an accident, had been ordered to the West Indies for a rest. For eighteen months RB had worked unceasingly through twelve to fourteen hour days. "He has taken no exercise, indulged in no recreation, has had no social contacts, went without vacation. And his work was of the hardest that any man can do." He had been going back night after night to the office until eleven or midnight. Indifference was no way to fight off erysipelas – a painful skin condition – and it had finally put him out. Even the 10 November 1931 edition of the *Winnipeg Free Press*, opposed to most of RB's policies, was sympathetic: "The Prime Minister has taken the duties of his office with the utmost seriousness, and has sacrificed his time and strength to the task of carrying them out with an energy that totally disregarded the limits of his physical capacity. Mr. Bennett has been working under great pressure and the strain is telling ... The Prime Minister's load has been far too heavy." When he was told to take a rest, RB's idea of following doctor's orders was to climb aboard a transatlantic liner and let ocean and England do the cure. That is what he did in November 1931, but instead of heading south, he went to dank, dark, foggy London to talk to British officials about next summer's Imperial Conference in Ottawa.[4]

The Canadian dollar continued to sink slowly against the US dollar, reaching about 80 cents (US) by the end of 1931. It gradually rose in 1932, reaching about 91 cents in April. By that time the advice that RB was receiving from knowledgeable bankers in Canada and London was to cut Canada away from so much dependence on American finance and banking. The US financial structure was in parlous condition. One of the most shrewd and sensible memos on the subject came from a young economist at the Royal Bank in Montreal, Graham Towers (1897–1975).[5]

By mid-December 1931 RB had returned from London restored to health and strength. British elections at the end of October had produced a British cabinet with a majority of Conservatives and a House of Commons top heavy with them. A little more buoyancy had developed in Ottawa; *Saturday Night* was slightly cheerful approaching the cranberry sauce that Christmas of 1931. RB was urged once more to get a finance minister, told that however able he was in that role, he could not do everything. Mark Robertson, an Edmonton friend, told him bluntly that as things were, he was committing suicide: "Alive, Mr. Premier, you are a great asset to Canada and the British Empire. Dead, you are quite useless ... You are mentioned in the British newspapers as the most important man in the British Empire next to King George V." RB's reply: "I am not anxious to commit suicide ... and if anybody for a moment believes that at my time of life I am working as I am just for pleasure they are of course mistaken, nor am I unwilling that others should do their share of the work, but continuity in certain offices becomes tremendously important, and that is particularly so with financial matters where we have problems such as this country has never had to deal with before."[6]

RB had in fact been trying in several directions to find a finance minister, Sir Thomas White, Borden's finance minister, 1911–19, being one possibility. White said he was too old, though he was only four years older than RB. One legislative change that made such appointments easier was a law that RB had put through in June 1931: appointees to cabinet no longer had to return to their constituencies for re-election. King had agreed to it but observed shrewdly that while the new law made it easier to get new appointees into cabinet, it also made it harder to resist potential aspirants to cabinet.

RB persuaded Edgar Nelson Rhodes, his minister of fisheries, to become minister of finance as of 3 February 1932. Rhodes had few illusions. He had at first refused RB's offer of a cabinet position, fearing that the Bennett government would be short-lived. In 1931 King met Rhodes at lunch at Sir George Perley's and they walked down Laurier Avenue together. Sir George Perley had never seen conditions so bad. Rhodes thought then that if conditions improved, Bennett would "score tremendously." If not, the government would be out in four years. Rhodes thought King was lucky to be out of power.[7]

Early in January 1932 a new recruit was added to the Bennett team: Arthur Meighen. In 1931 RB had offered him the chairmanship of the Board of Railway Commissioners. For whatever reason, Meighen did not accept, taking a less important job with Ontario Hydro. But in 1932 after a luncheon at the Rideau Club, RB came over to Meighen, put an arm around his shoulders, and asked him to come to his office. Rather to Meighen's surprise, RB offered him a senatorship, and with it the position of government leader in the Senate and minister without portfolio. Meighen accepted within a few days, with a couple of conditions. Since he was already working for Ontario Hydro, he would not regularly attend cabinet; also, he would not do any political campaigning. Finally, he reserved the right, on behalf of Senate, to propose modifications to government bills if he and the Senate thought it desirable.

RB accepted all the conditions; he was genuinely anxious to have Meighen in the government. There had been rumours of coolness between the two men, but RB admired Meighen's mind. He told Dr J.C. Webster of Shediac in 1929 that Meighen had the finest brain in Canada, comparing it to the brilliance of Lord Birkenhead. But to powerful suggestions that he appoint Meighen as minister of finance, RB replied with silence. Almost certainly he reserved that portfolio for himself, believing perhaps rightly that he had the better grasp of finance and its ramified connections domestically and imperially. In any case he wanted to apply his own style and methods, at least at first. There was a chorus of approval for his appointment of Meighen. Even the pro-Liberal *Winnipeg Free Press* joined in.[8]

RB needed Meighen for a number of reasons. Meighen represented Senate reform. It was worthwhile work to make the Senate a vital part of Canada's legislature. Bennett gave Meighen almost carte blanche. Ten years later Meighen recalled, "No Prime Minister ever before committed to the Senate constructive work of such consequence, or ever accepted from it with so good grace such a formidable catalogue of amendments to legislation." The most urgent need was to have Meighen control and direct the Senate Beauharnois inquiry – the only way the three offending senators could be got at. It had to be done discreetly but firmly. It could not be made into a witch hunt for Liberal wickedness. For one thing, the Senate majority was Liberal; the Senate Committee report, whatever it was, would need a majority. Thanks to Meighen's judiciousness and his mastery of the complex Beauharnois brief, it got a small majority of seven on 3 May 1932. It also owed not a little to the fair-mindedness of the Liberal-dominated Senate. McDougald resigned the day of the Senate report; Donat Raymond seemed ostensibly more sinned against than sinning and was left alone; Andrew Haydon was dying.[9]

RB would have Beauharnois on his agenda for many a month yet. That the project did not fail was fundamentally owing to its masterful conception and engineering, and not least to RB's backing. But there were many difficulties in completing such a massive, capital-eating project in 1931 and 1932, in the very depths of the North American depression. Everything depended on Beauharnois power coming on stream at its scheduled date of 1 October 1932. RB's mind was fixed on that. He did not want to take the project over; the Taschereau government of Quebec had set its teeth against the nationalization of Beauharnois, by province or by Ottawa. In any case, the burden of federal indebtedness with the CNR was heavy enough. In August 1931 RB made it abundantly clear that he wanted the Beauharnois construction to continue. Completion would keep thousands of men at work; it would protect a legion of small investors who had bought Beauharnois bonds, as well as shareholders and bankers. In January 1932 he reluctantly agreed to guarantee Beauharnois bank loans up to $16 million, but he urged the bankers and backers to be more positive and less niggling.[10]

In March 1932 a crisis arose over the 1 April payment of $1 million in Beauharnois bond interest. RB would not guarantee it. The subsequent default of payment of bond interest forced Sir Herbert Holt and the Montreal Power Company, who were greedy for Beauharnois but wanted it at a bargain basement price, to work harder. The history of the finances of Beauharnois became steadily more messy and complicated, with quarrels, for example, between Toronto and Montreal bondholders. Technically, Beauharnois was a dream coming true. The first four turbines were tested in mid-September 1932 and performed perfectly. On 1 October the power flowed as per contract. But there was another massive quarrel over a 1933 reorganization, and by that time RB had had about enough. Beauharnois was operational; let the financiers of Toronto and Montreal argue it out in boardrooms. In the meantime and for the future, the Beauharnois generators would hum sweetly and efficiently. In fact they did so for the foreseeable future. The ten turbines were finished before 1939, each delivering 50,000 HP (1 HP equalling roughly 746 watts of electricity). In 1982 an engineer would put a dime on top of one of the original generators to show how smoothly it still ran after half a century. R.O. Sweezey, prosperous and respected, died in Montreal in 1968 at the age of 83.[11]

Parliament opened on 11 February 1932. Almost the first thing Bennett did was to propose a civil service salary reduction of 10 per cent, to last until 31 March 1933. Some 65,000 civil servants were affected. The cut also included MPs. The government would pay pension fund contributions to any civil servant who got less than $1,200 a year. RB's argument was that the cost of living had dropped so much that even with the 10 per cent cut, civil servants in effect had no loss of salary at all. He also proposed extending the Unemployment and Farm Relief Act of 1931 from 1 March to 1 May. Ancient British law had always made relief of the poor and destitute a municipal issue. It went right back to Elizabeth I's Poor Law. In the BNA Act, Sec. 92, subs. 7, unemployment relief was clearly within the orbit of the provinces, which in turn had relegated it to the municipalities. By 1932 many Canadian municipalities had run out of money, and most western provinces had too. Ottawa's move in 1931 had been dictated by overwhelming necessity. It was even more relevant in 1932. Seed grain on the Prairies had been bought but not paid for. RB put it to the House: "There is a limit to what the [Prairie] provinces can do ... the only way in which the provinces can finance this situation is by loans from the dominion treasury."[12]

Out of that context five days earlier had come one of the most quoted debates in the House of Commons. It is usually pulled out of context and often misquoted: Chubby Power, MP for Quebec East, bilingual Irish, had a wicked gift of the gab and a considerable capacity for drinking. He often combined the two. Power rather admired RB but admitted there were blemishes. Bennett was not in the House when Power first rose, for which he was sorry, he said, for he would rather talk to RB than at him. He suggested to the government side that they could all go home rather than sitting day after day, silently watching the prime minister's every move and gesture, wondering if they'd get a smile from him. He went on: "They should be not unmindful of the somewhat inexplicable fact that personally I hold the Prime Minister in high esteem ... he has talents of no mean order. He is able and energetic ... His very talents may be those which if checked, controlled, and braked would make him an admirable constitutional Prime Minister but his very defects are those which I fear would lead this country into calamity and disaster if he were allowed to continue as the dictator thereof."

At about this point RB himself came into the House. Chubby welcomed him: "So that I can say to him in the manner of a kind, frank and candid friend – that I believe he is as inconstant as it is possible to be, that he is variable, that he is unstable, and that he lacks in character that ponderation, that prudence, and that wisdom which mark the truly great statesman."

MR BENNETT: Could you not find another adjective?
MR POWER: However admirable the Prime Minister may be in his private character, and in his private relations, I much regret to say that in his public relations here in this house he often exhibits the manners of a Chicago policeman and the temperament of a Hollywood actor.

Power was not finished yet; there was the hurt felt on the Liberal side of the House from "the weight of his [RB's] cudgels," his "elephantine sense of humour," his overawing of Parliament, and the law passed the previous session making himself supreme dictator of Canada. The government had been going around the country building "everything from sewers to cemeteries, from theatres to – well, in French they were called vespasiennes."

It would be easy to believe that Power's outburst was nourished by a long and bitter feud. But quite the opposite: the two men's relations had been harmonious. A week or two earlier both had attended a Canadian Legion dinner to commemorate the Battle of Vimy Ridge. Chubby was also living at the Château Laurier and RB had offered him a drive home. They had a friendly chat on the way, RB congratulating Chubby on his speech to the Legion's old soldiers and wishing he had had the same wartime experience so that he could better understand their needs. Then Chubby went on to reproach RB for his conduct in the House, saying that he often hurt members and sometimes was cruel. RB waved the criticism aside: "Oh, I can take it as well as I can give it, and it matters not what is said. I don't take these matters too seriously." But the contrast between Power's mild private reproof in Bennett's car and the more savage public attack in Parliament led RB to conclude that Power had been put up to it by others in the Liberal party, and had had a few drinks to help put some sting in it.

RB was properly and deeply offended. Walking out of the House with Tom Fraser, the clerk of the House, he said, "I will never forgive Chubby Power and will never speak to him again." Although polite and even on occasion complimentary when Power became minister of pensions in the Mackenzie King government after 1935, RB held to that hard resolution. In 1936 when Power and his wife were on their way overseas on the *Empress of Britain* to open the Vimy Ridge Memorial, RB was a passenger and had a table not far away. He made a point of stopping at the Power table to chat with Mrs Power, ostentatiously ignoring Chubby who looked like a little boy in a corner being punished for something – which he was. Years later, in Britain on RCAF business, Power was at a function also attended by RB. He went up to RB, thinking it was time to let bygones by bygones. RB shook his hand, but there was politeness only in it, no real forgiveness. RB's enmity went deep and was apt to stay deep. Power regretted that 1931 shot ever after.[13]

The story of Sir Henry Thornton (1871–1933) was bigger and more complex. He was an American railroader, one of the new breed, university educated, who got his start on the Pennsylvania Railroad. Brimming with energy, talent, and ambition, and a good mixer, Thornton joined to that his fundamental belief that in business, subordinates mattered. They were the lifeblood of any railway. He was close to the top of the most important New York commuter railway, the Long Island Railroad, when the British heard of him. In February 1914 the British board of the Great Eastern Railway offered him the post of general manager. That railway was then the busiest commuter railway anywhere, serving as commuter line for the northeastern suburbs of London. At once Thornton won the hearts of the Great Eastern railwaymen by inviting the first labour delegation that came to meet him to sit down. He then addressed them as "gentlemen." Thornton exuded North American business style, boldness, adaptability and friendliness. He went everywhere, talked to everyone, and soon had the whole Great Eastern Railway at his feet.[14]

After the war, Thornton was knighted by George V for distinguished service. But postwar Britain was not the glittering civilized world it had once been. J.H. Thomas, one of the Great Eastern's railwaymen, drew to Thornton's attention the Canadian interest in finding a new president for Canadian National Railways, and probably also notified Canada of Sir Henry's interest in a move. He arrived in Ottawa on 17 September 1922, where he at once met and charmed Mackenzie King, and his appointment as CNR president was established as of 1 December 1922.

Thornton insisted from the outset that the CNR be free of political interference. Big, sprawling, and debt-ridden, the CNR had from the very start of its life been a creature of political interference. The one thing to be said about its debt was that it was underwritten by the government. It had some 100,000 employees and 22,000 miles of track, of which 1,300 were in the United States.[15]

RB had long been a CPR lawyer, but he was not ill-disposed towards the CNR. The Château Laurier was a CNR hotel, inherited from Grand

Trunk days. In 1928 RB thought the grant for the new CNR hotel in Halifax should have been handled by government bill, not put in the estimates. Every year CNR estimates seemed to get heavier, but traffic was rising steeply, and an actual CNR surplus was on the horizon. But, RB warned on 8 June 1928, "It is all right to rejoice in these days of seeming prosperity and say we have ample moneys and let us spend them. But there comes a day of reckoning and that day you can almost see in the distance now."

In 1929 there was the issue of the partisan functioning of what was then called the Canadian National Broadcasting system, as it was run by Canadian National Railways. But its handling of political affairs broadcasts were, in RB's view, politically slanted. The government seemed to get all the free time it wanted, the Opposition only time for their leader. The CNR and its broadcasting system belonged to the people of Canada, RB said, not to the government of the day. He was anxious not to afford opportunity for people to attack the CNR for political reasons. But, he told W.D. Rodd, the CNR vice-president, its broadcasting system was "being used by the Government for the advancement of its fortunes, and against that I protest."

Then there was a massive row over a proposed new Montreal railway terminus. RB thought the King government should have had the courage to impose a union station on the railways; neither Thornton nor Beatty of the CPR could agree. Some 10 per cent of all the people in Canada in 1929 lived on Montreal Island. Why not, said Bennett, have the Board of Railway Commissioners determine what should be done? That was precisely the sort of thing they had been set up for. The commissioners made no decision.[16]

By 1931, however, with traffic and revenue steeply down, and CNR debt burgeoning dangerously, some creative and curative action was needed. The truth was, as D'Arcy Marsh observed, "In the period of prosperity expenditures were popular and the people clamoured for them; in the period of depression, economies were popular and the people clamoured for them." Should the two railways be forced to amalgamate? Public opinion was divided. The West opposed it. The *Winnipeg Free Press* thundered against it.

RB's answer now was a royal commission, as knowledgeable and non-partisan as he could make it. He began by consulting Sir Joseph Flavelle, the slightly austere millionaire Methodist who had been chairman of the board of the Grand Trunk, 1920–21, before it became the CNR in 1922. Flavelle was now chairman of the board of the Canadian Bank of Commerce. He and RB had several meetings about who should be appointed to the railway royal commission.[17]

The commission was struck on 20 November 1931. It was to inquire into railways and transportation in Canada, that is, road transportation as well as railways. Trucks and highways were already making palpable inroads into railway revenues. The Transportation Commission, as it came to be called, had seven members; its composition was a good example of how Bennett thought government should be run: by talent, knowledge, and fair-mindedness. The chairman was Lyman Duff, Puisne judge of the Supreme Court of Canada; members were Lord Ashfield, head of London's underground railway system; L.F. Loree, president of the Delaware and Hudson Railroad; Beaudry Leman of the Banque Canadienne Nationale, then president of the Canadian Bankers Association; Walter Murray, the Nova Scotian president of the University of Saskatchewan; Dr Clarence Webster of Shediac, NB, and Flavelle.

Thornton's fall as president of the CNR owed much to the absence from his inner circle of a hard tight-fisted financial adviser capable of riding herd on his flamboyance. It owed little or nothing to RB's enmity, though there were those who said it did. They had, for example, never been able to reach a mutually beneficial solution to RB's need for appropriate quarters as prime minister. In the late 1920s he lived at the Château Laurier as many MPs did, and after he was elected leader of the party in 1927 he continued there but needed more space. There were offers of houses in Ottawa and elsewhere that he did not take up. Early in 1930, as work began on enlarging the Château Laurier, Thornton asked Mildred Bennett to let him know if RB and herself needed bigger quarters. It could be easily arranged. For whatever reason, this offer was not taken up either.

As prime minister, RB needed still bigger quarters, and Thornton heard that RB was considering building his own house. Reluctant to lose so important a client, Thornton believed the CNR could justifiably fix up quarters for RB at the Château that "would measurably meet the facilities of a house." There were discussions and plans, rather extensive, involving some seventeen rooms, proposed and probably accepted in principle before RB left for England in late September 1930. Thornton's argument is fair enough: "I cannot see that anyone can criticize the railway company for providing suitable quarters for the Prime Minister of the country, provided he pays a proper rate ... It was a good deal for us to have the Prime Minister quartered at the Château. It lends prestige to the hotel, and indirectly brings us revenue from a good deal of entertainment."

Thornton cabled RB in London on 2 October 1930, in his confident manner and as usual in a hurry, that the revenue anticipated amply justified the proposed changes at the Château. The result could be leased immediately. Cost would be $50,000 at the outside. He needed RB's opinion as soon as possible, "as I want to get on with the job." At Ottawa, Sir George Perley, pro tem head of government, balked. He cabled that he did not like the expense or the proposed $40,000 as the cost of remodelling the railway car either. "I greatly fear political effect of such expenditure and request your permission to stop it. Nothing much has yet been done." RB concurred: "I agree that at cost indicated proposed alteration should not be made at Chateau or on cars. In any event had intended paying interest on capital expenditure on the Chateau." There would be in the end a yearly lease for his rooms, set by the hotel itself at commercial rates.

Ultimately, two years later, Thornton was forced to resign. A combination of a lavish personal lifestyle and poor fiscal control had left him with many enemies. Robert Manion, minister of railways, was convinced in May 1932 that Thornton would have to go. A majority of the directors on the CNR board felt the same way. Manion had hoped that Thornton would approach RB or himself with a proposal to resign, but he did not. He may have intended to do so, Manion suspected, but his personal debts made him hang on as long as possible. Convinced now that Thornton would not resign voluntarily, Manion suggested to RB that his salary be paid until October 1933. For $100,000 "we would be rid of him cheap." This brutal turn of phrase suggests Manion's position. RB ultimately agreed, though not perhaps with the blunt way the announcement was made on 19 July 1932. Thornton retired (or was retired) as of 1 August 1932. He died less than a year later in New York on 14 March 1933, at the age of sixty-two.[18]

On RB's heavy agenda for the spring of 1932 was the news, just out of London on 9 February, that the federal government now had jurisdiction over radio broadcasting. The story goes back to December 1928 when the Aird Royal Commission was set up by the King government, a little belatedly, for Parliament had approved it in June. The commission despatched its work with admirable celerity, and its report was handed down on 11 September 1929. At nine pages, it was a model of concision and decision. Canadians wanted Canadian broadcasting, it said, and suggested in general terms how it might be done. The commission had found radio conditions in Canada far from satisfactory, with the public demanding, as *Saturday Night* (21 Sept. 1929) put it, "better programmes of a national character ... [and] the creation of a national broadcasting monopoly in which the provinces and the Dominion would cooperate."

That was the first and major sticking point. Under whose jurisdiction was radio? When Quebec passed its own Broadcasting Act in 1929, King did not respond. His Quebec following was too important for him to cross the redoubtable premier of Quebec, Alexandre Taschereau. But when Bennett was elected, he acted. The jurisdiction reference to the Supreme Court was made in May 1931 and the decision was handed down a month later – fast work! The Supreme Court was divided 3-2 in favour of the federal government having jurisdiction over radio broadcasting. Quebec appealed the decision to the Privy Council, supported by Ontario. In Canada, a publicity battle was rapidly developing between pro and anti forces on public broadcasting. The Privy Council appeal was heard in London on December 1931, and that decision was handed down 9 February 1932, *In re Regulation and Control of Radio Communication in Canada, A.C. 394.* The first line of the decision: "That the Parliament of Canada has exclusive power to regulate and control radio communication in Canada." If RB wanted speedy judicial action, he certainly got it.

Action didn't stop there. A week after the Privy Council decision, RB proposed in the House of Commons a special committee to recommend legislation to Parliament based on the Aird report. The debate outside Parliament now developed apace. Dr Lee de Forest, the American inventor of the radio vacuum tube, deplored the commercialism of broadcasting. He wrote to the parliamentary committee, "We look to you in Canada to lead radio in North America out of the morass in which it is pitiably sunk. May Canada fulfil my early dream!"[19]

RB introduced the Canadian Radio Broadcasting Commission Bill on 16 May 1932, with second reading coming up two days later. Canada must be assured, he told the House, "of complete Canadian control of broadcasting from Canadian sources, free from foreign interference [a station in Windsor was already owned by Columbia Broadcasting]. Without such control Canadian broadcasting can never become a great agency ... by which national consciousness may be fostered and sustained ... [Furthermore,] private ownership must necessarily discriminate between densely and sparsely populated areas."[20]

The bill proceeded with remarkable support from both sides and all three parties in the House. Only one Liberal MP voted against it. This impressive support in Parliament for the Canadian Radio Broadcasting Commission (CRBC) disguised the array of powerful forces already marshalling against it. The great majority of Canadian newspapers and periodicals supported it, including *Saturday Night*, but a clutch of important papers that owned broadcasting stations took up arms against the fledgling CRBC: the *Calgary Albertan*, *London Free Press*, Montreal's *La Presse*, and the *Halifax Herald*, plus two important Toronto dailies that did not own broadcasting stations, the *Globe* and the *Telegram*.[21]

But perhaps the real resistance to the new government CRBC came from ordinary people, who over the previous few years in the large cities near the American border had become familiar with private radio. Much of it emanated from powerful American stations with their inexorable taste for the popular, their money from advertising, and their innate disposition to treat Canada as an extension of their own American bailiwick. This huge, heavy inertia of the status quo made the early years of the CRBC extremely difficult, worsened by the fact that Parliament had given it too little money to do its job properly. In the depths of the Depression, the CRBC found the going thin and hard.

Few of the politicians who supported the act in May 1932 had any real notion of how very instructive and illuminating well-run government radio could be. Few of RB's cabinet ministers had much idea either. He liked and admired the BBC, but in North America its great attributes were almost unknown. It made matters worse that Canadians had to buy a licence for owning a radio; that was British too and pre-dated the CRBC, but since Americans paid nothing for having a radio, the fee rankled and was widely evaded. Thus it was that RB was the highest, strongest, and most indefatigable defender of the CRBC. But whenever he was out of the country for more than a month, powerful attempts would emerge, seemingly out of the woodwork, to undo the CRBC. And they seemed to find little resistance in Ottawa and often some encouragement. When RB returned, the CRBC would be safe again. He said later, "Always insidiously is the attack made against the publicly owned facility and the effort made to destroy it."[22]

Shortly after the CRBC act passed, Parliament prorogued on 26 May 1932. Canada had less than two months before delegates would arrive in Ottawa for the Imperial Conference on which so many expectations and hopes now turned. Perhaps the best introduction to this conference is the poem that appeared in the London *New Statesman and Nation* in December 1931:

> So, as each imperial problem comes to tax our mother-wit,
> First we ask ourselves the question, "What do we get out of it?"
> And for each imperial partner I surmise the final test
> Is, "Do we get from the Empire slightly more than all the rest?"

Canada was better than Australia at trying to disguise its protectionism with high imperial sentiments, but in both cases the disguises were thin and easily perished in hard negotiations. Canada wanted as much preference as it could squeeze out of the British for Canadian wheat, apples, lumber, metals, and fish, all of which exports had suffered heavily from the new American tariff of 1930. The British wanted lower Canadian tariffs or free entry for their manufactured goods. Britain and Canada each wanted to give up as little as possible and to extract the most concessions possible from the other. Other Commonwealth countries, New Zealand, South Africa, India, Ireland (the Irish Free State), Southern Rhodesia and Newfoundland, each had reasons to be less pushy.

The Import Duties Act of February 1932 was Britain's decisive break with free trade. Some saw it coming. Beaverbrook cabled RB on 21 January 1932 to get High Commissioner Ferguson to pressure the British government into exempting the dominions from the proposed 10 per cent duty, at least until after the Ottawa Conference. Ferguson did that so successfully that Chamberlain's act exempted the dominions from it until 15 November 1932.[23]

Canada had never before hosted such a large conference. The colonial conference that Sir John Thompson called in Canada in 1894 (much to the consternation of the British) included six of the Australian colonies, Fiji, and a still independent Hawaii, but that conference was low key and concerned only with Pacific trade. In 1932 each of the nine delegations to the Imperial Conference brought advisers and support staff – close to three hundred. There were also two hundred representatives of industry and business, to say nothing of another two hundred journalists. The Château Laurier was filled to overflowing, awash in reports, rumours, and recreations. The 1894 conference had been able to meet in the Senate chamber; one measure of the difference in 1932 was that the House of Commons was now needed to accommodate the numbers.[24]

The event had taken a great deal of preparation. Canada had not only to plan the agenda of the conference but also to work out its own priorities and position papers. Much of the work fell on the shoulders of External Affairs. The agenda was produced scandalously late, as RB liked to put things through his own head. When the British held conferences, the agenda was generally ready four months in advance. On 11 March New Zealand cabled to find out what had happened to it. Sir William Clark, the British high commissioner, reported a week later, "the Prime Minister is waiting as usual until he can find time to deal with matters himself, and he talks of there being ample time after Parliament has adjourned. This is taking serious risk as the session may be prolonged beyond the first week in May." It was indeed prolonged, well beyond.

Parliament prorogued on 26 May; RB had cabled a draft agenda to London and the other dominion capitals two days before. There was much in that draft that London disliked. The agenda was not in fact ready in final form until early July, by which time the Australian and New Zealand delegates were already at sea on their long voyage to Ottawa. The late agenda was not wholly RB's fault. The Canadian civil service simply lacked the expertise for the huge drafts of time, energy, and not least knowledge that preparations for such a conference required. External Affairs were rushed off their feet morning to midnight every day, said senior civil servant Norman Robertson.

In an effort to remedy some of those weaknesses, RB had recruited W.C. Clark (1889–1952), a professor of political science and economics at Queen's University, for position papers. Clark was suggested by O.D. Skelton, and like many of Skelton's suggestions, proved so useful that RB prevailed upon Clark to assume the too long unfilled post of deputy minister of finance. It took a little tractability from both the university and RB to pry Clark out of Queen's with good grace, but it probably helped that RB was at that time chancellor of Queen's. Clark's appointment would be effective on 1 November 1932. He was a golden choice: he had talent, discretion, good sense, brains, and modesty withal. He was soon a pillar of the Canadian civil service and continued as deputy minister of finance until his death in 1952.[25]

In late 1931 Bennett's idea had been that if the British could commit themselves to a preference in natural products, then Canada would charge no duty on British goods that Canada did not produce. He thus needed to find out through the Canadian Manufacturers Association (CMA) what Canadian manufacturers could accept as free entry, what under preference, and what more heavily dutiable. It was a tall order. The CMA took its time, as did its members, whom RB found intransigent and unhelpful, cotton mills particularly so. They wanted to think of what they *might* be manufacturing as well as what they did manufacture. Not until 17 June did the CMA disgorge a list of 9,553 articles – not only terribly late but wholly unclassified.[26]

The British delegation left Britain on 13 July 1932 on the *Empress of Britain*, a gracious CP liner of 40,000 tons. The delegation came with lots of power to negotiate but much confusion over what terms it could accept. Basically, Britain wanted tariffs reduced within the empire. However, none of the Commonwealth countries could afford to reduce any tariffs unless they raised others. The vision of a wonderful, single multilateral trade charter was just a chimera. It did not happen, and indeed, given the British disarray and the Canadian and Australian anxiety (perhaps "greed" is the right word) for protection, it could not happen. It could only do so if the Commonwealth ministers were, to use Ian Drummond's phrase, "self-sacrificing saints." RB and Stanley Bruce of Australia did not answer to that description. Moreover, Canadian manufacturers had plenty of appetite for all the Canadian protection they could get.

However, the Canadian papers were full of great expectations, which RB's speeches had sedulously encouraged. Symbolic of these high hopes was a set of four postage stamps issued on 21 June 1932. The 13-cent stamp in green showed Britannia seated between two half globes, contemplating the future of her empire, her hand shielding her eyes as if dazzled by the brilliant prospect. That too was illusory. RB was getting a steady stream of advice from Beaverbrook that if Canada stood firm, the British government would sooner or later have to back down. The British had to go back to England with something tangible. Leo Amery, former secretary of state for the dominions (1925–29), who came to Canada, told RB the same.[27]

RB and the Canadian ministers met the British delegation at the Ottawa train station on Thursday, 21 July, escorting them up the platform to an immense cheering crowd and then, via the tunnel, to the Château Laurier. Chamberlain reported having a large suite with "a spraying chamber" (the term "shower" and its function presumably unknown in Birmingham in the early 1930s). That night RB and the Canadian government gave a dinner at the Château for 620 guests – Chamberlain used an exclamation mark to record the number. Mildred Herridge, who was returning to public life after the birth of a son, William Jr, in May, would hold a tea on the Sunday following. She and RB were both disappointed that Mrs Chamberlain had not come. (Mackenzie King reported that

Annie Chamberlain was the only woman in England he would have wanted to marry.) Chamberlain noted that the Canadian government had tried to cut down on the hospitality as much as possible but that there was still lots left.[28]

As the conference opened, RB was nominated chairman. He probably expected it, but perhaps he might have realized that the British expected a higher degree of impartiality in chairmen than he was capable of giving. In his opening speech, he asked Britain for substantial concessions both in preferences and in tariffs against products that competed with Canada, Australia, and the empire – for example, Russian wheat and lumber and Argentine beef. Stanley Baldwin, the British prime minister, replied that he hoped Canadian tariffs would be lowered. Thus were the polarities signalled almost at once.

Baldwin was the head of the British delegation, but his heart was not really in the conference; he would have preferred to be back in Worcestershire. He attended the plenary sessions but left the real work to Viscount Hailsham, Walter Runciman, president of the Board of Trade, and Neville Chamberlain. Chamberlain, as chancellor of the Exchequer, was the effective working head. Baldwin was the *suavitor in modo*, Chamberlain the *fortiter in re* with his essential and patient mastery of detail. His weakness was his woeful ignorance of Canadian realities. He and RB talked privately on Tuesday, 26 July, Chamberlain trying to allay RB's suspicion of British motives and putting to him the real difficulties facing the Baldwin government in these negotiations. RB said that he had told the Canadian cotton manufacturers to subdivide their classification, with the idea, Chamberlain assumed, of putting more lines into lower categories for Canadian duty. RB was obsessed about Russian wheat and lumber; Russian wheat, he had been told in England in 1930, was as good as Canadian wheat and could be landed in Liverpool at a highly competitive price. Chamberlain said the British were considering modes of action when the price of Russian commodities in general dropped below a certain level.

RB's worries about Russia kept surfacing throughout the discussions. In the midst of a denunciation of Soviet trade by RB on 27 July, Runciman interjected a sarcastic comment. RB hated to be mocked, and halted briefly. But behind his position were some decided stiffeners. He had given the negotiation of details of the Canadian tariff to R.W. Breadner, the commissioner of tariffs, who was devoted to protection as became a former employee of the CMA. Prime Minister Bruce of Australia and RB had agreed that Canada would take the lead in pressing the British; the Australians had a big loan to renegotiate in London after the conference and did not want to appear too rigid. Cahan, Stevens, and Weir of the Canadian cabinet were disposed to be hard-liners, and they came with RB when he addressed the British delegation on Thursday, 5 August, with the substance of the Canadian offers.

RB adopted, so Chamberlain recorded, a very aggressive stance, suggesting that British manufacturers were a flaccid lot, and that the Canadian free list was big enough now that they could save $55 million if they "were men enough to seize it." Chamberlain wanted to know if the Canadian offers had been made with the principle in mind of "domestic competition," that is, that the price of specific British goods landed in Canada would be equal to their Canadian equivalent. RB hedged on that, taking refuge in the new Tariff Board of 1931, not then fully constituted. He then laid down with strident emphasis what Canada expected from the British. That speech angered the British, so much so that Runciman, perhaps the best mind after Hailsham on the British team, came to see RB the next afternoon, still hot under the collar.

RB thought highly of Runciman; Runciman came on Friday, 5 August, and spoke bluntly to RB for over an hour. RB had called British manufacturers timid and unenterprising, whereas, Runciman said, they were the most successful in the world, winning their way over other countries' tariff walls without protection at home themselves. Canadians, on the other hand, had been nurtured and cosseted in a "protective hot house." Runciman warned RB sternly that the way things were going, any British-Canadian agreement was heading straight for failure. Canada was doing nothing for cottons or woollens, for example. How could RB ask for British duties against foreign goods and foodstuffs when all that Canadian offers would mean, on Runciman's calculation, was employment for 25,000 men? With British unemployment at 2,750,000, the British government that brought in that result would be "laughed out of the House. He [Bennett] no doubt had his own troubles but not more telling than that." What Canada was offering Britain was derisory, and the British "were not going to be such fools as to tumble into such a blunder." RB was willing to make amends for his remarks about British manufacturers, but his replies to Runciman were evasive and indefinite. The impression he left on Runciman was of a "shallow restless mind."[29]

RB may well have appeared so, but there were reasons. He was the focal point of a whole set of pressures. The Canadian cabinet were unhappy with the British offers. There was fierce lobbying from the CMA, admittedly encouraged by RB. He was also responsible, with Bruce of

Australia, for creating an anti-British group at the conference designed to box the British in, to force them to give concessions on Canadian wheat and Australian meat. So successful was this stance that, according to RB, within a week of the conference's opening, the Canadians had lined up behind them all the other delegations except New Zealand. But they had not reckoned on reporters or British resentments. The swarm of reporters, including those from the *London Times* and the *Manchester Guardian*, and some of the British delegates were not as close mouthed as they were supposed to be. RB named the *Manchester Guardian*, the *Toronto Daily Star*, and *Winnipeg Free Press* as culpable for the publicity that upset his conference cartel. As early as 10 August, the *Montreal Gazette* was warning of a possible breakdown of negotiations between Canada and Britain, blaming RB for his usual habit of taking on too much personally. "Canada stands now, more than ever at the parting of the ways." RB's stance was stiffened by a confidential letter (on Château Laurier paper) from H.A. Gwynne, editor of the *London Morning Post*, who summed up the dilemma neatly: the British couldn't leave with such inadequate concessions from Canada, and RB couldn't carry Canadian Parliament with what he'd got so far from Britain. Gwynne's main point was that the UK delegates could not go home and say they might have made a good deal with Canada but they had not wanted to hurt Russian feelings.

Beaverbrook was a further complication. RB told William Barclay, the Ottawa correspondent of Beaverbrook's the *London Daily Express*, that the conference was being wrecked because British ministers were under the thumb of old-fashioned civil servants like Sir Horace Wilson, the chief industrial adviser to the UK government. Educated at the London School of Economics, a British civil servant for over thirty years, Wilson was a formidable opponent. RB had developed what Chamberlain called a "vicious dislike" for Wilson. He "was not going to run this country," said RB, "though he had tried." One evening, Jimmy Thomas, British minister of state for the dominions, was dining with the Runcimans. A cable had just come with an account of the *Daily Express* attack on the British ministers. Thomas read it aloud and added, "'Ere's the Beaver in cahoots with R.B. to force our 'ands, stabbing us in the back. 'Ow the hell can you run a bloody Hempire with this kind of business going on. Please excuse my language, Lady Runciman, but isn't it a damned scandal!"[30]

By Friday, 18 August, the pressure had mounted on both sides. Prime Minister Ramsay MacDonald back in London wanted the delegation to avoid conceding duties on agricultural products – food duties, in current parlance – if it could be done without breaking up the conference. In the meantime the *Empress of Britain*'s departure was delayed at RB's request up to the evening of Saturday, August 20, or possibly even into Sunday. He was now not very hopeful about the conference, by which he meant the British-Canadian negotiations.

One Chamberlain grievance was the Canadian iron and steel schedules, which had supposedly been settled, but, as result of a last-minute decision by Canadian steel manufacturers, were now re-opened. It looked to Chamberlain as if Bennett wanted to wreck the negotiations. Bennett denied that but said the British "had given him nothing and that some of his colleagues had said he would be the laughing stock of the country if he gave such wonderful concessions" and got so meagre a return. Chamberlain asked him if he realized that failure of the conference would mean the end of the empire, something RB had once said himself. "Yes," RB said, "but an agreement like this?" Canadian newspapers were incensed at the lack of British concessions and at their refusal to put their cards on the table. Chamberlain believed that there had been Canadian leaks to Canadian papers.

It went on like that through Thursday, 18 August, even to the British suspicion that Canadians were listening in on their transatlantic telephone calls. RB was bristly and bad tempered, bringing up items the British thought had been settled. Chamberlain said, mildly enough in the circumstances, that the delegation was disappointed to find some things were not settled, "and we asked him to look at them again on their merits. And on his interrupting me with another passionate outburst, I reminded him that I had been deeply wounded myself" – at suggestions that Chamberlain had deliberately suppressed information that the Canadians ought to have had. Then at 7 PM they hastily adjourned for the official dinner the British government was giving the Canadians. Neither side was much in the mood for it, but apologies from Herridge and Weir did help.

Work went on steadily through Friday. It was not easy then either. British iron and steel would not agree to the last-minute Bennett withdrawal of his previous offer. The story in the Dafoe Papers is that this impasse so close to the end broke RB down, and he had to be led from the room by Manion and Herridge. But in the end it was the British that gave way. At 1:30 AM on Saturday, RB and Chamberlain finally initialled the copies of the British-Canadian agreement. "As for me," said Chamberlain, "I was fairly worn out but happy the situation had been saved." Later in the morning RB phoned to ask if Chamberlain would let him ask Baldwin to let Chamberlain sign the British-Canadian agreement. It was a gracious offer, and at 10:30 they met in the House of Commons, Chamberlain signing for the Canadian treaty, Baldwin signing the others. There had been no overarching imperial treaty: there were a series of hard bilateral ones, the Australian one being difficult. Bruce said he had to have a British duty on foreign meat. Two British ministers said they wouldn't have it. Chamberlain had got them to sleep on it. But the Canadian-British treaty was the hardest fought. The countries of the empire, said Chamberlain, "have been drifting apart pretty rapidly. We have been in time to stop the rot."

Chamberlain felt that most of the difficulties for the British delegation had stemmed from RB. "Full of high imperial sentiments he has done little to put them into practice. Instead of guiding the Conference in his capacity as Chairman he has stretched our patience to the limit. He has insulted us personally and still more our officials. He has been threatening and bullying in his manner, shifty and cunning in his methods." Bennett's underlying problem, Chamberlain wrote home to his wife, was "really inadequate preparation on his side. He has not a proper civil service and no ministers whom he trusts."

That was perhaps RB's fundamental problem: he took too much on himself, partly by instinct, but mostly because his ministers were never quite up to what he expected – indeed, demanded. He himself mastered subjects with uncanny facility, but he could not do everything, and given his volatile temperament, the strain made him more than usually irascible and impatient. In concentrating work on oneself, as he did, one has to be a monument of persistence, perspicacity, and patience. RB lacked patience, for which he was too apt to substitute petulance.

He said goodbye later that Saturday to Chamberlain and the British ministers. He admitted it had been a rough time, but trusted that Chamberlain would not carry away any feeling of resentment over anything that had occurred. Chamberlain the diplomat was reassuring, but his happy weekend's fishing for black bass on a rocky Canadian lake was no compensation. He told his wife, Annie, he never wanted to see Canada again. He never did. The train took the delegates straight to Quebec to catch the delayed *Empress of Britain*, with many a reminiscence shot through with ruminations good and bad.

Something of RB's side of this story begins in, of all places, the men's washroom of the Rideau Club, at lunchtime on Friday, 14 October 1932.[31] Grant Dexter, the *Winnipeg Free Press*'s Ottawa correspondent, was there talking to an Ottawa lawyer. A lavatory door opened and out came RB. As he began to wash his hands, he glowered at Dexter and opened with, "Well, what falsehoods have you been disseminating today?" Dexter replied, "None that I am aware of, Mr Bennett." Dexter was anxious to get away, but as he began to leave, RB shook his finger at him. "Why did you write so many falsehoods during the conference?"

"Mr Bennett, I am not aware that I wrote any."

"Oh yes, you are. You can't tell me that you were not actuated by malice."

"On the contrary, Mr Bennett, I had the very best reasons for believing that everything I wrote on the Conference was true."

"You had not."

At this point Arthur Meighen came in, smiling broadly behind RB's back. "However," RB said, "this certainly is not the place to discuss the matter." Dexter agreed it was not, and went on to the Rideau Club dining room, choosing a table by himself in a far corner.

Then RB came over. "Dexter, may I have lunch with you?"

"It is a very great honour to me, Mr Bennett," Dexter said.

"Not at all," RB replied. "I don't take my position [as prime minister] that way." They ordered lunch, Dexter soup, RB oysters, and RB returned to the attack. Said Dexter, "I had what I believed to be sound sources of information and everything I wrote was firmly based, in my judgment, upon fact. My job was to get the news and to write it, and I did my job, without malice to you or to anyone else, to the best of my ability."

RB then said that all the delegates had been bound to secrecy. "I kept my word. Others did not. Now I will tell you where you got most of your information. It came from British sources, from the British delegates themselves. Is that not true?"

"Between ourselves, Mr Bennett, it is true," Dexter answered, "not entirely but to a considerable extent. But the British sources that were available to me were very reliable indeed."

"Ah, I thought so," RB rejoined. "You see, Dexter, I knew what was going on ... Do you realize, Dexter, that the newspapers of the empire nearly wrecked the conference? ... When Napier Moore wrote in *Maclean's* magazine that newspapers came within an ace of breaking up the conference, he told the absolute truth ... Your despatches ... were malignant distortions of the facts. Why did you do it? One of the saddest consequences of this conference for me is that throughout the entire proceedings some Canadian journalists ... did everything in their power, stopped at nothing, to discredit your country's representatives and your own prime minister. Is that fair journalism, is it common decency?"

Dexter replied, "We are talking in the strictest confidence, Mr Bennett, and I want to tell you, sincerely, that I did not once distort a single fact, nor write anything that I did not believe to be true in basic information, fair in the way of comment."

RB rose to the occasion like a gentleman. "Dexter, I believe you." He went on then to describe how he and Bruce, with the advice of Amery and Beaverbrook, had planned to box in the British. The question for him was, could he hold out? Would his mind and body be sufficient for the strain? He was, he told Dexter, "a very exhausted man." The British had tried to win him over with flattery; Geoffrey Dawson, the redoubtable editor of the *London Times*, came to Canada having written in *Times* editorials that Bennett might well be on his way to the Valhalla of great empire statesmen. RB claimed to see through it and Dawson in five minutes. He did not have a high opinion of Baldwin, whom he thought weak but amiable. Hailsham was brilliant and formidable. So too was Runciman, though illness had weakened his effectiveness. As for Jim Thomas, RB described him as a trade union demagogue. Chamberlain had been a profound disappointment, not the man his father was, and it was Chamberlain, RB believed, who was responsible for the attacks on him in the *Montreal Gazette*. From RB's conversation it was abundantly obvious to Dexter that his policy at the conference "was to yield nothing and get all that he possibly could." Dexter and Chamberlain would have agreed on that.

Dexter wanted to know if in the future he could come and discuss important public questions with RB. "Telephone me, Dexter," RB said.

"I could not do that, sir," Dexter answered. He had never phoned a prime minister yet, and he expected RB would bang down the receiver. But Arthur Merriam, RB's principal secretary, was a good friend; Dexter could perhaps get in touch via Merriam and try to see RB when he was least busy. "Why, of course you could," said RB. "But would I be allowed to see you?" Dexter persisted. "Absolutely," RB replied.

Then followed an amiable interview about terms and conditions. "Here is a case in point, Mr Bennett," said Dexter, "You say you will not allow deflation of the dollar, but the western farmers are strenuously urging abandonment of gold and immediate inflation. You have said no, but your reasons have never been explained." He could write a column setting forth RB's reasons, which would be subject to the prime minister's corrections. At that point they were interrupted. As Dexter was leaving, RB turned to him and said, "Don't forget, Dexter, I will be looking for you."

Dexter's editor, Dafoe, told him by all means to take up RB's invitation. But then Dafoe added cold water: "If he were to address me in the terms in which he spoke to you, I should talk to him very plainly ... that the Free Press is at sword's point with him on practically every policy to which he is devoted, and ... it is both our right and our duty to oppose him to the extent of our ability." That position may well have settled any further rapprochement between RB and Dexter.[32]

The previous week, Parliament had resumed to pass the legislation required by the Ottawa agreements with the UK, Irish Free State, Rhodesia, and South Africa. (The treaties with Australia and New Zealand had been worked out in 1931.) Mackenzie King at once criticized the Bennett government's negotiating style: "I do not believe we shall ever see again within the British Empire another venture of that kind made ... relations came about as near to breaking point as it is possible." RB stoutly denied it. "There never was a moment ... when relations reached the state the right honourable gentleman has described ... except in the imaginations of base men who wrote in the newspapers stories that were entirely fabricated." He could prevaricate with the best of them.

Alan Lascelles from Government House wrote to Baldwin that November explaining RB's personality. He had a first-class mind, Lascelles said, but his legal experience was in western Canadian law courts, "abusing the plaintiff's attorney and pounding the table in shirt sleeves ... He was savagely sensitive to ridicule, with a child-like impatience of obstacles."[33]

The reaction in Canada to the Ottawa agreements was generally enthusiastic. Praise was heaped on RB's success. The *Canadian Magazine* of October 1932 offered a sharper assessment. The conference had trembled on the brink of failure; the problem for the British had been RB's manner and methods, "his bluntness, his impulsive impatience with opposition, his direct methods, frankness of speech." Even his own colleagues had not quite got used to him. He had shocked the British, quite upset them, in fact. Could even an empire trade agreement be worth all that hassle? "Really, you know!" they said. Baldwin later admitted that Bennett's tremendous pulling power did it: six cents a bushel preference on wheat, a more secure market for agriculture, lumber, mining, fish, and some relief from Soviet state-controlled competition. One Canadian minister called it "a damn good bargain." Manion added, "It has gone over big."

Indeed, within three years, between 1932 and 1935, Canadian exports to Britain were up 65 per cent, while British exports to Canada rose only 5 per cent. Meighen was close to being right in 1939, when at a dinner in Bennett's honour, he remarked, "the Ottawa Agreements ... were a really big achievement, a landmark in the history of this country. Wrapped in the body of those Agreements was a revolution in the fiscal policy of Britain." After the conference, Rudyard Kipling sent to Bennett a stanza from his 1897 poem "Our Lady of the Snows," still apt:

"The gates are mine to open,
As the gates are mine to close,
And I set my house in order,"
Said our Lady of the Snows.[34]

As the train carrying the Imperial Conference delegates steamed out of Ottawa at noon on that Saturday, 20 August, RB travelled by car to a rendezvous in Hawkesbury. He was met there by a chauffeured Rolls-Royce and whisked eastward through Quebec to Mascouche, the site of Le Manoir de Repentigny. It was owned by a wealthy Montreal widow, Hazel Kemp Colville.

Her acquaintance with Bennett seems to have begun in 1915–16. She was then a young married woman of twenty-six, acting as chaperone for her aunt Marguerite Gault, who was going through a messy divorce case in the Senate. Her husband's lawyers had spies out, hoping to upset her petition. Bennett was Mrs Gault's lawyer.

Hazel's husband, Francis Stephens, whom she'd married in 1911, had been invalided home from the First World War with trench fever; he died in the flu epidemic of 1918. The couple had a daughter, Frances, born in 1912. In 1920 Hazel remarried, to Arthur Colville, a well-to-do Toronto lawyer who had moved to Montreal in 1919 to work for Sun Life. Hazel and Colville had no children; she learned to her great dismay that he could not father children. In 1929 he was diagnosed with throat cancer, the cause no doubt related to his unfortunate taste for strong Egyptian cigarettes. Widowed a second time in May 1931, Hazel at forty-two was very well off, her rich senator father, Sir Edward Kemp, having died in 1929.

Hazel Colville was one of those women who attract men almost without trying. Beautiful, rich, spirited, intelligent, she liked men, and they came to her as moths to a flame. She could be swept by enthusiasms, which included men. She liked her social life, cigarettes, cocktails, and tennis. She was what one would call a society woman, well-bred, civilized, comfortable with her life and style and friends. In Montreal she lived at 1371 Pine Avenue and was in the process of developing an estate at Mascouche, northeast of Montreal, once the Manoir de Repentigny, which she had bought in 1930.

RB had been with her father in the short-lived government of Arthur Meighen, 1920–21. It was on 6 January 1930 that Hazel first wrote to RB. Was it "an imposition," she asked him, "for me, who must occupy a very shadowy niche in your memory," to ask a few questions? Then followed a series of queries, mostly about immigration policy. The letter closed with a PS: "Years ago I used to say 'R.B.' but that seems almost impertinent now to the leader of His Majesty's Loyal Opposition."

She soon learned it was anything but an imposition. RB's letters to her are signed "Arbee" or "R.B," the later ones "Dick," reserved for family and Beaverbrook. All of hers to him are missing except the one just quoted. It seems clear from RB's letters to her that their romance began to blossom in the spring of 1932, a year after the death of Arthur Colville. Certain it is that when the correspondence that we now have opens, the flame between them had been going for several months or more. Mildred referred to it in the spring of 1932. Perhaps that is what J.H. Thomas meant when he told Chamberlain on the way back to England that RB's "private life was very disreputable." If RB's visits to Mascouche to spend the odd weekend or a few days is what Thomas meant, it now seems exaggerated. On the other hand, in the 1930s single men did not as a rule stay in the same house with single women (unless they were relatives), even if there were servants around. Mackenzie King thought Hazel Colville had probably compromised herself.[35]

RB spent four delightful post-conference days at Mascouche; he remembered their walks and the sunlight, and he returned reluctantly to Ottawa for a civic reception in his honour on Friday, 26 August. Well used to public speaking, he was disconcerted when replying to congratulations for his conference work to see in his mind's eye Hazel's face, with tears in her eyes, "quite too real for words." As the day went on, he went through the motions, talking to friends. But, he wrote, "I was just thinking of you all the time." At a dinner that evening, his friends and public "eulogized me beyond all reason." His speech that night after an introduction by Sir William Mulock was a talk, unusual for him, about himself and his life. It must have been a wonderful performance, for after he was finished there was dead silence. The audience then rose to their feet as one and gave him a cheer that he told Hazel he would never forget.[36]

Calgary wanted to give him a reception, and thither he went by train, two of his devoted women with him, Mildred (up from Washington) and Alice Millar, his secretary since 1914, dumpy and devoted. They teased him all the way west. He almost didn't mind, for it reminded him of being with Hazel in Mascouche. "Do write me at the Palliser, Calgary," he wrote to her from the train. "It would so please me to see your hand-writing and have a few words from you. And I am not too hard to please & make happy you know." He added a rather arch comment,

> I hear that Toronto has quite a series of stories about you & I.
> Mildred says she saw Lady Kemp yesterday. She is ciphering out the relationship of a stepmother to a stepdaughter's husband!! ... But I miss you beyond all words & I am lonesome beyond cure without your presence & so I go with all my love
>   Ever your grateful & devoted old man.
> [PS] I am going to mail this without waiting. Oh my dear how I miss you. I really am just a poor weak emotional man, hungry for a sight of you.[37]

RB in love seems to have been acutely vulnerable, as if late in life love had caught him well and truly for the first time. *Spätlese* wine is sweet and strong and heady. RB's carapace of firmness, resolution, toughness even, seems to have been quite swept away by it; there he was, emotion-ally naked, quite stripped of defences.

For a bachelor of sixty-two to be so caught sounds like a sexual rela-tionship. That indeed is the question and there is no easy answer. Hazel's daughter, Frances Stephens, did not believe there were any sexual rela-tions between her mother and RB, but her disbelief is understandable; the young don't quite believe that sexuality exists much past forty-five years of age. RB by that standard would be over the hill. But when RB called at 1371 Pine Avenue in Montreal, Hazel would say to her daugh-ter, then about twenty years of age, "Couldn't you go somewhere?"

Hazel did not yet know whether she wanted to marry RB. He didn't like her cigarettes or cocktails and seems not to have hesitated to chide her every so often on the subject. With Frances he could be ponderous, as if his long exposure to Methodist sermons kept surfacing. His experi-ence with handling younger people had been mainly as schoolmaster at Douglastown, New Brunswick, half a century earlier. He was the genial but heavy-footed future stepfather. Kind, articulate, but rather stuffy and formal was the way Frances saw him.

As the west-bound train neared Fort William on its way to Calgary on Sunday, August 28, RB wrote to Hazel, pressing his suit a little:

After all we do know each other very, very well & it is not fitting that we should end our relations in just casual forgetfulness. For I cannot & will not forget. You are quite part of the greatest days of my life ... So you first [?] think it over carefully, won't you dear ? ... Mildred has been teasing me all day ... It is still like a real physical pain in my left side ... You will forgive me dearest if I suggest fewer cigarettes per day. You do smoke too much. And I only say it because your health is so important to us all. Hope you can read this letter as the train rocks so hard. The white-haired head & beloved face I have seen in all my waking hours. And do not think me silly for saying so. How I wish I could be with you. But that cannot be & I will with all my love & devotion sign myself
     Ever your loving old man, R.B.[38]

Back in Ottawa by mid-September, he sent Hazel a ring or bracelet as proof of his love and affection. He was happier than he had ever been. "But let me cling in happiness to my beloved word 'absolutely'; & with all my devotion & affection subscribe myself in truth ever & forever your own old man, R.B."
He was at Mascouche nearly every weekend, including Thanksgiving, 8–9 October:

But most of all on this day I render thanks for you & all dear heart you are to me with the hope that every Thanksgiving Day of this mortal life may find me having the same sentiments & thankfulness but stronger with the lapse of years – God bless & keep you my dear & may I sign with devotion and affection,
     ever yours in truth & fact.
     R.B.[39]

A week later he was in Toronto visiting Hazel's sisters in Rosedale. It was a family joke already that she would be the new senator for Repentigny, unless, Hazel's sister said archly, "she aspires to something higher!" To that RB added in a seven-page letter to Hazel, "I cannot say about the aspirations but I can say about the opportunity she has!!" He did not like Hazel's niece Sheila wearing lipstick; not being much of a diplomat, he promptly told her so. But writing to Hazel, RB was comfortably introspective:

> Life is a strange thing. We cannot determine by any action we may take what the results of such a given action will be. Think of all that has happened since April. It cannot be explained on any reasonable ground. But it has happened. What has happened? A new aspect to life: a new view of the future: a happiness made greater by the unhappiness, if that can be understood. "The wind bloweth where it listeth." No one can explain why the heart turns to that of another: For me I repeat that I am glad beyond words that the change has come to me even so late in life as it has – and so dearest of sweet-hearts I rejoice that a kind & benevolent Providence has made it possible to me with all my heart & mind & devotion & affection subscribe myself
>
> Ever & always your own R.B.[40]

He was at Mascouche the weekend of 28–29 October and wrote the next day. It is a letter that raises more questions than it answers, especially since it comes in RB's sincere, passionate scribble, and we do not have Hazel's letter that occasioned hs reaction:

> Dearest & best beloved – Just a note. You know of course that the P.M. in England sends a letter to the Sovereign at the close of each session of the House. I daresay you have read some of Disraeli's let-ters at such times. It is not near closing time but I will just send as I say a note to thank you for all your great & overwhelming kind-ness on the weekend – I shall never forget the last Sunday of Octo-ber 1932. It was so peaceful & somehow you did seem so very, very dear to me & perhaps you will permit me to say I seemed somehow dearer to you. But perhaps it was imagination. I cannot tell you of the effect of that letter. Never have I read such a moving communi-cation – I was right in what I told you yesterday. I do & should feel badly. But I will not fail you. I wish you had just sent it to me before. And now that I know all the terrible struggle why of course I will show to you that I can be of use & that my will[?] is not a total fail-ure. But dearest do not get into the awful habit of being introspec-tive. It is no good & will just ruin you – There is no need of resorting to heroic measures. Your old man will not be unworthy of your trust

– I am sure that impersonal ideal has been badly destroyed – But do not I pray you think it is lost beyond repair. Such a letter: How it has moved me. How often have I read it. Nothing dear that you have ever said or done has quite so touched me. It is quite beyond words. And I know that in the morrow [All Saints' Day] you will do just what the great Father dictates & that peace will follow & we will keep it ... And I hope that all you said in your note about me is true. Absolutely. Be his dearest. And of good report & do not worry. Ever my love & adoration dearest of women & sweethearts.

    Your own R.B.

And he was still thinking of it the next day:

I cannot permit the day to pass without sending to you[,] my dearly beloved, a note of grateful appreciation of thankfulness for all your consideration during the months that we have known one another so well. It is fitting that I should write such a note on the day so real & important to you. At 8 this morning I looked at the clock & said, "she is at church." & I knew that it would mean more than it had for some time recently ...

    It has meant so much to me to be able to go down to your place on the weekend: What delightful anticipation & joyous realization – Care has dropped from me as a mantle discarded & I have just lived & enjoyed myself altho' I wel [sic] knew that I have been very selfish for it has imposed restraint upon Frances & lessened your own hospitality to those who were your friends ...

    So today I thank the good Lord for you & all you are & have been to me & hope will ever be. And I want you to know that despite many, many things I shall ever hold that deep indescribable devotion for you that so strangely has come upon me at this late hour of life. And it has been good for me; sweetened my views of life & people & made me a much happier person even tho' I still find it irksome to be so held in leash by the party I lead – It is not only unfair but I cannot permit it to continue much longer. This is in the nature of a "peace offering." I am so happy when I am at the Manor House & with you ...

    Your own old man, R.B.[41]

Lowering on the horizon but coming closer, distantly hinted at in RB's letters, was the surprising fact that Hazel was a Roman Catholic. She had been brought up a Methodist, going with her family to Sherbourne Street United Church in Toronto, but probably during Arthur Colville's last illness she had become a Roman Catholic. Like many converts, she was sincere and dedicated. RB was on good terms with more than a few Catholic bishops, notably Bishop McNally of Hamilton, but his marrying a Roman Catholic widow would have been politically awkward, at least while he was still prime minister. Indeed, none of his many letters to Hazel actually mention marriage, though it may have been discussed between them.

The question of their future seems to have been precipitated by a large farewell dinner at the Château, 17 November 1932, that RB gave for Col. Hanford MacNider, the retiring American minister. Hazel's invitation was written in RB's hand. She was seated at the head table with members of cabinet and wives. Mackenzie King was at the dinner too and was introduced to her. "Lots of pearls but no distinction," was his waspish comment. Robert Manion, who took her in to the dinner, thought she was charming. Mildred was there too, without Bill Herridge. She said Bill was feeding the baby his bottle and couldn't come! They'd been having, King surmised, a row. He remarked that RB was more friendly that evening than he had ever been. King now believed that RB had so entangled himself with Hazel that, whatever happened, it would end his career.[42]

Then early in December 1932 a strange thing occurred. To King's amazement, he received a letter from Hazel Colville enclosing a letter to Vincent Massey. She did not have his address and would King be good enough to forward it? A week later in Toronto, Massey came to see King and revealed what the letter was about. She had written to him that King had made a great mistake in trying to advance himself as party leader by breaking up the "great friendship" between herself and RB. Whatever that meant, King's confidante Joan Patteson believed it meant the end of RB's romance. Indeed, on 24 November Hazel had put her Bennett letters into safekeeping at the Royal Trust in Montreal with the stern rubric: "Not to be opened by anyone. Can be given to my daughter in 1950 if not destroyed by me before that date."[43]

Perhaps she feared reporters. There had been a headline in the *Boston Advertiser* on Sunday, 23 October: "Premier Bennett to marry wealthy widow is report." RB instantly despatched a telegram to Boston. The Sunday issue, he said, "is greatly resented by reason of its unchivalrous and false article ... distribution in Canada of any newspaper so offending against the amenities of life is within our jurisdiction and invites action." The editor, J.W. Reardon, apologized, saying that his staff had been misled by a similar article in the *Toronto Daily Star*. Rumours flew. The *Ottawa Journal* reported on 6 December 1932 that RB and Hazel had been seen in the Château Laurier dining with the governor general and his wife. That was false: around 30 November, RB had sailed for England. And he sailed alone.[44]

What happened? The evidence is scattered and unsatisfactory. One concrete bit is RB's gold-headed cane, given to him on his sixtieth birthday on 3 July 1930, probably by Mildred. He left it behind at Hazel's Pine Avenue home in Montreal when he departed, angry and desperate, according to Hazel's daughter, Frances. He never returned for it. In 1989 Frances still had the handsome Irish blackthorn, its prickles rounded off. But we don't really know when that incident took place; it is supposition that it was in late May 1933. "She broke his heart" was the opinion of Alice Toner Tompkins, secretary to R.B. Hanson, MP for York-Sunbury. RB and Hazel remained on writing terms, probably on speaking terms, for some time, but for Hazel their love affair was almost certainly over.

RB wrote to her on her forty-fourth birthday on 12 May 1933, thanking her for the joys she had given him and rueful over the pain he had been put through. He had known her, he said, in her twenties, her thirties, her forties,

but none in a period so brief as 12 months have been in such close association as I for the last year. I have been in communication with you daily for about half that time. It has brought me great pleasure & happiness and also great disturbance and discontent, great sadness & unhappiness ... I am glad I have had the privilege of knowing you as I have & I hope and believe that with care & good will I shall not regret it for your sake & my own. I have had great contentment at your old home, greater pleasure in being with you and it is my very real desire to be of service to you to help you to be in a true and abiding sense your greatest & trusted friend ... Now dear girl can I better express myself than in the lines I quoted the other night I hope & believe indeed that your life will be

Like a river blest where'er it flows
Be still receiving while it still bestows.

My sincere hope too is that when another year is reached we may greet one another in terms of affectionate regard, for it is not by pure accident that our lives have been so interwoven during the last 12 months – Reason & hope have their place but after all Wordsworth knew the truth when he wrote:

> Oh! 'tis the heart that magnifies this life,
> Making a truth & beauty of its own.

God bless you, & keep you & make you a continued blessing to all with whom you come into association and believe me I am with all good wishes & affectionate regards
  Ever your faithful & adoring
    Dick[45]

There spoke philosophic resignation but shot through with hope of reunion. It was probably not religion that had split them apart, nor RB's being prime minister. Alice Tompkins was right: Hazel broke his heart, though without intending to. She breathed, she exhaled, a natural charm; it caught RB, as it had and would other men in her life. RB's later letters to her – they corresponded at least until 1934 – continued to leave the impression that one word from her would have brought him back. Perhaps she was never really in love with him. He was nineteen years older, little given to frivolity or sports, bridge or dancing or cocktails or cigarettes. He probably answered too few of her joys and her needs, and none of those needs was financial.

Back in September 1932 he had run across a set of three sonnets by poet Sara Henderson Hay in a popular American magazine – sonnets that he said reminded him of things that Hazel had said and written to him. He had read and re-read them. He sent the page to her to read and destroy. She kept it. The sentiments of the sonnets probably come close to what she was feeling about her late season romance:[46]

> In truth we might have known it from the start
> This path would have its turning; there would be
> No real alternative for you and me,
> Fashioned of honest earth, except to part.
> Whether the blow were mine to deal, or whether
> Yours the swift blade by which this bond were sundered,
> The hearts must bleed, because the feet have blundered
> Into a way we may not walk together.

Rebuke me not, beloved, in that I
Perforce do quickly that which needs must be –
I am as one who fights because she fears
A darker wound, a deadlier agony
Than fronts her now. And if I say good-bye,
Believe me that I say it through my tears.

5

Battle for Solvency, 1933–1934

Bruised, brooding, and chastened by his failing love affair with Hazel Colville, weary with the growing burden of intractable difficulties, RB returned from England, probably spending Christmas 1932 with his brother Ronald in Sackville, New Brunswick. Through the dank, dark English December, he had been busy. H.A. Gwynne of the London *Morning Post* had promised him "a right royal welcome" for his arrival on 9 December, and he had got it. However disappointed he might have been at the end of his romance, publicly he was in good form. Rudyard Kipling heard RB on 14 December, probably at a club, and wrote in appreciation, "Bless you for last night ... I think it got under their skins. *Keep it up*. Ever with admiration, Kipling."[1]

Kipling's admiration was flattering, but RB was returning home to a thicket of problems that could only grow worse. Indeed, RB told Robert Manion that another year like 1932 would "break the whole capitalistic system." His supreme worry was unemployment and how best to deal with it. How to cope with its too obvious consequences, the shoals of single men, especially in the West, who roamed the country looking for food and work?

He had sought advice from General A.G.L. McNaughton, who suggested construction camps for employing single men in useful public works. He had consulted Charlotte Whitton in April 1932 and commissioned her between May and October to study the current state of unemployment relief in the West, where the worst of the unemployment was. A brilliant student at Queen's University, Whitton had developed a great interest in and knowledge of social work just as its professionalization was beginning. After completing her master's degree at Queen's, she was hired by the Canadian Committee on Child and Family Welfare and soon transformed it into Canada's most respected social work organization. RB found her social values and ideas a tremendous asset. Her 800-page report when she completed it was something of an eye-opener, confirming what he had half suspected, that about 35 per cent of those getting relief in the West were not really entitled to it. Casual workers normally employed for half the year had moved easily onto full-time relief. Moreover, municipal relief offices were wretchedly staffed by the incompetents thrown up by local politics. Whitton urgently advised tightening up relief administration.[2]

RB's first major engagement of 1933 was the Dominion-Provincial Conference that met in Ottawa 18 January 1933 to discuss unemployment insurance. Back in April 1931 he had promised the Commons to bring it in before his term of office was over. Canada's population in 1931 was 10.4 million; of that, some 372,000 heads of families and individuals were on relief. If one added their dependants, the total was frightening: some 2.6 million, 26 per cent of Canada's population. By January 1933 joblessness was even more pressing. Clifford Clark, RB's deputy minister of finance, warned that the four western provinces municipally and provincially were overwhelmed and could not finance their relief expenses. Relief totals had climbed inexorably from 600,000 in May 1932 to 1,114,000 in October. On the other side, RB's finance minister, Edgar Rhodes, had in December quite emphatically told John Bracken, the premier of Manitoba, that "the Dominion Government had no undertaking with any province to continue to provide the whole cost of direct relief." Nevertheless, said Clark, "it does seem that the four western provinces are facing a crisis and that a major change in policy may have to be considered."[3]

Unemployment relief was one thing; insurance for it another. Joblessness was immediate and pressing, insurance against it longer term. Clark and RB's executive assistant, Rod Finlayson, were both convinced that unemployment insurance as such would do "nothing to meet the present difficulty." But since relief from unemployment had always been a provincial responsibility, RB wanted to get at its legal and constitutional foundations. It wasn't right to go on dishing out federal money to the provinces for something that they were legally responsible for. But there had not been sufficient preparation on the issue before the conference. The government needed extracts from the 1931 Census data, which were only ready on 10 January, too late to be of much use. Although the January conference served a number of useful purposes, there was no agreement on unemployment insurance. Ontario, Quebec, and the

Maritimes would not offer RB the blank cheque for the necessary constitutional changes.

The western provinces were very disappointed but said they would not stop their campaign to have Ottawa pay at least 50 per cent of direct relief. Manion, minister of railways and canals, said RB had handled the conference well, closing it "by giving them merry hell the last night, particularly the western provinces, who have been getting so much and thanking so little."[4]

The questions of unemployment insurance and actual relief for the jobless were both fraught with acute dangers to Canada's financial stability. The business community was overwhelmingly hostile to unemployment insurance. Moreover, now in January and February 1933 the North American business climate was even more dark and foreboding. In 1931 J.M. Keynes had warned that the American banking system was the weakest point in its whole economic system. Since 1930 over five thousand American banks had suspended payment. There was a state-wide bank collapse in Nevada in October 1932, and heavy clouds were on the horizon for other states even as RB met the Ottawa Conference. The Michigan bank failures came on 15 February, triggering the debacle that followed, the swift spread of that infection across the United States. The new president, Franklin Roosevelt, was sworn in on a gloomy Saturday, 4 March 1933. At that point it was said that Roosevelt could have nationalized the whole American banking system with hardly a murmur of protest. In a much less drastic move, all American banks were peremptorily closed until Monday, 13 March.[5]

RB feared not so much the Canadian banking system (which had survived its own crisis in 1931) but inflation. His answer was in his address to the 1933 meeting of the Board of Trade on 23 January. Jim Macdonnell of Edmonton introduced him with Tennyson's hopeful lines, "Yea let all good things wait / On him who cares not to be great / But as he saves or serves the state." Inflation had often been suggested in various forms and guises to remedy deflation, RB said, but "Canada dare not depart from sound money." England's abandoning the gold standard in September 1931 was, he said (emphasizing each word) "the greatest single disaster ever to befall this country." Canada's debt in England was now easier to pay off, but Canada's big American debt, designated in gold in New York, had suddenly become steeply more expensive. Moreover, with continually declining export markets, the country had been buying more than it was selling.[6]

RB met with the railwaymen's union two days later on Thursday, 26 January. He told them he had been expecting a railway problem ever since Laurier's huge and expensive adventure with the Canadian Northern Railway in 1904. (One still marvels at the flamboyance of the Canadian Northern's tracking in the Fraser Canyon, crossing and re-crossing the Fraser, exactly where the CPR had done the reverse.) RB spoke gently, in a tone of regret. It was not the railwaymen's fault that the railways were in a mess. The Duff Commission of 1932 found the country's railways in much worse condition than it expected, so its findings had to be drastic. "No words that I could use," said RB, "would exaggerate the seriousness of the difficult problems facing this country. It is our business to keep the railways going, but if we continue as we have gone in the past, where is it all to end?"[7]

This mood of sober realism was part of a newer, sadder RB picked up and noted by a young, perceptive *Toronto Daily Star* reporter, Wilfrid Eggleston, late that January 1933. Eggleston (1901–86) was English born but raised on an Alberta homestead, went to Queen's University, graduated in 1926, and by 1929 was Ottawa correspondent for Reuters and the *Star*. In January 1933 he had known Bennett out of office and in for four years and rather liked him; certainly Eggleston had not imbibed, as Grant Dexter came to, the prejudices of his boss. In recent months, Eggleston reported, a marked change had come over the prime minister's manner: "It was a new 'R.B.' who came back from England." The impression in Ottawa was that he was growing mellow, not from age or philosophy but from sheer weariness of mind and spirit. The old pugnacious and domineering Bennett was being replaced by a prime minister more likeable, more human and reasonable – "more winning, in a word." Once upon a time RB's mode had been to begin an interview with attack, as if that were the best defence. In January 1933 he seemed to have abandoned that mode, as if not being able to spare the nervous energy. He was a very model of reasonableness when he met with railwaymen, and again on Friday, 27 January, with organized labour delegates. No political rancour or acrimony crept in. "In four years' contact with him at Ottawa," Eggleston wrote, "I never saw him more like a statesman, less like a petty politician." His usual breeziness, his occasional rotund oratory, were absent. In place of his former grandiose images of how wonderful Canada was, how Canadians were paragons of all the virtues, he now painted a sombre picture, calling for loyalty and cooperation and recognizing that great sacrifices would be needed before Canada emerged from the Depression. "With that skill at creating moods of which he is a master, he played on the feelings of those stolid labour delegates until I felt a similar atmosphere to that induced by eloquent clergymen in fervent prayer," Eggleston wrote. Some of RB's words were indeed from the old hymn "Abide with Me"; Eggleston quoted from the second verse:

Swift to its close ebbs out life's little day;
Earth's joys grow dim, its glories pass away;
Change and decay in all around I see;
O Thou who changest not abide with me.[8]

RB may well have quoted the whole of it. He confessed that he had never supposed when he took office in August 1930 that he and his colleagues would be called upon to solve such fearful problems as those that had now been heaped upon Canada. However, he said, looking at Rhodes, Gordon, and Duranleau, the three members of cabinet at the railwaymen's union meeting with him, "We went out to get it and we got it. Now we'll stay and fight it out."

By this time a subterranean but very real fear haunted many Canadians. Even those on fixed incomes, whose standard of living had been quietly rising inch by inch since the Crash of 1929, could not avoid the contagion: the dark figures on the roofs of freight cars, men huddled together at downtown corners, the tramps, as they were called, looking for a meal or a handout of some kind at the back doors of homes. Sir Robert Borden told RB in August 1931 that two-thirds of the men who came to his home at Glensmere in Ottawa looking for something to eat were genuinely down on their luck. Lady Borden invited them in; so did most women in similar circumstances. The men would sit at a kitchen table and tuck in, glad of the food and often of the heat from a stove. Then they would move on, as a rule pathetically grateful for what they had been given – especially for that one great gift, the milk of human kindness.

Between 1930 to 1935, Alice Millar answered several thousand sad letters looking for help from the prime minister. Usually something was sent. RB had long been used to living at arm's length from hungry men knocking at the door looking for food or odd jobs. In Calgary he had lived on the seventh floor of the Palliser Hotel, and in Ottawa on the second floor of the west side of the Château Laurier above the Rideau Canal. His mode of life insulated him a little from the world. Statistics tell their own brutal tale of these long years of demoralization. Canada's labour force was heavily into primary production, farming, logging, and construction, all seasonal and most heavily dependent on exports. Agricultural exports plunged from $783 million in 1928 to $283 million in 1932, wood products from $289 million to $131 million. The burden of that bleak and sustained unemployment fell on the labour force, especially the young. By 1936, the Dominion Bureau of Statistics estimated that two-thirds of new labour coming onto the market each year could not find sustained work. The result was massive unemployment among the young.[9]

G.G. Coote (MP for Macleod, CCF) said that since Parliament adjourned in November 1932, he had been beset with questions in his riding: "Is Parliament going to do anything for us this year? Is Parliament going to do anything to make conditions better?" Those questions were often driven by fear. The answers were neither simple nor easy. RB's two great preoccupations were unemployment and somehow keeping Canada solvent – maintaining if at all possible, as he told Parliament on 3 March 1933, "the integrity and credit of this country." In the past year the four western governments had borrowed $17.5 million from Ottawa and owed another $24.5 million from the previous year. In addition a Manitoba provincial savings bank had gone broke in 1932, and RB felt it incumbent upon the Dominion government to spend $12 million to rescue its many small depositors. How would the Opposition have dealt with all of this? he asked the House. If they wanted to defeat this government, well and good: "Certainly, if this country desires that we should give place to my honourable friends, we should only be too glad to do so in that sense, but from the standpoint of the safety of the country, in view of what we have heard today, I am perfectly certain that no one could contemplate such a thing without apprehension of the gravest disaster to the body politic." King would not have agreed, of course, but many a time between 1931 and 1933 he confided to his diary that he was glad – indeed, he thought himself lucky – to be out of office. He wrote on 21 March 1933, "the Dominion & provinces alike are heading towards bankruptcy. It is really an appalling situation." In the House, RB added, "Conditions now are uncertain enough, but in the future they are quite unknowable." In 1932 he had asked for and got power to act by order-in-council if necessary – "Not that we want power for the sake of power, but that we may be able in an emergency to preserve the state from destruction. That is all we have tried to do." This power was renewed on 23 March 1933, the terms still sweeping enough: "when parliament is not in session, to take all such measures as in his [governor general in council's] discretion may be deemed necessary or advisable to maintain within the competence of parliament peace, order, and good government throughout Canada." King was consulted on this amendment but still felt obliged to vote against it. The government's majority was, however, decisive, 89–46.[10]

The new Co-operative Commonwealth Federation (CCF) Party had been formed in August 1932. It made RB uneasy; he feared its socialist ideology and distant communist connections. When Woodsworth announced its formation to the House, saying that it aimed at "the socialization of our economic life," RB asked him what he would do with the constitution of the country as it now stood.

"I presume it would remain as it is today," Woodsworth replied.

"It would not," retorted Bennett.

He put his dislike for the new development in a speech reported in the *Toronto Globe* on 10 November 1932: "The swing to the left behind Mr. Woodsworth is towards a government soviet in its character ... they seek to capitalize on the unrest that exists ... and we know that throughout Canada this propaganda is being brought forward by organizations from foreign lands that seek to destroy our institutions. And we ask every man and woman to put the iron heel of ruthlessness against a thing of that kind."

Woodsworth denied that the CCF had any connection with Russia – "none whatsoever." That did not much comfort RB; he hated communists for what he viewed as their constant conspiracies against peace and order. To his mind, there were many worse things in the world than peace, order, and good government. But his remark about the "iron heel of ruthlessness" would inevitably get pulled out of context, for it seemed to fit the image he himself was charged with.

RB lacked the large reserves of pity that his sister Mildred had in abundance. Put more generously, his hatred of riot and disorder overwhelmed his rudimentary compassion. For someone like him who had come up the hard way through his own sweat, privations, and long hours (as well as a modicum of luck), it was difficult to unbend his sympathies. RB's private charities were enormous, amounting to 10 per cent of his gross income, but his tolerance of things he thought improper, immoral, or treasonable was narrow and hard-bitten.

His moral belligerence came to the fore (the mellowness Eggleston had earlier noted nowhere in evidence) in an interview he gave to a young woman reporter from the University of Alberta's student paper, *The Gateway*, on 13 October 1933 at the Edmonton train station. RB had made a speech to the students the day before; the young woman said the students had enjoyed it but there were certain things they could not agree with. "Naturally," said RB. The reporter said the students couldn't finish their courses owing to lack of money, and those who did finish couldn't find jobs. "Why can't they find work?" RB asked. "It is because they feel entitled to make a choice. There is plenty of work to be done – but it is not the kind of work they wish to do ... How many girls do you know who would want to do housework? Not many! Everyone would rather look to the government."

The reporter then put forward the suggestion that payment of debts should be discontinued when it meant Canadians should suffer in order to pay interest or pay back loans. RB exploded, "What! Repudiate our debts! I am ashamed that any Canadian student should think of such a thing."

Earlier in the year he had been quoted as saying, "We are not masters of our fate. We are in the grip of forces over which we have no control." "What are those forces?" the reporter asked. RB said, "In 1930 we were dealing with a national condition. In 1933 we're faced with a situation which is universal. Ten and one-half million people can exercise tremendously little influence on a situation that is universal." Now at the top of steps of the rear platform of the train as it prepared to leave, he reverted to what was bothering him. "I am appalled at any Canadian woman who would suggest repudiation." He pointing a finger at her in stern rebuke. "Young lady, you will have to reform your ideas – do you understand? You – a university student – must reform your opinions."[11]

In the House that spring, he had explained the ideas that lay behind his stern argument. It was perhaps his most luminous lecture to the Commons, on the interrelations of gold, currency, and debt. While technically Canada was not on the gold standard, what mattered was that most of its external obligations and debt were payable in gold or its equivalent. Gold debt was paid back by services, trade, or the bullion itself. In 1932 had Canada shipped south some $60 million in gold, the product mostly of Canadian mines, to redeem debt maturing in New York. That, he said, sustained the credit of the country. Australian debt in 1932 was worth only 50 cents on the dollar. Canada's was fully funded. RB's speech evoked great praise from the other side of the House. King thought privately it "a most admirable presentation [of monetary policy] & I agree with every word he said." William Irvine (United Farmers, MP for Wetaskiwin, Alberta) thought it the ablest defence of the gold standard he had ever heard, though as a good socialist he had to disagree with RB's conclusions. It was characteristic of those two very different men that King reserved his praise of Bennett for his diary, while Irvine's expressed his openly in the House of Commons.[12]

At Roosevelt's invitation, RB went to Washington on 23 April 1933 for a discussion of monetary and other economic matters. In the hurly-burly of the Hundred Days, it was amazing that Roosevelt thought of Canada at all. Perhaps he was kept in mind of it by his summer home on Campobello Island in the Bay of Fundy. The two leaders met on 29 April and issued a joint communiqué that touched several economic issues. They agreed to look for ways to increase trade between their countries. RB returned to Ottawa well impressed by Roosevelt, but the new administration was at sixes and sevens between a rise in domestic prices (which Roosevelt desperately wanted) and the removal of barriers to trade (which Cordell Hull, his secretary of state, wanted). A large American delegation set sail to the World Economic Conference of 1933 "in a fog much denser than anything they might encounter in the North Atlantic."[13]

The Canadian delegation at the conference was small, cohesive, and expert: RB, Clifford Clark, Rhodes, Ferguson, Dana Wilgress of Trade and Commerce, Norman Robertson and Georges Vanier of External. RB had been working with Arthur Merriam and Alice Millar right up to the minute the ship sailed. The Canadians left from Quebec City on Friday, 2 June, on the new CP liner *Duchess of Bedford*. To RB's surprise, there was something of a send-off. Canadians viewed the 1932 Ottawa Conference as a Canadian triumph, and the World Economic and Monetary Conference seemed to promise well too. Along the St Lawrence there was, so RB wrote to Hazel Colville, "a vast multitude of people," and "great goodwill – apparently– all along the river the whistles tooted & all the ships had their flags up." He had had many messages of encouragement but, he added, "I will tell you the truth I cared more for the one signed 'H' than all the others ... Yet so strange are the workings of the human heart that I think more of the one that spoke to me as a human being than of all the others who spoke only to the figure – a P.M."

He had seen Hazel in Montreal en route and was delighted by how much better she looked than he'd expected, for he knew she had not been well over the winter. She was forty-five years old in May that year. It was obvious that he still carried a torch for her; the two letters he wrote to her that day spoke volumes. He worried about her mental outlook. Do let me help you, he wrote: "Just treat me as one who wants to be a real help to you who has for you a very real and close [?] affection but who does not wish you to be worried by reason of that fact." Summer was coming, and she would be living and resting at that lovely place, Mascouche:

> Just be Hazel ... just be your own dear natural self – I do appreciate being able to see you again. I am afraid you were rather annoyed at me – but with all my faults & I know them, I pray for you daily & think of you so often always kindly, always helpfully always affectionately & only wish I could help you in all your trials & tribulations: and they are many. Drop me a line as you used to. It will help you I feel certain to a fairer appreciation of things. Hypocrite you say & rightly. Yet the other me says not. The real me tries to help & to be helped ... Why won't you understand? I tried to explain that all those troubles are not yours alone. Let us bear them without regret. And above all you know I try not to write so as to displease you. But you are "such a woman" that one does not perhaps always act with that cold precision of thought that should govern say a P.M.!! ... Do take care of yourself your child & family & your ever devoted and faithful friend & more. Dick.
> P.S. You cannot make me cease to be what I have so often told you must be –

In a telegram later that afternoon she had wished him a safe journey, but, he said, "You did not wish me a safe and quick return!!"[14]

Six days later after a benign crossing, the *Duchess of Bedford* docked on Thursday, 8 June, at Greenock on the Clyde, the vessel's first stop. RB had immediately to disembark and take the train to London, for a meeting of British Empire delegates was set for Saturday morning. He hoped that the "same good circumstances" that had attended him at Ottawa in 1932 would again do so in London. Would Hazel's face be again at his shoulder as last year? By now, though, he was beginning to understand that she did not want to listen to his sentimental memories. She had them herself; last winter in Europe she had kept seeing RB's face as she went from place to place and often at singularly inopportune times. She pushed such memories away. The measure of the gap between them was that she regretted her memories, while RB cherished his: "I don't forget the girl who helped me when I needed it, who went with me in my difficulties, comforted me & did not fail me."

He told Hazel that he was going to face a very different situation than at Ottawa in 1932. The impression out of Washington, not least from the American secretary of state, Cordell Hull, was that the Americans would try to ease trade barriers. Hull had said as much as he embarked for London. However, while he was at sea, President Roosevelt withdrew the reciprocal trade agreements bill then before Congress. Thus Hull arrived in London with empty hands. RB said that Canada's position had some advantages; Canada understood the Americans better than most of the other delegations – useful, since American intentions were wildly contradictory.[15]

The World Economic Conference in London was a League of Nations enterprise, encouraged to meet in London by Ramsay MacDonald. There were three main positions represented: first was that of the French gold bloc and its European and other adherents, whose sovereign remedy was international return to the gold standard. The second was that of the American inflationists who wanted price levels raised and an end to continued bumps of deflation; it was a position J.M. Keynes supported and Roosevelt was becoming enamoured of. The third position was a multilateral agreement to lower tariffs and end trade barriers. That was Cordell Hull's aim. The American delegation had elements of all three positions. Canada wanted better prices for wheat, lumber, and other primary commodities; in that sense the Canadians were Rooseveltian.

The conference opened on Monday, 12 June, in the Geological Museum in South Kensington. George V officially opened the conference and Ramsay MacDonald presided. Every country in the world was represented, including Liberia. As MacDonald read out the names of the sixty-six governments present, from Allemagne to the U.S.S.R., Norman Robertson was surprised to find that Canada was omitted, included only as "a representative of the British Dominions." It was as if the Statute of Westminster had never happened. He turned to RB and said, "I think we ought to object to that." RB was loath to obtrude that constitutional issue, but to Robertson it mattered, and he stuck to his guns. "After ten minutes of heated argument," RB reluctantly conceded Robertson's point. Canada was added: now there were sixty-seven nations present.

The truth probably was that RB (and MacDonald) had not yet come quite to terms with the Statute of Westminster. It had been passed a short eighteen months before in December 1931, and there were philosophical tangles in it. It was a little like the doctrine of the Trinity: the

Crown was both indivisible and divisible. The king of Great Britain and the king of Canada were one and the same; how could the king of Canada have different policies from the king of Great Britain? It puzzled the mind. William Hughes of Australia called the Westminster Statute "an almost metaphysical document." Not much liking metaphysics, the British, Canadians, and many others of the Commonwealth simply ignored the contradiction in dominion status. It would not be the first time in the Anglo-Saxon world that gross philosophical contradictions had been glossed over. Every Sunday since the "black rubric" had appeared in Elizabeth I's prayer book over three hundred years ago, the Church of England's communion service was a declaration of transubstantiation and at the same time an assertion that it was simply remembrance. Not all Elizabethans were able to live with that contradiction, but most were.[16]

On 25 June RB reported that the conference was going better than he expected. He was on the Management Committee for reporting the position of the British Commonwealth and Empire. The Commonwealth delegations continued to meet outside the main conference. That part of it was really intra-imperial, its main concerns being oversupply of primary products, which implied mainly quantitative control. It was hard work, RB said, as they wrestled with how to regulate overabundant supplies of wheat, meat, cheese, apples, and livestock. He sent Hazel a newspaper photograph of himself in earnest discussion with two other senior empire statesmen at the Geological Museum, Ramsay MacDonald and Neville Chamberlain; RB is listening to MacDonald with intense concentration. At the end what emerged was a wheat marketing scheme, over which RB laboured, that urged restrictions on wheat output. By the time various amendments had been added, however, it made no effective attack on the basic problem of glut.

In the main conference a tariff truce had been negotiated beforehand, agreeing during the conference to suspend all tariff changes prior to 12 June and to continue the suspension after the conference adjourned, upon a month's notice of withdrawal. Some fifty-three governments agreed to the truce.

After initial opening statements, the conference had agreed that exchange stabilization was an essential precondition for the revival of trade, and according to RB there was "an excellent international atmosphere and attitude of mind on the part of the delegates." Then, he said, the Americans asserted that they were going to ignore all that and go their own way. After that, Professor Raymond Moley, a top FDR advisor, arrived, said RB, and "they burned incense before him." Moley in turn urged Roosevelt to accept the exchange stabilization principle.

By this time it was clear that there was a basic split among the major nations over whether exchange rate stabilization or a rise in domestic prices was the answer. For the gold bloc, led by France, the answer was easy: stability in exchange rates was the essential thing; let domestic prices rise or fall as they might. The gold bloc attitude seemed to be "We are on the gold standard, and all the rest of you should be on it." Canada, like Britain, wanted some domestic price increases, but RB wanted to avoid real inflation. By the third week of June, newspapers began to carry stories of imminent exchange stabilization at, say, $4 or $4.25 to the pound. On 3 July, fearing the French and the European gold bloc were walking off with the conference, Roosevelt sent a peremptory message, its tone brusque, uncompromising, almost insulting. Those who would seek mere exchange rate stabilization were all wrong; instead, they should aim at curing what he called "fundamental economic ills."

The message hit London like a bombshell. Indeed, it came to be called just that. France and the gold bloc were furious and threatened to pull out of the conference immediately. Keynes and Moley concocted a more benign version of the Roosevelt message, which cooled the heated atmosphere a little. Still, Keynes wrote in the London *Daily Mail*, Roosevelt was right. This the *Daily Mail*, in the style of popular English papers, headlined on 3 July 1933, PRESIDENT ROOSEVELT IS MAGNIFICENTLY RIGHT.

RB did not think Roosevelt was right at all. He had sent, RB told Hazel, "a very insolent message, the terms were even worse than those employed by the P.M. of Canada!!" Nevertheless he thought the conference should stay intact, that the French should not leave. It had already achieved important agreements. Cordell Hull thought the same, and he, RB, and others fought to keep the conference going. A conference committee had already presented a resolution supporting adjournment, laying the blame for failure squarely on the United States. Hull, Neville Chamberlain, and Bennett managed to get the Management [viz., Steering] Committee to agree to meet on 6 July. When it met, Hull gave a strong speech urging that the conference continue. Second only to Hull's speech, said John MacCormac in the *New York Times*, were the arguments of Prime Minister Bennett. Indeed, said an observer, Bennett put the climax on Hull's speech, "but he was more vehement." If the French were to pull out, said RB, they would be accused of wrecking the conference. It was, he wrote to Hazel that night of 6 July, "a long hard struggle with the French. They [the conference] give me unfairly credit for saving it. But it has been an awful day. From 10 till 6.30 with a short respite and I had to bear a good deal of the burden."[17]

A few days later RB lunched at Londonderry House with the marchioness of Londonderry, a noted socialite and philanthropist of the time. He described her as "the guide" of Prime Minister Ramsay MacDonald. Lady Londonderry called RB the "strongman" of the conference. He was amused and flattered. "You know what a misnomer that is, don't you?" he wrote to Hazel. "I am able quietly though to do considerable in the way of directing the channels of thought. That is not egotism & don't you think so!" William Bullitt of the American delegation wrote to Roosevelt, "The most striking feature of this Conference thus far [8 July] is Bennett's desire to cooperate with us and I think if you have any plans for reciprocal tariff negotiations with Canada the time is very propitious."[18] The World Economic Congress adjourned on 27 July 1933 with hopeful noises made for the future, but it never reconvened. Oddly enough in the circumstances, its main legacy could be said to be the Reciprocal Trade Agreements Act (RTAA), passed by the U.S. Congress in June of the following year. The act transformed the direction of U.S. trade policy, moving it away from protectionism and towards free trade.

Most of the Canadians boarded the *Empress of Britain* on Saturday, 29 July. RB, worn out from work and heat, left the next day for a fortnight at the Yorkshire spa of Harrogate. Hazel had suggested a French spa, but he preferred "the England I know to the France I do not know." They had everything in Harrogate, he told Hazel on 8 July, for "'heavies', for 'brain fag' (that's me), 'obesity' that's me too, a trio." At the Grand Hotel, five hundred feet above sea level and close to a grassy two-hundred acre park known as "The Stray," he rested, bathed, and doubtless drank sulphur water of different taste and density from thirty springs. He worried about Hazel's well-being. She worried instead about their relations: how to establish greater distance between them without hurting RB too badly. Only a year before, they had been back and forth to Mascouche together; RB remembered all of it and reminisced sentimentally about it. On his hotel dressing table he even kept a picture of Mascouche, where he and Hazel had been so happy. But for her, wanting arm's-length relations, all that wouldn't do.[19]

In August she invited Alice Millar to visit Mascouche. Hazel thought of it as a "vicarious" farewell. RB wrote at once to thank her for inviting Alice but may have swallowed hard, for Hazel's letter sounded very close to a farewell – a real farewell, pushing him too hard, too soon. He summoned up his pride. "I assure you," he wrote to her, "no one could so well represent me, for this month she [Alice] enters her 20th year with me. And her loyalty & devotion to my interests have increased – if possible – with the passing of the years. Can more be said?" As for the burthen of Hazel's letter,

I am not wholly lacking in understanding. Yet the time may come – you never can tell – when I can in some way serve the "imaginary woman" and I assure you that I shall be ready and willing to render that service, however small or humble it may be, equally to the "imaginary woman" or the "real woman".

For the rest I will not add to your worries by either contradiction or argument.

With my best wishes always,
Believe me I am
Ever yours sincerely, D

From London he addressed a letter to her as "My dear." It had a heartfelt PS: "& please do not leave me all alone!! Ever your devoted Dick."

But she did. A line from "Field of Honor" of the previous September may tell something of her anguish: "The heart insolvent, but the conscience freed." But it may well be that what Alice Toner Tompkins said was right: "Hazel Colville broke his heart."[20]

RB returned to Canada by the beginning of September in time to meet with the Macmillan Royal Commission on Banking and Currency, just beginning to wind up a whirlwind tour of Canada's banks. Finance Minister Rhodes had announced plans for the commission to Parliament earlier in the year on 21 March. Only six months later the report would be submitted – a record that for brevity and dispatch few Canadian royal commissions have beaten.

The Canadian branch banking system as it stood had many strengths. It was financially conservative, it was far reaching, and it was safe. In the words of the 1933 Macmillan royal commission, it gave "admirable evidence of security, efficiency and convenience." Canada had not had a bank failure since the demise of the Home Bank in 1923. It would not have one now, though there had recently been some bad moments in bank boardrooms and in Ottawa. Canada was, however, locked into a fairly rigid monetary system, which could only be eased by the cumbersome manipulation allowed by the Finance Act of 1914. The banks borrowed from the federal government money that served as legal tender. That allowed the banks to increase their cash reserves, which in turn allowed for monetary expansion. But all that was only when it suited the banks; it was an awkward mechanism for the government to use when it itself wanted monetary expansion. Thus Canada had little or no experience at managing its own currency. In fact, in the early 1930s the banks tended to enforce a regime of tight credit, to protect, as Duncan MacDowall notes in his history of the Royal Bank of Canada, "their own solvency." Different banks did it in different ways, the Bank of Montreal being the most conservative, the Royal most liberal, but the net effect of all these varieties of orthodoxy was to harden the dollar and exacerbate deflation.[21]

Near the end of 1932 after a strong push of "moral suasion" from RB under an order-in-council on 28 October 1932 (confirmed in Parliament on 8 November 1932), $35 million in new money had at RB's insistence been spread between the banks. He met with them and said, "I want each of you to borrow a certain amount so that no one can point the finger at the other, and that the intense deflationary things will be to that extent relieved." The Bank of Montreal, which had reason to preen itself on its conservative approach to monetary questions, was furious, and another of the banks was very unhappy, but RB swung considerable weight and the bankers agreed to take the loans. This informal method of expanding bank credit was highly unsatisfactory, however, and it may have been the tipping point in RB's mind that Canada needed a central bank. It was certainly something that Clifford Clark was increasingly certain of. Clark had indeed agreed to become deputy minister only after ascertaining that Bennett would support a central bank.[22]

The other push in the same direction came from senior officials at the Royal Bank of Canada. The Royal had long been RB's bank. It had started as a Maritime institution, kept its roots, but moved and branched westward, eventually south to Cuba and beyond. Rather a maverick among the chartered banks, it was aggressive, forward looking, a young man's institution. "It gave promising young men plenty of leash, trained them to be cautious and promoted them expecting boldness."[23] RB had been a director until he gave that position up along with many other directorships on becoming leader of the Conservative Party. But he remained a major shareholder. His close ties with the bank and its officials did not make him give in to strong suggestions in 1932 about a central bank from Morris Wilson, the Royal's general manager and the most knowledgeable of its senior officials, or from Wilson's assistant, young Graham Towers, but he weighed and stored what they had to recommend.

Towers was a brilliant young economist with the Royal's head office on St James Street in Montreal. He had graduated from McGill with high honours. The Royal had been aggressive there too, for Canadian banks hardly ever hired university graduates; in 1920 Towers was the second university graduate the Royal had taken on. He was fluent in French and, as a result of visiting the Royal's Caribbean and South American branches, spoke some Spanish as well. By 1933 at the age of thirty-six he was assistant general manager. He had worried about Canada's too-close financial association with New York bankers and the Washington of Herbert Hoover, fearing that it would infect Canada with "useless deflation," as he termed it. He wanted to pull Canada away by closer association with the sterling bloc – or better, wanted Canada to have its own central bank, manage its own currency, and settle its own bank rate.[24]

Once the Royal Commission on Banking and Currency in Canada had been announced to Parliament, RB lost no time. He had had more than one meeting with Sir Montagu Norman, governor of the Bank of England, and Norman undoubtedly persuaded him of the importance of a central bank. RB had observed from his own wealth of experience in England how important the Bank of England was. He also knew that most of the chartered banks would be opposed to a central bank. Western Canada was generally supportive; so was Mackenzie King. But the dead weight of the powerful financial institutions of eastern Canada would be against a Bank of Canada. So who the commissioners would be was important. Both RB and Clark considered that a chairman from outside the country was essential.

Numerous names were considered, including American suggestions from Clark. There had recently been a major British inquiry on finance and industry in 1929–31, directed with dispatch and success by Lord Macmillan. In June 1933 while in London at the World Economic Conference, RB saw Macmillan and convinced him to serve as the Canadian commission's chairman. Macmillan in turn suggested a second British member, Sir Charles Addis, an expert in central banking. RB had already secured one Canadian appointment, Sir Thomas White, Borden's wartime minister of finance. Cables sent from London brought in, reluctantly, Beaudry Leman, general manager of the Banque Canadienne Nationale, and J.E. Brownlee, the premier of

Alberta. The five commissioners were appointed by order-in-council on 31 July 1933. By that time the two British commissioners had already sailed for Canada.

They arrived on 4 August, and hearings began four days later. RB gave them a very free hand. The speed of the commission was breathtaking: they went across Canada and back, finishing their hearings by 11 September. Their brisk, nine-page recommendations were in RB's hands by 28 September. Perhaps because of the extreme time constraints, the commission split 3–2 in recommending a central bank for Canada. White and Leman were opposed, with Brownlee submitting a memorandum indicating his unhappiness with private ownership of Bank of Canada shares. Altogether it was a near thing. A week later, over the new CRBC national network, RB announced that Bank of Canada legislation would be introduced at the next session of Parliament.

When the news got out, RB was subjected to a great deal of pressure, people wanting this change or that. F.D.L. Smith, senior editor of the *Toronto Mail & Empire*, suggested to RB that he take the Canadian Bankers Association into his confidence and work with them on the Bank of Canada bill. RB's reply was characteristic: "If the people must engage in conflict with those who worship profits as their god and who regard the welfare of the nation as being of secondary importance then I know in which camp I will be enlisted." As one student of the subject observed, "The extent to which Bennett held firm to his convictions in the face of such pressure is probably both a mark of his greatest asset and his most obvious weakness as a politician." However, it is almost certain that, had Mackenzie King been in power, there would have been no central bank constituted as the Bank of Canada came to be. RB's opinion was that the chartered banks were powerful enough to get their own way against a timorous government, but they were not going to do so against his.[25]

While the commission was moving towards the conclusion of its work, one of the commissioners, Premier Brownlee, was having his own private problems. On 22 September 1933 the *Edmonton Bulletin* published in full the statement of claim by lawyers for a Vivian MacMillan (no relation) that she had been seduced by Brownlee, not once but constantly over three years since 1930. She (and her father) wanted damages under the Province of Alberta Seduction Act of 1922. It was the juiciest scandal to hit Alberta in many a year. Brownlee denied all of it and submitted a counterclaim. He offered his resignation to the Macmillan commission, but both Lord Macmillan and RB turned it down. Brownlee was probably as much sinned against as sinning, but he had sinned generously too. What saved his career was that those who sought to expose him were evidently using their own nasty quiver of dirty tricks.

RB had a high opinion of Brownlee. He had the ablest mind of any of the law students who had worked for him at the Lougheed and Bennett firm. RB took an interest in Brownlee back then, asking him what he was studying and then offering an impromptu lecture on the point, giving specific legal references. At first Brownlee did not quite believe what he was hearing, but time and again RB's summaries proved accurate. Brownlee went on to become attorney general of Alberta from 1921 to 1924 and then was elected premier in 1924 as head of the United Farmers of Alberta. RB told him, "You're the one government in Canada that has played the game one hundred per cent with us. We have never found one instance in checking your accounts where you have tried to put something over on us under the guise of unemployment relief." In the tough letter to all four western premiers about constraints on federal relief assistance, he added a private note to Brownlee: "You've dealt with conditions better than any one of the Western Provinces."[26]

RB had returned on 1 September from his three months' sojourn in England restless and dissatisfied; his role as Canadian prime minister and head of the Conservative party was becoming a terrible burden to carry. He had not expected much joy and delight in it, but the never-ending litany of problems and criticism that came his way was a constant vexation to his spirit. The party was faring badly. The Conservatives lost two provincial elections in Nova Scotia and in British Columbia and three federal by-elections on 23 October in New Brunswick, Quebec, and Saskatchewan. All of that shortened his temper and compounded an atavistic desire to be out of it all.

He could be generous to colleagues, as to Manion on his fifty-second birthday on 19 November 1933. Manion was a doctor, and he had been instrumental in getting RB to reduce his weight a little and take a modicum of exercise. RB sent him a personal note: "Your native Irish wit, your charm of manner, & the spontaneous generosity of your great heart endear you to all who are privileged to know you ... R.B." But Bob Manion was special, one of the few in cabinet who could talk back to RB. At one cabinet meeting in 1932 Manion criticized him for using the CNR as a whipping boy. RB came right back at him; Manion demurred. RB persisted. "My first ambition," Manion shot back, "is that some day I may make a speech that will meet with your approval." RB fairly fumed at that. Then the next day he telephoned Manion in a friendly way, and it was all over. A measure of his regard for Manion was the MacNider dinner of 17 November 1932 when RB had asked him to escort Hazel Colville to the head table.[27]

It was to Manion especially that RB seems to have made his first remarks about wanting to get out of office. (He had also said so more than once to Hazel Colville.) Shortly after his return to Ottawa, he and Manion met at a large Canadian Bar Association luncheon given by RB. They talked for three and a half hours about his trip. He was charming, Manion said, but it was as if his months in England had further weakened his resolution to carry the burden of leadership. He said he was going to quit by the next King's Birthday (1 June). That autumn he would repeat it at almost every cabinet meeting, Manion wrote in his diary, "*RBB vont résigner – Il va à H.E. pour nommer successeur.*"

Early in October, RB had a long talk in Toronto with F.D.L. Smith, chief editor of the *Mail and Empire*. Smith was shocked at RB's "renewed threats to resign," though he found it difficult to take them seriously. The two men had had a continual close working relationship, especially since 1930. RB had kept Smith constantly informed, and Smith realized fully what a sacrifice in time, money, and energy being prime minister had entailed. But RB should not retire, said Smith, not at least until he had accomplished some of the things he had promised in Winnipeg in 1927. "You complain that your efforts are not properly appreciated even by your own party," he said, "but are not you yourself, and your colleagues partly to blame, if not wholly to blame? You have not taken the public into your confidence, you have been content to do good by stealth, keeping your achievements in a dark cellar. Have you not steadfastly refused to provide the nation with the necessary flow of adequate explanation and propaganda?" Sir John Willison, the *Globe*'s editor from 1890 to 1902, had told Smith that to get a simple truth through to the public, it had to be repeated a dozen times. RB needed a publicity bureau, said Smith. As it was now, several party stalwarts, when they heard rumours about his retiring, got panicky. And "thousands of better-class Liberals would be just as appalled. Lots of Canadians may grumble," Smith said, "but there is a pretty universal agreement that you were sent by heaven to save the nation."

RB's reply is not extant, but something of his rueful state of mind comes through in a revealing letter to Manion of 22 November 1933: "Nothing could more clearly indicate why I desire to be honourably discharged from my task than the letter which you have received from Art Clark [minister in the Tolmie government]. Why don't these people do something? Why turn to R.B. for everything? How can we in Ottawa control the situation in B.C. Art Clark & others are as responsible for the mess in B.C. as anybody else. Why didn't he take the matter in hand? Why didn't he direct Tolmie along proper lines ..."[28] Manion was well aware of his chief's talents but critical of his failures. Before RB's return, Manion and Herridge had lunched together in Ottawa, and both felt strongly the need for a Bennett program for the future. They agreed that Manion would put his proposals in writing to RB and that Herridge would press them personally. The letter went to RB the day after Manion left for the annual fall meeting of the League of Nations, driving his own car across Europe. Manion suggested to RB that $100 million should be spent on public works, to be called the "Bennett Recovery Programme." RB did not answer, not right away at least, though once or twice he rather made fun of the proposal. By the end of 1933, however, he had begun to accept it, as if, said Manion, "after long pondering he had just thought it out."[29]

Manion's besetting complaint was RB's apparent indifference to party organization. After the 1930 election, the party headquarters on Wellington Street was closed. RB did not want to finance it out of his own pocket; neither did he attempt to appoint anyone else to look after it. It required a driving force that he had neither time nor inclination to put in gear. A secretary or two were answering letters but that was that. Manion and others pointed out to RB time and again, especially after the South Huron by-election defeat of 3 October 1932 (which the Conservatives badly wanted to win and didn't), that energy, effort, and dollars had to be provided if Conservative fortunes were to be turned around. But RB would not finance the Conservative party by himself, and money was tight everywhere.

He was also temperamentally, philosophically, and morally against kickbacks, slush funds, and some of the more earthy forms of patronage. Even appointments well within his power to effect were long postponed. H.A. Bruce, the lieutenant governor of Ontario, was appointed in 1932 only after a year's delay. Both H.H. Stevens and Murray MacLaren had to remind RB several times of the need to appoint deputy ministers to their departments of Trade and Commerce and Veterans Affairs. Party work, party strategies, party appointments, party bosses, little men with greedy eyes and big pretensions – the whole rather seamy side of politics that some of his colleagues quite enjoyed the rough and tumble of – RB shied away from as if distasteful. It may well have been against his grain. Thus the lament of Manion to his son at the Canadian Legation in

Tokyo: "This inaction and a good deal of his own out-bursts regarding quitting are causing the spread of the tale that he is looking forward shortly to getting an estate in England and a lordship ... this is awfully demoralizing; it is particularly so when one knows that he has such abilities from the brilliant side and could do so much to put things across if he would really, not only face the issue as he so often expresses it, but do something about it."[30]

RB's own agenda had always mattered more, and truth be told, it was an austere one, giving the people of Canada what he believed they ought to have and really ought to want. He could fairly be said to be authoritarian, convinced of the rightness of his own inner beliefs and apt to regard those of others as obtrusive or even irrelevant. Perhaps that is what Hazel felt, and it may have ruined their late season romance. Certainly her daughter felt it was so.

RB left Ottawa on Saturday, 23 December, with Mildred and Bill Herridge and their new son up from Washington. They were bound for Christmas in Sackville, New Brunswick, to spend Christmas with Ronald Bennett. RB saw Hazel on his way through Montreal; he had been worried about her health but was delighted to find her so "bright & happy":

> Will you be annoyed when I tell you that your being happy & well
> will comfort me very much ... remember that I would not consciously
> give you pain or make you unhappy. And I think of you always as a
> friend or more & always with the desire to be trusted & esteemed
> by you even though 'a colossal egotist' – And you have been of real
> help to me as you know. The report of the Conference will be bound
> for you ... if at any time you are resentful or cross or annoyed at
> me, read a few lines of the report & think that you at least helped in
> making it all possible. So I wish you Peace at Christmas Time ...
>   Ever yours faithfully,
>   D.

At the top of that letter he wrote, "East of Montreal, Saturday night (Rough track.)" It is the last letter from him that Hazel kept.[31]

Indeed, their track had by now come to an end. His separate one was going to get rougher. The last of their meetings seems to have occurred in 1934 when RB visited her at her Pine Avenue home in Montreal, and walked out so agitated that he left his handsome Irish blackthorn cane behind. "Poor R.B.," wrote Frances on 16 August 1989; "he becomes one in a procession as Mother grasps for the impossible emotionally after A.B.C.'s [Arthur B. Colville's] death. She was not a happy lady."[32]

Later in 1934 Hazel went to live in Italy, moving in high circles in Rome until the Ethiopian War after October 1935 made her Rolls-Royce too conspicuous. Some Italians threw stones at it. That decided her to return to England. By 1942 she was in the Bahamas, where she was invited to play bridge with the Duke of Windsor; the duchess did not play bridge. For that matter, neither did RB.

From the moment he returned to Ottawa in January 1934, RB would be working flat out. Delegations innumerable wanted to see him. Mackenzie King did not as a rule meet delegations; he would refer them to a minister. RB believed in meeting and talking, for he could hold his own in almost any situation. He was at interviews daily from 9 AM to 6 PM, except for meetings of cabinet or caucus. When J.B. Carswell of Burlington Steel Hamilton complained that decisions for public works in the spring of 1934 were not yet announced. RB replied politely how appreciative he was of Carswell's suggestions. He told Pigott of Pigott Construction that he was working as hard as he could to overcome delays and backlogs in his correspondence. Because of the Depression, he was seeing as many delegations as he possibly could. And, he added, "if I say to you that I have only one ambition and that is to be honourably discharged from this office, I think you will understand the point to which this incessant toil has driven me."[33]

His toil encompassed many things. He was quick on the uptake if something vital to Canadian history was at issue. In 1932 the original sketch for Robert Harris's famous 1884 painting, "The Fathers of Confederation" was found in the basement of the National Gallery. The huge original painting itself had burned up in the terrible fire of February 1916 that destroyed most of the Centre Block. The sketch was not small either, thirteen by nine feet. When it was brought to his attention by Hugh Stewart, minister of public works, RB agreed that it should be rescued and placed in the Railway Committee room "without further delay." RB also saw that a handsome stamp was issued in 1933 to commemorate the 1833 voyage of the *Royal William*, the first steamship to cross the Atlantic; 1934 would be the four hundredth anniversary of Jacques Cartier's first voyage to Quebec, followed by the hunded and fiftieth anniversary of the United Empire Loyalists, and the founding of New Brunswick in 1784. RB had once taught history in Douglastown, New Brunswick, and now he enjoyed commemorating it.[34]

Another historic preoccupation of his was the revival of honours –
something he'd had in mind for a long time ever since the House of
Commons, after a run of not very good knighthoods, had passed a resolution on 22 May 1919 asking King George V not to award any more.
The resolution had been pushed by W.F. Nickle, MP for Kingston (Conservative), much aggrieved, it was said, that the presidents of the University of Toronto and McGill were both given knighthoods when his
father-in-law, principal of Queen's University, was not. He first tried his
resolution in 1918, but Sir Robert Borden blocked it. In 1919, however,
Borden was off in Paris at the Peace Conference and Nickle got his way;
the resolution passed 96–43. (RB was not then an MP; he had not run
in the general election of December 1917. Mackenzie King was not in
the House either; he had been defeated in the general election of 1911.)
An attempt to derail it back to committee failed. But the Nickle resolution did not go to the Senate for the simple reason that it would have
been defeated there. So it remained an expression of Nickle's pique and
the earnest sincerities of others. Borden was much annoyed, and so, it
appeared, was King George V.

Peter McGibbon, Conservative MP for Muskoka, said in 1929 that
the 1919 resolution had passed owing to "a kind of war hysteria." In
February 1929, C.H. Cahan attempted to revive the debate by moving
for a committee to consider the advisability of revising the resolution.
RB supported Cahan strongly: in a democracy, merit should "be given
some recognition by the state." And what was wrong with titles? One
addressed a judge as "Your Lordship." Still, as the *Vancouver News-
Herald* later observed, it was difficult for any democratic government to
keep the flow of honours within the limits of good taste. Prior to 1919
the awarding of honours, titles, and decorations had amounted, it said,
"very nearly to a public scandal."[35]

RB was well aware of this history as well as the thicket of opinions,
prejudices, and jealousies surrounding knighthoods and honours. When
approached on the subject in March 1931, he said it was much too soon
to think about it. A year later, in February 1932, he felt it was still too
soon to consider it; indeed, to suggest it right then would be "to suggest
the dissolution of the present government." By May 1933, however, with
the prospect of his government being re-elected dimming almost month
by month, he felt that if ever that 1919 resolution were to be overruled,
it would have to be by his government – and soon. His own convictions
were clear about the lack of constitutional efficacy of the 1919 resolution. It was only an opinion of a majority of the House of Commons on

an April day in 1919. True, it had been transmitted formally enough to London and was acted on by the imperial government, but as RB put it to Lord Bessborough, then governor general, "formality, however great, cannot clothe with validity that which is invalid."[36]

Nevertheless, RB now approached the whole subject obliquely. A week before Parliament prorogued on 17 May 1933, Paul Mercier, Liberal MP for Montreal-St Denis, asked if the recent promotion within the Order of St Michael and St George meant that Canadians could accept such promotions. RB replied, "It is the considered opinion of His Majesty's Government in Canada that the motion of 22 May 1919 was not binding on His Majesty or His Majesty's Government in Canada."

Mackenzie King pricked up his ears. What was meant? he asked. Was the House to be given a chance to discuss it? He wanted assurance before any titles were given that there would be a full discussion in the House. RB replied he would not promise any such thing. It was a matter of the sovereign's prerogative and Canada's executive government. King became heavily sarcastic, saying how he would hate to deprive the right honourable gentleman of his chance to become a peer. An acid exchange followed, but in effect nothing much happened; there was no outcry. Mackenzie King wished there were.[37]

The 1934 New Year's honours were announced in London on 31 December 1933 and published in Canada the next day. Contrary to rumours, neither RB nor Ferguson was mentioned. There were two knighthoods, Lyman Duff, chief justice of Canada, and Joseph Tellier, chief justice of Quebec, both eminent jurists. RB believed that, whatever action might be taken by cabinet or Parliament, "in the end it falls to the Judges of the Country to determine the true intent and meaning of such action." In addition to the two knighthoods, there were honours for thirty-two women. Most of them received an OBE (Order of the British Empire), primarily for social work. Charlotte Whitton of Ottawa was given a CBE (Commander of the British Empire).

Mackenzie King said that same day that the government's actions in so reviving honours were an affront to Parliament. But Canadians, said the *Halifax Herald*, were not worried about any implied threat to democracy: "Beyond any doubt, they are against hereditary titles in this country; but when it comes to direct recognition of unusual merit and devoted service, the people will refuse to be stampeded." Indeed, it said, let those who urged an end to honours turn in their own. That was a direct cut at King himself: he held a CMG awarded in 1906 and had been made a member of the Imperial Privy Council in 1922. He was thus entitled to be called "Right Honourable," and in the House of Commons he was. What King had done, said the *Herald*, was to dissolve "the pearl of independence in the vinegar of obligation."[38]

As for implied social discrimination, RB wrote to one critic, most of the forty people named in the 1934 New Year's honours did not have more than $25,000 in the world. And "why should not the services of women who have worked their hands off for many years in the interests of the needy be recognized by their sovereign? So far as I am concerned, I will be content to be deprived of office on an issue of that kind."[39]

There was not much chance of that on the honours issue. The newspapers generally liked the return of honours. "I am amazed at the sycophancy of the Press," Mackenzie King told his diary in disgust. The *Toronto Star* and the *Winnipeg Free Press* supported his attack on the renewal of honours, but few others did. When Sir William Clark, the British high commissioner, said Mackenzie King had gone too far, King told his diary that Clark had "better mind his own business." One of the most percipient appreciations of RB's new departure came from Sir Thomas White, president of the Canadian Bank of Commerce in Toronto:

> My dear old friend,
> My hearty congratulations upon your courage in dealing with the matter of honours. You are absolutely right of course. A resolution of the House of Commons – one branch only of Parliament is wholly ineffectual to cut down the King's prerogative on most any line. "Intestinal Fortitude" is a rare quality but highly desirable in a P.M. and you have it in a marked degree ... All our talk about winning great constitutional freedom is so much buncombe and hypocrisy because whatever we ask for is readily accorded.[40]

In the summer of 1933, Canadian political parties had all launched broad-ranging political seminars about the state of Canada and how it could be improved. Liberals had their go at it; so did the fledgling CCF; the Conservatives had their gathering at Newmarket, Ontario. At that time RB was coping with the World Economic Conference in London and then recuperating in Harrogate. He was not in any event much of an enthusiast for think tanks or the professors who frequently inhabited them. In January 1931, when Harry Stevens suggested a council on unemployment with advisers from industry, labour, and the universities, RB came back with, "Why talk such nonsense? Do you think I want a lot of long-haired professors telling me what to do? If I can't run this country, I will get out." In October 1931 he had been much offended when R.A. MacKay, a thirty-eighty-year-old political science professor at Dalhousie University, published an article in *Maclean's*, "After Beauharnois – What?" The article was not vituperative, but it had not taken account of recent revelations in the House of Commons committee. When MacKay learned his article had been accepted by *Maclean's*, he read over his draft and realized he had gone further than the evidence warranted. But it was too late; the magazine had already gone to press. The gist of the article was that both Liberals and Conservatives had been guilty of accepting tainted campaign contributions. Since the federal Conservatives had not accepted any Beauharnois money, RB was properly indignant. He was a governor of Dalhousie since 1926, having been a considerable benefactor, giving money to Dalhousie through Jennie Shirreff Eddy for a women's residence and on his own a house for Dalhousie's president. He thought MacKay should be fired and was aggrieved when Dalhousie refused to do it. In the end the university managed to keep both MacKay and RB onside, but RB grumbled that, while MacKay might well be the idealist Dalhousie said he was, "I am sure you will agree that untruthfulness and idealism are not synonymous and that idealism is not usually expressed in slanderous or libellous words." RB could be heavy-handed; the article had little of either in it. On the other hand, he told Bob Manion in March 1933, "an injustice is an injustice – it matters not how it may be supported." That could work both ways. In August 1932 when he was hip deep in the Imperial Economic Conference, a Workers' Economic Conference was convened in Ottawa. In his address to them, RB was stern on civil disobedience. We have laws, he said. "You break those laws and I say that, as sure as the sun rises, you will pay the price for it." To him, peace, order and good government mattered.[41]

Early in January 1934 RB asked Harry Stevens, his minister of trade and commerce, if he would take over a speaking engagement in Toronto to the Retail Shoe Merchants and Shoe Manufacturers Association for Monday, 15 January, at the Royal York Hotel. (RB had to be in western Canada.) Stevens had his speech ready well ahead of time, as he usually did, but in the few days prior to his leaving Ottawa, he had received delegations from three different bodies: needleworkers, livestock farmers, and owners of small businesses. Their submissions had a common theme: they were being squeezed out of their livelihoods by big business cutthroat practices. And he said in his speech, "My mind was so filled with these conditions that I ... [could] not remain silent." The burden of his refrain was that large retailers used their tremendous buying power to extract what seemed to him as vicious price concessions or else lose business to someone else. For example, he blamed large meat-packing firms for paying farmers only one and a half cents a pound for beef and selling it to butchers at 19 cents. "I am getting to the point where I see there must be action taken of some kind. It will be a sorry day for Canada when these independent citizen-businessmen are crushed out." The effect on manufacturers was bad too. In order to meet the prices dictated to them, they had to squeeze their own workers hard. The worst part of it was that there was no publicity for such conditions; in order to keep their advertisers sweet, newspapers would not discuss such things. [42]

Stevens's militant declarations, said the *Toronto Globe*, "came with machine-gun precision," and when he concluded, the entire gathering stood to its feet and cheered. That fairly put the fat in the fire. The next day the *Globe* headlined it but made rather more of stern denials from Eaton's and Simpson's. The matter was soon enough on RB's desk, and he called Stevens on the carpet. Stevens had promised action, and that quite possibly meant government commitment. He had gone too far; he had formulated policy without consulting colleagues or prime minister. Stevens abruptly resigned. [43]

RB did not want to lose Stevens; he had a popular touch that many others in cabinet did not. If Stevens pressed his resignation, RB said, he would be forced to resign as well. That assertion comes through Stevens's son, the Rev. Francis Stevens, in 1969, based on a letter his father had sent many years before, but it is a plausible scenario. RB thought well of Stevens. Both were Methodists and teetotallers and had been parliamentary companions since both came to the House in the 1911 election. They had fought many parliamentary battles together, not least the major battle in 1926 that briefly unseated Mackenzie King. Stevens had become the parliamentary workhorse, conscientious, willing, one that every party needs. He could be carried away by his own sincerity. Discreet he was not, especially when his social sympathies were aroused. He was a not unsuccessful businessman, but his occasional business troubles allowed richer cabinet colleagues, Cahan and Ryckman especially, to sometimes sneer at his acumen, obloquy that Stevens sharply resented. During business difficulties in 1929, he had talked of getting out of politics for the sake of himself and his family; RB persuaded him then to stay on, that he was quite indispensable to the party. A year or so earlier RB had helped to rescue one of Stevens's sons – perhaps Francis – from an unfortunate entanglement by arranging to have the young lady, a civil servant, transferred from Vancouver to Ottawa. Stevens was grateful. But there was more than gratitude in Stevens for RB; there was admiration. In June 1931 a Conservative colleague in Victoria, Sam Maton, asked him what the prime minister was like. "Sam," said Stevens, "he is a perfect marvel and he came through the long [1931] session without a scar – he looks like a million dollars – is as fit as a man can be and I want to tell you that he can mop the floor with the opposition any time he feels like it. Our premier is the greatest man that Canada has produced."[44]

RB did not accept Stevens's resignation, putting it aside as if from a petulant boy. Stevens wanted a royal commission to investigate his charges; RB offered a parliamentary inquiry, with the promise of a royal commission should the committee's work outrun the parliamentary session. There was every expectation that it would; the scope of the committee's instructions was vast. Consisting of eleven members, it was to investigate "the causes of the large spread between the prices received for commodities by the producers thereof, and the prices paid by the consumers therefor; the system of distribution in Canada of farm and other natural produce, as well as manufactured products." And more specifically, it was to look at "the effect of mass buying by department and chain store organizations on the retail trade of the country." While they were at it, the committee was to report on labour conditions in industry, the relations of flour milling and bakeries, and the marketing of livestock. RB was aware of these issues; any Canadian who read American news would have known of the work of Roosevelt's National Recovery Administration, set up to deal with analogous problems but also making the effort to have industries regulate themselves (with decidedly mixed results).

RB introduced the resolutions in the Commons on 2 February 1934. In the light of the stir that Stevens's Toronto speech had made, he added a cautionary note: "I thought it was not desirable to enter into a discussion of specific instances, because it might be regarded as a tendency to prejudge the matter." It was a reminder to Stevens to be careful with his allegations. Of course, said RB, there would have to be witnesses called, papers and documentation brought forward and examined. It was a huge agenda. Stevens was off and running within a week.[45]

A month later, Robert Weir, minister of agriculture, brought in the Natural Products Marketing Act. Weir was a dozen years younger than RB, wounded at Passchendaele, and after the war raised cattle in Saskatchewan. He knew the West and its problems intimately. The Marketing

Act's aim was to firm up agricultural prices by controlling marketing through local boards for each industry, apples, cattle and others, set up by the growers themselves. Obviously it was a complex act, constitutionally dicey. RB got around that by offering concurrent legislation with participating provinces and by delegating authority to them to act as agents for Ottawa. The boards, provincial and national, were given power to set prices. J.-A. Bradette, MP for Temiskaming, asked if the effect would be to take money without parliamentary sanction. Of course it would, RB replied, and in one of his characteristic trenchant asides added, "there is no legislation that does not involve a curtailment of the unrestrained and unlimited liberty of everyone. That is what parliament is for." It was also typical of him that after one of King's long and rambling speeches on the issue, he could not resist needling King that the speech reminded him of Mr Pilgrim in John Bunyan's *The Pilgrim's Progress* meeting Mr Facing-Both-Ways. The Marketing Bill passed second reading with a robust majority: 120–60.[46]

It was RB who brought in for second reading in June two further major pieces of financial legislation: the Farmers' Creditors Arrangement Act and the Bank of Canada Act. His finance minister, Edgar Rhodes, was dealing with the sudden loss of his wife, Grace Pipes. The couple had gone to the movies on Saturday night, 5 May, and Grace was dead the next morning. King and RB were pallbearers at her funeral at Christ Church Cathedral on the following Tuesday. Rhodes did not want to "stick it" alone and considered dropping out of public life. RB doubtless talked him out of it. (King noticed at this time that RB looked unwell, tired and worn out. RB told him he had not been sleeping properly.)[47]

The Farmers' Creditors Arrangement Act was one of those pieces of legislation whose unlovely title masked a considerable achievement. By 1934 the farm debt problem had become widespread and serious, especially in the West. The problem fundamentally was that too much farm debt had been contracted when mortgage rates were high. That did not matter much at a time when farm production was good and prices were too. But it mattered very much when commodity prices hit bottom and high-priced mortgage debt remained, a heavier and heavier albatross. RB told the House, "I can say from my own personal observations and experience that ... the inability of the mortgagor to pay his debt has been one of the most fruitful sources of the present disaster." Every MP had a pocketful of distastrous tales to tell. "Everybody knew of cases where a mortgage company refused to make any concession to a hard-pressed farmer, foreclosed the mortgage, and then resold the farm for a fraction of what its customer had owed," journalist James Gray has written. That was often the way with foreclosures. The mortgage companies soon saw that too, and in time concluded that a live farm, even a heavily mortgaged one, was much better than a dead foreclosed one.[48]

There is a delightful history about this legislation from George Curtis, later dean of law at UBC, 1945–1971, then a young lawyer in Regina. Between briefs he would help out at the Saskatchewan farm of his uncle Leonard Curtis. After delivering a load of grain to the elevator, they stopped to have a beer and struck up a conversation with a local farmer who was saying how hard things were. Curtis's uncle tried to be reassuring, saying there was sure to be a good crop next year. "That may be true, Len," said the old farmer, "but if we have a good crop from now until I die, I'll never be out of debt." The remark lodged in young Curtis's mind. A few months later he was working for M.A. Macpherson, attorney general of the province. "This may be a silly idea," Curtis said to Macpherson, "but I noticed the other day that Parliament passed a Creditors' Arrangement Act for business that called for the scaling down of debt to avoid bankruptcy. Why couldn't we have that for farmers?"

"I don't know," Macpherson said. "That's federal. But I like the idea. Give me a memo on it. I'm going to Ottawa in a few days' time and I'll see the prime minister." A week later Macpherson was back. "Not a bad idea," Bennett had said. "But wait a minute, Macpherson, constitutionally we can't do it." When this was relayed to Curtis, he said, "I've thought of that. The BNA Act doesn't just say bankruptcy is federal; it says bankruptcy and *insolvency*."

The cause was taken up by Ottawa. The first draft of the bill offered to RB contemplated a voluntary arrangement between the farmer-debtor and his creditors. RB was not satisfied with that; he wanted legislation that went much further, that would give authority to officials to adjust both principal and interest on the debt to the productive value of the farm. This radical idea seems to have thrown Clifford Clark into something of a panic; nevertheless RB asked him in March 1934 to arrange a meeting of loan companies, insurance companies, and banks, the principal holders of western mortgages. The bill was revised on RB's lines after consultation with the companies that held most of the farm debt. This comprehensive consulting process was essential; by common law no compromise could be made by an individual with his creditors except on the basis of 100 cents on the dollar unless all creditors agreed. Both Ontario and Quebec had passed laws mitigating the old common law rules, but elsewhere in Canada they still stood (or better perhaps, stood still). The point of the bill, as RB explained to the House, was "to keep the farmer on the farm; if possible to help him cultivating the land." The farmer could thus begin once more to rebuild "his fortune and his future." The administrative costs would be borne not by the farmer nor by his creditors but by the federal government.

The act passed Parliament without serious opposition. Indeed, Mackenzie King said it would meet with general approval. The measure of RB's radical achievement was that in the eighteen months to 31 March 1936 some 19,000 farmers submitted proposals to official receivers and nearly as many meetings with creditors were held. Many thousands more meetings were arranged outside the immediate aegis of the act but fostered by it. The total farm debt reduction averaged 30 per cent. In short, the legislation was a considerable success. The end of the George Curtis story came half a century later in 1982 when he met a United Nations official on tour in Canada. "Do you know, Curtis," the man said, "that in 1934 the Canadian Parliament passed an act that saved the West?" "What was it?" Curtis asked. "The Farmers' Creditors' Arrangement Act," the official replied. In James Gray's view, the act was R.B. Bennett's greatest achievement.[49]

RB himself thought the Bank of Canada was. Clark drafted a clever preamble to the Bank of Canada Act that he persuaded RB to include: "Whereas it is desirable to establish a central bank in Canada to regulate credit and currency in the best interests of the economic life of the nation ..." There was substantial support in Parliament, though the debate dragged on interminably, mainly over three issues. One issue was solid and substantial. RB wanted the bank set up as a private corporation, like the Bank of England, to keep it as far away as possible from government interference. Mackenzie King and the Liberals wanted it as a government bank. RB insisted that the experience of the world generally went the other way. True, some countries had publicly owned central banks: Australia, Russia, Sweden. Some central banks were part public, part private. Many others were private. To all intents and purposes, the Bank of Canada itself was "a publicly owned bank" but had the security of being distant from the immediate pressures of the government of the day.

The other two issues were minor, one of them quite inflammatory and both of them unworthy of the House of Commons. Both cut closer to MPS' passions and prejudices. Who was to be appointed governor of the Bank of Canada? RB emphasized time and again how important and independent the governor's position would be. But, he asserted, "there is not one general manager of a bank in Canada who would undertake this position ... I put it to them in committee; I asked them then and there. Anyone who is appointed governor of the Bank of Canada would have to get experience." That did not mean, RB said, that a Canadian would not be appointed; however, as of June 1934, no Canadian appeared to be qualified. And he deplored the tone of the discussion raised by the Liberals, that it was intended that the Bank of Canada be an adjunct of the Bank of England. Nothing of the kind, RB said – he would use brains from any country. Premier Taschereau, when he needed a head for Quebec's Statistics Branch, had to go to Paris to find the right candidate. Henri Bourassa too deplored the tone of the Commons discussion, especially when the House had all along been fundamentally committed to the principle of a central bank. He remarked in his mature way (he had been an MP from 1896 to 1907 and again since 1925), "I think the two ablest men in Canada ... even with all their defects, are the Prime Minister of Canada and the Premier of Quebec."[50]

But the most heated discussion was yet to come. What language were the new Bank of Canada banknotes to be printed in? Raised early in June in the banking and commerce committee, the issue was soon a hot one in the Quebec papers. The banknotes, said the original legislation, were to be printed "in the French and English languages." What exactly did that mean? RB's firm opinion was that it meant English for banknotes in English Canada, and in French for French Canada. What on earth was wrong with that? But French Canadians on both sides of politics wanted bilingual banknotes. RB was definitely not having that! Lapointe moved an amendment in the Commons that both languages be used on Bank of Canada notes throughout the country. RB said Lapointe's amendment raised a question of "very serious moment" – and why now? In 1930 just before leaving office, the King government had ordered bills printed separately in the two languages. But RB had the bit in his teeth. "Nothing is more fatal than an effort to impose on a majority the will of a minority if the rights are established by law. Since when has it become the law of Canada that the will of a minority shall prevail over the will of the majority?" For years, he said, Canada's statutes, Canada's debates, had been issued in the two separate languages. In 1896 he supported the Tupper government's Remedial Bill for Roman Catholic schools in Manitoba. But then it was the law; now, he said, "I see my fellow citizens from Quebec ... subjected to those attacks in the press, so vicious in character, so uncalled for, denounced as traitors to their race ... I ask, is it fair, is it right, is it just?"[51]

Bourassa tried to cool off the sulphurous debate. All politicians, he said, make the most they can out of any question. Lapointe played it softly because he knew it was explosive; the prime minister, "disquieted as he rightly is, from appearance, at least, by the tone of some of the papers on the province of Quebec, has rather exaggerated." He had known the people of Quebec a long time, Bourassa said; the French Canadian farmer or artisan did not give a damn what language his money came in. It could be "in French or English or Chinese or any other language." It was money. At least, he said, we'll be doing away with those lugubrious old banknotes with the pictures of bank presidents and general managers on them, "some of them good, honest people, some of them –"

Here he was interrupted by MP Chubby Power: "– Less honest."

Bourassa finished his sentence: "– High class crooks." He added that throughout his often agitated life he had always tried to get French Canadians to understand English Canadians, and vice versa. "If we do understand each other we can accomplish wonders." So a heated, passionate, and characteristic Canadian debate was mitigated by Bourassa's common sense.[52]

In banknotes there lay another characteristic Bennett departure. Those issued by the chartered banks were secured by the banks' own gold. For the banks the difference between the cost of the gold and the total value of their banknote issue was free capital. The banknote issue was thus profitable, and the banks did not want to give it up, nor the gold that secured it. The Bank of Canada Act accepted the principle that the banks' notes would be gradually extinguished, and the gold would be taken over by the Bank of Canada. The question was, at what price? The old price, at which the banks themselves had acquired the gold, was $20.65. It was now $35.40. The banks wanted their gold taken over at the new price. RB thought it iniquitous that the banks would make a capital gain of 75 per cent on the backs of Canadian taxpayers. He met with the bankers around 30 May 1934 at the Château Laurier. It was anything but an amiable exchange. Dr G.D. Stanley, MP for Calgary East, was waiting for RB when he emerged afterward. "I never saw R.B. quite so worked up and wrathy, almost vicious, as I saw him on that particular occasion ... I was never so impressed with R.B. as that morning. It took a man of capacity and determination to stand up against the bigwigs of finance and tell them where they got off at."[53]

Another MP, James Stitt, MP for Selkirk, went to RB wondering if the gold transfer to the Bank of Canada was even constitutional. "He listened to me carefully," said Stitt, "then turned to me and with his eyebrows bristling like quills on a fretful porcupine said, 'Jimmie Stitt, you quit worrying. We are going to get that gold and it is just about time for us to find out whether the banks or this government is running this country.'"[54]

On Tuesday, 28 June 1934, holidaying at Murray Bay, Graham Towers, the assistant general manager of the Royal Bank, received a phone call from a Mr Rose in the Department of Finance at Ottawa. On his returning the call, Finance said there was no Mr Rose: was it possibly Mr Rhodes, the minister? It was. Towers did not know Rhodes "from a load of hay," but Rhodes wanted to see him. So did Bennett.

Towers went to the meeting and was offered the governorship of the Bank of Canada. He really did not want it but asked for time to think. RB said he was leaving for Paris the next day: would Towers report his decision to Sir George Perley, acting prime minister? Towers liked his Montreal life but decided that if he had to move to Ottawa, he'd better have a decent salary. He was not wealthy and he had watched his father go bankrupt. He accepted RB's offer and, despite his initial hesitation, never regretted doing so. Nor, it soon appeared, did anyone else. The appointment was made on 10 September 1934, and within five days Towers and his wife sailed for Europe on the *Empress of Britain*. That was RB's suggestion: a quick start, avoid awkward questions, and get off to Europe for central banking consultation and advice from European central bankers. It was to be Paris first, then Stockholm, Basle, Brussels, and Amsterdam, and then for the last two weeks of October, London. Towers won golden opinions everywhere. The Bank of Canada would open its doors on 11 March 1935.[55]

RB's own voyage to Europe was from New York for the September 1934 meeting of the League of Nations. He had with him a thirty-seven-year-old official from External Affairs, Lester Pearson. Mike Pearson's cleverness, ductility, and vivacity came with smiles and bonhomie. External Affairs was RB's own department. He liked it and quite enjoyed the international circuit and indeed was good at it. He had found Mike Pearson exceptionally useful, first as secretary to the Royal Commission on Grain Futures, 1930–31, and again in 1934 when he made Pearson secretary to the far more exigent Royal Commission on Price Spreads, when the Commons committee had outrun its time and had to be reconstituted. Pearson could also work from 9 AM to midnight, seven days a week if needed. RB liked that about him. When they boarded ship in New York, he noted that Pearson looked worn out; Pearson was quite capable of faking a little of that so that RB would send him off on a trip as a bit of a break. It was perhaps on this trip that RB told Pearson that he had intended in August 1930 to fire Skelton but had simply found him too useful.[56]

RB believed in the League of Nations. The advent of Hitler as German chancellor in January the previous year made him very uneasy. He said in London, Ontario, on 8 December 1933 that "the transcendent duty of every lover of peace – and that means every Canadian – is to support the League of Nations in its struggle for the maintenance of peace, for the obligations of the Treaty of Versailles are being flouted." But privately he admitted that Canada as a country of ten and a half million people – a little more than Belgium – could only do so much. Nevertheless, Canada should stand up in the League of Nations and do its part. On that front Mackenzie King was much more pusillanimous. The two as ministers of External Affairs were quite different, in thought, word, and deed. They agreed, however, that secrecy in international relations was essential. A prime minister, RB said in 1936, often had information that others had not, and if in his view the public interest would be served by not revealing it, then so be it. Thus he supported Mackenzie King in May 1936.[57]

In External Affairs, as across the rest of the government's Inside Service (viz. Ottawa), the Civil Service Commission's writ ran strongly. The CSC had been created in 1908. RB had supported the idea of a nonpartisan civil service all his life. He hated political interference. He and Sir Robert Borden were of the same mind, nurtured in the same school of thought. Brought up in Maritime societies that were steeped to the lips in patronage, both reacted sternly against it. Both would have derived wry amusement from the idea in Gilbert and Sullivan's *Iolanthe* (1882) that members of the House of Lords should earn their peerages by competitive examination.

The most interesting example of RB's dislike of political pressures on civil service appointments was in 1933–34. In 1933 R.B. Hanson was MP for York-Sunbury, and he was not a Maritimer for nothing. He was pushing the appointment of Douglas Woods, a bright young constituent, for third secretary in External Affairs. RB was not having it, not even from a New Brunswick supporter whom he liked. "I would be unfit for this office," he told Hanson sharply, "if, in view of the open character of the [External Affairs] examinations ... I were to indicate [a preference] ... it would be most improper to indicate to the Civil Service Commission what I wanted them to do." Thus chastised, Hanson apologized, but offered as defence that the postmaster general, Arthur Sauvé, whenever opportunity offered, would "load the dice" with secret instructions to the rating officers. A recent example, Hanson said, was the appointment to the postmastership at Campbellton, New Brunswick.

RB refuted that presumption. Hanson was to let him know of any such interference by the postmaster general or anyone else in Civil Service Commission recommendations. A Montreal postmastership appointment had gone to an English speaker over French Canadian protests. As for the Campbellton appointment, that went to the csc nominee.

Hanson did not give up. There are back doors in such matters, and he tried through Arthur Merriam, RB's private secretary, at least to find out what happened. Merriam told him that Woods had passed the External Affairs examinations all right but that some three hundred applicants had written those exams. Woods and several others had been interviewed by the Selection Committee, RB, Skelton, and the commission. But Woods's chances were not good: some eighteen candidates had passed the examinations with better marks. RB told a supporter in September 1930 that "he had never attempted to exercise political influence with the Civil Service Commission and doubt[ed] it could be done."[58]

It can thus be said that RB's view of what politics ought to be was much more rigorous than that either of his colleagues in cabinet or many in caucus. He had an income big enough to be scornful, sometimes not without arrogance, of the political world in which he moved. To him it was a high calling to serve the Canadian state as he believed it should be done by those called to its service. He had said so in Winnipeg in 1927 and would reiterate it again in Ottawa in 1938. Public life, he said, "is a philosophy of service, not of opportunism. Not of power, except to serve. Not of place, except as a means of service, not of the party but of mankind, for the high and low, for the poor and rich, for equality under the law." He might well have agreed with Marley's ghost in Dickens's *Christmas Carol*: "'Business!' cried the Ghost, wringing its hands again, 'Mankind was my business; charity. mercy, forbearance, and benevolence, were all my business. The dealings of my trade were but a drop of water in the comprehensive ocean of my business!'" RB did not always succeed in living up to that stance, but he would try. He was a Methodist, and an unusually devoted one. His private secretary, Andrew MacLean, remarked in 1934 that RB believed those in government should be the ablest and the best. Mackenzie King, MacLean added, faced with a political decision, would ask himself, "What do the people want?" RB on the other hand would ask, "What would be in the best interests of the people?" RB could well choose an unpopular course of action if he believed it was in the public interest. Elitism? Of course it was elitism. In RB's eyes that was what government was about, the wisest and the best governing, as near selflessly as possible in the best interest of the many.[59]

That perspective perhaps helps to explain RB's attitude to the press. Newspaper editors and reporters were never high-minded enough for him. He disliked intensely their distortions, their peremptory, loaded questions. Those jostling journalists of the newspaper world sought not truth but exposés, snippets to titillate their readers. They made the business of governing much harder. So RB was frequently scornful, dismissive, angry, even at friendly newspapers and their owners and their editors, if they violated what he believed were the proper canons of reporting news. He wrote an angry letter in February 1934 to the managing director of the *Ottawa Journal*, the Ottawa Conservative paper: "It has always been matter of wonder to me that the newspapers in this country never admit that anyone connected with them can make a mistake ... I think I can say to you that there is not a day goes by that I do not detect an error, that sometimes is very serious in one and sometimes several of the newspapers that pass through my hands." The problem was a report of an interview between the Trade and Labour Congress and the Government over section 98 of the Criminal Code. The reporter said the TLC had not asked for repeal when in fact it had. Norman Smith, the president of the *Ottawa Journal*, replied the same day. "This time you certainly have us – on toast ... [it] only proves that reporters, like politicians and even some statesmen are human, make blunders that are more or less unfortunate." But Smith wasn't going to be allowed to get away with that. RB came right back: "While politicians, statesmen and even reporters are always ready and willing to admit they make mistakes, those who employ reporters never are."[60]

The same ruthlessness of mind girded him in facing opposition. Sometimes it is better labelled gall. In early days, electioneering in Alberta, he stopped at a farm where a farmer was digging a well, which was half dug. They talked politics, but the farmer couldn't make up his mind. Finally RB grabbed the ladder and shoved it back down the well. "You go ahead and finish your work and then we'll talk." The farmer looked at RB for a minute and then said, "Any man that's got as much gall as you deserves my vote." In giving speeches, RB quite enjoyed hecklers, for he could usually face them down. Dalhousie student debates, the Alberta legislature, western courtrooms, and his own quickness of mind, his vast store of information on law, history, and wheat had given him a carapace not easily penetrated. He was not easily cowed, not readily given to being cast down by adversity. He had been through much of it in his life; he had triumphed over it. His government would do so too if he could possibly manage it.[61]

By the autumn of 1934 the party had become gloomy enough; the Liberals under Mitch Hepburn in June had swept the long-established Ontario Conservative government out of office; Jimmy Gardiner had brought the Liberals back in Saskatchewan. Of six federal by-elections on 24 September, Bennett's party had only taken one. By October 1934 everyone in the party was anxious and a bit dismayed about the future; the political outlook was grim and the economic one the same. The Conservative MPs and senators gave a dinner at the country club in Hull in RB's honour. He was marvellous at rallying the "boys." He made a speech of half an hour; after that the whole roomful felt as if they owned and commanded the earth, and like the mouse, they could have cried, "Bring on your damned cat!"

Going home afterward in his car with an old Alberta friend, Brig.-Gen J.J. Stewart, RB was in a very affable mood. There was a mutual glow of appreciation. Stewart asked him how he could understand the thoughts that troubled ordinary men. At the right time, Stewart said, RB could cheer them up "& force us to admire & worship you." And RB said, "John, I'll always remember the pit from which I was digged [sic] & the long uphill road I had to travel. I'll never forget one step."[62]

6

Reformer Redux, 1934–1935

RB was looking at drafts of radio speeches that he was going to give in the new year of 1935. Rod Finlayson, his young executive assistant, had put together some ideas from Bill Herridge in Washington. "You'll look like a reformer," Finlayson said.

RB's eyebrows shot up. "Reformer? Of course I'm a reformer." He got Finlayson to bring down from the shelf the 1911 *Commons Debates*. There, in the Address in Reply to the Speech from the Throne, on November 1911, was the neophyte Conservative MP's reform ideas: unemployment insurance, workmen's compensation, non-partisan civil service, government boards to control railway rates, government this and government that, and through it all a high-minded impatience with pump-priming politics. RB had been forty years old then, newly elected MP for Calgary, with plenty of gusto, quite ready to push his party into reforming Canada. Not for him the seventeenth-century scepticism of Molière: "*C'est une folie à nulle autre seconde/ Vouloir se mêler de corriger le monde*" – "'Tis the worst of follies if your plan/ Is to try to start reforming man." But that was not the way of Methodists. Methodism was eighteenth century, not seventeenth, and optimistic, not sceptical.[1]

RB was still a reformer, all right. The trouble was, he did not look the part. Height five feet, eleven inches, with a generous belly (corporation, as it was called then), meticulously groomed, he looked the epitome of a cartoon capitalist.

The mandate of the Seventeenth Parliament of Canada would run out by the end of 1935, leading to a dissolution of Parliament and a general election. The radical proposals in RB's radio broadcasts of early January made it look like he had undergone a death-bed repentance. So said Mackenzie King and others. But RB denied that in the House of Commons on 21 January 1935 just after Parliament opened. He admitted that his proposals could indeed look like that. But he stoutly maintained that it was the improving economy, the slow upward plane of prosperity – too slow, indeed, but upward – that allowed him to propose the major reforms that now were in train. He had had them in mind for some time, but until the fall of 1934 they were simply too dangerous to attempt. The whole energies (and revenues) of the government had been set on keeping the country from following the example of Australia, where a major state, New South Wales, defaulted on its loans; the Canadian ship of state, to use his metaphor, was being steered safely into harbour. "We were concerned with the problem of saving this country from absolute ruin," he told the House, "from bankruptcy. Day in and day out, week in and week out, month in and month out, year in and year out our concern has been the safety of Canada."[2]

In power, his own hopes and ambitions were chastened by three realities, RB said: what was financially feasible, what was constitutionally possible, and what he could get his cabinet to accept. It is often said that his cabinet was afraid of him; indeed, many in it were, but their fear could not prevent them from resigning if their ideas were too grossly affronted. The cabinet was as divided on the question of reform as on the question of inflation, between hard line Conservatives like C.H. Cahan, with the *Montreal Gazette* behind him, or Edmond Ryckman of Toronto (who had died in December 1933), or seventy-seven-year-old Sir George Perley, and the more reform-minded like H.H. Stevens and Robert Manion. Prior to late 1934 it is probable that RB could not get his cabinet to accept the reforms he would have wanted. By December, however, some of them were more willing to listen to some radical rhetoric or at least not resign over it. In any case RB did not ask them to approve the new departures. The January broadcasts came as a surprise to the cabinet, pleasant or unpleasant, as the case may have been. Cahan was appalled at the constitutional stretch required to justify some of the legislation.

In 1950, RB's brother, Capt. Ronald Bennett, told Robert Rogers, an early Bennett researcher, that before 1934 the reforms RB wanted to set up were "far in advance of public opinion and of opinion in his party." His position is well illustrated by a convocation address he gave to Rensselaer Polytechnic Institute, at Troy, New York, on 16 June 1934. We live, he said, in an interdependent world: the shot in Sarajevo on 28 June 1914 that launched World War I was felt along the Saskatchewan River in Canada. And the pursuit of liberty alone led only to anarchy, as the search for security as an end itself led to autocracy. "Fear," he said, "is the father of despotism." What could be done to overcome this fear, to restore security? "Is the day not passed when that government governs best which governs least [?] ... The intervention of the state then is inevitable in the economic field – not to destroy freedom; not to curb initiative, but to preserve freedom and release initiative; not to create socialism but to destroy economic feudalism. The intervention of the state is not revolutionary – it is restorative."³

There was also a major and sustained push for reform from RB's brother-in-law, Bill Herridge, Canadian minister to Washington. From the time that he and Mildred arrived in Washington in 1931, he had been a success. Quick, intelligent, adaptable, and shrewd, he soon won golden opinions; this was especially true with the Democratic administration of Franklin Roosevelt, sworn in on 4 March 1933. Herridge struck up close acquaintance with several of the "brains-trusters," especially Raymond Moley, who seems to have taught him something of the new economic theories of John Maynard Keynes. To be in Herridge's presence, said Dean Acheson, Roosevelt's under-secretary of the Treasury, "was to be alive, to be moving, and to be breathless."

By 1934 Herridge had also developed a fairly robust opinion of the talent and political astuteness of William Herridge. "I think by this time," he told Rod Finlayson, "the Government should have it in its head that when I recommend a thing it is generally right." There was a headlong quality to his mind, and too often he suited his actions to his thought. Quick to assimilate new ideas, he was also quick to launch them, even before they were mature enough to be launched. He had a natural talent for hyperbole. He was not a diplomat and it showed. In Ottawa he had not been known as "Wild Bill" for nothing.

It was a great pity, he told Finlayson, that Canada's destiny was being arbitrated by "the type of halting intellect which characterizes the personnel of the Tory Cabinet." (His opinion of the Canadian civil service was no better. Bob Coats of the Dominion Bureau of Statistics seemed to be "one of the few oases in the awful Ottawa desert of wooden-headedness.") Herridge claimed in May 1935 that he had never had any fixed view of what the best social and economic changes should be; nevertheless, he continued to believe that laissez-faire was "far more dangerous to our [Canadian] peace and prosperity than the so-called radical ... Resist the forces making for change and you provoke chaos. Work with those forces and direct them and you make progress."⁴

But he had something of the impatient Keynesianism of the Roosevelt New Dealers, and he had retailed it with long and frequent harangues to Finlayson through 1934, some of that time chuckling to himself over how he would steal a march on King by using ideas from King's own *Industry and Humanity*. The most notorious public display of Herridge's indiscretion was a speech he gave to the Ottawa Canadian Club on Saturday, 15 December 1934. RB, Mackenzie King, and Sir Robert Borden were at the head table at a huge luncheon in the Château Laurier. There was economic good sense in some of Herridge's long speech, but it came in a cloud of rhetoric, some of it unpalatable. "Had I the power," said he grandiloquently, "I would throw over our economic system in a flash, if I thought there was a better one available." But he added later on, "Let us search through this system and see what is wrong with it and what we can do to right it." That was sensible. The trouble with Herridge was that he let loose the preacher in him inherited from his father; his speech was prolix, hortatory, demagogic. After it was over, RB turned to Borden beside him and muttered, "That speech arouses in me distinctive [*sic*] antagonism." Borden replied, "In me, also."

RB himself had already made five speeches in December in eastern Canada in which he promised to curb the excesses of business manipulation, a preview of his four radio addresses that began on Wednesday, 2 January 1935. They were heavily Herridge but shorn of Herridge's exaggerations and rhetoric. Even so, they were dramatic enough: "The old order is gone," RB thundered over the air waves. "I am for reform. And, in my mind, reform means Government intervention. It means Government control and regulation. It means the end of laissez-faire." What followed in the next three speeches was discussion of the legislation that was to come. The rhetoric was stern: "Selfish men, and the country is not without them, whose mounting bank rolls loom larger than your happiness, corporations without souls and without virtue, these fearful that government might impinge on what they have come to regard as their immemorial right of exploitation will ... call us radicals ... the first step on the road to socialism. A ten per cent surtax on incomes over $280,000."

Sir Robert Borden thought RB's government was certainly on the right track but admitted that the "socialistic tinge of his addresses was rather disconcerting at first to leaders in business, industry and finance." It was also so to some in the cabinet, which had not been consulted about the speeches. Bennett's reason for this fait accompli was almost certainly that consultation would have disrupted cabinet. Cahan was soon on the verge of resigning. In general, however, there was a chorus of appreciation from the party. Borden observed, "Undoubtedly, the Prime Minister has entirely changed the current of political thought in Canada by his enunciation of these policies. It is a remarkable achievement and illustrates his high courage." All would depend, Lord Atholstan, owner of the *Montreal Daily Star*, told Borden, on the concrete proposals submitted to Parliament.[5]

The trouble was that the legislation to implement RB's ideas was by no means ready. Indeed, when he made his speeches, it had not even yet been drafted. King got wind of this through the shrewdness of Sir William Mulock, the bearded ninety-one-year old Liberal veteran. Mulock came to Ottawa on 15 January, two days before Parliament opened, to suggest strategy. King usually found it a trial entertaining old Mulock, but now the effort was well rewarded. Don't try to fight the government, said Sir William. Offer cooperation. They're not ready; in any case, all they want to do is to box you into a corner called laissez-faire. Don't let them do it. Indeed, that was exactly what Herridge had in mind. Then would RB & Co. go to the polls and saddle the Liberals with opposing important and progressive legislation. King told his senior colleagues what he thought should not be done – that is, they should not fight the government at all. Under the watchwords "unity and secrecy," the Liberal caucus was to be told nothing yet of this plot but were implicitly to trust headquarters.[6]

Parliament was to meet on Thursday, 17 January. Before it did, there was a crisis over the speaker of the House, George Black, Conservative MP for Yukon. A New Brunswicker, Black had gone to the Yukon in the gold rush of 1898. Speaker since 1930, he had now developed a psychiatric disorder, possibly the result of a brain tumour, and his language was out of control, his swearing enriched by a Yukon vocabulary of obscenities. RB said to King, "What a terrible thing mental affliction is." There was a scene at the big Château Laurier dinner that RB gave for the new Japanese minister, Iyemasa Tokugawa. Speaker Black came in, and Bennett said sharply to him, "Black, what are you doing here? You go to bed." According to King, RB spoke so roughly that Mildred broke into tears. Black gathered up what dignity he had and said that for Mildred's sake he would go. The next day he wrote RB a venomous letter telling him just what he thought of him, and resigned as speaker. Nevertheless, when Parliament opened, Black attempted to take his seat as MP in the Commons and had to be restrained by the sergeant-at-arms. Put in his office under a guard, he smashed a window or two trying to get out. The irony of the story is that, presumably cured of his illness, Black was re-elected for Yukon in 1940 and in 1945. He remarried in 1957 and died in 1965 at the age of eighty-two.[7]

The 1935 Throne Speech was deliberately upbeat. The "anxious years" were passing. Changes were, however, necessary to correct "grave defects and abuses in the capitalist system." Proof of the need for change lay in continuing unemployment and want. Parliament would therefore be presented with measures to reform the capitalist system "to remedy the social and economic injustices now prevailing." As to why such legislation had not been introduced earlier, RB explained later, the parlous state of the economy had enjoined controlling measures to keep things from getting much worse "during the four long years I have been endeavouring to sail this ship of state safely into the harbour."[8]

Prominent Liberals, said RB, had come to his office to thank him for the legislation already put into effect to stabilize the ship. Mackenzie King interjected, "Who?" RB replied, "Burton of Simpson's, for one." In the previous four years, he added, he and his cabinet were concerned with saving the financial and industrial structure of Canada; now he wanted to ensure that such a situation could never happen again: "We were concerned with the problem of saving this country from absolute ruin, from bankruptcy. Day in and day out, month in and month out, year in and year out our concern has been the safety of Canada ... When the evidence became clear that the greatest danger of the depression had passed, that the country was on the upward grade and moving towards complete recovery, I conceived it my solemn duty to introduce to the House such measures as I believed would prevent a recurrence of those dangers."

When the government came into power on 7 August 1930, RB had ordered a survey of what the government's financial condition really was. It was frankly awful. Whole layers of contracts had been issued by the King government in its last ten days in office as if there were no tomorrow. Almost at once the Bennett government was faced with having to raise a loan of $100 million. They did it in New York at 4 per cent. So the measures now being proposed in 1935 were anything but a death-bed repentance; the government simply could not do them before. Stark evidence is RB's heartfelt letter to Sir Robert Borden from the depths of October 1933, as Canada faced what he saw as the greatest crisis of its history: "The real difficulty is that we are subject to the play of forces we did not create and which we can neither regulate nor control. We are between the upper and the nether millstone. We are a debtor country ... Our people have been very steady, but they are depressed and having listened on the radio to so much 'ballyhoo,' they are now demanding Action! Action!! Action!!! Any action at this time except to maintain the

ship of state on an even keel and trim our sails to benefit by every passing breeze involves possible consequences about which I hesitate even
to think."[9]

Now, in January 1935, the government was groping for time, for light
and air, so to speak, in order to get its legislation drafted and ready. On
28 January, RB moved the House into committee to discuss "the expedi-
ency of introducing a bill to establish a national employment service" –
in effect, unemployment insurance. The full bill would have to await the
report of the Price Spreads Commission. On 31 January a private member proposed a resolution that the 1932 Ottawa Agreements merited the
approval of the House. That peculiar resolution had the virtue of bringing out some statistics, that the total Canadian exports to the empire had
gone up 60 per cent since 1932. Fundamentally, however, it was a mark-
time resolution. Early in February, RB brought in legislation covering
International Labour Office rules, the eight hour day, and the forty-eight
hour week. To assuage doubts about the constitutionality of the legislation, he was counting on Section 132 of the BNA Act allowing the
dominion government to implement international treaties. The debate
on that proposal took up some fifty-five pages of the Commons Debates.

At 11 AM on 21 February, RB's secretary phoned King's secretary for
an appointment. Could RB meet King at King's room in the Commons
at 12:45? At first the two men talked about Queen's University. RB was
chancellor of Queen's, now three years into a six-year term, and had
just returned from a visit to Kingston. Both agreed that Queen's turned
out "more men of real value to the country than any other college." RB
said that Dalhousie had been like that a few years earlier, implying that
it had slipped somewhat since. He had not forgotten his row with Dalhousie (he was on the Dalhousie board of governors) over Professor
R.A. MacKay's Beauharnois article in Maclean's in 1931.[10]

The purpose of RB's visit to King was to discuss arrangements for
George V's Silver Jubilee on 6 May 1935. Would King serve on a small,
senior bipartisan committee with Cahan and Sir George Perley? He had
had more experience with such things than anyone else except perhaps
Perley. King was willing though not anxious to assume new responsibilities. As RB was talking, King realized that his request meant RB would
not be in Canada in May but in England.

RB talked frankly about himself and his problems. He was very tired
and needed rest, and he did not know how or when it could be managed.

They then talked about Cahan. King had been told by Cahan that he'd given up a law practice worth $40,000 a year on coming into RB's cabinet. RB said Cahan had been much disappointed at being offered only the post of secretary of state; he thought he deserved a bigger portfolio than that. Nevertheless, he had done a remarkably thorough job in the office. The trouble with Cahan, said RB candidly, was that he was difficult to work with and irritated other colleagues with his harsh, strident voice. That was part of the reason why H.H. Stevens resigned from cabinet in October 1934, RB said. "Now, Harry, you must do this and do that," Cahan would say at the top of his voice across the cabinet table. It had exasperated Stevens terribly.[11]

However, Stevens's resignation was much more closely linked to his activities with the Price Spreads committee and the following royal commission. In the eyes of many in the cabinet, he and his parliamentary committee had been overstepping the mark, accusing Canadian capitalists of price-fixing. This issue came to a head when Stevens's address to the Conservative Study Club on 26 June 1934 was printed up as a pamphlet and some three thousand copies were sent to a very wide distribution. The *Winnipeg Free Press* received a copy and published it. RB found out about the pamphlet when C.L. Burton, president of the Robert Simpson Company, threatened to sue unless Stevens retracted his remarks. On being contacted by RB, Stevens claimed he'd had nothing to do with it being published. But James Muir of the Dominion Bureau of Statistics told RB that Stevens had gone over the text very carefully. RB left for Geneva shortly thereafter. At the first cabinet meeting after his return on 25 October, just prior to his arrival at it, Cahan had gone after Stevens for the report's inaccuracies, and the inappropriateness of the chairman of a royal commission speaking out before all the evidence and the views of his commission colleagues were in and taken into account. Stevens thereupon tendered his resignation, not expecting it to be accepted. But it was.

Now RB and King talked about the governor general, Lord Bessborough, who wanted badly to return to England; Lady Bessborough found the Ottawa winters very trying. Bennett was trying to persuade Bessborough to wait, for his term had another year or more to go. He had had a difficult time replacing Lord Willingdon in 1931. Candidates were usually peers of the realm, and they usually had several directorships of large companies, which they would have to give up on becoming Canadian governor general. Once given up, such positions were not easy to get back. As to a new governor general, King told RB candidly that his government no longer had the confidence of the country, and in those circumstances RB really did not have the right to make any such appointment.

King then said that prior to Bennett's New Deal speeches, he had intended to oppose the government in the 1935 session, but now, "I felt it was our own policy and a matter [in] which I had personally been deeply interested and that it would be necessary in the circumstances for me to change tactics and let him get through his social legislation. Personally I would be glad to get anything furthered that would help labour." However, King thought RB should be chary about making appointments. RB said only that the appointments he was mainly thinking of would be to the new (and not yet legislated) labour exchanges, for he wanted to get them established as soon as possible.

He then returned to the question of a new governor general. Would King, he asked, think over some names for the position? No doubt he would prefer a Liberal peer. Here King ventured a new departure. Perhaps, he said, "the time had come in the affairs of our country when it would be wise to choose someone who would stand for the same idea as [James] Bryce stood for when he went to the United States." RB was much taken with that idea. Bryce had been British ambassador to the United States from 1907 to 1913. His 1888 book, *The American Commonwealth*, "was the best thing the Americans had ever had." And indeed for that time, and for many a year afterward, it was a leading text in the United States.

King then suggested that John Buchan, a well-known British author, would be a good choice. A Lowland Scot, a writer of enthralling adventure stories, notably *The Thirty-Nine Steps* (1915), he was currently a British MP and thus familiar with parliamentary ways. True, said King, he was a Tory, but he would be able to rise above any narrow partisan attitude. RB embraced the idea of Buchan with enthusiasm. He had never thought of the House of Commons as a source for governor generals. "I will say to you frankly" he told King, "that [it] commends itself to me very much. I doubt if anything could be better."

King added that government Houses of Parliament in general, both in Ottawa and in the provinces, were in precarious balance, that scholarship and worth should now be more the criteria for governor generals and lieutenant governors, that Canada could not go on filling these offices with aristocrats and millionaires. Unless criteria were changed, they would be hastening the day "when there would be no Governor

General at all." He did not like what Hepburn wanted done in Ontario, closing down Government House in order to save money. RB noted that Alberta had tried the same thing but was forced by public opinion to revive it.

Their meeting ended with RB reiterating what an excellent idea appointing John Buchan was. He would talk to Lord Bessborough directly. "Our conversation," said King, "lasted for about an hour and from beginning to close was most friendly and genuinely pleasant. Bennett could not have been nicer and it seems to me he was genuinely glad to have a talk of the kind."

That was on Thursday, 21 February. RB was in Toronto two days later giving a rather *richesse oblige* speech on how God had been good to him and how in return he was working to show his gratitude. But the Toronto trip seems to have been too much for him. He got a cold; it got worse, and on Monday, 25 February, had to take to his bed. F.D.L. Smith, editor of the *Toronto Mail and Empire*, saw him the next weekend and reported him much worse than was generally understood. Ned Rhodes told King that RB had never quite got over the illness that had affected him in Geneva in September 1934.

By early March most of RB's ministers, without RB's imperious presence, seemed adrift from moorings. King reported that the House of Commons without him "seems a sort of a morgue." Rhodes was handling the House fairly well in the circumstances, but Cahan was difficult. Stevens had not shown up at the House yet, though he was at the Royal Commission on Price Spreads, continuing to leak tidbits to the *Toronto Star*. The cabinet covered up the exent of RB's illness, and Sir George Perley issued mild medical bulletins. Neither cabinet nor RB wanted it known how serious his condition was, though he did not mind telling King, who had written him a commiserating letter. In an appreciative reply on 6 March, RB said he was like Oliver Wendell Holmes's "one-hoss shay" that goes on and on, built so superbly that the chaise doesn't wear out until it finally breaks down.[12]

There was premonitory truth in RB's whimsical observation. He had been planning to return to the Commons on Thursday, 7 March. When the nurse came into his room at the Château that morning, she found him in a chair unconscious, white as a sheet and bathed in sweat. It was a heart attack, a blood clot somewhere around his heart, brought on by the diabetes for which he was already taking insulin. He was delirious with a high fever and was, it seems for the first time, really concerned about himself. There were conflicting reports; the government continued to give out anodyne statements that the prime minister was much better. The probable truth was that he was much worse – more so, certainly, than anyone had been allowed to believe. Dr Stevens, his physician, was asked by cabinet to issue a statement that the prime minister's illness was slight and that he was getting on fairly well. Indignant at such a suggestion, Stevens said he would do nothing of the kind. Before he would even express an opinion, the prime minister would have to go to bed for a fortnight. And it would be a much longer time before he could resume any work. If he kept very quiet, got well rested, moved to another climate, and took things very easy, he would have three years of life ahead of him.

Manion, who saw RB that Sunday and spent three hours with Stevens, had seen the electro-cardiograms and confirmed a heart attack. He urged RB not to go to England for the Jubilee, citing Dr H.A. Bruce, lieutenant governor of Ontario (1932–37), and other Conservatives in support of RB's staying home. At that suggestion, said Manion, RB "fairly hit the roof ... and unless something strange happens, he is going to go and nothing can stop him, irrespective of the results."

Meanwhile, RB's cabinet were in disarray. He carried so much of what he was planning to do in his own head that they were in the dark about too many things, and found it "greatly embarrassing." Rhodes had a candid report for Sir Robert Borden, wintering in Augusta, Georgia: "The situation in the House is most curious. My colleagues are taking up various Bills which stood in the name of the P.M., but, as was his custom, he had kept the contents of the Bills and the material to be used with them, entirely to himself, with the result that we are now in the position of having different Ministers coached by his Secretary. Poor Sir George is daily worried that we will not have sufficient business with which to carry on. At the end of each day we fall back on Estimates ... It will be news to you that the Government at any time, and especially before an election, is embarrassed in securing sufficient work to prolong the session."[13]

The *Toronto Star* of Saturday, 9 March, echoed the widening speculation: "After Mr. Bennett, who?" The Conservative caucus would probably have voted 60 per cent for Harry Stevens, the cabinet for Rhodes. Ned Rhodes was not well known, for he had never made an effort to be known. Stevens was known far and wide; he enjoyed publicity and indeed cultivated it. He had been attending the Price Spreads Commission but until 15 March, a week after RB's heart attack, made no appearance in the Commons. Then he came to the debate on the Minimum

Hours bill (to implement a League of Nations Convention) and attacked Cahan savagely. He was, as King put it, heavily demagogic. "I shall not soon forget the Ministers looking chagrined beyond words," King said. "Perley crouched beside Guthrie, both their heads down, others were in similar attitudes."

Stevens was clearly making a fairly brazen attempt to position himself to be the leader of the party. He said, dripping sarcasm to annoy Cahan, "I am a layman, one of those stupid laymen who are more or less incapable of appreciating the intricacies of legal matters." He had the zeal of the convert and the rhetoric to go with it. His argument was that no federal government had sufficiently tried to occupy the federal field of trade and commerce. Cahan, by no means a friendly witness, told King that in all the years he had known Stevens in cabinet, "he had never known him to say a word about social reform or ratification of any [international] conventions." The Conservative party seemed wracked with feuds, sharpened by RB's absence. The rank and file of the party tended to side with Stevens; the elders thought him an agitator, perhaps sharing King's view that he was "largely an adventurer, prepared to break through the most evident rules."[14]

The report of the Price Spreads Commission appeared in the *Toronto Star* of 8 April, leaked, it appeared, by Stevens who feared its emasculation by cabinet. It dismayed King that even his own followers were inclined to measure Stevens's strength by the extent to which he was applauded by what King called "the 'down and outs,' the dissatisfied elements, the discontents. What is to become of government," he wondered, "if that state of things goes on?" He especially deplored Stevens's ignorance of economics, his lack of a solid grip on theory and functions of the business world that he was so stridently criticizing.[15]

Despite talk that RB would soon be back in Parliament, the best he could manage was to see the governor general and meet with cabinet in private. On 18 April he phoned King to say that he had King George's permission to offer him a GCMG, Grand Commander of St Michael and St George. It was King's great opportunity to become Sir William Lyon Mackenzie King. He was delighted and much touched by the offer, but of course, as RB suspected, it was not an offer he could accept.[16]

King thought that RB would be travelling from New York on the *Berengaria*, at that time the biggest liner on the North Atlantic, 50,000 tons. King wished him a pleasant voyage. "Well, I don't know about the voyage," RB said. "I am going to have 'me' heart looked at when I am over there."

Parliament was adjourned for a month, until Monday, 20 May, not without complaints from MPs that it was a very long adjournment. Whatever King's source of information, RB crossed the Atlantic out of New York on the *Paris*, a French liner, and with Mike Pearson, of External Affairs, who had been seconded by RB as secretary of the Price Spreads Commission. Pearson had just completed an exhausting run of work getting the commission's report out and welcomed RB's invitation to accompany him overseas. It was indeed for a second year running, for they had gone to Geneva together the year before. RB liked Pearson; he was well read, intelligent, hard working, with a deft and infectious sense of humour. RB stayed, as he always did, at the Mayfair in Berkeley Square. One evening he and Pearson went for a walk in Green Park, just the other side of Piccadilly, when suddenly RB said, "I've put you down for an OBE in the Jubilee Honours, Pearson. What do you think of that?"

Pearson never had nor ever would have much of a taste for fuss and feathers, and replied with the casualness so characteristic of him, "I would rather have settled for a twenty-five-dollar-a-month raise, sir." There was a frozen silence, and Pearson wondered if he had put his foot in it properly. Would there be a price to pay for such unseemly sincerity? But after a while RB asked what his salary was. It was $296 a month – not at all bad, Peason said, but out of this he had to pay for a good deal of departmental entertainment and support a wife and two children. That at times made for thin going. In the end he got both. Later that summer he was playing tennis at the Rockcliffe Club when the governor general's ADC, Sir Alan Lascelles, came by. "Here's your OBE," he said, tossing the precious case containing it to him. Pearson was amused; RB would certainly not have been.[17]

RB went through the Jubilee ceremonies limply, still unwell. The highlight for him was a meeting of Commonwealth prime ministers at St James Palace to pay tributes to the king. RB said that his address to the king included Queen Mary and observed that she was in tears at the end. He added that the Jubilee story that most delighted the king was one heard from an old Eastender in London who, on hearing the king's broadcast, said to his wife, "The old bloke is just like any of us when he came to talk about his wife, he couldn't help crying." What most impressed RB was the way the English public cherished the royal family's home life. There was a lesson in that; the Prince of Wales, nearing his forty-first birthday, was developing his intense relationship with Wallis Warfield Simpson and seemed almost helpless to do anything about escaping from it. The king's disgust with was well under way too.

In April he had given orders that Mrs Simpson was not to be asked to any Jubilee functions nor to the Royal Enclosure at Ascot.[18]

RB arrived back in Ottawa on 17 May. King thought he looked anything but healthy, his eyes contracted, his breath bad. He told King that the London doctors said he had fatty degeneracy of the heart and should get out of public life. That, indeed, seems to have been his intention as he made his return voyage westward. Who, then, would take the leadership of the party? His idea was Rhodes, the ablest and most sure-footed of possible successors. But it was soon obvious that Rhodes, aged just fifty-eight, was no more able than RB in terms of health to undertake the work and the strain of being prime minister. He would be off for a day or two, but the moment he engaged the gears of work again, was back where he started. He went home at the end of May feeling unwell and found he had a temperature of 104F. He was then out of Parliament for ten days. Early in June, he told RB that he could not take on the leadership. Rather pathetically, he confided to King privately, "I don't know what I am going to do. I have no money and I have no profession." After being so long in political life, his lawyer's work had dried up. King sensibly suggested that Rhodes consider taking a senatorship – to which, indeed, RB appointed him in July after the session was over.[19]

Meighen was another possible successor, three years older than Rhodes but a good deal healthier. However, Meighen was still impossible for Quebec to accept, and he was not unhappy as a senator, a senior statesman in a senior position, respected and comfortable. What RB would not accept, could not accept, was the awful possibility that he might be succeeded as leader by Harry Stevens. So he would soldier on, come what may.

Before leaving for England, RB had made arrangements that the Price Spreads report, as soon as it came out (which it did officially on Friday, 12 April), was to be turned over to the law officers of the crown to have legislation prepared on its recommendations. Then, when the draft bills were ready, they were to go to special counsel, who would check out their constitutionality. Five modest bills had already gone to cabinet on 21 May. The larger, more comprehensive bills might not be proceeded with. RB told King, "I am not going to make Parliament a farce by flying deliberately in the face of the courts." Nevertheless, RB presided over cabinet debating these hard questions for at least another six days, perhaps longer. Cahan and his colleagues in cabinet suggested that RB's conception of constitutional law was too abstract, not sufficiently in tune with political realities. When asked in council to bring in a measure that violated his ideas of law, RB replied to cabinet, "There is something which a man must preserve at all costs, and that is his self-respect." It was deeply felt. While recounting this event to King, Cahan's voice broke. Two colleagues in cabinet had suggested to him, "Could you not work with Stevens and work out a compromise?" To this Cahan replied with feeling, "My God, have we come to that time in Canada when a Government is to bow before a man like Stevens who has no responsibility at present and who is simply stirring up feelings which he knows are not justified?" At that point Cahan did not know whether he would be in cabinet a week longer.[20]

Though no longer in cabinet himself, Stevens had his supporters in cabinet. Moreover, he still had support and pulling power in caucus. There was always something of the promoter in Harry Stevens. Optimistic, flamboyant, earnest, like most promoters he really believed in what he was saying. Western Canada certainly had its share of promoters, though as Max Aitken's career shows, eastern Canada was not devoid of them either; young countries need them. In Parliament, Stevens delivered his ideas with dash and flair, with the full force of his earnestness behind them. He was inclined to believe that what the public wanted, they ought to have, and the task of government, certainly that of the minister of trade and commerce, was to try to give it to them, Law and laws were all very well, but they could get terribly in the way of things that one felt just had to be done. That position does much to explain the rise and fall of his chairmanship of the Price Spreads Commission. As RB told the House of Commons on 19 June 1935, one difficulty of the commission was that "it did not adequately understand the extent to which existing legislation granted a remedy." Indeed, what Stevens lacked was what Sir John A. Macdonald used to call "heavy metal."[21]

When RB said in January that he proposed to implement the changes recommended by the Price Spreads Commission, he believed it would be urging changes that were *intra vires* of Parliament. The constitution needed changing; RB admitted that, but it couldn't be done by means of making certain actions crimes. The power to make and remake the Criminal Code did not give the government power to override constitutional law. As RB put it, "if the people of this country have been led into the belief that this parliament can pass any kind of legislation it likes regardless of the constitution, the age of lawlessness is upon us. Let there be no misunderstanding about that ... The first step toward dictatorship in Europe was what? It was a prejudicial appeal to the little man, that was first. Then followed the inevitable, the utter disregard of constitutional limitations."

Nevertheless there were powerful forces in cabinet and caucus urging reconciliation with Stevens for the sake of the party. With the election looming portentously on the horizon, it seemed to be of considerable urgency. About the middle of June, Stevens was somehow persuaded to return to caucus. But for whatever reason, RB seemed to pay no attention to his presence. Not having been at caucus for some little time, Stevens expected some notice, some hint of welcome. He didn't get it. Angry, he got up abruptly and left. RB later said he was busy with the caucus agenda and did not notice Stevens at the back. That was possible, with ninety to a hundred MPs in the room. Moreover, RB was still not well.

In the end Cahan stayed and Stevens went. A politician more adept and less rancorous than RB might have been able to keep Stevens in the party. But Stevens was proud, sensitive, his ego swollen by the success and the publicity for his work on price spreads and his ambition whetted by party friends and, not least, by his own family. By 19 June 1935 the cleavage between him and the rest of the Conservative party was visible, palpable. That day in the Commons, RB got the Tory applause; there was little for Harry Stevens. In the evening there was a banquet in RB's honour given by the party. That was when he announced that, barring any further breakdown in his health, he would be leading the party in the elections.[22]

RB's strong defence of constitutional proprieties against Stevens on 19 June was followed three days later by his robust, strident, indeed hectoring defence of law and order on Saturday, 22 June. He met the eight delegates from the On-to-Ottawa march in his East Block office late that Saturday morning. Perhaps "confrontation" is the word that best describes it. Neither side was willing to give very much, but the government was the more recalcitrant, backed as it was by a strong swell of newspaper opinion urging it to stand firm.

Like most *émeutes*, this one had a history. Canada had long had a resource-based economy, and since the turn of the century its immigration policy had been designed to feed it by bringing in large numbers of unskilled workers from Great Britain and Europe. Skilled workers were not discouraged, of course, but Canadian railways, lumber camps, farms, and mines needed raw manpower. The preponderance of unskilled workers was especially noticeable in the 1920s after the United States closed its doors to them after 1919. Thus the Canadian unemployment problem as it developed after 1930 was quite different from that in the United States, being concentrated far more heavily in single males, many of them recent immigrants. (Of the eight delegates of the On-to-Ottawa trek who met RB in Ottawa on 22 June, all but one was born outside of Canada.) Foreign born, unemployed single males formed a substantially larger percentage of the Canadian population than they did in the United States, and they were regarded by Canadian newspapers and the public as potentially more threatening. Thus both provincial and federal governments reacted early to this problem. In the winter of 1932–33, while American unemployed were still at the mercy of private charities, the Canadian federal government was already paying the cost of caring for something like 46,000 men under the Unemployment and Relief Act of 1932.[23]

The first employment relief camps were established in British Columbia, and they were originally proposed for both single men and men with wives. Major-General A.G.L. McNaughton suggested the idea to RB in October 1932, and he adopted it almost at once, though soon shorn of the amenities that British Columbia was already finding too expensive. The camps under the Department of National Defence were for single men, homeless, able-bodied, and unemployed. The camps soon held 11,000; by the time they were disbanded in 1936, they had taken in 170,000. To get in, a man had to be physically fit, not known as a political agitator. He was given work clothes, soap, towels and three fairly square meals a day. In British Columbia he got a single bunk bed (in the East they were double), and so there he had his own space. The bunkhouse was usually a tar-paper shack heated with a kerosene stove and furnished with showers, indoor toilets, and a laundry. Recreation and education were provided by Frontier College, the only federally supported college. Founded in 1899 in Ontario, it became national after 1918. University undergraduates would work in the camps in the daytime and teach in the evenings. In return for room and board, the labour camp men put in an eight hour day, forty-four hour week, mostly on road and airport construction.

As an idea, the federal relief camps were not all that bad. RB summed it up in February 1936, "Why did they come into being? For some government purpose? No. Did they come into being to provide homes? No. They came into being for the purpose of providing places where men might find food, clothing and shelter until they could find employment." The largest number of men in the camps at any one time was, he said, between 20,000 and 25,000. The average stay was ninety-five days. Long enough: the food was nourishing but dull. The pay was very low at twenty cents a day. Life must have been especially difficult there in the winters but at least there was food, shelter, and warmth.

RB, unannounced, visited two of the camps and told the Commons that "many, many Canadians are not nearly as well provided for as those who are living in those camps." In short it was not such a bad system if – and it is a big "if" – it did not last too long or if you were an older man. The *Vancouver Province* wrote," The young man has ambitions, and urges. He wants to be out and doing ... He wants to try his wings." For most of the workers in the camps it seemed a complete dead end, as if they were parked there like old cars rusting away in obscurity. One inmate wrote in his diary, "We are truly a lost legion of youth – rotting away for want of ... something to do and something for that doing."[24]

Into this bunkhouse world came of course radicals of various types, older, wily, experienced, disciplined, some of them communist sympathizers. They set up committees for this, committees for that, and in British Columbia worked up a strong union, the Workers' Unity League. It was communist affiliated, its organizer Arthur "Slim" Evans (1890–1944). Born in Toronto, tall, tough, brooding, looking a little like Boris Karloff, Evans was an agitator born and bred who seemed to think of nothing else but the class struggle. He was often up to the edge of the law and sometimes over it. In the camps there was, perhaps inevitably, a fair bit of tepid tea and some hot Marx.

There were so many complaints about the BC camps that Sir George Perley, as acting prime minister, on 30 March 1935 appointed a royal commission to report and make recommendations on them. It was headed by a former chief justice of the BC Supreme Court, W.A. Macdonald, and was almost certainly done with RB's advice and approval from his bed in the Château Laurier. The commission reported on 31 May 1935. They found not all that much wrong with the BC camps: minor complaints there were indeed, but fundamentally the unrest stemmed from young men too much in isolation, cut off from normal life. And they were not being paid an adequate wage for their physically demanding forty-four hour week. As one young Frontier College teacher/worker remarked, "The communists could not have engineered it [the strike of relief camp workers] unless they had a ground basis to work on and that basis is craving for life." It was the dead-endedness that rankled. How long, O Lord, how long?[25]

"Work and wages" was a marvellous slogan, but what could any democratic Canadian government, federal or provincial, do about meeting it? Hitler solved an analogous German problem by means of National Socialism and the Nazi Party, by frenzied rhetoric, Keynesian economics, and the *Autobahnen*.

The relief camp strike began 4 April. Vancouver was soon visited by some fifteen hundred unemployed; they were set up in four divisions of about four hundred men each; they would march in ranks of four, army style. It was impressive to many, intimidating to authority. There were committees for everything. In the words of one of the trekkers, "We couldn't slice a loaf of bread into five bologna sandwiches without appointing a committee to see that it was done according to plan. Discipline was an absolute must." By the last of May, however, the initial impetus was lost. Strikers were drifting back to the camps or leaving town, despite union pickets in the railway yards. The relief camp strike, after nearly eight long weeks, had little to show. A spontaneous snake dance through the main downtown Hudson's Bay Company store on Granville Street on 24 April got out of hand and resulted in Mayor Gerry McGeer reading the Riot Act. Prior to that, McGeer had done all he felt he was able to do and was soon fed up with strike and strikers as well as with Ottawa. He was not too happy with Victoria, either. There was another rampage at Woodwards on 18 May. The Vancouver public had been patient, but their sympathy and support was wearing thin by the end of May. Still, the union hung on. At a union meeting 30 May, two-thirds of the 909 ballots cast were resolutely in favour of keeping the strike going.

But if it were to be kept going, what next? One striker got up and said, "Comrades, I think we are through with Vancouver ... They [the federal government] won't come to us, so I say let us go to them. I hereby move we go to Ottawa to discuss work and wages with the federal cabinet." Slim Evans seconded the motion. It electrified the meeting, which went on all night. The issue was concluded by the next day. There was hardly a man at the meeting who was not a veteran of riding freight trains; the three thousand miles to Ottawa was a long way, but the idea was infectious, indeed dazzling. It was going to be, as one of them said, a great adventure. Departure was set for Monday evening of 3 June. Thus started the On-to-Ottawa trek.[26]

It was not all that easy. True, the fast freight trains stopped at divisional points and often waited obligingly while trekkers made for town where local supporters had sandwiches and coffee ready. In Golden, BC, in the upper Columbia valley, they stopped for a day. By then the trek had shed about a hundred not-so-stalwarts, and the organizers spent the day regrouping to count heads and make sure "division captains and platoon corporals" knew what was to be expected of them and their men. The hardest part of the trip was the spiral tunnels on the west side of Kicking Horse Pass, although the eleven-mile Connaught Tunnel through the Selkirks had not been a picnic. At Field, BC, just before the spiral tunnels, the train stopped, and two local Mounted Police and a railwayman briefed everyone about the dangers ahead from heat and smoke and from the lurching of the freight cars around those very tight curves in the tunnels.[27]

On Friday afternoon, 7 June, the trekkers arrived in Calgary. The city knew they were coming and tried to get the Edmonton government to fund their stay. Edmonton said it was Calgary's responsibility, so there was a certain amount of individual initiative required. The trekkers had their own tag day. They also blockaded the downtown office of the Alberta Relief Commission to the point where Edmonton relented and disgorged $600 for two meals a day. That blockade was perhaps a tactical error, for it became known as "the siege," and it reverberated badly in Ottawa. Calgarians seemed generous enough. They were impressed with the youth of the trekkers and their discipline. Marching to the freight yards to catch the 10 PM freight southeastward to Medicine Hat, some new recruits broke ranks and started "horsing around" with female spectators. The organizers jumped on it at once. "What the hell's going on here? Have you bastards gone mad? Do you think we've spent years building our organization to have you come and wreck it?"

The discipline impressed the public. At Swift Current, J.S. Woodsworth joined the trek at the behest of the *Winnipeg Tribune*, the Conservative paper. As the train pulled in, he expected the trekkers to invade Swift Current like a mob. Nothing of the sort! They formed fours immediately – standard British/Canadian armed forces formation until 1942 – and waited until all the men had climbed down from the freight cars, then marched into town "in real army style." Woodsworth was impressed with their youth, most of the men in their twenties but some just sixteen or seventeen years old. Their discipline and army-style marching had differing effects, however. It impressed the public but began to worry the government.[28]

RB's position, asserted time and again, was that the responsibility for law and order rested squarely with the provinces. Ottawa had nothing to do with it, he reminded the House of Commons. The federal government could not take any measure toward law and order and criminal administration except at the behest of provincial government. (As recently as 1970, Quebec asked Ottawa to intervene in the FLQ crisis.) Technically in 1935 (as in 1970), between a municipality like Vancouver or Montreal and the federal government, there was no legal point of contact. "The province and the province alone is the competent authority with which the dominion deals." If a province could not keep law and order, it could call on Ottawa. For, RB went on, "there can be no trifling with anarchy, there can be no playing with chaos ... mob violence, mob threats, mob law will not be the means by which to deal with matters of this kind between the province of British Columbia and the Dominion of Canada." That statement was made in the Commons on 21 May, the day after RB returned to work.[29]

BC Premier Pattullo in May and June 1935 did not ask for federal help. He and Vancouver were delighted to see the trekkers off eastward to oblivion beyond the borders of the province. In Saskatchewan in June 1935, Premier Gardiner, the recently elected Liberal premier, had not asked for federal help and appeared to have no intention of doing so. Thus the point of federal entry was narrowed to the Railway Act. Both CPR and CNR agreed to declare the trekkers' mode of transportation a trespass on railway property that would not be further allowed.

Another difficulty was that the government of Saskatchewan, not Ottawa, exercised control of the RCMP in Saskatchewan. Did Ottawa have the legal authority to order the RCMP to stop the trek in Regina, as Ottawa was now determined to do? There was thus a division between Ottawa and Regina, not only about the authority for action but what action was to be taken. RB sent Robert Weir, his Saskatchewan-born minister of agriculture, and Robert Manion, minister of railways, to see the Saskatchewan cabinet and then the trek leaders. They met severally on Monday, 17 June. There were thus a number of cards in play that Monday: the RCMP, the Saskatchewan government, the mayor of Regina, the Regina police, the CPR, the trekkers, and their leaders. Regina and its government, civic and provincial, wanted the trekkers peacefully out of town as soon as possible, in either direction, east or west.[30]

There were rumours that the trekkers wanted to leave that very evening on a fast freight, direction Ottawa. Manion successfully headed that plan off. He suggested that a delegation from the trekkers go to Ottawa by regular train at government expense – that is, inside the cars with berths and meals rather than on the outside of freight cars with smoke and wind and rain. They would meet with cabinet in Ottawa. In the meantime the rest of the trekkers would be fed and housed in Regina until the delegation reported back what the results were. That proposal was taken to a trekker meeting that afternoon. Manion reported to RB that the situation was very delicate. The leaders were radicals, very much in earnest, and should be cosseted as much as possible. In the end the trekkers accepted the Manion proposals, reluctantly. They seemed to feel that they had been "snookered."[31]

The eight leaders, with Slim Evans as their spokesman, met the federal cabinet in Bennett's East Block office on Saturday morning, 22 June, at 11:30. Most of the cabinet were there, RB and eleven others. H. Oliver, a regular parliamentary reporter, was brought in, probably by RB, to record exactly what transpired. RB told the House of Commons later that he was on his best behaviour, that he was trying to keep the talks as unruffled as possible: "I declined to indicate the slightest sign of temper, although heaven knows there had been good excuse for it, and I restrained myself from any violent statement of any kind despite the provocation. But when I heard [Slim] Evans say what he said as to his purposes, and Collins [Cosgrove] make the statements he did, I felt I would be recreant to my duty if I did not say to them that law and order would be maintained in the country because it was the duty of the federal government to preserve peace, order and good government." He added that, had Woodsworth been present, "he would have been amazed at my moderation – amazed at it."[32]

His representations to the contrary, RB was not very amiable, nor was it an amiable meeting. Most of the time it was hardly polite. There they were, RB for the government, Slim Evans for the trekkers, two tall fighting cocks, each conscious of his power and neither liking the other nor holding it back much. RB asked each man to introduce himself with names and places. After some minutes of Evans's statement of grievances, RB asked each man how old he was and where he had originally come from. It was a little too much like a drill sergeant. Only Evans was born in Canada, in Toronto. Of the other seven, three were English, one Scottish, one Irish, one Danish, and one from Newfoundland. Six of the men were single. Evans did not admit that he was married, though he was. Their purpose in coming to Ottawa, said Evans, "is to demand from you this programme of work and wages." RB answered that the camps were not established for that purpose. "That is passing the buck," Evans said, "we want work and wages."

MR BENNETT: "Just a moment."
MR EVANS: "You referred to us as not wanting work. Give any of us work and see whether we will work. This is an insidious attempt to propagandize the press on your part, and any body who professes to be Premier and uses such despicable tactics is not fit to be premier of a Hottentot village."

MR BENNETT: "I come from Alberta. I remember when you embezzled funds from your union and were sent to the penitentiary."
MR EVANS: "You are a liar. I was arrested for fraudulently converting these funds to feed the starving."[33]

It was as if Evans deliberately set out to get RB's goat, not always too difficult. After Evans and Cosgrove spoke, RB explained to the House of Commons, "I felt I would be recreant to my duty if I did not say to them that law and order would be maintained in this country."

He was soon in his sharp and bristly form, not at all forthcoming with soft answers. It was enough, said Agnes Macphail, who was fond of him, to make people communist who weren't already. The trek delegates left RB's East Block office angry. It was a pity, Woodsworth said later, that Evans had a criminal record, which "of course discounts him;" but Woodsworth believed RB had behaved "despicably." Nevertheless the general opinion of the newspapers supported Bennett, that he had not much option but to stand firm for law and order. That was not difficult for him; it was position long and firmly held.[34]

The truth was, however, that RB was worn out and irritable, putting a brave face on his many adversities. On 26 June, two days after the meeting with the trekkers, there was a provincial election in New Brunswick; the Liberals took every seat. They had done the same in Saskatchewan the year before. That was on top of provincial Liberal victories in British Columbia, Ontario, and Nova Scotia. The federal Liberal MPs were cock-a-hoop, parading around Commons corridors. King wondered how RB could carry on with the constant jabs and jibes from the Liberals across the floor.

When the House adjourned on the evening of Thursday, 27 June, RB came across to King's seat to confer about a resolution thanking the governor general, Lord Bessborough, now at the end of his term. They talked. King said RB must have had a difficult time altogether with his ministers. RB looked at him, glumly. "You've no idea how hard it was. Poor old Ned Rhodes is not half the man he was a few years ago. Guthrie is almost done for. I myself am done for. I am good for nothing more." King answered with a touch of drama: "There was nothing that saved those of us who sat on the front row of the last Parliament from the grave but the defeat of 1930."[35]

As for the trek delegates, after leaving RB's office they had called a meeting for the next evening, Sunday, 23 June, in an Ottawa theatre. There they threatened to come back to Ottawa from Regina, not with eight men but with thousands. En route west again, Evans allegedly said that "blood would flow in the streets of Regina." Attitudes hardened on all sides. The Saskatchewan government would not support the trekkers with funds for meals; the trekkers did not like the federal government's offer of shelter and meals in bell tents at Lumsden, twenty miles north of Regina. Under Evans's impassioned lead, the trekkers wanted to keep coming east to Winnipeg, where they could be greatly reinforced. That day the railways ended hitchhiking on freight trains. On Wednesday, 26 June, Evans put out a call for trucks to take trekkers to Winnipeg. He also tightened controls to prevent desertions to the Lumsden camp. Then on Thursday, Manitoba announced it would not accept the eastward movement of the trekkers. They were in effect boxed in at Regina – that is, unless they chose unwelcome federal options. On Saturday, 29 June, an editorial in the *Regina Leader-Post* announced the "End of the Trail."[36]

At 5 PM on 1 July, arrest warrants under Section 98 of the Criminal Code were issued for seven of the trek leaders. It was local Regina police with Mounted Police backup enforcing those warrants in the midst of an apparently peaceful rally in Market Square that set off the riot. One Regina policeman was killed, many were injured, and much damage was done to shops and property nearby. The relief camp strikers said they were merely defending themselves when attacked. Premier Jimmy Gardiner blamed not so much the local police or the Mounties but Bennett and the federal government. With the election a few weeks distant, the whole saga could be seen as Bennett saving the country from the communists. Former Winnipeg Mayor Ralph Webb blamed the BC Liberals for having sedulously encouraged the whole trek movement.[37]

The next day, as Regina began to pick up the pieces, and with the trek leaders including Evans and Cosgrove in custody, RB offered explanations in Parliament. "Not a mounted policeman had a bullet in his holster; not one. The instructions were definite ... They were obeyed." As for the naive young men who had joined the trek, they had looked upon it as a lark, as an adventure, but what they found, said RB, was that once they were in it, it was not easy to get out: "They were terrified and controlled by their leaders." The trekkers movement was "not a mere uprising against law and order but a definite revolutionary effort to usurp authority and destroy government." He chided Woodsworth with encouraging the strikers; he should realize now that it was "far too late to quell the monster, the Frankenstein that he has invoked."[38]

In the debate that followed RB's speech, Mackenzie King said almost nothing. He was persuaded by Lapointe not to speak too strongly against the government, lest he offend the Quebec bishops, who were death on communists. On the other hand he warned his caucus not to be too generous to Bennett for "stamping out communism." That wouldn't do either. The effect was that it was Woodsworth who led the criticism of Bennett in the Commons. He was hassled and heckled a good deal by the Conservatives. "What are you grouching about?" asked one. "You have enough to eat." But in general, except by the CCF, the Bennett government's action was supported rather than opposed. Even Harry Stevens, now at odds with the government, remarked that it had no alternative but to do what it did. Agnes Macphail said she was not condoning the strikers' conduct in the prime minister's office "any more than one would condone his [RB's] conduct."[39]

By 5 July the trekkers had gone back to their several camps or homes, most of them to British Columbia, by regular trains at Saskatchewan's expense. An inquiry into the riot was being set up in Regina. Premier Jimmy Gardiner and his attorney general, Tommy Davis, went off on hard-earned holidays. Parliament was winding down too. Perhaps surprisingly, its mood was sad and sentimental, at least as King described it. He thought the Conservatives all recognized that their defeat in the election to come was inevitable. King rose and asked the honourable members on the Conservative side to stand who expected appointments to the Senate. That produced a roar of laughter. Then F.P. Quinn, Conservative MP for Halifax (who was in fact appointed to the Senate two weeks later) asked the Liberal MPs who were hoping for a cabinet position in a future Liberal government also to do the same. King said he'd never seen the Commons in such a friendly mood. He went over and shook hands with RB. The Commons sang "Alouette," "Show Me the Way to Go Home," and "Auld Lang Syne." And so ended the long and hard Seventeenth Parliament.[40]

Summer was already on in earnest; it reached 90 degrees Fahrenheit (30C) that day. At the official prorogation in the Senate, Bennett and Meighen in full Windsor uniform were not very comfortable. That evening, Joan Patteson, King's often prescient companion and hostess, told him, "I believe it is the last time you will ever sit as the leader of the Opposition in Parliament."[41]

Two days later, on Sunday, 7 July, Stevens called a press conference to announce the formation of his new Reconstruction Party. It was to be based on the ideology of small business, against burgeoning monopoly capitalism, holding on to the system but, as he would have said, shorn of its excesses. What separated Stevens from Bennett was as much temperament as politics; he was ambitious, and his ambition was whetted and nourished by the plaudits that followed his arguments and forensic drive on the Price Spreads inquiry. Stevens was conservative with a small "c"; RB had a much bigger "C," that is, Conservatism within a firm framework of law, with an acute awareness of constitutional possibilities and limitations. There was room in the party for both positions but it required from RB a gift for political accommodation, for flexibility, that seems to have been foreign to his nature.[42]

On the cultural scene he was much more ductile. The birthday honours of 1935 are a good example. He had been trying to ensure that honours for Canada were retained; to do that, he had to keep the control of recommendations strictly in his own hands and make it abundantly clear that he had "no selfish interests to serve." That meant that political recommendations would be left mostly alone. Indeed, he had offered Mackenzie King a knighthood, although King felt he had to turn it down on principle. The OBEs went mostly to professional women, nurses, social workers, librarians, and authors – among them Lucy Maud Montgomey, author of *Anne of Green Gables*. The few knighthoods went to culture and civilization too – as of 3 June 1935, the conductor of the Toronto Symphony, Sir Ernest Macmillan, the French-Canadian historian Sir Thomas Chapais, and the poet Sir Charles G.D. Roberts. RB wrote in a personal note to Roberts, "My earliest recollections of Canadian literature are intimately associated with your name."[43] (Not all new knights, even poets, alas, behave with decorum. At a dinner given by an elegant Hamilton hostess to honour Sir Charles, a maid was passing behind his chair with the soup. She gave a short scream and dropped the soup. Upon the hostess upbraiding her, she flushed angrily and pointed to Sir Charles. "He pinched me!" Theodore Roberts, Sir Charles's brother, at the same table, defended the maid. "Yes, he did, madam, I saw him do it!"[44])

The public response to RB's honours recommendations was exactly what he was hoping for. The *Vancouver Province* said that once upon a time the bestowal of honours in Canada "amounted nearly to a public scandal." That's why it had been shut down in 1919; it was indeed difficult for any democratic government to regulate the flow of honours and keep it within the bounds of good taste. "Mr. Bennett, however, would appear to have achieved the impossible." The *Winnipeg Tribune* added that RB had "scored heavily by the nature of his recommendations ... the awards are so precisely right."[45]

RB invited another famous literary figure to stand for election as a Conservative in Simcoe North, Ontario. Stephen Leacock, formerly professor of political science at McGill, lived at Old Brewery Bay on Lake Simcoe. Simcoe North had been a mostly Conservative riding since D'Alton McCarthy's time in the 1880s and had voted Conservative since 1925. Leacock, a year older than RB, was flattered, amused, and charmed, but said "my life has been for so many years in an academic and literary ground that I feel I must finish in that furrow to the end."[46]

Four weeks later, 15 August 1935, Parliament was dissolved. Elections were set for Monday, 14 October. RB had set it as late as he could.

The *St. Thomas Times-Journal* shortly before the election ran a short piece of doggerel verse that aptly summed up the reasons why RB could have well justified leaving the field:

If I were R.B. Bennett, do you know what I would do?
I'd write a letter to the press and tell 'em I was through;
No more would I before a desk slave sixteen hours a day;
A-straining brains and body powers and getting worn and gray
In efforts to, in some strange way, a miracle perform
And put this country on its feet (now with depression torn);
No more I'd stand for critics who played football with my name,
As though my task had been a joke and politics a game ...
If I were R.B. Bennett I'd grow tired of taking knocks
And wrap my old pajamas and a pair or two of socks
And chuck 'em in a club-bag with a razor and a pipe
Fill up the 'Liz' with gasoline and leave this scene of strife.[47]

But the cut-and-run philosophy was not RB's style. He had all the grit he needed to sustain adversity: he met it head on. A cartoon published in the revived *The Canadian* of September 1935 shows him clad in sou'wester against wind and rain at the helm of the sailing ship *Canada* in stormy seas under a glowering sky.

From early September to 12 October, he took the campaign at a blistering pace. Some forty meetings were scheduled in the nine provinces. He had big audiences everywhere: 8,000 at the Sherbrooke Armouries, 12,000 at the Montreal Forum, 15,000 at the final rally in Maple Leaf Gardens in Toronto on Saturday, 12 October. There were hecklers, of course. RB seemed almost to enjoy them, for he was quite willing and able to knock their pitches into the left-field stands. Perhaps the most vivid account of him on campaign is that of Bruce Hutchison, reporting for the *Victoria Times*. The Royal Theatre in Victoria was packed to capacity. Hutchison arrived late and groped his way backstage to the press box. In the dark wings, slumped hugely in a small chair, was RB. To Hutchison he seemed no longer "the lusty, vibrant Bennett I had watched so often as he hurled his thunderbolts across the House of Commons. The man on the chair looked ill, almost unconscious ... deserted, drained." When the curtain went up, there was an instant metamorphosis: RB sprang to life, strode to centre stage, tail coat and all, master of himself and, as it soon appeared, the crowd. When the hecklers started, he shouted them down with voice and argument. The next night in Vancouver the crowd was even bigger and more hostile, the hecklers even more determined. The whole thing seemed to be perched on the rim of a riot. RB triumphed there as well, his vibrant spirit came piercing through on a voice like the trumpets of Jericho. If votes hung on speeches like that, Hutchison said, he would have won the election.[48]

On 6 October there was a student debate at UBC on the motion that Bennett was a greater statesman than King. The side for RB won 3–1. Such events do not necessarily win elections, but there were those, certainly, who believed RB could win. F.D.L. Smith, senior editor at the *Toronto Mail & Empire*, had written to him just before a radio address in Toronto on 9 September that he and many others had been vastly encouraged by RB's vigorous campaign: "I feel more and more confident you are going to win," Smith said. The *Globe* said that RB had put up such a strong campaign that he had rescued the party from "the grave position it was in two months ago." Then there had been a *sauve qui peut* feeling among the weaker mortals in the party, but RB's energy and action had put new life into Conservatives. He was not going out with a whimper! Manion even indulged hope the party might win. King, while certainly not willing to be defeated, knew that victory would not be an unmixed blessing. He had a very good idea of what was in store for him and his colleagues should they be victorious.[49]

RB's four September radio addresses provide an illuminating perspective on his five hard years. He was not trying to duck anything. It was true, he said, that he had promised in September 1930 to end unemployment. As he had put it in a private letter in July 1935, "We cannot accept unemployment as a natural and necessary consequence of a social system." He had been working at it ever since, and the government now felt it had found the means to do it, principally unemployment insurance and more recently an accelerated rate of retirement for older workers, the latter not yet put into legislation. The problem with liberalism was not its ideas so much as the anachronism embodied in them. For the time and the circumstances, liberalism had worked very well. Then indeed business could be left to "run itself" – which it did. But now "in this modern world," said RB, "it is but a ghost." In the modern world of economic nationalism, monopolies, and business concentrations of every kind, new measures were needed. That was what the Conservative government had tried to put into place. RB recited his government's record with some pride: the Bank of Canada, the Farmer's Creditor's Arrangements Act, unemployment insurance, minimum wages, a Wheat Board Act, and several others. And remember, he concluded, "we know where we are going." The Liberals' philosophy had left them drifting, rudderless. "I want you to think without like or dislike of me, of what I tell you," he said, concluding his first address. "Vote ... not for party, but for yourselves, your children, your welfare, your country. Vote as your duty to these compels you to vote."[50]

If he had wanted to abandon ship, RB had reasons a-plenty, and medical opinion in Canada and England was unanimous in recommending his retirement from public life. On the other side, both his sister, Mildred, and her husband, Bill Herridge, wanted to see his mandate renewed. Mildred's dearest wish was to see her brother continue as prime minister. As for Herridge, he was pushing hard for RB's re-election, hoping to be able to use an imminent reciprocity treaty with the United States to boost the Conservative campaign. His memorable phrase from the 1930 election, "Blasting our way into the markets of the world," neatly embodies Herridge's style. He was pushing too hard for RB. They seem not to have been on speaking terms after RB's return from England in May. RB had long been in the habit of getting his own way; so too Herridge, whose confidence in himself had increased to the point of arrogance with the years. So their relations could suddenly cool. Herridge found a more receptive audience in Rod Finlayson, RB's executive assistant. Herridge's letters to Finlayson in July and August 1935 are full of impatience: "If you can devise some dynamic force to pierce the dead wall of hostility ... But why go on? I have taken you over this ground several times. I am so utterly weary of talking, arguing and urging." Finlayson should talk to Bob Coats, the Dominion Statistician, one "of the few oases in the awful Ottawa desert of wooden-headedness."[51]

Herridge thought he had the trade agreement virtually in hand. By May 1935 it had almost been ready. Then the United States cooled. Roosevelt was hesitant; he feared a repetition of twenty-five years before when a proposed reciprocity treaty that Laurier had negotiated became the issue in the Canadian election of 1911. "No truck nor trade with the Yankees!" Conservatives said, and won the election with it. The inclination in Washington in 1935 was to move cautiously. That caution disappointed both RB and Herridge.

Professor Elliott of Harvard told King on 4 June that he'd been in conference with President Roosevelt before coming to Ottawa; Roosevelt did not want to embarrass the Liberals, for he and the US administration believed that the Conservative government would be defeated. But for that *arrière-pensée*, a reciprocity treaty might have been concluded some time before. Indeed, prior to Roosevelt's inauguration on March 1933, RB's view was that Canada should not show undue haste; now it was the other way round. The other element in this complex quadrille was the fact that King and Roosevelt were both Harvard men, King a PhD in 1900, Roosevelt a BA in 1904. That mattered. Roosevelt seems to have intervened in at least two directions: via Professor Elliott of Harvard in June with King and with the American negotiators on 26 September. Reciprocity would finally be signed in Washington with Roosevelt, King, and Cordell Hull in attendance, on 9 November 1935.[52]

It was not the only foreign policy question that obtruded into the 1935 election. There was another more fraught with problems, one that brought Canada to international attention, quite where King had no wish to be. It was the proposed League of Nations sanctions against Italy for its attack on Ethiopia at the beginning of October. RB had always been a supporter of the League, though with reservations about what a country of less than 11 million people could do. Nor did he have great faith in the League's possibilities, but he felt that Canada had to stand up and play its part in world affairs as it had during the war. That did not signify an independent line in Geneva, but rather that of a major member of the British Commonwealth and the only important League member in North America. The Canadian government's support of the League, distant but real, was brought sharply into focus by Italian threats against Ethiopia in September 1935. The Italian point of contact was in Eritrea, once a northeastern province of Ethiopia over against the Red Sea but Italian since 1890. Canada's chief representative at the League was Howard Ferguson, high commissioner to London, assisted by W.A. Riddell of External Affairs, who had been in Geneva for ten years.

The League met on 9 September, its annual meeting, but its immediate agenda was to try to prevent Italian aggression against Ethiopia. Britain and France made strong statements supporting the League Covenant against any Italian aggression. At that point the Canadian cabinet were off on the campaign trail, scattered across three thousand miles, but RB, still in Ottawa, pricked up his ears and thought that Canada's position at the League seemed pusillanimous. So did Ferguson; Riddell as well was happy to find some spunk in Ottawa. RB had a tussle with Skelton at External Affairs, but a statement went out that Canada would join other members of the League "in considering how by unanimous action" peace was to be maintained. On 14 September, Ferguson made such a statement at the League Assembly. On 3 October, Italy invaded Ethiopia.

Now what? The Canadians at Geneva wired for instructions. On 9 October, RB and Skelton agreed that in view of the elections, now just five days away, Canada "should refrain from voting at the present juncture." But should Canada thus abstain? Skelton's instructions meant that Canada would join Italy, Austria, and Hungary in abstaining – not a happy prospect. Ferguson talked to Pearson, one of the trio of Canadian officials, about what Skelton's instructions meant. Did they really mean that Canada would have to abstain from labelling Italy an aggressor? "Yes," said Pearson. "Nothing doing," said Ferguson. Pearson then suggested that he phone RB to have the instructions changed. It was lunch time in Geneva, breakfast time in Toronto. Pearson seemed to feel that a positive decision from RB might depend on how well his breakfast had gone. It must, he said, have been a good one, for RB was jovial and jocular. He told Ferguson to ignore instructions if he saw fit. Thus Canada voted to label Italy as aggressor.

That was not the end of it. Ferguson agreed later on to serve on the Committee of Eighteen that the League set up to plan what sanctions would be imposed on Italy. Skelton argued that Canada had always opposed sanctions. RB was firm that if Canada opposed aggression, sanctions against it could not be evaded. In an angry Toronto-Ottawa telephone conversation with Skelton, he was characteristically blunt: "We went into the League, took benefits, [and] must assume responsibilities, not try to hornswoggle ourselves out of it if it meant we didn't get one vote." That was on Thursday, 10 October. The elections were now only four days off.[53]

When the election results came in, RB sent a jocular cable to Ferguson. "The operations of the Italian-Ethiopian campaign were extended generally along the Quebec front with heavy casualties. In other sections the disaster was almost as great ... the people have expressed their pent-up feeling of resentment against conditions." Major-General A.H. Bell, a former Calgarian, sent his consolations at once: "You may feel confident that the verdict of historians will be far different & that your loyal & devoted work in the service of the country will receive its just recognition." RB responded that he had expected to be defeated "in a general way but had not expected [it] to be so great a disaster." But he was glad he had stayed with his troops "and met disaster with them rather than attempting to escape it, as I might have done last spring."[54]

It was not just the defeat in the popular vote that shocked the Conservatives, although that was substantial: 30 per cent for Conservatives against the Liberals' 45 per cent; it was the loss of seats. Had the 245 seats in the Commons been divided on the basis of the popular vote, Conservatives would have had 74 seats to the Liberals' 110. But as every student of single-member constituencies knows, it doesn't work out that way; the Conservatives actually won only 40 seats to the Liberals' 173. Stevens's Reconstruction Party carried 9 per cent of the popular vote and by that calculation would have had 22 seats. They got one, for Stevens himself.[55]

RB had long known that defeat was coming. He pretended he didn't; he acted and fought a strong and virile campaign. King admired him for it and told him so when they met the day following the election. RB sent an early note to King at Laurier House, offering his congratulations on King's victory, and asking to talk about the turnover of government. They met at 5 PM on 15 October in the leader of the Opposition's quarters in the Parliament buildings.

RB arrived a few minutes ahead of King. Owing to a mix-up of doors locked and doors unlocked, he found himself locked in the Leader of the Opposition's office! It was strangely prophetic. RB apologized to King for having held the election so late, but said various adventitious circumstances had kept it having to be put off, the last being the Yom Kippur Jewish holiday at the end of September. The most urgent matter RB had on his agenda was funding a replacement issue of CNR bonds, now due early in November. King said he would be ready to take over by the middle of the following week.

The talk turned to Stevens and the pamphlet of June 1934 that had led to his being fired from cabinet. "You should have dealt with him then," King told RB. To that RB admitted he had been wrong, but that he had had to go to Geneva. At the first cabinet meeting after his return on 25 October, just prior to RB's arrival at it, Cahan had gone after Stevens for the report's inaccuracies, and Stevens thereupon resigned. From that day forward, RB told King, he had only seen Stevens once, and then gave him only a casual nod. After RB's illness in March 1935, Stevens seems to have found the opportunity too good to miss and proceeded to collect parliamentary support. "Your men were more alarmed at Stevens's possible success than I was," he told King "I never thought he would get anything." RB seems to have consistently underestimated Stevens's popularity. After his return from England in May 1935, his cabinet kept coming to him and asking what he was going to do about staying on as prime minister, what he really wanted to do. "You may think it strange," RB told King, "that I should say my reason for staying on. If I had dropped out, and Stevens succeeded, with the kind of extreme stuff he was talking, you would have become the Conservative party." Thus the reason that RB stayed on as prime minister was to save the Conservative party from Stevens.

"You've no idea," RB added, "of the kind of man he is. Years ago when Dick McBride [Sir Richard McBride, 1870–1917, BC premier 1903–15] was alive, he told me, 'If you ever form a government, do not trust that man Stevens; he will betray you.'" RB could not forgive Stevens's breach of trust in 1934 or his efforts to make his way to the leadership of the party in 1935 in RB's absence.[56]

RB and King talked for nearly an hour and a half. When RB rose to leave, King said, "Before you go, Bennett, let me say to you that I have admired very much the way you have fought on, knowing, as you must have known, that you were sure of defeat. I hope you have not taxed yourself too much." To which RB replied, "Yes, I have known I was defeated for some time past." They walked to the elevator together; it wasn't working, so RB walked down the stairs. King remarked how friendly it had been, especially the last half hour or so when Bennett had been talking to him as a colleague in cabinet would, as if he had been looking for comfort in the Stevens affair that must, King thought, have been the most trying of his whole administration.[57]

That same evening, Tuesday 15 October, the Toronto *Evening Telegram* summed up R.B. Bennett's five long years: "A great statesman [has been] defeated by a poor politician."

7

Leader of the Opposition and Elder Statesman, 1935–1938

Wednesday, 23 October 1935, was the day set for the change of government. The prime minister's office was emptied and ready. So was the leader of the Opposition's office at the far southwest corner of the Centre Block, Room 301, as far away as possible from the prime minister's world in the East Block. Mackenzie King's future cabinet ministers gathered in 301, awaiting word that their leader had arrived at the PMO's office from Laurier House. On that signal the whole new cabinet, newspapermen in tow, trooped across to the East Block. There they were sworn in by the chief justice, Sir Lyman Duff, acting for the new governor general, Lord Tweedsmuir, John Buchan, not yet arrived from England. Meanwhile RB and his executive secretary, Rod Finlayson, RB's hand on Finlayson's arm, King observed, for Finlayson was lame, walked unobtrusively behind the buildings to the Château Laurier. Thus it was that RB retired from being prime minister.[1]

A few days later RB invited the whole of his office staff to dinner at the Château Laurier to thank them all for their loyal service. In his most sepulchral tone, he growled, "The reign of terror is at an end."

"No, no!" they cried. Mildred Herridge rose to say that with her wonderful brother there was no reign of terror: he had always strewn her path with roses.[2]

RB appeared neither rueful nor sad. On that day that his government resigned, he wrote to one lady correspondent that Canadians were entitled to express their resentment against conditions, and he was philosophical about defeat. "Personally, I have neither complaint to make nor regrets. I accept my discharge with no feeling of resentment against anyone, and can console myself with the thought that at least I did not abandon the ship or seek to avoid punishment by retiring last spring as I might have done." But to a sympathizer in England who sent him a consoling cable, he admitted that he had not expected quite so great a disaster. For it was a devastation in almost any way one looked at it. The great and only redeeming feature was the core 30 per cent of the Conservative popular vote across Canada: it was a bit better than that in the Maritimes and Ontario, almost that in Quebec, Manitoba, and British Columbia. Otherwise the defeat was shattering. Only forty Conservative MPs were elected: one from each of the three Maritime provinces, one from each of the three Prairie provinces, five from Quebec, six from British Columbia, and the other twenty-five from Ontario. Of RB's former cabinet, only six were re-elected. Dick Hanson of New Brunswick and Bob Manion of Ontario went down to defeat; the six who were re-elected were either very old (Sir George Perley and C.H. Cahan) or else young and inexperienced, brought in in the last weeks of RB's government. Larry Glassford puts it succinctly: the Conservative caucus was "decimated ... in terms of quantity, quality and regional balance." Canadians, said RB, deeply resented the conditions of the last five years and could not get used to it. They expressed their dissatisfaction by "soundly defeating the government."[3]

In any case, RB could not have worked harder than he had done in his term of office. He sent a consoling letter to all the defeated Conservative candidates: "You can, however, take pride in the magnificent fight you waged against overwhelming odds." As to that, an Ottawa widow sent him the last lines of Shelley's "Prometheus Unbound" (Prometheus, it may be remembered, was the Titan in Greek mythology who stole fire from the gods and gave it to humankind): "Neither to change, nor falter, nor repent; / This, like thy glory, Titan, is to be / Good, great and joyous, beautiful and free; / This is alone Life, Joy, Empire and Victory." She told RB that in 1925, before her husband died, he flourished a newspaper at her and said, "R.B. of Calgary is going to run for the Federal House. If Bennett gets to Ottawa, there will be fireworks."

RB much appreciated that letter, especially the Shelley. "Whether my work was good or bad, I at least did all I could for Canada during the last five years." He told Lord Glendyne, a friend and senior official at the Bank of England, "It was inevitable that the people would vote against the Government and for a 'change.' Canadians greatly resented conditions. Hardship was something to which they were not accustomed." One Englishwoman in Ottawa was not sure whether he needed sympathy or congratulation. "I cannot help feeling," she said, "you must be glad to be relieved of the burden. I remember you told me there's nothing in the world you want." At that point it was simply some peace and quiet.[4]

That was now going to be possible. After completing his move into the Centre Block by early November, he was footloose and fancy-free for a few weeks. Parliament would not meet before February, so he and George Robinson, an old Calgary friend going back to the early days of Lougheed & Bennett, were going on a sea cruise out of California.[5]

Robinson was been an insurance and real estate agent in the same Clarence block in downtown Calgary as RB. They had become friends early on, and when RB went into politics, Robinson became his campaign manager. Robinson was an unreformed smoker, and cigars at that. He was the only person who could walk into RB's office and keep on smoking. RB's office staff were strictly prohibited from smoking and were aghast to see Robinson doing so. Long familiarity also allowed him to tease RB with impunity. Once when the Bennett entourage had arrived in Medicine Hat, he noticed that the room charge rose significantly. For those rates, he told the hotel, "women must be included!"

The two men left Calgary about 18 November by train for Seattle and then Los Angeles to board the ss *Pennsylvania* (33,375 tons), sailing 23 November for New York via the Panama Canal and Havana, Cuba. It was, RB told a London friend, a "very pleasant trip." That's about all we know, though one detail surfaced in the House of Commons two months later. As they were going through the Panama Canal, they learned from newspapers, both English and Spanish, of W.A. Riddell's initiative at Geneva on sanctions against Italy: if nickel and copper were to be embargoed, why not steel and oil? King and Skelton promptly quashed Riddell, leaving him hanging out to dry, and Rome, according to RB, rejoicing.

After landing in New York, he returned to Calgary and was still there as late as 23 January 1936.[6] Once back in Ottawa, he was met by a development of talks he had begun in Calgary about the purchase of an English estate. Avon Castle in Hampshire was available at $400,000. RB read the description "with great interest." But the first and most important question for him was: how many miles was it from London? On learning that it was a hundred miles miles away – about three hours' drive even on good roads – he cooled off.[7]

For some time this had been rumoured to be his intention: to retire to England and take a peerage. He was comfortable there, comfortable with English style and manners, the way they did things – often too slowly and ponderously, true, too inclined to accept "as it was in the beginning, is now, and ought to continue," but still it was a civilized world. The other element in his considerations was the way that he had for five years been treated by Canadian newspapers and magazines. There were reasons, good ones, for his bad press, not a few of them of them his own doing, mostly because of the nigh-impenetrable carapace of his own personality, preconceptions, and prejudices. In February 1936, *Maclean's*, which had been quite anti-Bennett, published an article "Fair Play, Please." Roy Cox of Vancouver wrote to *Maclean's* in response, saying in effect that at long last they had something good to say about R.B. Bennett, namely, that he had tried to prevent the Americanization of Canadian magazines. RB sent Cox an appreciative letter revealing something of his stored-up animus. In the immediate post-election weeks, he may have said that he harboured no rancour for his treatment, but he did: "I do not suppose, in the whole history of Canadian political life, any man has been attacked as I was during the five years I held office. It was part of the policy of the Liberal Party and, to some extent, I think, they succeeded in creating an adverse public opinion against myself personally ... [Many now realize] that, after all, I had no selfish purposes to serve and desired only to do my best for the country in which I was born."[8]

Parliament convened on Thursday, 6 February 1936. Even before the Speech from the Throne, RB made a singular move, opposing the election of Pierre-François Casgrain for speaker. The newspapers had announced sometime earlier that Casgrain had been nominated by Mackenzie King. Casgrain promptly acted on the assumption that he had the speakership already. It was not done that way, however: the practice was for his nomination to be seconded by the leader of the Opposition. Casgrain had again jumped the gun by ordering the sergeant-at-arms to fire, as of 31 January 1936, some 120 House of Commons employees, most of whom were permanent. Some of them had served, said RB, under four sovereigns: Queen Victoria, Edward VII, George V, and the new King Edward VIII, just come to the throne on 20 January. RB did not believe that Casgrain's dismissals had had Mackenzie King's approval or knowledge; indeed, RB thanked and congratulated King when he cancelled Casgrain's order. What Casgrain then ought to have done, in RB's opinion, was to resign the nomination as speaker. But he didn't. J.S. Woodsworth supported RB's refusal to accept Casgrain. Of course, with 135 seats (of 245), the Liberals got Casgrain as speaker as they wanted.

The new Liberal government was not above showing its teeth from time to time, nor was it above crowing over its big electoral victory. There was a certain amount of *Schadenfreude* in King's remarking, "I have never had a band of colleagues who deserted me on the eve of battle" and in the fact that the Conservative party had been humbled, not to say humiliated, with a corporal's guard of only forty MPs. Indeed there was not enough room on the government side of the Commons, and so some Liberal MPs now had to sit to the speaker's left.[9]

But as RB acknowledged in thanking King for his action in the Casgrain affair, the Liberals could also be generous. Arthur Slagt, the Liberal MP for Parry Sound, congratulated RB on his record handsomely: "I count the house and the country fortunate that in the years ahead of us we are to have the benefit of his courage, his industry and his wide experience of passing the laws of our country." Soon enough, however, would politics intervene; soon enough would the Liberals say, as RB satirically put it, "We have the votes; we are going to do it ... call up the guards."[10]

RB was very critical of the Canadian-American Trade Agreement, negotiated in Washington just three and a half weeks after the October election. J.C. Elliott, who became postmaster general, had said during the election campaign, "Put us in office and we will have a trade agreement with the United States within ninety days." He had good reason for saying that: King knew and his cabinet knew that Roosevelt was not going to conclude any last-minute trade agreement with the Bennett government. King was anxious for an agreement; not for him fussing over the minutiae of most-favoured nation status, or the complex rates of the intermediate tariff. There were officials to handle those nuts-and-bolts things. What he was after was a trade agreement, not quite *à tout prix* but almost. That was RB's objection to King's haste with Washington. RB was not alone in his objections – Dana Wilgress, Canada's chief negotiator, thought too much had been given away. As C.P. Stacey remarked, "King got his quick agreement, but he had paid a price ... The extension of the intermediate tariff to imports from the United States was revolutionary." Most Canadians neither knew nor cared much about the whys and wherefores of the intermediate tariff, but RB knew. So did the American negotiators. "The Canadian agreement," they told the president, "is so favorable to us that in six months it will be recognized generally as a great political and economic asset."[11]

That was the gist of what RB told the House of Commons on 10 February 1936. The most favoured nation status and the six hundred to seven hundred items of the intermediate tariff were of such enormous importance to the Americans that, as RB put it, "I felt they should pay and pay handsomely." In November 1934, at Wilgress's earnest suggestion, he had offered intermediate tariff status to the Americans, but then he had wanted a lot more for it than King had asked. As it was now, RB said, the government was sacrificing the interests of Canada "to a mere chimera." This agreement was arrived at in a headlong rush – "Fancy! – just a few hours and it was all over." The trade figures for 1935–38 bear out RB's contention. Canadian exports to the United States rose by about 40 per cent, while Canadian imports from the United States were up 60 per cent.[12]

But RB did have some good things to say about what Liberals were doing. The establishment of the National Harbours Board was one thing he approved of. The previous arrangement was a series of individual harbour commissions administered by the Department of Marine. RB thought the system inefficient and cumbersome and in 1931 appointed Sir Alexander Gibb to study and report. In 1932 Gibb recommended in effect what would later become the National Harbours Board. But there was a good deal of resistance to sweeping away the old Harbour Commissions, and RB had found that he simply did not have the power to do it. Nor, in 1932, did he have the money: "I do not think the government could have carried this through in the midst of that Parliament," he admitted. So he warmly congratulated the new minister of transport, C.D. Howe, for having effected what he would like to have brought in himself.[13]

A measure that he did achieve himself in June 1935 was the Grain Board. Western farmers had long been critical of Winnipeg grain dealers and their forum, the Winnipeg Grain Exchange. In the 1920s, farmers had created voluntary wheat pools to get around Winnipeg dealers, and by the end of the decade about half of western wheat production was being handled by the pools. Then in 1930 wheat prices plunged steeply downward. The chartered banks, which had advanced money to the pools (which had paid the farmers for their wheat), were now faced with serious, indeed crippling losses. Europe had been a considerable importer of Canadian wheat, and now that market had all but dried up. Wheat subsidies in many countries and tariffs against foreign wheat meant that Canadian, Australian, and Argentinian wheat prices all fell precipitously. After having averaged well over a $1 a bushel in the 1920s, wheat fell to below 40 cents. The pools, which had advanced money to farmers based on, say, a price of $1.25 a bushel, were broke. In the United States, local western banks failed in shoals. In Canada, where the branch banking system made for much more flexibility, the wheat crisis by 1932 brought banks to the edge of bankruptcy, especially those with large western commitments – notably, the Royal. That's when RB acted, appointing J.I. McFarland, an experienced Winnipeg grain dealer and an old friend, to head up a system of government buying and selling. With RB's approval, McFarland bought wheat futures with the aim of strengthening the market. But wheat prices refused to be strengthened. Not even the disastrous western crop failures made a difference; Canadian wheat surpluses piled up in Grain Board warehouses. At least farmers were paid something. RB claimed in 1935 that McFarland's grain operations had averted "stark, complete, absolute disaster beyond the ability of any man to see."[14]

One of RB's last measures in June 1935 was to introduce Grain Board legislation, by which not just wheat but all grains were to be marketed. RB pushed hard for his idea of a compulsory grain board, but there was some resistance in his own caucus, and in the end it went to a special committee with him as chairman. The bill then became the Wheat Board bill, shorn of its command over other grains, and further allowing farmers to choose between selling their wheat to private dealers or to the Wheat Board. The new board's compulsory power forced the Liberals to declare a policy, which was difficult for them too. Charles Dunning, who had a great deal of experience in Saskatchewan farming and politics, concluded by then that some form of federal intervention in the grain market was inevitable. By the election of October 1935 the Wheat Board owned some 200 million bushels of wheat. McFarland had established the price at 87.5 cents a bushel, above the market price for the 1935 crop.

The new King government wanted that big surplus got rid of, rather than waiting for wheat prices to rise as McFarland (and RB) had been doing for years. In late 1935 there were some indications that those long-held expectations might have some hope of realization. In any case the new King government wasn't having just hope, and they weren't having McFarland either. In December 1935 they asked him to resign. When he refused, he was fired by order-in-council. That action drew fierce criticism from Bennett, who used several technicalities in the drafting of the OIC to chastise the King government. It was a long, arid (and acrid) argument about details. Stung by Liberal taunts, RB at one point told J.G. Ross, the Liberal MP for Moose Jaw, that he (Bennett) was not going to be refuted by "a poor rural rustic." The honourable member for Moose Jaw came back and said that with more rural rustics, the House would get through its business a lot faster than having "a bunch of lawyers splitting hairs all afternoon." But one did not tangle with RB lightly. He had spent a lot of time in tough Alberta courtrooms. His answer:

"The honourable member for Moose Jaw has said he is a poor rural rustic; there is no reason why he should prove it."[15]

The real enmity across the House was between RB and Jimmy Gardiner, King's minister of agriculture. Gardiner had not forgotten Ottawa's handling of the trekkers' drama in June 1935, for which he blamed Bennett. He now delighted in pointing out RB's failings. He claimed that 52 per cent of the time of the House of Commons was taken up with RB's speeches on one thing or another. If one were to mention the name of one of the ships in the British Navy, said Gardiner, the leader of the Opposition would proceed to name them all. RB refuted at least the charge of taking up so much of debate time. He had taken the trouble actually to ascertain the exact figure, and it was less than 25 per cent. Besides, as leader of the Opposition (and paid as a cabinet minister) he had a statutory duty to perform. He was doing that duty every day the House was sitting, from 3 to 6 PM and 8 to 11 PM King chimed in to say that most of the House would agree that the leader of the Opposition had earned his salary.[16]

The King government was determined also to make the Bank of Canada a publicly owned bank. RB had set it up to be at arm's length from the government, with private ownership of its shares like the Bank of England, though he and Bank of Canada supporters avoided mentioning that inflammatory precedent. Graham Towers, now the bank's governor, liked it that way and liked RB's legislation. But with the election of 1935, Towers knew he might as well face the inevitable. That came in two stages, in 1936 when a majority of Bank of Canada shares became publicly owned, and in 1938 when all of them were.

The most acrid part of the 1936 Bank of Canada debate developed around matter quite minor to many MPs then, almost absurd to most now: the language on the new Bank of Canada banknotes. RB was clearly upset by having the French language openly juxtaposed with the English on the face of the bills. To make his point, he reviewed the whole history of Canada since Confederation. What had stuck in his mind was his vivid – probably too vivid – memories of the hard language debates that racked Canada in the late 1880s and 1890s. As a young law student at Dalhousie, he had cut his teeth on that issue, on D'Alton McCarthy, on E.A. Freeman's ideas in *Comparative Politics* (1873), that language had and always would determine nationality. By Freeman's argument, Switzerland with its three languages of German, French, and Italian was an artificial creation, thrown together by the pressures of the big countries around it, and was bound to fail. RB had met Sir John Thompson in

1890 and might better have remembered Thompson's memorable reply to D'Alton McCarthy in the Jesuit Estates debate of 27 March 1889: in matters of race, religion, and education, "for the sake of the prospects of making a nation," one should leave such subjects severely alone. Thompson's children were sent to French schools. He thought it a matter of courtesy to learn to speak French.

The irony was that in both Thompson's and Bennett's positions, their arguments were directed toward making Canada a better, more united nation. The premises of each, however, were very different. RB had developed his adult life in the Canadian West where English had become the *lingua franca* of several other languages including French. Nor had he really taken in the Quebec world of the 1930s. He had met Duplessis, *le grand Maurice*; they were both Conservatives, but their lives, habits, and ideas were swung in very different orbits. Thus RB argued in June 1936, "Each one in his own conscience must answer whether or not in a community that is overwhelmingly British the circulation of notes of that kind is not fraught with the gravest danger to harmony between the races in other parts of Canada." The whole hard, tense debate led the freshman MP from Weyburn, Tommy Douglas, to read the Commons a lesson in common sense: "I have been amazed, amused, and I am afraid a little pained to see this house spending a day and a half discussing what to many people in Canada is a very trivial aspect of the bill. There are hundreds of people across the prairies to-day who would be very glad to get money no matter in what language it was printed."[17]

Though they differed on this point, Douglas came to appreciate RB. It did not, however, begin that way. From a distance Douglas had what might be called the *Winnipeg Free Press*'s perspective of Bennett as "a blustering bully." He found the real Bennett quite different when he actually got to the House of Commons; he soon realized that RB was one of the best informed men in the House and could deliver his information skilfully, indeed eloquently. Moreover, to Douglas's surprise, RB was kindness itself. He congratulated both Douglas and M.J. Coldwell, both CCF MPs, on their maiden speeches and asked them if they needed any help. Neither of the new MPs were lawyers; Coldwell was a school principal and Douglas was a Baptist minister; both needed lessons about the way Parliament worked. When he was out around the Parliament buildings, RB would call Douglas over and gossip about life and politics, RB telling about his life as prime minister. He was amiable, friendly, and forthcoming. Then and later, Douglas was admiring and grateful.[18]

RB was not a romantic; poetry he appreciated intellectually rather than romantically. What he liked in Browning's poetry was its muscular strength, its tough graininess. Nor did he seem much caught by the beauty of nature. Mackenzie King loved nature in its many moods; every so often he would invite RB up to his country acres at Kingsmere. Apparently, however, RB never did visit Kingsmere. One has the impression that he was bored by the idea of a day in the country. For many years RB was MP for Calgary West, which included Banff National Park, yet in his letters there is hardly a single reference to the physical beauty of the mountains and vistas within his own constituency. Even the spectacular Banff-Jasper Highway, which he had ordered built in 1930, he seems to have thought of more as an important transportation link to Jasper than as a way to view the glorious panorama of the Rocky Mountains. His appreciation of the British Empire tended also toward the concrete – its productions, its lands, and its people. Now in the summer and autumn of 1936 he would see something of it for himself.

He appears to have thought he could make such a trip as an ordinary tourist without anyone really knowing who he was. Alice Millar warned him otherwise. She told him he would be dined and wined and that he would come home early in 1937 tired and worn to a nice restful session of the House of Commons to get his health back. She was close to being right.[19]

Departure plans were made and unmade. It was a busy summer. RB, Mildred, and Alice went west to Vancouver and Victoria in early July. From there RB returned to Ottawa via Calgary (the annual dinner of the Rangemen), where he stayed until August. Norman MacLeod of the Parliamentary press gallery telegraphed him with best wishes for a pleasant trip and, not all that well informed, hoped that "the bride survives the voyage." That created some amusement; RB's "bride" was his valet, S.G. Brooks, who a few months before had been the elegant doorman at the Bank of Canada.

By this time the Australians were fully aware of RB's coming, and were well into the process of filling out a packed itinerary. The day that RB finally left Ottawa on 11 August, J.A. Lyons, the Australian prime minister, cabled to invite him to stay at Government House in Canberra. He was due there 11–13 October when the Australian spring was nicely under way. During his stay, the cable said, he was to be guest of the Australian government. The Australians had not forgotten the Canadian/Australian conspiracy of 1932 that had extracted benefits for both countries from the reluctant British. RB responded, "Greatly honoured by invitation which quite overwhelmed me. Anticipate availing myself of your all too kind proposals."[20]

He and Brooks sailed out of Long Beach, Los Angeles, on 19 August aboard the ss *Monterey*. One of the four "White Fleet" ships of the Matson Line, newly built in 1932 for the Pacific passenger trade, the *Monterey* carried 472 first class and 228 cabin class passengers. It was an odd proportion, but on the long Pacific Ocean voyages, passengers who had the time and money preferred to be as comfortable as possible. It was almost five thousand nautical miles to Fiji, where the ship made its first stop at Suva in among some three hundred of the Fiji Islands. RB had lunch with the British governor, who met him at the dock. From there it was a further one thousand nautical miles to Auckland, New Zealand. There, and for the rest of his three-week tour of New Zealand, RB was to be the guest of the New Zealand government. Travelling incognito he certainly was not.

New Zealand is over eleven hundred miles from north to south. RB covered its length from Auckland southward, eventually returning to Wellington, the capital, to take his departure. He found New Zealand delightful, its people in style and habits not unlike Canadians of a generation earlier.[21]

Australia was to be quite different. It was a three-day voyage, about twelve hundred nautical miles. RB, aboard ss *Wangenella*, was met on arrival at Sydney Harbour on Sunday, 27 September, by W.M. Hughes, the former Australian prime minister. RB's Australian schedule had been set up by Prime Minister Lyons in consultation with the premiers of each of the six Australian states. The itinerary – compressed between RB's arrival in Sydney on 27 September and his departure for South Africa from Fremantle on Australia's west coast on 9 November – was formidable; they were going to show a visiting Canadian ex-prime minister what Australia and Australians were made of. The British high commissioner in Canberra wrote to RB that he was sorry to miss him (previous commitments) and hoped his visit would go well, but that "certainly it looked strenuous."[22]

It was. The day after landing, RB addressed the luncheon meeting of the Sydney Millions Club. His speech was about the similarities and, more important, the dissimilarities of Canada and Australia, their people and their resources. RB thought Australia had at least one big advantage over Canada: "You are a homogenous people." True, like Canada, Australia had difficulties with climate and distances, but it also had wonderful export opportunities with southern hemisphere fruit, wine, and wool, as well as sugar and tea from Australia's tropical north. What it needed was good immigrants, as Canada did, preferably from Britain, to maintain the homogeneity of the Australian people. That perception of RB's tells much about his distance from French Canada. In this respect he was still a thorough Calgarian: bring other races with other languages into the country, of course, but be sure that the English language and the history and culture of the British Empire are an integral part of the proper process of immigrant assimilation. As the *Sydney Morning Herald* said two days later, "We are linked [to Canada] by a common heritage of the English tongue and British traditions." In a Rotary Club speech a day later, RB chided Australians a little for thinking of Canada as an appendage of the United States. No nation exercised suzerainty over Canada, he said: she was proud of her place in the British Empire, as she proved in France and Flanders twenty years before.[23]

Now early in October, it was already hot. Sydney recorded 85 degrees Fahrenheit (29°C) on 2 October while RB was being shown the environs of Sydney. Sydney Harbour has an opening from the sea only a mile wide, but behind Sydney Heads the harbour spreads out into a huge indented shoreline, some 155 miles (250 km) of it. The Sydney Harbour bridge, a major achievement, had been built two years before RB's visit. RB was also taken fifty miles (80 km) west to the Blue Mountains – blue because eucalyptus trees ("gums" in Australian parlance) exude a bluish haze that gives an attractive miasma to Australian wooded landscapes, especially in heat. RB did not complain of the temperatures; but then he complained of very little during his stay. Indeed, he seems to have been delighted with Australia and Australians, their vivacity, their energy, and their very Australian version of Britishness. "Poms" or "Pommies," they called the Brits, not always with flattery in mind: "You can tell 'em any place by the way they look around as if they own the place but don't want it," one Australian said.[24]

After being based in Sydney for a week, RB left for the tropical north and Brisbane, capital of Queensland, for a further week. Queensland seemed to outdo everything so far. "Amazing hospitality," he cabled Alice Millar in Canada. Then it was Canberra, 185 miles (300 km) south of Sydney, where RB stayed at Government House with the governor general. There was a state dinner on 12 October and the next day a government luncheon. RB's speeches stressed Canadian-Australian trade and relations and support for the League of Nations by both countries. He would re-emphasize his delight in Australia on his journey southward to Melbourne in the State of Victoria. Australians, he told a Melbourne civic reception, were too modest about their own country; he himself "was lost in admiration for a country with resources so rich." Did Australians fully appreciate what they had? Robert Menzies, attorney general of Australia from 1935 to 1939 and twenty-two years RB's junior, teased him with an old Ottawa joke, that RB's ability was so highly regarded that when he needed a cabinet meeting, "he had only to take a quiet walk by himself."[25]

A break from this huge round of speeches and dinners – though RB's appetite for both seems to have been considerable – was a trip by air to Tasmania where he enjoyed four days of cooler weather but a still brisk itinerary. From there he went to Adelaide, the capital of South Australia, a state of considerable diversity, with the great deserts, the Simpson and the Sturt, to the north and the Great Victorian to the northwest; heavier rainfall southward allowed grape cultivation in the Barossa Valley and the growing of wheat on the Eyre and other peninsulas. The old steel-hulled sailing ships still took their cargoes of Australian grain to England out of Port Lincoln, Port Augusta, and Port Adelaide on the Great Southern Ocean. Indeed, until 1939 the grain race for the best times to Falmouth was an annual event for those beautiful old square riggers. The evolution and the dying of those spectacular vessels somehow evoke Hegel's aphorism, "Minerva's owl takes flight in the gathering dusk."[26]

Of all the six Australian states he visited, RB seems to have felt most at home in South Australia. It was the only Australian state that had not originally been a penal colony, and its style and its history showed. Named after the queen of William IV (1830–37), Adelaide was called by other envious or sarcastic Australians "Wowserville" – "wowser" being old Australian slang for the puritan-minded. Perhaps that is why RB found Adelaide so agreeable. At the formal parliamentary dinner celebrating South Australia's centennial, he was ribbed in a poem, "Richard Bedford Bennett," sung to the tune of an old Australian ballad, "Abe, My Boy,"

What are you waiting for now?
They say you are wealthy,
Don't smoke, and T.T.
A shining example to folk such as we.
These remarks are just playful, we think you'll allow,
But what are you *living* for now?

Judging by the picture in the *Adelaide Chronicle* of RB in white tie and tails smiling at Lady Dugan, whom he had taken in to dinner, he seems to have been enjoying himself thoroughly. He later wrote to Sir George Murray, chief justice of South Australia, of another Adelaide occasion, "I do not know that I enjoyed myself at any time more than I did at the Attorney-General's dinner in the old Club at Adelaide."[27]

North and west from Adelaide lay the Great Victorian Desert, miles upon brutal miles of it. The Great Western Railway across the Nullabor ("no trees") Plain runs for one hundred miles without a curve. After a full day's run out of Adelaide, the train crosses the state line into Western Australia at East longitude 129 degrees, carving north and south across the whole continent. Western Australia, the largest state, takes up a full third of the country. It is a further half day's journey before the train steams into Kalgoorlie, an old gold rush town. The whole journey, Adelaide to Perth, reminds one of Henry Lawson's magical lines from "The Roaring Days": "The flaunting flag of progress / Is in the West unfurled, / The mighty bush with iron rails / Is tethered to the world."[28]

Perth, the capital of Western Australia, was another 125 miles (200 km) or so to the southwest, on an attractive bend of the Swan River, just in from the coast of the Indian Ocean. RB was greeted at the Adelphi Hotel by telegrams from Adelaide praising his speeches there as "the most elegant ever delivered." He kept it up in Perth. At a civic reception on 3 November he confessed that though he had read much about Australia before he came, "I say to you that I had no real appreciation of its greatness." In this expansive mood he suggested his own imperial sentiments. "We [the British Empire] occupy one quarter of the world's surface and we represent one quarter of the world's population ... That is a tremendous responsibility. Never before has there been an empire such as ours. There has been no centralization of power; every section has had the opportunity to develop a character [of its own]."[29]

He went down to see the great hardwood forests of the well-watered south, the karri and the jarrah forests at Pemberton, beautiful dark strong woods rather like a rich mahogany. He was given a jarrah walking stick on his departure from Fremantle, the port of Perth, on 7 November. "I came to Australia a few weeks ago as a stranger and I leave as a loyal and devoted friend," he said in his farewell speech. But Brooks, RB's valet, breathed a heartfelt sigh of relief. The itinerary had been packed, comprehensive, wonderful but exhausting. "Anyway," he wrote to Alice Millar in Canada, "we have finished it with flying colours and he [RB] is having a great experience with the Australian people." Now, Brooks said, they would have a good rest on the sea trip to South Africa.[30]

It is 4,300 nautical miles across the Indian Ocean from Fremantle to Durban, an ocean that even in summer can get rough. On the previous voyage of the ss *Ceramic* (18,750 tons), a lifeboat was smashed and one of the crew badly injured. RB and Brooks reached Durban on 19 November without incident.

The South African leg was much more low key than either New Zealand or Australia. For one thing its government was a thicket of Boer War veterans. The prime minister, General James Hertzog, six years older than RB, had fought as a Boer general and was as fervent an anti-imperialist as ever he had been in the war. Prime minister since 1924, he would remain so until 1939. The main government effort put forth for RB in South Africa came from the governor general, Lord Hyde, and Lady Hyde, who invited him to stay at Government House in Pretoria on his way northwestward to Victoria Falls in Southern Rhodesia (now Zimbabwe). South Africa is a big country. It is 560 miles (900 km) from Durban to Pretoria and almost 930 miles (1500 km) south to Cape Town.[31]

The 1932 Ottawa Conference had not done much to ameliorate South African attitudes to the empire. Dr Nicolaas Havenga, the finance minister, had even tried to avoid sending a South African delegation. The British preferences on wine, brandy, and fruit affected only small sections of South Africa, and where the Hertzog government was not strong anyway. Boer farmers looked for concessions on meat, but all four dominions were after that, their appetite for concessions all limitless. A quid pro quo for such a concession was difficult too; the Havenga budget of 1924 launched protection for selected industries looking toward industrialization, to afford poorer whites entry into a new labour force. So the chances in 1932 of intra-imperial trade had been limited. And memories of the Boer War were only a generation old.[32]

All of this conspired to limit the South African government's enthusiasm for a visit by an outspoken Canadian imperialist. RB had interviews with Hertzog and with Jan Smuts (1870–1950), but cut short his visit to South Africa by a week, probably in part because he learned at Victoria Falls on 3 December that the Canadian Parliament would open on Thursday, 14 January.[33]

Victoria Falls on the Zambezi River was named in 1855 by its white discoverer, David Livingstone. The mighty cataract was more than twice the height of Niagara, with a roar so loud that Livingstone claimed he could hear it from the river's mouth. Although it was now the dry season, RB found the falls "indescribably magnificent." His reaction was a little like Rupert Brooke's reaction in 1912 to Niagara; blasé poet that he was, he had hoped not to be impressed, "but I horribly was."[34]

After a visit to Bulawayo, RB came south through Johannesberg to Ladysmith where in late January 1900 the British army had fought and lost the hard battle of Spion Kop. He continued southward through Kimberley to Cape Town and embarked from there on 18 December in *Edinburgh Castle* (13,000 tons) for Southampton via Madeira. Though the ship was heading into northern winter, the weather was benign. RB found Captain Bickford's table "amusing and at times interesting!!" – an arch comment that suggests good female company.

North of Madeira, on New Year's Day 1937, RB penned an appreciative letter to Alice Millar. She had now been with him for more than two decades, since 1914. One of the many points of difference between him and Mackenzie King was their regard for staff: King was always grumbling, expecting too much, while RB was genuinely concerned for the welfare of those who worked for him. The New Year, he wrote to Alice, should induce a feeling of gratitude for the year past, "so his first one must be to you for all your devoted service and loyal cooperation during 1936. No man was more fortunate & if at times you think I did not fully appreciate my good fortune I assure you that you are mistaken. I do not suppose I could have taken this trip were it not for you."[35]

His travels had obviously done him good. A friend told him after seeing him at Southampton on 4 January 1937, "I have never seen you looking so well." RB stopped in London briefly for a Park Lane lunch and a BBC broadcast about his travels (also heard in Canada). Then he was immediately off to Glasgow to catch the CP *Montclare* for Halifax. Once in the brutal North Atlantic winter, the 16,400-ton *Montclare* made heavy weather of it and was late arriving at Halifax. Parliament opened on Thursday, 14 January (the earliest since 1905, except for 1926 when it opened 7 January). RB sent a radiogram that he could not reach Ottawa before Saturday, 16 January, even by special boat train.

The coronation of Edward VIII had originally been set for 12 May; after his abdication on 23 December 1936, the new king George VI stepped in and accepted the ceremonies already arranged for his elder brother. RB had met Edward as Prince of Wales several times, and each time seems to have found him a bit more weary, a little more jaded, the nightclub life he had been leading showing up all too often, much to his father's disgust, giving more evidence that he was not born to be a king. What RB thought of Wallis Warfield Simpson is not known. On his first day back at the House of Commons in Ottawa, RB approved of Mackenzie King's loyal support of George VI, and of what Stanley Baldwin had done in engineering the first British abdication since that of James II in 1689. The situation had bristled with difficulties and dangers. In the Canadian House of Commons, RB, not without sympathy for Edward, quoted *Othello* with singular aptness: "I pray you, in your letters, / When you shall these unlucky deeds relate; / Speak of me as I am, nothing extenuate, / Nor set down aught in malice; then must you speak / Of one that loved not wisely but too well."[36]

RB had returned from travelling "around the world," as his fellow MPs referred to it, a man changed and calmed and much more at ease. The relief from the pressures of responsibility for Canada's welfare had come slowly; it had taken him time to unbend that heavy bow, the very considerable tension that had driven him since 1930. He still had lively memories of what it had been like bearing those troubles on his shoulders. Nor was it altogether simple to adjust to "the role of a candid friend, especially if he recalls, as sometimes he must, what he had to endure [from the Liberals]." But now he seemed to be relaxed, smiling, good humoured. Mackenzie King was struck by it from RB's first appearance in Parliament on Monday, 18 January 1937, in the debate on the Address. He was "exceedingly nice ... really in a wholly different frame of mind than I have seen him in any previous year." Two days later RB crossed the floor to give him a new book on the abdication that he had bought in London. "I do not recall," King told his diary, "in all my years in the House, Bennett having crossed over to my side of the House to speak in a friendly way and to make a gesture of the kind he made today."[37]

Early in March, invited by Roosevelt to come to Washington to discuss European affairs. King at once consulted RB. Go by all means, RB advised, as long as it would not delay the session. Parliament had to end in time to enable King and several key ministers to get to the Coronation on 12 May and an Imperial Conference afterward. Moreover, King was already exhausted and needed the break. He would be away in Washington until nearly the end of March.[38]

The most memorable debate in that unrancorous 1937 session was occasioned by the decisions of the Privy Council on Bennett's legislation of 1935 – in particular, the centrepiece of it, the Employment and

Social Insurance Act of summer 1935. It had established unemployment insurance. King claimed that much of it was beyond Ottawa's powers. Within a fortnight of his government being sworn in on 23 October 1935, a reference had gone to the Supreme Court of Canada to test the constitutionality of the act. The court ruled 4–2 that the Employment and Social Insurance Act was *ultra vires*. The ruling was then appealed to the Privy Council.

The nub of the problem for both the Supreme Court of Canada and the Privy Council was that it was impossible to separate those parts of the legislation that were clearly within the Parliament of Canada's power from those that were more doubtful and which a majority of the Supreme Court held were *ultra vires*. So the whole act fell to the ground. King crowed a little; he had always held that in the act RB had bitten off too much. RB, on the other hand, maintained that it was within Canada's powers. The Privy Council decisions (there were others) came down late in January 1937. They infuriated Cahan, who said in the House, "May I respectfully, but emphatically, express the opinion that Canada is not willing to accept obligations, either domestic or international, which are deliberately imposed ... on this dominion by the government of the United Kingdom ... The ominous fact that this question of dominion subserviency is now again deliberately raised by the judicial committee of the privy council of the United Kingdom demands the careful consideration of this government and this parliament."

Born in Yarmouth in 1862, Cahan had come to know many of the Maritime Fathers of Confederation. He had been a colleague of RB's at Dalhousie in 1890–91. In 1935 in debate on some of RB's "New Deal" ideas, he roundly asserted that the nation's founders had never intended that the property and civil rights section 92(13) should have the sweep and range that the Judicial Committee had given it. RB quoted an earlier Privy Council decision he had cited in the 1928 debates: "There must be a national entity in Canada ... that has power to make laws for the national well being." He complained that in 1937 the Liberal government lawyers had given the case away by replying to one of the judges' questions, "Yes, in all these cases, in every instance, the [dominion] legislation affects property and civil rights." Ernest Lapointe, King's minister of justice, said, "And it was true." RB replied, "Of course it is true, but the phrase in section 92 is not 'affect' but 'in relation to.' There is no legislation that can be passed by this parliament which does not affect property and civil rights." He agreed with Cahan that the Privy Council judgments were "most unfortunate." [39]

The legal community in Canada was more outspoken. W.P.M. Kennedy, at the University of Toronto, long a friend and admirer of RB's, was outraged. His remarks in the *Canadian Bar Review* are too delicious to pass by: "The federal 'general power' [peace, order and good government] is gone with the wind. It can be relied upon at best when the nation is intoxicated with alcohol, at worst intoxicated with war; but at times of sober poverty, sober financial chaos, sober unemployment, sober exploitation, it cannot be used."[40]

Behind RB's position was the idea that the Privy Council's decisions of 1937 made revision of Canada's constitution imperative – either that or abolish appeals to the Privy Council. The latter was controversial; RB did not want it, but something had to change. He seems to have had in mind a constitutional conference, but with Quebec's Duplessis and Ontario's Hepburn that route did not seem promising, Moreover, as Sir George Perley explained to King, the time and manner of RB's putting it forward, as the Privy Council decisions were being announced, made his suggestion look as if he were trying to cover up any reflection on his own judgment in creating the laws in 1935.[41]

Two days before the end of the 1937 session, King asked RB to see him about a draft coronation address to King George VI. RB offered some critical changes, which King promptly accepted, and they went on to talk. King said that he had heard on the radio that RB was going to retire. Was that true? RB answered obliquely, saying his heart was not strong enough to carry him and his party through another general election and he wanted to give the party time to look around for a new leader. His own leadership had cost him $165,000, which was owing to the bank. After the coronation he would take a rest and then decide. King read that, perhaps correctly, as meaning that RB did not want to give up the leadership but wanted to push the Conservative Party into having to requisition it.

King's useful habit of recording conversations included one a few days later with Sir Edward Beatty, president of the CPR. Beatty was in town to discuss CP steamships, one of which, the *Empress of Australia*, King was taking to England for the coronation. RB had told Beatty, so King recorded, that Mildred's health was worrying him, especially so since she was "more than a sister to him." If anything happened to Mildred, RB said, "he would certainly leave public life and leave Canada."[42]

RB's six-month trip around the world, albeit with his valet, seemed to have made him more conscious of his aloneness. King even had the impression in 1937 that RB was thinking of marrying after the coronation, but to whom he does not say. RB's advice to Mackenzie King on the last day of Parliament was that if he should ever think of doing a trip round the world, he shouldn't do it alone. So it was not surprising that Mildred (and a maid) accompanied RB on his way to the coronation early in May, along with Alice Millar. RB and Mildred met Mackenzie King at Buckingham Palace at a post-rehearsal reception two days before the coronation; King remarked how well Mildred looked. However, Mildred had been diagnosed with cancer, and in cancer patients, appearance can be deceptive. After the coronation RB and Mildred, with a nurse, went on to a German spa, Bad Nauheim, north of Frankfurt-am-Main. They were there for most of June, for baths, massage, light walking, and rest. Mildred enjoyed herself thoroughly: "It was all so wonderful & so unexpected," she wrote RB from New York, where she went for further treatment. The German eye specialist had been much impressed that RB could read fine print without glasses. A report from Bad Nauheim on 9 July to RB's London doctor noted that he weighed 228 pounds – after treatment, not before. That was still too much. The German doctor recommended he lose a further ten pounds. RB's pulse rate had improved; it was 90 when he arrived, 60–70 when he left. He still had auricular fluttering and his liver was slightly enlarged. RB asked Alice for the moment to say nothing to anyone of his heart condition. He would ask Finlayson to arrange a summer meeting of Conservative MPs.[43]

RB's return to Canada was greeted by an appreciative editorial in the July *Saturday Night*. Over the past two sessions of Parliament, it said, Mackenzie King has been a less conspicuous and less admired figure than Bennett. His recovery of personal prestige was not so much due to him as party leader but as a brilliant parliamentarian. If there were to arise any international crisis, it was good to have in the government "a man who is highly unsusceptible to the influence of powerful individuals outside of or in the background of politics ... The Conservative party may be able to develop, and learn to follow, a leader of similar attainments."

Mildred had gone to New York for cancer treatment but, perhaps inevitably, found the New York hospital depressing. She observed the people going for treatment, children clinging to their mother's skirts and crying as she left them. "The quarry of the old – the low and the high" was the way Mildred described it. She looked at the other patients and said to herself, "What has Capitalism done for you?" That was the Candida in her speaking. But she was still positive about RB's political future: "Cheer up dear old brother of mine, we will make you Prime

Minister again & then you can do as you please but you will be glad and love us for it."[44]

In fact, RB had come home having decided to resign the party leadership. A party caucus called for Saturday, 31 August, did not go well, at least not according to RB's wishes. As he put it to a friend, "I frankly felt that I was entitled to be released [from the party leadership]. I had definite plans as to how I might spend the remaining years of my life." But, as he told another, "our friends were so insistent on my remaining that I could not bring myself to quit and be regarded as a coward and so I will do my best." He stayed not from inclination but from duty. Indeed, he called that August Saturday "one of the most difficult days of my life." Whether or not he could be of service to Canada he was not sure, but there was no doubt that he could be useful to the Conservative Party. So on he would struggle, as he put it, despite an uncertain heart. Press, prospects, and friends gave him some encouragement: "There never was a time when your experience and ability was as much needed," Aubrey Davis wrote to him. Caucus agreed that there should be a larger meeting of the party to discuss finances, organization, and policies. It was scheduled for the weekend of Saturday, 5 March 1938, when Parliament would, of course, be in session.[45]

The new Conservative MP for Vancouver South, Howard Green, a staunch Bennett supporter, called on him at his Centre Block blue-upholstered office that mid-summer of 1937. RB looked blooming, Green thought. Green wanted to introduce Bruce Hutchison, the reporter from the *Victoria Times*. Hutchison was ostensibly Liberal, but he was impressed. RB was immaculately dressed, trousers pressed to a knife edge, one leg carelessly draped over the arm of his chair. He was in a genial mood, particularly so with Green, who thought the world of him. People might think they knew Bennett, Hutchison said, but they didn't. They might know the old R.B. Bennett of the Depression years, who for five long years "brooded over this capital like a perpetual thunder cloud, with occasional lightning." But a world tour and a year away from being prime minister had resulted in "an entirely changed man."

"They say," Hutchison reported, "that he will retire before the next election but no one really knows. Tomorrow, with one of those sudden bursts of enthusiasm, 'the streaks of boyishness that are the most attractive things about him,' he can change." Bennett had launched into a lucid, amusing two-hour talk, punctuated every so often by his hitting his fist on his desk for emphasis: his memories of New Brunswick, his verdict on Oliver Cromwell's revolt against Charles I (RB was a Cromwellian), a judicious assessment of Ming pottery, a detailed history of the Boer War, plus a philosophic view of the human comedy as he had observed it across his sixty-seven years. This final phase of his career, Huchison said – that is, if it was the final phase – was the most attractive of all. His encyclopedic mind, which seemed to remember almost every fact he ever learned, "is part of the strange fierce fire which yet burns within him."[46]

The streak of boyishness that Hutchison remarked upon was still strong. RB was fond of his young nephew, William Herridge Jr, who had returned with his parents, Mildred and Bill, probably in late November 1935, to live in Ottawa. The family had a house in Sandy Hill on Goulburn Avenue and would flee the Ottawa heat every summer to St Andrews, New Brunswick. On one visit there, RB's bathroom shower had just been started when young William, all of four or five years old, happened by, all dressed to go out. He had never seen a shower before and was curious. "Why not go in?" said his uncle with mischief in his eye. "It's nice and warm. Go right in!" A few minutes later Mildred found her son shrieking with laughter and delight and very wet. Young William continued to be a great admirer of his uncle. During callisthenics with his schoolmates at Osgoode Street school, the teacher said, "Now children, hold your stomachs in or you will never grow to be big strong men." William replied, "My Uncle Dick is a big strong man and he certainly doesn't hold his stomach in!"

The Herridge household was within walking distance of the Château Laurier and Room 301 of the Centre Block. Alice Millar reported (10 September 1937) to RB, then in Sackville, that Mildred had visited her with young William in tow. Mildred was "looking wonderfully well, and William is a real fellow ... he lets Harrison [Captain Ronald Bennett's son] swing him around by one arm and one leg, to my complete terror, but he shrieked with laughter and asked for more."

RB probably spent that Christmas with the Herridges. His first duty in the New Year 1938 was to be pallbearer, with Mackenzie King, at the funeral of Sir George Perley, who died in his sleep on 4 January 1938 at the age of eighty-one. RB and King drove to the church and the cemetery together, talking European and American politics on the way. RB thought the American domestic position serious. He saw desperation in the US federal government's supplying services such as night classes in education to try to create jobs and stimulate the economy. The concept did not seem to trouble King, even though he was a stickler for the proper spheres of the federal and provincial. Standing around at the cemetery later, RB told a group that he could not understand why King had bothered going to Germany in May 1937 to see Hitler when at his doorstep in Ottawa he had in R.B. Bennett a dictator to equal a Hitler and a Mussolini together! He still had a sense of humour and was ready enough to make fun of himself; he just did not like others doing it.[47]

Parliament opened on Thursday, 27 January 1938. King introduced four new MPs to the speaker, three of them Liberals and two of those from old and traditional Conservative seats, the result of 1937 by-elections. RB took the loss of Victoria, Tolmie's seat, hard. Except for a few years from 1902 to 1908, it had been a Conservative seat since 1873 when British Columbia had joined Confederation. King reported that RB looked crushed. And for once in debate, he had the tables turned on him by King. When RB made reference to the large number of Liberal MPs elected by minority vote, King replied that by that criterion, Conservative members would be reduced to four![48]

It was a long-standing tradition of Parliament to recall and remember MPs who had died since Parliament had last met. Objective the tributes generally were not: the rule seemed to be the old Latin motto "*de mortuis nil nisi bene*." But they were often worth listening to. Tolmie's genius, RB said, was his delight in friendship and his sense of humour. Sir Robert Borden, who had died on 10 June 1937 while RB was in Germany, RB had known well. They had disagreed more than once and seriously, but in recent years, certainly since RB had become prime minister, Borden had been an understanding, perceptive, and appreciative colleague, well aware of what Bennett was facing and doing. He was, said RB, a man of infinite patience: "I have never known a more patient man. But once he had made up his mind he was relentless."[49]

The Rowell-Sirois Commission on Dominion-Provincial Relations that King had created in 1937 RB opposed from the very start. His position on Canadian federalism was basically that "we cannot have a Dominion of Canada and nine Sovereign Provinces at the same time." He wanted an open discussion in constitutional conference. At least through questions one could get answers and bring disagreements into the open. But as King had organized it, there was merely going to be a long academic discussion on "re-confederation." As to the commission members, while RB knew and trusted Newton Rowell, the Ontario co-chairman, he was particularly critical of John W. Dafoe, editor of the *Manitoba Free Press*, and R.A. MacKay of Dalhousie University; RB believed both men to be political partisans to the core. Dafoe, he told the Commons, "is a man who has managed by one means or another to insult all those who do not agree with his political opinions." As to MacKay, "for bitter political partisanship I have never known his equal." That last cut was unfair; it went back to a disagreement in October 1931 at the time of Beauharnois scandal. RB had a habit of nursing and indulging his memories of bruises and abrasions, as if they had never healed, as if they were a true reflection of reality. ("Isn't he a hard bugger though?" Herridge once said to Rod Finlayson after the death of Sylvia Stevens, when RB refused to meet the train carrying her body, Stevens with her, back to Vancouver.) Norman Rogers, minister of labour, who knew MacKay – both were political scientists in Nova Scotia – answered RB's criticism: MacKay had "never made a political speech and has never appeared in a political platform."[50]

RB was convinced, however, that the Canadian people needed something more effective than an anodyne royal commission. "We must conquer poverty." Later in the session he put it more dramatically: "We are now fighting a greater war in one sense than we have ever been engaged in. It is a war against unemployment; it is a war against poverty; it is a war against conditions the like of which, despite our richness as a new country, we have never known before." In the debate in the reply to the Speech from the Throne on 31 January, he moved regret that the government had taken no steps to deal with the level of insecurity and unemployment in Canada. The debate went on for a further eleven days. By that time, the newspapers had begun to question RB's leadership. According to Mackenzie King, at the end of the debate on 11 February when RB rose to speak to his 31 January amendment, there was no applause from his thirty-nine Conservative followers. King reported that "every man behind him was as silent as death. It was as humiliating a spectacle as I have witnessed in the House of Commons." Two and a half years after the 1935 election, said King, Bennett was beginning to be seen as a defeated man. With those 1937 by-election defeats as a new and sharp reminder, King's ninety seat majority, 132–42, the throne speech debate seemed to confirm it. Three weeks later, on Saturday, 5 March, as a lead-up to the Conservative conference, RB announced his resignation as Conservative party leader.[51]

The Conservative Party conference of March 1938 was to be an inquiry into the party's affairs, financial and organizational, and inexorably into Bennett's leadership. He knew it was coming but gave no sign of what he intended to do. The truth seemed to be that he disliked giving up the leadership; but sometime in February 1938 there had been a change in his heart rhythm. The doctors told him it was "absolutely imperative for him to abandon ship." RB did not seem to worry as much about dying as becoming a permanent invalid. He told the House of Commons and the public that although for the last few months his health had been better than for some time past, that was no index of the state of his heart. Certainly he could not take the party through another general election.[52]

King watched all this with keen interest. Notwithstanding his frequent diary outbursts against RB and his irritating superiority of knowledge, style, and footwork, King wrote, "it is a tragedy. It is like seeing a man mangled at one's feet." His own cabinet was divided over whether he should make any public comment in the House on RB's decision to go. But he overruled that and was glad he did. So was RB, although he could not resist a barb over what he had endured at Liberal hands during his time as prime minister: "I can only say, Mr Speaker, that I would like to thank the house for this manifestation of good will though, perhaps, if it had been expressed in more strenuous times, it might not have been necessary at all." Alice Millar remarked in a letter, à propos of this Liberal badgering of Bennett, "they wore themselves out trying to wear him out." Her Toronto correspondent had written, "There wasn't a man in Canada that could have accomplished what he did during the depression."[53]

Many of RB's friends thought so too. How sad we are, wrote the governor general's secretary, Willis O'Connor, that "our dear R.B. is leaving the leadership. He has served the country so well. He did such wonderful work during the hard times. When history is written he will come out in large letters." So said many academics and colleagues, not least Harold Innis, the great University of Toronto economist, whose appreciation sums up the outpouring of recognition:

Your leadership of the party especially during the years when you were Prime Minister was marked by a distinction which has not been surpassed and will not be surpassed in our time. No one has ever been asked to carry the burdens of an unprecedented depression such as you assumed and no one could have shouldered them with such ability. I am confident that we shall look to those years as landmarks in Canadian history because of your energy and direction. I hope you will long live to enjoy the growing appreciation which is bound to come with the future.
Yours sincerely,
Harold Innis

RB confided to S.L. Cork, supervisor at the Royal Bank in Winnipeg, that while he and others knew the Depression was coming, they could do nothing to stop it nor to keep the country from going headlong into it. "We had to content ourselves with saving the country from disaster. It is difficult to say whether the majority of Canadians are yet aware of the terrific conditions with which we as a Government were faced."[54]

A cartoon in the *Vancouver Province* of 10 March 1938 showed a future candidate for the party leadership looking at those huge Bennett boots: "It's like to be quite a job." RB was no doubt gratified with the flood of praise, but his replies more often than not carried a rueful overtone as if the country had given him a hard time and had been a long while marshalling up its gratitude. Moreover, the range and depth of his 1935 defeat, whatever philosophy he may have brought to bear upon it, still rankled.

But in April 1938, RB's main concern was not politics but Mildred. The Ottawa and New York doctors kept making soothing murmurs about her recovery from cancer, and so indeed did Mildred herself. But she had a rasping dry cough and a leg infection that made RB very uneasy. She was now in a New York hospital undergoing treatment. During the Commons' Easter adjournment, 8–25 April, he went down to New York to see her. They much enjoyed each other's company, as they always did. She wrote to him, "My nurse is down at supper so I am sending you a few lines to say how wonderful it was of you to come and see me yesterday and how much good it did me to see my dear old brother who has always gone ahead of me in life and scattered roses in my path ... I'll be back soon to living [?] life with you again. " RB returned to Ottawa and his parliamentary duties feeling cheered and somewhat more hopeful. Then on the evening of Wednesday, 11 May, came sudden news from New York that Mildred had died. She was only forty-nine years old.

RB was devastated. Mildred was the woman he was closest to in the world, who understood him, who could counsel him, who could even upbraid him if she thought it necessary. Now she had vanished from his life forever. He shut himself up in her old room in their Château Laurier suite, mindlessly pacing, then reading aloud the Book of Ruth: "And Ruth said, Intreat me not to leave thee, or to return from following after thee: for whither thou goest, I will go ... nought but death part thee and me."

An outpouring of tributes followed the news of her death. Alan Lascelles at Buckingham Palace wrote of "the bright sunshine of her presence." He and his wife asked themselves, "What will he do without her?" well knowing "the cruel significance, that there was no answer." O.D. Skelton wrote from Rockcliffe, "It is only once in a generation that the world is blessed with a woman of such charm and friendliness and understanding." From the Senate, Arthur Meighen was exceptionally warm and solicitous. Even H.H. Stevens sent a note of sympathy. Lapointe, who had crossed swords with RB more than once, exclaimed, "What a tragedy! What a shock!" Old R.S. White (1856–1944), MP for St Antoine-Westmount, spoke of her as "so amiable, so beautiful, so good and so beloved" and quoted the old lines, "None knew her but to love her, / None named her but to praise." Many thought of William, her six-year old son, now left motherless.[55]

RB took it all as manfully as he could, but one of the mooring lines to his life in Canada had clearly given way. Nevertheless, he was still the member for Calgary West, and he was staying on as leader of the Opposition until his party should choose his successor. Parliament was still in session. In a foreign policy debate on 24 May, he said that "the party with which I am associated" would doubtless have a foreign policy statement to make. He was speaking mainly for himself now.

But across the Atlantic there were important issues looming ever larger. The Anschluss of Austria and Germany had taken place on Friday, 11 March 1938. Before that time the German word had no particular connotation, simply meaning "connection" or "joining." But it could also mean "annexation," and that is the signification it soon acquired: the German annexation of Austria. It put all Europe on edge and threw into sharp relief the question of what Canada might do in the event of a European war that involved Britain. In May what Canada's role should be was debated in the House of Commons. It was not so much about what Canada's status in the British Commonwealth was – though that was vague enough – but what military consequences flowed from it. RB distinguished, in a slightly academic way, five positions, ranging from being in lock-step with Britain to being completely neutral. He put Canada in the middle position, of consultation with Britain and the other dominions, thus to "hope to arrive at a common policy." Such a position was, he said, "the essence of common sense" – but in a time of crisis, it was not a very workable stance. He deplored what he seemed to view as King's backsliding toward a fourth position of quasi-neutrality. How could any kind of neutrality be possible? Did Canada have any defence principle at all? Canada still relied almost entirely on the British navy for its defence, almost as it had in 1917 when the Germans laid mines off the coast of Nova Scotia. According to RB, King's position was acutely embarrassing. Canada needed Britain for its defence and yet did little to help.[56]

In the spring of 1938 Britain renewed an initiative that it had offered in 1937, to develop an air force training school in Canada manned by the Royal Air Force for training RAF pilots. Mackenzie King shied away from the idea like a frightened horse. But in the summer of 1938, with the Anschluss just four months old (and not a very pretty process), a British commission came to Canada to discuss aircraft production and air force training. King had no objection to the former (provided that none of the meetings took place in Ottawa) but he had serious objections to the latter. RB asked in Parliament, "If it is essential that we should depend on the British navy for our national life, is it inconsistent with our position of free association with the people that provide it that they should have an opportunity to establish a training school in Canada ... ?" In the end Canada agreed with some reluctance to allow 120 Royal Military College graduates each year to go to England for training and to be short commission officers. The question of training RAF pilots in Canada was left to a time still more urgent than the summer of 1938.[57]

It was RB's last debate in the Canadian House of Commons. King made a graceful farewell speech to him; RB replied that in the course of their eleven years opposite each other in the House, they had each given and taken some hard knocks. "It is all part of the rough and tumble of public life. It is a tiresome task. It is a wearying task. It is an ungrateful task." Yet someone had to do it. The most generous farewell came from A.A. Heaps, the Yorkshireman who was CCF member for Winnipeg North Centre. It might be, said Heaps, that Bennett's heart and soul were in Alberta, but "I think his real heart and soul have been in the work carried on here." RB, he said, was the hardest-working member of the House. The rest sat and marvelled "at the way the right hon. gentleman attends here day after day, week after week ... and at the wealth of information which he has drawn upon ... it is difficult to think of this house without him."[58]

Parliament prorogued that day, Thursday, 1 July 1938. R.B. Bennett, MP for Calgary West since 1925, never returned to the House of Commons again.

The Conservative Party convention took place four days later in Ottawa. As they gathered, the dearth of powerful and compelling candidates became uncomfortably obvious. Robert Manion was already in the field, and "fighting Bob" was well thought of. Arthur Meighen, however, did not think so highly of him, though Meighen also said firmly that he himself was not in the running. A search had developed for a new great leader – in vain, though there were several candidates. That first night, RB gave a banquet speech, and he spoke again the following afternoon, his powerful voice reiterating his social reform ideas of 1935, that the Conservatives still had to fight two great enemies: poverty and unemployment. There emerged a "Draft Bennett" movement led by Howard Ferguson: get Bennett somehow to change his mind. Not least among those pressures came from Herridge, who told RB that Mildred's dearest wish had been that her brother be prime minister again. At the last minute, two "Draft Bennett" men came to see Meighen to get him to push RB in that direction. Meighen called on him at once. He discovered that although RB did not say outright that he could be drafted, it seemed that he could. It was very late in the nomination process, the deadline for close of nominations less than an hour away. Meighen was frank: he was already supporting Murdoch MacPherson of Saskatchewan, another last-minute candidate, and RB's candidacy at this late hour would be unfair to MacPherson and to Manion, both of whom had put themselves in the running on the firm assumption that RB was not, and would not be, a candidate. Besides, Bennett could very well be defeated. If he were, it would be deeply humiliating to him and might very well split the party.

Meighen's argument was decisive. Mildred's seductive idea came and vanished, and Manion emerged from the convention as party leader.[59]

RB's gloss on this is in a letter to Pelham Edgar, a professor of English at Victoria College in Toronto. "I think you will agree," RB wrote, "that I could not yield to the pressure that was put upon me at the Convention … to have declared myself a candidate to succeed myself, at the eleventh hour, would have been rather dishonourable." That's not quite the way it was – RB's ego was a delicate plant.[60]

In Alan Lascelles's letter in May about Mildred, there was a PS: "If you are thinking of a home in England, let Joan and I know." RB had been thinking along exactly those lines. In May 1937 following the coronation, he and Mildred had inspected properties together but found none suitable. After he announced his retirement a year later, he received a letter from Max Aitken, Lord Beaverbrook: "Now I hope you will come here to live and let me see you often." RB replied that while he had no specific plans for the future, as soon as he could get away from Canada he would come over and they would discuss whys and wherefores.

"Please think of me, and the possibility of my being in some public service in my declining years."

In Canada he had received many offers of promising positions, from president of a bank to president of a university, as well as overtures from several large commercial enterprises. But he really did not now want to live in Canada. There were too many sharp edges to memories of the Depression that he had come to symbolize. He had done his best to pull Canada through it, but it was disconcerting to be surrounded with so many unhappy reminders and unpopular designations. "Bennett Buggies" was the most notorious: cars whose owners no longer had the wherewithal to run them. Furthermore, as he put it to Beaverbrook, "I have been too much in the political arena to ever be trusted as a neutral or dispassionate observer." He told friends and newspapermen, "I could see nothing left for me but to go to England to reside. Lord Tweedsmuir [the governor general] thought I should do so." As to a place in the House of Lords, often enough rumoured in Canada and actually mooted by the British in 1932, RB was low key. He still nourished the hope, but it was doubtful now that Neville Chamberlain was prime minister (1937–40).[61]

Beaverbrook had a large country estate in Surrey called Cherkley, near Leatherhead, an hour by train or car south of London. (The English pronounced it "Charkley," the Beaver with his stubborn Canadian accent "Churkley.") It was a huge undistinguished mansion with rooms for thirty guests. Beaverbrook had bought it in 1911, and before long it was the busiest country house in England. South of it half a mile or so was Juniper Hill, a much older and larger estate, with some ninety-six acres of mostly woodlands. The house, built in the 1780s, had been empty for half a dozen years and on the market for some time. Now it was run down, its price dropping steadily. Beaverbrook wanted to protect Cherkley against any adjacent development and had taken an option on it. When RB arrived in England in September, Beaverbrook offered to let him take over that option. RB came, saw, and was delighted. He bought Juniper Hill on 1 November 1938, the purchase to be completed when he returned from his Canadian farewells.

They were to be long and emotional. However experienced a world traveller RB was, he seems to have quite underestimated how hard it would be to pull up his deep Canadian roots in Calgary, Toronto, Ottawa, and especially New Brunswick. Britain on close acquaintance was not Canada, nor British ways Canadian ways, he would discover. Three years later in 1941, he and John Stevenson (1883–1970), chief

Canadian correspondent for the *London Times*, were in New Brunswick, looking out over the Shediac River and the low wooded hills beyond. "It may not be a good thing to tear up one's roots as I have done," he told Stevenson. "I've spent the happiest summers of my boyhood here in New Brunswick. I love it with all my soul. All I have asked to do is to serve the land in which I was born."[62]

He returned to Canada on 19 November 1938 and announced a few days later from the Château Laurier that he had bought an estate in England where he was now going to live. He was "utterly amazed," he said, at the public reaction, a positive torrent of letters and telegrams. He arrived in Calgary on 21 November to a glowing tribute from the *Calgary Herald*: "Few men who ever sat in the House of Commons had greater intellectual equipment and debating power. His marvellous memory, his cogency of argument, his keenness of repartee will be sorely missed." Back in Ottawa at the end of November, he left again for the West "to close up Calgary affairs." Code telegrams from Calgary to London early in December instructed Beaverbrook to get his London architect, Robert Atkinson, to work on the extensive renovations (Beaverbrook called it "reconstruction") that Juniper Hill required.[63]

Winding up his Calgary and western affairs was not simple, and it was mid-January before RB was back east in Toronto for a testimonial dinner at the Royal York, presided over by Arthur Meighen. Meighen gave a major speech, generous, open, frank, succinct. Of course, he said, R.B. Bennett was bound to be defeated in 1935: "There are times when no Prime Minister can be true to the nation he has sworn to serve, save at the temporary sacrifice of the party he is appointed to lead. Without a question there never was a Prime Minister who could have done so in the years Mr. Bennett was in office." Some people, Meighen went on, reacted to Bennett's "New Deal" legislation as if it were a nightmare. But the legislation was enlightened: it was the rhetoric that frightened. The laws themselves had almost unanimous approval by Parliament.[64]

The 1939 session had already started when RB finally arrived back in Ottawa. There is no evidence that he attended the House of Commons; there were already enough – and more than enough – farewells. Just saying goodbye to the staff at the Château Laurier, including the Château's barber, was emotional enough. But when RB left for Montreal and Saint John, only three MPs were at the Ottawa station to see him off: Howard Green, Conservative MP for Vancouver South, Ernest Perley, Conservative MP for Qu'Appelle, and Tommy Douglas, CCF MP for Weyburn,

Douglas was not forgetting the many times RB had helped him understand the ways of Parliament three years back as a new thirty-one-year
old rookie member. But that January it was as if, as Douglas commented,
RB was being shunned by his own party. RB took it that way too – that
is, badly.[65]

It was not easy for a proud man to be so treated. He nursed his grievances en route to Montreal and was not taking calls in his Montreal
hotel. Frank MacKinnon, a twenty-one-year-old student from Prince
Edward Island attending McGill, was asked by a PEI doctor (a Liberal
at that) if he would convey the doctor's personal good wishes to RB.
Somehow MacKinnon's phone call got through. RB was delighted and
said so more than once, but MacKinnon was disconcerted, believing that
RB was quietly sobbing between his sentences of thanks. It was as if his
emotions had at last given way.[66]

Saint John did its best to make up for Ottawa's letdown with a huge
Conservative dinner at the Admiral Beatty Hotel on King Square. The
next day, CP's 18,400-ton ship *Montclare* sailed for Halifax with RB, his
brother Ronald, and Alice Millar aboard. Ronald and Alice would leave
the ship in Halifax, but RB wanted his last touch of Canadian soil to be
in New Brunswick.

The Nova Scotian Conservatives, however, were not to be outdone by
Saint John. George Curtis at the Dalhousie Law School, with the help of
Sir Joseph Chisholm, chief justice of Nova Scotia (one of RB's knighthoods) and Sir Edward Beatty, president of CP Steamships, arranged to
deprive the other passengers of their lunch aboard *Montclare* in Halifax
harbour and so sent them ashore. It was Saturday, 28 January 1939. RB
had just mailed off his resignation as MP for Calgary West when some
292 Nova Scotian Conservatives crowded aboard the ship. It was a fes-
tive farewell luncheon. Sir Joseph presided. When RB rose to acknowledge Sir Joseph's tribute, he needed a handkerchief to wipe away tears
"that streamed down that strong, resolute face."[67] At the end he quoted
Byron: "Fare thee well, and if for ever, / Still for ever, fare thee well."

The *Montclare* sailed that evening for Greenock, Belfast, and Liverpool.

8

Becoming Squire of Mickleham,
1938–1947

In the five or six days at sea between Canada and Britain, old horizons melt away and new ones come into view. RB never commented on this shift, except in the poem "The Crossing Paths" that he wrote down in 1890.[1] Neither did he ever talk much about the differences between Canada and London. He had come a long way, but he never forgot that long road out of Hopewell Cape. He never scorned his upbringing, of which his mother had been head and centre, though he did tend to distance himself from it, not so much by deliberation as by experience and knowledge. His style came finally to measure the distance he had travelled. Not for him, even in Calgary, cowboy boots or a Stetson hat. Informality was too close to his humble origins. He first encountered England in 1905, and eventually his clothes all came from Chancery Lane or Saville Row.

RB mastered social ideas and niceties on both sides of the Atlantic and moved effortlessly between them. It was as if the six days on the Atlantic Ocean was the moral and aesthetic distance necessary to effect the adjustment. In this respect he was unlike Henry James, whose whole literary oeuvre celebrated his profound sense of the differences between North America and Europe. One of James's eerie short stories, "The Jolly Corner," ends with a doppelgänger encounter between an American who returned after twenty years in Europe to encounter his alter ego who stayed at home in New York. It was a terrible shock. But James was American, and his contrasts were between the United States and Europe; RB's were between Canada and Britain. There's a difference. With RB, certainly, it was as if Canada, Britain, the empire even, were all equally part of his inhabited world. The Armada of 1588 was his victory; his great-grandfather had fought on the British side at Louisbourg in 1758 and at Quebec in 1759. Spion Kop in South Africa in January 1900 was his disaster.

In January 1939, on his way east from Calgary he was interviewed in Ottawa by Frederick Griffin of the *Toronto Star Weekly*. No longer leader of the Opposition, RB was just MP, Calgary West, in an ordinary MP's room. Griffin asked RB, now on the eve of his departure for England, if he did not feel sad, if he were going into exile? RB looked at Griffin steadily from beneath those quill eyebrows. "No, my friend," said he gently, "I shall be going, shall we say, home?" He then quoted Henry V's lines before the battle of Agincourt (1415): "This royal throne of Kings, this happy breed of men, this little world, this precious stone set in a silver sea, this earth, this realm this England." The main Roman road between London and the south coast went right through his property at Juniper Hill, and in his mind reverberated the tramp of Roman legions two thousand years earlier. "The call of that little island is terrific," he told Griffin.

Afterward Griffin spoke to Alice Millar, asking her if she didn't think Mr Bennett might be lonely. "He lives in a welter of work," she said, "of thought, of action. Besides," she added, "he is not of a lonely nature."[2] Moreover, RB would not be alone in England: as his personal and financial secretary for many years, Alice would be joining him. He would also have as his closest neighbour his old friend Max Aitken.

Max Aitken, 1st Baron Beaverbrook, had outgrown Canada and Canadian life in perhaps the same way that RB had. Charming, greedy, generous, intensely curious, avid for information about all things (others' sexuality not least), he remained devoted to the old New Brunswick friend who had helped him in his first steps in business. Aitken had begun life with mischief in his heart and after that he was mischief on the make, in Chatham, Calgary, Halifax, Montreal, and then London. He was made a baron in 1916 by Lloyd George, with the help of the New Brunswick born Bonar Law, prime minister of Britain in 1922–23. Aitken was mocked in London as "Lord Ratstream," and the origin of his peerage derided: "As propagandist I'm sublime / A peer without a flaw, / But to such heights I ne'er could climb / Loved I not Bonar Law."

Beaverbrook and RB shared a passion for the greater glory of the British Empire. In the minds of both men, there was the thought that in a generation or two, when British coal had run out, the residuary legatee of Britain's role in the empire might well be Canada. "The centre of Empire is passing westward," Beaverbrook told RB when he first became leader of the Opposition in October 1927. The idea was not put forward publicly, but noted in reflective moments in letters between them.

For the present, however, RB believed that Canada needed the British Commonwealth. In his mind there was no real conflict between Canadian nationalism and British imperialism. The imperial idea was a vital Canadian counterweight against the insidious and heavy gravitational pull of the United States. "Unless we remain within the British Empire," he said in 1938, "we will ... lose our identity as a nation and be absorbed in our great neighbour to the south."[3]

RB had many important English acquaintances, among them Neville Chamberlain, now prime minister. At the turn of the century the imperial sentiments of Chamberlain's father, Joseph Chamberlain, had inspired both Aitken and RB as young empire-minded Canadians. Neville Chamberlain had a mind and style very different to his father's. There was a narrow-gauge quality about him, a lack of humour, a complacent earnestness, and, as he himself admitted, a nature too trusting, too easily taken in – by Beaverbrook in 1930 or by Hitler in 1937. On the other hand, he had a long memory, and he had not forgotten how difficult RB had been in Ottawa in 1932.

The question of a peerage for R.B. Bennett of Canada arose in the spring of 1939. Sir Samuel Hoare, the home secretary, had welcomed RB to England, and a few weeks later RB went to see him about the peerage that had been mooted in 1932. Hoare was enthusiastic, but Chamberlain was dubious: RB had not been living long enough in Britain; the Canadian government could well object. Hoare saw Chamberlain about it several times that summer, but his suggestions fell among thistles: Chamberlain's brooding memories of Ottawa. When Hoare went to Madrid as ambassador, Beaverbrook took up the cause with even less effect: one slippery Canadian recommending another obdurate one for a British peerage did not commend itself to Chamberlain. RB's peerage went to a back burner – well back.[4]

When RB arrived in England early in February 1939, he took up residence at his old stamping ground, the Mayfair Hotel in Berkeley Square. Juniper Hill was far from ready. It had been vacant for some time, and Beaverbrook had originally been intending to let it go to rack and ruin and to replant the estate with larch and beech. The house was badly run down, but it was a well-designed brick Italianate structure, built by Robert Adam in the 1780s. In 1928 the owner was said to have refused

£40,000 for the property. After he died, the estate deteriorated and the price with it. But there was a problem with an ancient right-of-way, and in the end Bennett got the property for only £9,750. He was enthusiastic. "I have acquired," he had written Alice Millar "one of the finest pptys [*sic*] in Surrey."[5]

Juniper Hill was potentially a lovely place, half surrounded by National Trust properties. A path ran up the hill through the woods to Beaverbrook's Cherkley. About one-quarter was parkland, where eventually RB would graze five or six head of Highland cattle, though he never could bring himself to have them killed. There was an apple orchard and rose garden combined and a walled kitchen garden that grew pears, plums, cherries, peaches, and nectarines. Beds of asparagus and strawberries were planted at the front of the house; RB ate both in profusion. He was even able to find and employ the old Juniper Hill gardener, William Christison. The house certainly needed a stern, even ruthless refurbishing; it also needed that Canadian essential, central heating, and lots of hot water for several new bathrooms. The large elevation between the main entrance hall and the first floor – some twenty-five feet – to RB's eye enjoined an elevator ("lift" in English parlance). He liked movies, so a small movie theatre was to be installed. Happily, the old house could sustain the massive changes. The architect Robert Atkinson proceeded to engage contractors to carry out the extensive improvements. Juniper Hill was to be ready for RB's occupancy by 30 June 1939. He had cabled early in January 1939: did the architect need him urgently? No. As it turned out, the English architect and contractors had yet to become acquainted with RB's impatience. They soon would.

He was exigent and particular with the changes he wanted but seemed to know little of what could be expected in England from architects and contractors. The contract with John Greenwood Ltd. gave the builders possession of the property as of 11 February 1939. They had undertaken to have the work completed by 30 June, agreeing to a penalty of £25 a day for every day it ran over schedule. RB did not think it could be done in that time, but he was anxious to move in. Trouble arose over the ancient right-of-way, and he agreed to a new deadline of 31 July. He hired domestics for August, but the work was not complete even by the end of September. Nevertheless, he moved into Juniper Hill on 1 October 1939.

The long argument with both architect and contractors would extend into 1941 over what RB claimed was inadequate supervision and sloppy workmanship. While he was grateful to Atkinson for advice with furnishings and for his general readiness to help, that appreciation would not, could not, prevent RB from expressing his honest convictions: "I am very much disappointed in the working out of the contract at Juniper Hill. I feel I am paying far more than I should and that the work was not adequately supervised ... just what 8½ per cent of the expenditure made at Juniper Hill has secured for me I confess I find it at times difficult to ascertain ... I will never look back upon this whole work except in terms of the bitter treatment I have received from the contractors."

Atkinson replied tartly that it was "not part of the architect's duty to be on the site constantly." He relied on the honesty of the contractors. RB did not. He even got down to going through the day-work sheets. The conflict did not exclude his "explosive telephone conversations" with Atkinson. It would finally be sorted out by April 1941 with the help of the more tractable Alice Millar. The original contract was for £8,000 plus architect's fees; the final one was £16,223.[6]

At the other end of the scale was RB's adventure with chairs for Juniper Hill. He found eight antique chairs in W.J. Mansell's, a long-established firm in the Fulham Road, but he wanted a dozen. Mansell's thought that the family from whom the eight had been originally bought might well have four more. RB closed with buying the dozen at £85. A few months later, in a shop of a "manufacturer of antiques," he discovered an exact copy of his chairs: they were not antique! (In Beaverbrook's version, the shop was owned by an old Jewish gentleman with a slow smile and an ingratiating manner.)

Back went Bennett to Mansell's with Alice Millar and Atkinson in tow, demanding his money back. The clerk said the firm could not do that. RB filed a claim with his solicitor on 27 February 1940. Mansell's protested that they were a reputable firm, that they'd never had legal action before; they would take the chairs back "on the distinct understanding that we do not admit that the chairs are aught else than represented to Mr. Bennett" – namely, that they were sixty years old. RB wasn't having it. Mansell's might not have wanted litigation, but they were going to get it. He believed with good reason that his chairs were all of two years old and wanted an apology and an admission of fraud, failing which the firm would be exposed in court. No doubt the firm was old and established, he said, "but I do not propose to become a victim of conduct on their part that amounts to fraud." In January 1941, he got his apology, and legal proceedings in the West London County Court were withdrawn. "It's a poor business," said Alice, "to try to scalp Canadians." At least one could say it was wise not to try it on R.B. Bennett.[7]

With the onset of war in 1939–40, RB was increasingly involved with the Canadian Red Cross. He had been a power in the Alberta Red Cross, and over the years this interest had expanded to the national level. Almost from the moment he arrived in England, he became chairman of the London Advisory Committee of the Canadian Red Cross. It was in this role that he crossed swords with the Masseys. When Mackenzie King had returned to power in 1935, within a fortnight he had appointed Vincent Massey (1887–1967) as Canada's high commissioner to London in 1935 – much to Massey's delight and to his wife's. RB had deprived him of the post in 1930. RB had never liked Massey; he thought him priggish, precious, and effete. That dislike was reciprocated. Of course, when RB arrived in England in 1939, there was no love lost between Juniper Hill and Canada House. That enmity certainly included Mrs Alice Parkin Massey.

Alice Massey was honorary president of the Canadian Women's Club and chair of its War Emergency Committee. She wanted to pull the Information Bureau out of the Canadian Red Cross and put it with her group. When she informed RB of her intention, he informed her bluntly that it was certainly not on. The Women's Club executive backed him, and there was a fat row in which they descended on Alice Massey's office and put all files and correspondence out of her reach. It was a technique similar to the one RB had used in his quarrel with Sir James Lougheed in 1922. He then went off to Canada for Christmas in December 1939 to make clear where he stood with the Canadian Red Cross. He won on all fronts.[8]

One of RB's early discoveries was that as owner of Juniper Hill he had an official pew in St Michael's Church, Mickleham, a quarter-mile away. St Michael's was an ancient establishment, its unlovely squat bell-tower dating from AD 946–75, even before the Domesday Book of 1086. The rest of the church had been largely rebuilt in 1823. Buried there was Beaverbrook's first wife, Gladys Drury of Halifax, Nova Scotia, who had died in December 1927 of a brain tumour.

Just before leaving for Canada, RB made a Christmas contribution to St Michael's for Mickleham children and evacuees. On his return in January 1940, he invited the Rev. R.M. Langdale-Smith, rector since 1936, and his wife to Juniper Hill. He learned from them that the church needed £4 a week just to keep going, and that the average Sunday collection was only £2. RB funded half the difference on a per annum basis. He liked the way the church was run. "Nothing could be better," he told the treasurer, "than sending to the various supporters of the church an indication of just what sums are required." And so he became a patron, and an important one.[9]

Mickleham was in the new diocese of Guildford, created in 1927. Guildford Cathedral was begun in 1936 on Stag Hill on the northwest edge of town. It was an imposing design, some 365 feet long, and money was being raised to complete it. Exactly when RB's interest in Guildford Cathedral first surfaced is unknown, but Bishop John Guildford MacMillan had first met him in London in August 1939 when he was still living at the Mayfair Hotel. RB thought the cathedral's size required more ample land around it, and in 1941, on condition of secrecy, gave Bishop MacMillan £10,000 to buy land that had become available around the cathedral. The news came out in 1946. A plaque in Guildford Cathedral commemorates the gift.[10]

In late January 1940, RB was recommended to the Lord Lieutenant of Surrey as justice of the peace and was so appointed. He sat on the bench at Dorking Magistrate's Court on Wednesday mornings every fortnight, though in later years less often.[11]

RB had early acquired a reputation in London as a gifted and entertaining speaker. Almost as soon as he was in England, before even he was settled in Juniper Hill, the British Council (founded in 1934) had recruited him for talks in Europe about Britain and its empire. In June 1939 the council's chairman, Lord Lloyd, asked him to undertake a strenuous lecture tour of Northern Europe. There were two lectures in RB's portfolio: one on the British Empire, with details from his 1936 tour of New Zealand, Australia, and South Africa, the other on Canada. The itinerary was formidable: he was to leave London on 4 November 1939, going to Copenhagen, Oslo, Helsinki, Riga, Kaunas, Warsaw, and Lvov, ending in Cracow, December 9–10, then returning to England by train through Berlin. This program was overtaken by the German invasion of Poland on 1 September, and Britain's declaration of war on Germany of 3 September. But the British Council was indefatigable, returning in November with a new program of lectures in countries still neutral.

RB was willing; the Canadian Red Cross was not yet taking much of his time, and he was ready to devote himself to "any useful purpose for the Empire." However, he added, "I feel that if the [war] crisis develops it will be the most serious in the history of our Empire since the Armada. I can only hope it will not occur." The new British Council northern itinerary would cut out Poland and Finland but include the Netherlands,

Denmark, Sweden, and the Baltic States. It would have RB leave London on 16 March 1940, returning by air from Riga on 15 April. Lord Lloyd emphasized how valuable such a tour would be: "The Germans are working extremely hard in the area you are going to visit and I cannot think of any step more likely to draw the attention of the peoples of Denmark, Holland and Sweden than a visit of the ex-Prime Minister of Canada." But the Germans were working even harder than Lord Lloyd suggested, and this tour too was overtaken by events. The German invasion of Denmark and Norway came on 9 April 1940.[12]

Within a month, RB had become an unpaid senior official in Beaverbrook's Ministry of Aircraft Production. Beaverbrook was appointed minister on 14 May 1940, and a fortnight later RB was there too, trouble-shooting for his old friend in a variety of tasks. He commuted regularly from Juniper Hill to London, leaving about 9 AM and returning in the evening. Although his work for the Canadian Red Cross continued, it was now largely overtaken by important and serious work at Beaverbrook's ministry.

Bennett became Beaverbrook's roving commissioner on strategic metals, especially aluminium and magnesium. He reported in mid-June 1940 that by the end of the year the available stock of aluminium would be almost exhausted; the controller should be required at once to replace the eight thousand tons he had taken from the ministry's supply. Beaverbrook gave RB a good deal of authority, signing without further ado letters that RB had drafted. In July 1940, RB was sent to South Wales to investigate the supply of non-ferrous metals. Beaverbrook was appreciative. "I am deeply conscious without your guidance I would not have got the question to the present degree of order." Three weeks later he wrote, "You know what your support has meant to me in the past months. All I ask now is that you should continue to give it. Of that I can be certain."[13]

Beaverbrook (and others) used RB to give ringing patriotic speeches at British industrial centres and war factories, something that he liked and was good at doing. In May 1940 he agreed to go to Hull to give a speech about savings certificates. Much publicity had been laid on, but air raids threatened and the audience was small. That only put RB on his mettle. He discovered how much money Hull had already raised and at once concluded that the last thing Hull needed to hear about was savings certificates. The English didn't talk about their achievements, so he proceeded to do it for them. He told the citizens of Hull of the indebtedness of the world at large to the British Empire and all that it had stood for. His speech came as a surprise – "possibly a pleasant shock."

Major Morris, the local commander, wrote that it was "the most inspiring and moving address I have ever heard ... It created a tremendous impression."[14] His success as a speaker was such that he was soon lined up: for example, Cambridge on 25 November, Oxford on 30 November (substituting for Beaverbrook), Godstone on 7 December, and a rash of speeches for 1941. Frank Hall, the organizer for both National Savings and War Weapons Week, apologized for giving him such a load, but what could they do in view of "the chorus of praise which has reached us from every place in which you have spoken on our behalf?"[15]

But moving around England in the blitz was risky. One of RB's adventures in this regard can do for many. He was to give a speech in Birmingham on 7 October 1940. The Ministry of Aircraft Production persuaded him not to attempt to reach Birmingham by car but to take the train. After the speech, RB missed his return train but found another due at Euston at 7:25 PM. It was attacked en route and arrived late. Finding no taxis at Euston Station, he walked to Warren Street, got the tube to the Strand, and from there walked through the bombing to the Athenaeum Club. It was one of the fiercest night raids so far; "as I walked towards the Athenaeum, wearing a tin hat, and alone with fires burning fiercely, shrapnel exploding in the air & bombs falling, I wondered if I were struck whether it would ever be known how I had perished." At the Athenaeum he found that his chauffeur and a house guest at Juniper Hill, J.A. Noonan of the Royal Bank of Canada's London office, "blown into the Club." Fortunately the car was intact. They got back to Juniper Hill at 11:30.[16]

RB's work for Beaverbrook also meant unravelling problems that others in the Ministry of Aircraft Production were too slow or too rigid to deal with effectively. One example from late August 1940: T.A. Macaulay, chairman of A.C. Cossor Ltd (the firm made valves in Yorkshire) complained that the ministry was being too refractory. Its policy was to compensate for losses from air raids, but officials insisted that each contract must be recalculated separately. "We can't do it," Macaulay wrote Bennett, "we have 100 contracts for valves, and 50 more for other things ... I am directing this to you because I believe you will get a solution for the problem quicker than anybody I know at the Ministry." RB acted, Beaverbrook phoned, and within three weeks the difficulty had been put to rest. Letters to Bennett at the Ministry of Aircraft Production would sometimes end, "Can you get some action?" They were directed to the right place; one of RB's earliest maxims was, "Make things happen."[17]

After the fall of France and the Dunkirk evacuation in June, when the only organized army element in Britain was the 1st Canadian Division – and it was ill-equipped – with the threat of German invasion imminent, the British government had ordered the internment of enemy aliens. That order also encompassed Jewish refugees, who were rounded up and sent to quarters on the Isle of Man. Beaverbrook arranged for a German-speaking friend to go there and interview those with technical skills; by ministerial fiat he pulled them back to the factories from which they had been taken. That fairly put the cat among the pigeons in Whitehall. One critical factory was Loewy Manufacturing in Bournemouth, whose work was extrusion presses for aluminium. Was an enemy alien, Ludwig Loewy, to be relied on in such critical work? About some of his workmen there was even more uncertainty. To get Whitehall off his back, Beaverbrook asked RB in August 1940 to investigate the firm. Bennett did, and did not approve of Beaverbrook's releasing enemy aliens back into Britain's war factories. Beaverbrook countermanded Bennett's recommendation, saying that he needed them. Loewy himself would eventually prove innocent, but it was a complicated story that Beaverbrook simplified to his own tune later.[18]

Loewy seems to have been naive in employing Germans and Czechs of decidedly dubious background. Chief among these was Adolf Lendl, the first serious case that RB encountered. Born in old Austria in 1902, Lendl was a metallurgical engineer who had come to England in 1937. A former Czech army officer, he had at one time been associated with Henlein groups in the Sudetenland. A letter of 6 May 1939 to Lendl from his mother suggests the problem RB had to consider: "We are so happy to be German citizens under the leadership of Adolf Hitler. It was endlessly beautiful ... The Prague Citadel, the waving swastika flags, thousands of men in front, then the Führer ... What do you think of the Poles? What swine!"

Lord Rothschild of the Security Service in the War Office and RB both believed that Lendl should be interned. Rothschild could not believe that he was "completely indispensable," as Beaverbrook asserted. In early October 1940 the Home Office began putting an internment order for Lendl in motion. It was blocked; as Lord Rothschild put it, "they were frightened of Lord B[eaverbrook]." In the end the compromise was a police guard. Rothschild and RB were vexed that Lendl was allowed thus to remain at large. "We've been struggling for years," Rothschild told RB, "to dispel the idea that any foreigner in this country in time of war is friendly until he has been actually caught committing some overt act against the State."[19]

In late October 1940, Loewy was compromised by a Frenchwoman, Mlle Bette Bertelot, who landed in England on a flight from Portugal. It was discovered she had letters to several German refugees in England sewn inside her skirt. Among them was a letter to Ludwig Loewy. RB now felt thoroughly vindicated. He wrote to Beaverbrook in a tone of aggrieved righteousness, reciting the story: "It may interest you to know ..." But Beaverbrook was still convinced that Loewy was more sinned against than sinning. He phoned the director of military intelligence and said impatiently that Loewy should either be arrested or bloody well left alone. He was left alone. Intelligence was finally convinced he was reliable, but Lendl was still a serious risk. Lord Swinton, chairman of the Home Defence (Security) Executive, told Beaverbrook, "I see from the papers that Bennett is familiar with it all." RB's complaint was the lack of evidence that Lendl and others like him had renounced Hitler. However, on this issue he did not have power of final decision; it rested with "others" (read, Beaverbrook). "It is also the reason," he told Rothschild, "why the whole situation has been so difficult." He never did like being thwarted when he thought he was right. He sulked for a week, but he was at Cherkley for Christmas dinner.[20]

He retained a basic distrust of enemy aliens. Treat them with tolerance, he said, "see them fed and clothed and employed, but not placed in a position where they can give effect to 'Once a German, always a German.'" His charity was to support German refugees, but his instinct was to regard them with suspicion.[21]

By early 1941 wrecked German aircraft were showing that the Germans were using magnesium alloys. RB was set to investigating supplies. He estimated that the 1941 requirements would be just under 16,000 tons, and that experts were too optimistic about supply. Extraction from seawater was not going well. Private sources in Canada could in a short time produce 1,500 tons, but RB concluded, "Your magnesium supply should not in any case rest on conjecture." He kept urging Beaverbrook to go after 10,000 tons of magnesium, for it would soon be needed. So much did he urge this point that Beaverbrook minions were convinced that their master was being harassed. RB thought of Henry II's remark in 1170 to his minions against Thomas à Becket, "Will no man rid me of this turbulent priest?"[22]

But the turbulent priest was kept on to the end of Beaverbrook's ministry. Indeed, when Beaverbrook became minister of supply in late June 1941, his personal assistants were RB and an Australian senator, W.D. Elliott. Beaverbrook retained a high opinion of RB's work, writing to a Canadian friend from Washington in December 1941, "R.B. has won a most splendid position with the British public. And I count myself a very fortunate man in securing his wisdom for my guidance."[23]

By this stage RB had become a viscount. It had taken some time. Beaverbrook had pressed his claim on Chamberlain, but outside of smiles and thanks for Beaverbrook's support in the *Daily Express*, it availed nothing. Churchill was better disposed, and Beaverbrook was an indispensable minister. Churchill wrote to RB on 21 May 1941: would he accept a viscountcy in the coming birthday honours? RB was delighted. The highest rank in the peerage ever offered a Canadian, it was announced in *The Times* on 12 June, his viscountcy heading the list of honours.[24]

There was a chorus of approval on both sides of the Atlantic. The minister of information, Brendan Bracken, wrote from 10 Downing Street, "For nearly three years the bureaucrats have discovered every sort of reason for depriving the House of Lords of the best legislator the Empire has ever produced ... Our dynamic little Max brushed aside the sorry and superficial objections." And, he added, how thoroughly pleased Churchill was! Vincent Massey sent a telegram from Canada House.

If Mackenzie King refused to allow the Canadian House of Commons to send congratulations, disapproving as he did of all imperial honours, still he cabled "good wishes for the opportunities." A.A. Heaps (CCF MP, 1925–40) and M.J. Coldwell (CCF MP, 1935–58, CCF leader, 1940–58), though they may have disapproved of honours, both sent Bennett their best wishes, Coldwell adding, "as one who sat in the House of Commons with you and grew to respect your great gifts and services." Sir John A. Macdonald's granddaughter, Daisy Gainsford, wrote from Winnipeg, "Yes! Canada misses you. She did not know your worth until too late. I have heard some hard-boiled Liberals say, 'Mr. Bennett should be here.' Our present Prime Minister [Mackenzie King] is doing his best – but both you and I and a large number have no faith in him."[25]

The honour entailed for RB some delightful preoccupations: researching his pedigree and designing his proposed arms, his motto, his title. For the Bennett arms, he ingeniously proposed a New Brunswick moose on one side and a Calgary buffalo on the other. The College of Arms hoped their artist would be able to do justice to the North American wildlife. His motto, he decided, would be "*Premi non opprimi*": "Press but do not oppress." He consulted Calgary friends about his title. They wanted simply "Bennett of Calgary." He added Hopewell and Mickleham. For his induction to the Lords, "in these difficult times," Ede & Ravenscroft of Chancery Lane offered a viscount's robes "not quite new," which RB availed himself of at 55 guineas.

Two fellow viscounts, both old friends, Lord Hailsham and Lord Greenwood, took him to lunch and presented him to the Lords on 23 July. Three friends and Alice Millar were in the gallery. RB was nervous and excited; although he disclaimed it, he was, a few layers down, sentimental, and the House of Lords was the height of his ambition. In his long letter of thanks to Beaverbrook, begun 12 June and finished only the day of his formal induction, the new Lord Bennett recited the story of the crossings and entanglements of their two lives starting at Chatham, New Brunswick, in 1889 to London in 1941. No one, RB said, has "greater pride in your success or holds you in more affectionate regard than your friend of boyhood days who still subscribes himself ever, 'Yours, faithfully, devoted and affectionately, Dick.'"[26]

When the Lords was in session, RB attended every Tuesday, Wednesday, and Thursday at 2 PM when he was in England, which was most of the time. He did his committee work; he enjoyed the Lords thoroughly. On 10 August he even sat with the lord chancellor to give George VI's assent to the bills passed by Parliament. He told his brother in New Brunswick, "It is a long far cry from the school house at the Cape ... I will be careful not to say too much for a good long time. They are very kind to me."[27]

In the meantime, as custom decreed, he answered his congratulations by handwritten letters. At five a day, he was finished by Christmas, in time to prepare his maiden speech in the Lords. He gave it on 28 January 1942, on a subject which would become a perennial favourite of Canadian graduate students in British universities: an overview of the way the British Empire had evolved since the first Colonial Conference in 1887. He spoke with pride of the work of Sir Robert Borden, especially in urging in 1918 "continuous consultation on all important matters of common Imperial concern." The British Foreign Office could never seem to get its mind around the idea that anyone else might have a finger in the making of empire foreign policy. Constitutional evolution was going quite the other way, ending with the Balfour Declaration of 1926, translated into the Statute of Westminster of 1931. Though at the time of its passing he had been less than enthusiastic, Viscount Bennett now thought that statute "one of the great landmarks in our history." It was a statute of at once recognition and renunciation ... What this great Parliament did was to renounce completely its legislative control over the whole of these vast Dominions." The dominions were now held together only by the Crown. As RB put it in a later debate, "the Crown is the Crown. It is the Crown in Canada, the Crown in Australia, it is the Crown in South Africa and it is the Crown here."

Lord Chatfield, former first sea lord, praised Viscount Bennett's speech as widening British counsels "from a rather narrow and insular point of view." How fortunate that the Lords were to have a "great Imperial statesman in their midst." Beaverbrook, who was away with Churchill in Washington, was fulsome: "I have heard on all sides of the immense impression which your first speech made upon your audience in the House of Lords."[28]

For a year now RB had been speaking across England about the contribution of Britain and Britain's empire to world civilization. In the last hundred years there had been nothing "more remarkable than the development of the political relations of the British Empire." Other countries, he told the Birmingham and Midland Institute, centralized power: Britain decentralized it. He told a Sheffield meeting on 16 March 1942, "I sometimes think that you in England little realize what you really have done." At times his expression of pride was near arrogance, as he quoted Tennyson: "We sailed wherever ship may sail / We founded many a mighty state / Pray God our greatness may not fail / Through craven fear of being great." He was invited to join the War Policy Group in the Lords and was asked to support Lord Elibank's motion on 1 July 1942 for the maintenance and strengthening of the British Empire.[29]

The low point of the war for Britain had now been reached. "I have never been so agitated and concerned about the fate of the British Empire as I have in the last few days," RB said on 1 July. German tanks were within a fortnight of sighting the oil derricks at Maikop in the Caucasus; Rommel's army was at the western borders of Egypt. The carnage in North Atlantic shipping could not be sustained much longer. Japan's success in overrunning the Philippines, Malaysia, and Singapore had spread outward to the bombing of Darwin in Northern Australia and to threats on Ceylon. The Germans called the years 1940–42 "*die Zeit ohne Beispiel*" ("the time without equal"). RB's speech in support of Lord Elibank's motion is as near to a *cri de coeur* as one finds in Bennett:

I have from my youth up thought it [the British Empire] was almost a sacred thing ... I believe it is the greatest instrument for the maintenance of civilization, for the promotion of friendly feelings between peoples, and for the maintenance of order and justice that the world has ever known. But I see it disintegrating under my very eyes. Its richest possessions are now in the hands of the enemy ...

I have always remembered the words of Lord Roseberry when speaking of the British Empire. He said that it was a product of men's minds and brains and that he would indeed be a cynic who did not see within it the finger of the Divine. That thought has been with me all my thinking life.

That same day a motion of censure against the government was raised in the Commons. Although the Battle for Midway Island in the Pacific on 4 June 1942 had halted Japanese expansion, its effects had not yet been grasped. In mid-August Churchill brought in General Alexander as commander in chief in the Middle East with Montgomery as general of the 8th Army. After a very bad couple of years, the war began to look a little more hopeful.

It was also starting to add weight and momentum to the centrifugal principles latent in the 1931 Statute of Westminster. For the present it was disguised by the struggles and the patriotism of war, but in March 1944 RB raised in the Lords an alarm over what he had seen in a Canadian Army pamphlet. Canada owed allegiance to the King of Canada, it said: where then was Canadian allegiance to the King of Great Britain? After RB's protest to the Canadian Army, apparently the offending pamphlet was withdrawn. "But," RB told the Lords, "it is a terrible thing to have that idea get abroad ... and we must see to it that our [British] foreign policy is the policy of all these Dominions." There was later to be ache and disillusionment for him on how long that position could be maintained.

RB also took a firm position in a Lords debate in May 1944 on Newfoundland. He had been prime minister in 1932–33 when Newfoundland was forced to default on some of its public debt. Ottawa and London both agreed to a shared temporary bailout, on condition of Newfoundland's accepting a British royal commission with sweeping powers to look into its public finances. The resulting Baron Amulree Royal Commission came out to St John's early in 1933, visited Ottawa in November, and reported in 1934. It recommended sweeping changes. In return for Britain's taking over and refunding Newfoundland's public debt, the colony would give up responsible government and instead be governed by an appointed commission that would stay in place until it could again look after its own finances. Lord Amulree's recommendations were heavy handed, but there were few options available. Canada could not afford to buy Labrador, a possibility that been mooted.

The war and the skilful commission government had now steadily improved the colony's financial outlook, and in May 1944 the Lords debated what was to come next. RB rose to say that whatever else Britain might urge, it should not allow Newfoundland to revert back to responsible government: "It is perhaps a dreadful thing to say but in Newfoundland it may be best to begin again ... and develop effectively the institutions [to] ... make possible the full development of the country and its people." Five years later, in March 1949, in effect that is what confederation with Canada did.[30]

Since the start of the war, RB had presided at Juniper Hill over wide-ranging, felicitous hospitality, especially for Canadian soldiers. It included drink as well as food; RB now knew a little about wines and spirits, and he had ample advice about what to buy from Beaverbrook up the hill. The result was praised by Thomas Cotton, his doctor, at Christmas 1943, as "the best company in the world, with food and drink that could not be surpassed even in the days of Lucullus when he entertained our mutual friend Cicero." RB also offered Juniper Hill as a weekend refuge to the Women's Volunteer Service, an invitation which its head, Stella, dowager marchioness of Reading, gratefully accepted. On many of the weekends through the autumn and winter of 1939–40, two or three wvs women, occasionally as many as five, would get "a lovely break from grim London," as one of them put it. Alice Millar had to explain in February 1940 to Miss P.Y. Betts, the wvs coordinator, that for most of February 1940 the weekends were taken up, as Mr Bennett had "filled the house with Canadian soldiers." In March one maid was off with German measles, and another was showing signs, but if Miss Betts didn't mind turning to and doing maids' work, she was welcome to come. "Actually, I miss your cheery presence,"[31] Alice wrote.

There was another cheery presence that would inhabit Juniper Hill periodically for the next few years, perhaps the most vivacious of Bennett's many devoted women friends, Jane Lamb Carton. A children's writer, she had married Ronald Carton, the former Far East correspondent of the *Times* and currently the editor of *Country Life*. He was the *Times* chief editor for their special numbers. Jane Carton was a spirited young woman with wit and dash who made requests of RB with amazing aplomb. The war had released her inhibitions, she said: could she come down for the weekend? "Will you tell me where to meet you with my little bag?" Another visit was in connection with the *Times*

Christmas number for 1940. The *Times* library had been badly damaged in the blitz, and she needed a week's work in a good library to help her husband prepare the *Times* general knowledge Christmas quiz. RB suggested one question: the source of the quotation "*Veni, vidi, Deus vincit*": "I came, I saw, God conquered." It was from Jan Sobieski's report to Pope Innocent XI on 12 September 1683, after having lifted the Turkish siege of Vienna. RB had always had a high opinion of that great Polish endeavour. The suggestion was greeted with enthusiasm by Jane and her husband. Jane's letter of thanks is a delight:

How truly grateful I was for the chance I had to produce my magnum opus in such circumstances of peace and loveliness. I believe I should have done something quite good with my modest equipment of brains if I'd had the luck to live in such an environment in my youth. But then I should have been, I expect, an intolerable bluestocking – instead of which I get as much fun out of life as can be got, I fancy ... You are nice. It suddenly came upon me ... Did I ever tell you so? ... The first time I met you, you waved me to a chair, sat down opposite and did your famous seeing-through-one-at-a-glance act and said brusquely, "Who are you?" I was so taken aback I just answered meekly, "I'm Jane!" What an idiot I must have seemed ... what I like best about you is that you've never missed the point of one of my little jokes ...

Are you likely to be seeing us or me for Christmas? You know I don't mind in the least your saying "no" – I think lots of conventions are just ridiculous.

... Love to you all from
    That I[nterfering] B[itch][32]

A couple of months later, perhaps in March 1941, she wrote,

Dear Kind Richard –
Do you miss me and my noisy ways? I hope so, else I shan't be able to say with confidence what I want to, which is that I miss you! How nice you have been to me in these lovely days and what fun! (I kinda think, Mr. Bennett, that you had a little too!) Remembering, I'm quite amazed that you endured me so long. Ronnie was delighted that you got the last word with your dry invitation to "come again some time when you can't stay so long." He couldn't stop laughing at that. Catherine [her mother] said: "Oh, Jane, I should have died of

mortification ... " Never mind, you will have some nice intellectual companionship this weekend more appropriate to an Elder Statesman than the gaiety of that terrible Janie ...

It's getting dark but not too dark to finish by sending my love. Of course in the real dark I could always put an x. How nice to know that your mind is the mind that will see the nice little *double entendre* in that! ...

When shall I come again?
Ever your affectionate
Janie[33]

"Do ask me down some time when you are free," she said, "so that we can read together." Their reading was sometimes serious; in April 1941 she said, "I can't get over your theory that man has been terrified into acceptance of law and order." This is the first hint that RB may have begun to believe with Hobbes that the life of man in a state of nature is "nasty, mean, brutish and short." A prime minister who took Canada through the bitter Depression years may be excused for being diverted from eighteenth century Methodist optimism, the "heavenly city," as Carl Becker once put it, to the tougher seventeenth century world of Thomas Hobbes. "Isn't it the negation of the gospel of love?" Janie asked plaintively. But nothing changed her affection for RB and for Juniper Hill, even if he did "tick her off" now and then for being, as she sometimes signed herself, an "Interfering Hussy." "How refreshing it is," she wrote in 1944, "when kind hearts are allied to coronets!"[34]

They were not always so allied in RB's old friend up the hill at Cherkley. Beaverbrook was capable of flattery, cajolery, enmity, trickery, bribery; all of those gears he usually managed to engage smoothly, for he had a prodigious and accurate memory. He also collected papers, those of Bonar Law and others, sometimes out of sheer spite to prevent someone else's use of them. He had as well a vast collection of his own papers (some nine hundred boxes and one hundred volumes, now in the House of Lords Record Office). He loved a good story, and to round one off, he could and would invent. He was expert at omission when historical accuracy would clutter or spoil his narrative, as his account of the 1941 Lendl affair illustrates. His weakness, and his strength, came from his desire (perhaps passion is the better word) to be read and widely read, talked about not only in the street but also in the corridors of power. He liked to be in both himself. He also had a few vendettas that he pursued with cheerful and unabashed malice. It was more fun to criticize than to praise, but he could be lavish both ways.

Friends is Beaverbrook's 1959 tribute to his long fifty-year friendship with RB. He published it mostly because he had been unable to find a suitable biographer. It is a good read, revealing sides to Bennett that no one else could know. That is the problem: when *Friends* was published, few people were alive who knew him. Beaverbrook had almost a clear field and knew it. What he wrote of RB was often right, sometimes wrong. Alice, RB's secretary from 1914 to 1947, was by then seventy-one years old and living in Vancouver; Beaverbrook had been helpful to her in so many ways that she probably did not wish to criticize. All RB's brothers and sisters were dead save Ronald, who would die in 1962. Two of Bennett's nephews were dead, and the other two were children when Bennett left Canada. Disproving *Friends* is complicated and messy; Peter Fraser's 1982 criticism of Beaverbrook's fabrications in *Politicians and the War, 1914–1916* suggests the difficulty. In *Friends* Beaverbrook praises RB's courage and vigour and often runs him down in little asides. To take one example: Beaverbrook gives the impression that Bennett's enjoyment of music was mostly confined to tumpy Methodist hymns, rising to the level of Elgar's "Pomp and Circumstance" marches or Sibelius's *Finlandia*. How does one disprove that? Mostly by accident. When Bennett spent Christmas 1928 with Mildred in Vienna, they went to Christmas Eve mass in the Stefanskirche and on Christmas night to the opera to hear Richard Strauss conduct his own *Der Rosenkavalier*. It was by then a Viennese Christmas tradition. RB wrote to Alice in Calgary about it. He had much enjoyed the sumptuous evocation of eighteenth-century Viennese life. Strauss and Methodist hymns are not the same; one can, however, like both.[35]

That is the point with Beaverbrook on Bennett or on other subjects: he may be right but what does he leave out? What is twisted? Bennett comes through sometimes as portly and temperamental; no doubt he was some of the time, but the book leaves one wondering where lay the basis for Beaverbrook's devotion to him. For devoted to RB Beaverbrook was. In 1947 Alice was surprised how deep it went. But a dozen years later when Beaverbrook was writing *Friends*, that devotion was not proof against his irresistible temptation to tell a good yarn. He was a compelling writer, but his old habits, his lifelong delight in making mischief, was at age eighty armed and pointed by a comprehensive memory and a cheerful vindictiveness.[36]

The social circles that Beaverbrook and RB moved in had a few points in common but were essentially different. RB spent Christmas of 1940 at Cherkley but after that seems to have kept more distance. Beaverbrook had been a widower from December 1927 onward; his political friends, some of them rather racy, would certainly not all have suited RB. Sir James Jeans, the astronomer, and his young second wife, Susi Hock of Vienna, were more RB's style. So were Ronald and Jane Cartons, and his doctor, Thomas Cotton, and his wife – not the raffish characters from politics and society that often aroused Beaverbrook's consuming interest in other people's politics and sexuality.

In 1939 Beaverbrook had given seventy-three acres of Mickleham Downs to the National Trust. The trust's secretary had asked RB in February 1939, since he was himself on the very edge of National Trust land, ought he not to consider being a member? He had not yet moved into Juniper Hill, but he did join and in 1941 was invited also to become a member of the Box Hill Trust, a local committee of the National Trust that met every quarter. RB thought the Box Hill Trust was well qualified without him, but if they wanted him, he would join.

The trust wished to purchase Juniper Hall (not to be confused with Juniper Hill), where in 1793 Fanny Burney was married to Alexandre d'Arblay, a French exile. The Hall was established some twenty years earlier and was half a mile south of Juniper Hill. The purchase depended upon a donation from RB of £3,000 which would be given after the completion of certain covenants affecting his own property. It is not known how these issues were resolved, but the purchase was completed in 1944.

By 1946 RB had become chairman of the Box Hill Trust. That year he reported that the trust had planted three thousand saplings of oak, beech, larch, and box. An enthusiastic tree-planter, he belonged to an organization picturesquely called "Men of the Trees," as a life member and in 1946 on their council. In the absence of the president, he presided at council. After his death, their publication, *Trees*, remembered him fondly: "He was always courteous, considerate and fair, giving every member his or her due. He had a subtle and sometimes boyish sense of fun."[37]

Despite the stress of the war years, RB gradually recovered his health, which in March 1940 he reported as "very good." The atrial fibrillation had diminished. What remained was his incipient diabetes, not helped by his delight in the maple sugar, maple syrup, and chocolates sent from Canada by friends. In effect, these indulgences were his substitute for smoking and drinking. They also made him overweight, but he came from an age that still believed stoutness was a sign of good health. His youngest (and favourite) nephew, William Herridge, now aged eight, admired his uncle's big stomach.[38]

William's father, Bill Herridge, had desperately wanted to be in the war, but at age fifty-two in 1939, was too old. Bennett tried to warn him off by pointing out that the British call-up ceiling was forty-three years of age. Herridge came to London anyway, telling RB with almost no notice that he would be there for less than a week. "I want to see Winston and possibly Eden and Hankey. I have a very real contribution to make and am going over to England for the sole purpose of making it," he wrote. Would RB make the appointments? What emerged is uncertain, but Herridge's ego a few months later seemed unscathed. In July 1940 he was still convinced that if he were attached to Eden's staff, he "could do a lot for him." He returned again a year later with no more success.[39]

In addition to young William, Bennett had a niece and three other nephews. Joan Bennett was the offspring of his brother, George, who had been installed about 1924 in Fort McMurray, Alberta. As a drinker, George was not quite out of harm's way even there, for he would make unexpected descents to watering holes in Edmonton and Calgary. It was then the job of H.R. Milner in Edmonton, or a little task force in Calgary, to get him home somehow. George died in January 1938 in Fort McMurray.[40]

As for the three other nephews, Richard Coates was the son of RB's sister Evelyn. After leaving Dalhousie University in the 1930s without graduating, he ended up in Montreal. The other two nephews were Ronald's sons, Ronald Jr and Harrison. Both young men completed university before the war caught them up. RB was appalled to get the news that Ronald, aged twenty-three, was thinking of getting married! RB's letter to his brother says something of Depression mentality and much about the two senior Bennetts: "A young man who has never earned a cent has no income of his own no house no profession to marry is to end[?] all hope of making a career for himself. I had hoped for a finer sense of responsibility ... I wonder where we would all be had you & I taken that course."[41]

When both nephews came overseas with the Canadian Army and visited Juniper Hill on leave, RB's attitude to them soon changed. Alice thought Lt Ronald Bennett (later captain, then promoted to major in the field) near perfection. She felt the same way about Harrison when he arrived a few months later. The household staff at Juniper Hill, not always enamoured with some of the many visitors, loved both the young Canadian officers for their lack of punctiliousness, willingness to pitch in, and gratitude for whatever might be done for them – in short, their Canadian openness. Epps, RB's butler, an old soldier, could not do enough for them, polishing buttons and cleaning uniforms. Mrs Epps, the cook, adored them. Harrison went to the kitchen to say goodbye to her whenever he left. He loved Juniper Hill and after going with his uncle every morning on a pre-breakfast walk, would then turn to and help the gardener.

The brothers went over to Normandy with the Canadian Army in the invasion of June 1944. Within two months, both were dead. They were killed in the battle for Caen, Ronald on 5 August and Harrison two weeks later. For RB it was "such an overwhelming disaster" that he hardly knew how or what to write to his brother. Nor was it the end of Ronald Bennett's tragedies. His wife, Elva, died in January 1945. There seemed to have been no discernible illness. She died, RB said, "of a broken heart if anyone ever did. She could not stand the awful shock of the loss of both of her boys." He wanted to go to his brother in Sackville, but transport was so tightly controlled that it was impossible.[42]

After the disasters of August 1944, RB would not soon recover his joy in life. He manfully kept on with his work in London, the Canadian Red Cross, the House of Lords, and the shoals of committees on anything and everything. Gradually he began to resume familiar duties, however disheartened he was at first. In the summer of 1945 he was finally able to visit Canada. Back in England, he wrote to his brother in September that the recent months had been filled up with engagements, although his eyes were bothering him. "I cannot do what I once did," he admitted. "I guess at 75 one has to think of breaking up." On the Friday before Christmas, 21 December 1945 he took to his bed with a temperature and indications of pneumonia. New drugs helped, but he spent Christmas and New Year's in bed. Alice presided at his Christmas dinner for eight. By March 1946, sugar in his blood was confirmed: he had diabetes. His local physician, Dr Tait, now came every morning half an hour before breakfast to give him an injection of insulin.[43]

In the autumn of 1946 Ronald Bennett determined to come over and see the graves of his two sons in Normandy. RB warned him that the weather would be terrible in late November and that he would not be able to go to France with him. Daily injections of insulin made RB a virtual prisoner at Juniper Hill. But the old sea-captain came anyway;

winter storms in the North Atlantic were nothing much to him. RB arranged a car with a French-speaking chauffeur, Captain Bennett took Alice with him, and off they went to the rain-soaked cemeteries of Normandy in the second week of December.[44]

That year RB had lost a good deal of weight. The *London Times* photograph of him used in Ernest Watkins's *R.B. Bennett* (1963) is barely recognizable. Other friends from Canada were struck by how thin he had become. But his life at this point was not quite the usual gloomy catalogue of an old man in decline. His visits to town were not all for doctors' appointments. He still entertained. Alice recalled a dinner on Thursday, 6 February 1947, when Lady Susi Jeans came and left him in a particularly happy mood. He and Alice and Epps the butler then set off for Sidmouth on the Devon coast for some sunshine and mild weather. RB returned to London looking and feeling much better, his taste for maple creams quite undiminished. Two boxes arrived for him on 14 May, and he finished most of one on the first day. And London very soon claimed him again. As Alice put it, "These people in London are so anxious to have him here, there and the other place, it is hard for him to break away."[45]

She, however, was going to do just that. She hadn't seen her brother in Vancouver for four years and managed to get passage for 24 May 1947 to Victoria and Vancouver via the Panama Canal in a new cargo steamer. She worried about RB, but when she talked about putting off her trip, he wouldn't hear of it.

Alice was now fifty-nine years old, a healthy, vigorous woman with a quick intelligence, her determined manner offset by a lively sense of humour. She was not at all prudish. Over the years she had become essential to RB's work, corporate, political, public, and private. By the 1930s she was reputed to be something of a dragon, guarding access to him; as time went on, he relied upon her more and more. He was deeply conscious of her devotion and her capacity. For some time past when he was ordering stock or bonds, he would order a block for her. By 1940 she was, if not wealthy, certainly comfortably off, enjoying her life in England with him. Bonar Law's daughter later wrote to her, "How much your companionship helped him." In March 1943 when RB finally sold his Eddy shares to Garfield Weston and was bailing out of his other Canadian investments, he instructed F.J. Crawford's of Toronto to turn the rest of his account over to Alice.[46]

With some regrets and heart-wrenchings, she embarked on her long voyage from Milford Haven in a new one-funnelled steamer, the

Lochgarth. She wrote to RB frequently from the ship. A letter from the west coast of North America she signed with "Affectionate respects and regards," and added, "Spinster still." She reported to RB *Time* magazine's English news that "although Mr. Chisman and Mrs. Pole Carew had been in bed together there was no reason to believe there had been any misconduct." That improbability amused her. She hoped that Bennett was not managing too well without her – otherwise, "You won't want me back!" And she had one specific instruction: "Don't take one of those midnight baths of yours without letting Epps know. It wouldn't do for Bill [R.B.'s dog] to have to occupy the bed all night by himself." That was on 17 June. They exchanged cables that day, RB reporting that his peaches were at their best.[47]

Since returning from Sidmouth he was feeling better. Diabetes was a problem, he was thinner, and he was starting to show his age, but life was still good. Garfield Weston, the Canadian philanthropist who also served as an MP in the British House of Commons during the war, had reported him in 1943 as "happy as a clam," and many friends cherished, as did Rosalind Hayes, daughter of RB's close friend Viscount Finlay, "those happy serene days at Juniper Hill when the world was on fire all around." Certainly he found peace, joy, and delight there. Catherine, wife of Julian Amery, entertained RB at Eaton Square in mid-June 1947 and found him showing his age "but happy and ... so charming and interesting." James Duncan, chairman of Ontario Hydro, and his wife, Trini, lunched with RB at the Savoy Grill a few weeks earlier. While he was in "one of his best and most talkative moods," they found one of his remarks unsettling:

> I remember we sat in the Savoy Grill until we were alone at the table and the waiters had placed green covers on all the others. I think he enjoyed talking about Canada and mutual friends. At about 3:30 in the afternoon he got up to go, and as he put on his coat my wife said to him that we were returning to London in about six months and she hoped that he would come to lunch or dine with us, to which he replied that would not be possible because he would no longer be here when we returned. My wife, misjudging his meaning, asked him if he was going travelling, to which he replied, "My dear, I am not going travelling but I am going for a long trip from which I won't return."[48]

Yet his actions belied this ominous note. On Wednesday, 25 June, he presided at the 193rd annual meeting of the Royal Society of the Arts as its president, and was promptly re-elected for the following year. His diary was already studded with duties for the rest of the summer and on into 1948. The Box Hill Committee was set down for 5 July; his duty on the Dorking Magistrates' Court was for 16 July and 3 August.[49]

"Sunny and warm" was *The Times'* forecast for Thursday, 26 June 1947, with temperatures around 77 degrees Fahrenheit – fairly hot for London. RB was driven up as usual; he had a meeting at Mansion House with the lord mayor for 10:15 to 11:00 AM, and after lunch there were other meetings. He came back to Juniper Hill late in the afternoon and walked in the grounds. Even now it was hot. Beaverbrook came over with two houseguests and suggested RB join them at Cherkley for dinner, promising good soup and lots of asparagus. But RB decided to stay home; he'd had a long day. He had a quiet supper, read, watched the slow summer gathering of the evening (the sun set at 10:21), and soon after took his elevator upstairs. He told Epps he would not take a bath, so the butler bade him goodnight. As usual he read a chapter of the Bible. He then decided he would have a bath after all and ran one himself. He liked them hot.

The following day, Friday, Janie Carton came down to breakfast at 1 Canonbury Place and said to her husband, "Ronald, I must ring up RB, for I've been dreaming about him in the most extraordinary way." He had died in his bath, where Epps found him that morning. RB's heart had given out at last.[50]

The Times' obituary came out on Saturday, 28 June:

> He had a vein of unorthodoxy which ... sometimes shocked the more staid elements in his own party ... he held that changed conditions had revealed flaws and weaknesses in the capitalist structure, which could only be saved by drastic reforms in the line of State intervention ... he was a highly competent Parliamentarian and a commanding presence was reinforced by an authoritarian temper and forceful manner of speech. His industry was immense, and, supremely self-confident, he was slow to delegate his responsibilities. Although he instilled respect, it cannot be said that he was ever a well-loved or popular figure.

It was a Canadian rather than an English slant and not acceptable to all readers; Lord Bessborough was one. He had been Canada's governor general from 1931 to 1935, his term almost coinciding with Bennett's time as prime minister. Bessborough suggested other sides to Bennett. "His main preoccupation was always for the public service," he wrote to *The Times*. "He attached the highest importance to the impartial administration of the law ... A warm-hearted, affectionate, sentimental man ... he was as easily moved as a child."

Bessborough's letter was published the day of Bennett's funeral, on Monday, 30 June. It was a service Alice desperately tried to get to. She was told of Bennett's death by wireless aboard the *Lochgarth*. Devastated, she was whisked ashore at Victoria, BC, to catch Trans-Canada Airlines for the east and for London. But the plane developed engine trouble in Montreal, and she arrived too late for the service.

The little church at Mickleham was crowded. The Bishop of Guildford presided; Lady Susi Jeans was the organist. Beaverbrook represented the Lord Lieutenant of Surrey. Churchill's doctor, Lord Moran, and his wife, and the Hailshams came, as well as many from Mickleham village and the household staff from Juniper Hill.

A memorial service was held in Westminster Abbey on Friday, 4 July. It was a large congregation. Prime Minister Attlee and the lord mayor of London attended, with many lords and ladies. By this time Alice was there, as were Janie and Ronald Carton, Brendan Bracken, and others. "O Canada!" was sung after the blessing. Viscount Addison, secretary of state for the dominions, was present, but as of 3 July, he had a new title: secretary for commonwealth relations; there was some irony in that. A friend in St Michael's churchyard after the funeral recalled RB just recently speaking of his love for the British Empire and the fellowship that it had meant to him. RB had then mused aloud, "Alas, no one but me thinks that now." It was protested, that utterance, but it was coming to be true. As James Morris would later write, "For the Americans irrevocably damaged the British Empire and Commonwealth Wherever they went the Americans presented an overwhelming image of opulence, vigour and generosity more compelling by far than the dry modes of Empire. They cheerfully disregarded the old imperial taboos ... They lacked the proper sahibs' aloofness, they laughed at the carefully devised orthodoxies of the imperial system, passed so reverently from generation to generation of imperialist."[51]

RB's's neighbours in Mickleham grieved for him. They wrote to *The Times* that the obituary for RB had neglected his work and hospitality as the Squire of Mickleham. He who had sought peace and tranquillity in the Surrey countryside had during the war traversed the length and breadth of the country on war work, and in his many speeches he had offered a ringing affirmation, in a Canadian accent, of the old common empire ideals of law and justice. To his Mickleham neighbours, he was a wise counsellor and a delightful host. It seemed to them that if he had not been a "well-loved or popular figure" in Canada, "the benignity of our Surrey countryside wrought in him a great change." He had become, as Rosalind Hayes remarked, "the beloved laird of Mickleham."[52] He is buried in its churchyard.

Epilogue

R.B. Bennett's institutional legacy was important and lasting. He was instrumental in establishing the Canadian Broadcasting Corporation and the Bank of Canada; he initiated unemployment insurance and the prairie farm legislation of 1934–35. He told the Conservative Party faithful in July 1938, "One purpose, and one purpose only, can make the party an instrument for the good of Canada. That purpose is to use the collective power for the general good."[1]

He was a statesman betrayed not by his ideas, most of which were well founded, sensible, even brilliant, but by his imperious temperament and unforgiving nature, and sometimes by the rhetoric that went with both. Nor was he really a team man. The Hopewell Cape of his birth had been a seafaring world; his father and grandfather were shipbuilders, his brother was a sea captain. A ship's governance is teamwork on deck but hierarchy from the bridge. At sea the captain's word is the supreme law. RB was the captain of the Conservative ship; he tended to put down grumblings. Mutineers could be jettisoned overboard.

Even as a youth he had never been much of a one for games. He seems not to have ever quite known how to play. In his mature years his close friends were few. He could command the loyalty but not always the affection of party faithful, certainly not as Sir John A. Macdonald or Sir Wilfrid Laurier could. Respect, even admiration, he could and did earn, but at times he also baffled his followers. Sometimes his mind worked in oblique and even elliptical ways, like a poet's, like Robert Browning's. His sense of humour was real enough but apt to be whimsical and ironic.

He was not used to failure. He had made a success of almost everything he had undertaken. His fortune and standing in the world were proof of it. But his confident promises of 1930 were impossible to realize. His sincere love affair in 1932 with Hazel Colville failed in the end.

Ottawa rumours that she broke his heart have to be set against his 1935 remark to a close friend, "I do not deal in regrets."[2]

Nevertheless, his crushing defeat in the election of 1935, whatever he might have said in extenuation, rankled. To have his name associated with cars whose owners could no longer afford to run them, dead cars harnessed to live horses – "Bennett buggies" – must have been cumulatively galling. It was especially so to a proud man who gloried in having done the best he possibly could to pull the country through a mountain of difficulties.

The onward thrust of his mind is revealed in his reply to a Canadian Medical Association request that the federal funds transferred to the provinces for unemployment relief should include medical care. CMA representatives met with him in Ottawa on 6 October 1933. His reply: "I have every sympathy with the point of view you have expressed." However, he said, the constitutional impediments were formidable. He would invite each province to submit such a request. In the end, it appears that nothing materialized from this initiative.[3]

RB's great strength lay in the range and depth of his blazing intelligence. Grattan O'Leary of the *Ottawa Journal*, who knew him well, said he was "highly, perhaps perilously, endowed with intellectual gifts."[4] He served Canada with fanatical zeal; to his intelligence was conjoined an immense capacity for work. But he also had a vast and sensitive ego. He might make jokes about himself, but he did not relish others doing it. He could be impatient and short. He was generous in many things but not much in praise or forgiveness.

There is a story about him in 1937 that illustrates something of his style. A young man from Prince Edward Island studying at Dalhousie University was working in Ottawa that summer as a waiter. He had saved enough to pay his Halifax room and board for the next college year (1937–38), but at summer's end he still needed $250 for tuition. A bit desperate, he took up a friend's suggestion that he might try appealing to R.B. Bennett, who was on Dalhousie's board of governors and known for generosity to needy students. Greatly daring, he phoned RB's suite at the Château Laurier. The secretary answered, but a gruff voice interjected. "What do you want?" The student explained his predicament. "Come around at 11 o'clock tomorrow," he was told.

The next day the student was duly ushered in to RB's suite. He gave an account of his current position. "What do you think of Carleton Stanley, Dalhousie's president?" RB asked. (President Stanley had leftish leanings and had been making a few waves in Halifax.) The student thought he'd better be truthful, diplomatic, too, if possible. He said that Stanley had been personally kind to him and that the president was considered a reputable scholar. "That's right," said RB. He proceeded to write out a $250 cheque. "But how shall I arrange to pay it back to you?" the student asked. "Pay it back I will." RB replied, "You don't pay it back to me. You do the same for someone else."[5]

Many Conservatives who saw RB off in January 1939 at Saint John and Halifax felt the sadness of his parting from Canada, as if they were sending him into a lonely future. Perhaps he felt something of that himself. But he was soon comfortable in England. As he was starting to settle down in Mickleham, he received a transatlantic phone call from the Bank of Montreal. Its president, Sir Charles Gordon, had just died, on 30 August 1939. Would RB consider being president? RB consulted his brother in Sackville. Although Ronald urged him to accept, RB discovered that he did not really want to return to Canada; the urbanity of Britain, its civilized and deeply layered society, and the glorious Surrey countryside were closing in about him. Juniper Hill, his new home – his first real home since leaving Hopewell Cape fifty years before – was, he told his brother, "becoming very beautiful." He realized that he really "had no intention of going back to Canada."[6]

Within a few months the village of Mickleham had taken the big generous Canadian to its heart. Within a few months too, as the war came on, RB's great success in wartime speeches across Britain helped him feel welcomed and recognized in British society. Recognition was important to him. Being made a viscount in 1941 by Winston Churchill, at the top of the George VI Honours list, was the splendid culmination.

Richard Bedford, 1st (and last) Viscount Bennett, is buried at the front of the churchyard of St Michael's, Mickleham's parish church. To be buried there was his choice; there in its village he had come to be respected and loved.

Notes

CHAPTER ONE

1 I owe this delightful recollection to Jeffrey Simpson, of course, who was in Halifax in 1987 doing research for his 1988 book on patronage, *Spoils of Power*.

2 For Bob Edwards, see Grant MacEwan, *Eye Opener Bob*. The Gilpen story is on p. 146. Also see James H. Gray, *R.B. Bennett: The Calgary Years*, 85–6, 89, 91. On Bennett's being "it," see University of New Brunswick, R.B. Bennett Papers (hereafter RBB Papers), M-919, #17148, Harriette Gordon-Cooper (née Wells) to RBB, 13 Oct. 1927, from Chilliwack, BC. She was recalling the 1911 election in Calgary when Bennett was first elected to the House of Commons.

A word about the style of citation for the Bennett papers: across the past fifty years, scholars have used three modes. One is by volume number, established when the papers were first put together – useful no doubt, but since a volume comprises some five hundred items, not very specific. A second mode is the microfilm number, set up when the whole Bennett collection was microfilmed by the National Archives in the 1960s and 1970s. This has an even greater disadvantage, since a microfilm can comprise two thousand items. The third mode is the serial number established during the microfilming. This is cumbersome but accurate, and so here I have usually preferred the serial number.

3 RBB Papers, M-3140, #543181+, is a run of papers about the history of the Bennett family. The Bennetts were not Loyalists. In current historiographical parlance, they were "planters," coming to Nova Scotia before the American Revolution to take up the vacant Acadian lands. See Library and Archives Canada (hereafter LAC), MG 28, Progressive Conservative Party Records, Bennett file. The biographical note is not friendly in tone,

but in respect of what it says about RBB and the Eddy Company, it is accurate.

4   "The Use of Money," in Outler, *The Works of John Wesley*, vol. 1, 279.

5   See Grayson and Bliss, *The Wretched of Canada*, with its valuable introduction.

6   The lines from "Mary Garvin" are in John Greenleaf Whittier, *Complete Poetical Works of John Greenleaf Whittier*, 50; for Wesley on tolerance, see Jackson, *The Works of the Reverend John Wesley*, vol. 8, 345.

7   New Brunswick Museum, Saint John, Alma Russell Papers, RBB to Alma Russell in Victoria, 1 Nov. 1914, from Calgary. As often with RBB's hand-written letters, this one is undated except marked "Sunday." The envelope, however, has been kept by discerning archivists, and the postmark gives the date. This important small collection was brought to my attention by the New Brunswick Museum's archivists. Alma Russell was RB's friend from the Douglastown/Chatham days, 1889–92. She moved to the West in 1892 with her family, married Fred Yorston in Victoria, BC, then separated, and resumed her maiden name. Yorston ended in Montreal editing the *Montreal Standard*. Alma Russell remained in touch with RB until his death. There is a long letter from her with her fifty-nine-year-old memories of RB to Alice Millar, who had solicited them. See RBB Papers, M-3140, #543794, Alma Russell to Alice Millar (hereafter AEM), 12 Nov. 1948, from Victoria.

8   RBB Papers, M-3140, #543820, interview with Miss Annie Morrison of Douglastown, NB, by Robert Rogers in 1948. She was in grade 8 when Bennett taught at Douglastown and recalled this poem as one of his favourites, almost certainly learned from his mother. The cobbler's poem comes from an interview by Robert Rogers with William Hickey of Chatham, Sunday, 2 July [1950], M-3140, #543887.

9   This paragraph is based on diverse sources: *Annual Report of Schools of New Brunswick 1889*; Smith, "The Maritime Years of R.B. Bennett," 78–9; RBB Papers, M-3140, #544148; *Ottawa Morning Journal*, 21 May 1932.

10 RBB Papers, M-3140, #544537, Diaries, 27 Jan. 1891. At this point RB was twenty-six years old, Dunn twenty-two, and Aitken seventeen. The date of the picnic is uncertain, 1896 being my best guess. The reference is in the Beaverbrook Papers, House of Lords Record Office, G/39 Harold Girvan to Lady Beaverbrook, 19 April 1956, from Victoria, BC. This file is marked, "Only available after Lady Beaverbrook's death."

11 *Calgary Herald*, 3 Jan. 1939.

12 RBB Papers, M-3141, #545727, RBB to C.H. Parker, Nanaimo, BC, 5 March 1903, from Calgary.

13 Knafla, "Richard 'Bonfire' Bennett," 354; Knafla has a comprehensive analysis of Bennett's legal cases, 320–76.

14 Gray, *The Calgary Years*, 201–6.

15 Mann, *Buddenbrooks: Verfall einer Familie* (Berlin 1901) reprinted (Frankfurt 1981), 426; the citation here is the English translation by H.T. Lowe-Porter originally done in 1924, from the 1984 New York edition, 343.

16 Gray, *The Calgary Years*, 119–29, 189–90.

17 House of Lords Record Office, Beaverbrook Papers, vol. 66, RBB to Max Aitken, 10 Dec. 1909; Gray, *The Calgary Years,* 140–4.

18 RBB Papers, M-3141, #544913, RBB to Borden, 3 June 1903.

19 This quotation from Leacock's *Sunshine Sketches of a Little Town* (1912) is from "The Candidacy of Mr. Smith."

20 RBB Papers, M-918, #15550, RBB to P.C. Shaw, secretary, Amalgamated Civil Servants, Calgary, 4 May 1928.

21 *Calgary Herald*, 21 July 1902; Gray, *The Calgary Years*, 66–7.

22 House of Lords Record Office, Beaverbrook Papers, vol. 66, RBB to Max Aitken, 13 Nov. 1910.

23 RBB Papers, M-3156, #567741. The Cardinal Manning quotation is written in RB's hand on the back of a telegram. One might guess the date as December 1934. Manning was a convert to Catholicism from Anglicanism. The remark about a quiet mind is a reply to Mark Irish, a young Toronto admirer (M-3156, #567534, RBB to Irish, 31 Dec. 1934).

24 Beaverbrook Papers, vol. 66, RBB to Max, 9 Dec. 1911, from Ottawa; also Gray, *The Calgary Years,* 127–8.

25 Canada, *House of Commons Debates*, 26 March 1913.

26 Ibid., 14 May 1914, 3758–60.

27 *Calgary Herald*, 15 May 1914; Gray, *The Calgary Years,* 156; Smith, *The Treasure-Seekers,* 18.

28 Beaverbrook Papers, G19, AEM to Beaverbrook, n.d. but late 1957, from St Lawrence Hotel, Barbados: "For reasons known to himself he [Bennett] was unfit for military service." Alice Millar's trip to Barbados was almost certainly paid for by Beaverbrook. See also LAC, William Lyon Mackenzie King Papers, Diaries (hereafter King Diaries), 29 July 1930, for discussion of RB's medical problems.

29 Beaverbrook Papers, vol. 65, RBB to Beaverbrook, 5 Aug. 1916, confidential.

30 RBB Papers, M-3140, #605082, J.H. Dunn to RBB, 16 March 1934, private and confidential from New York. The jingle is recalled by Alma Russell, RBB Papers, M-3140, #543794, Alma Russell to AEM, 12 Nov. 1948, remembering days at Fredericton sixty years earlier.

31 RBB Papers, M-3140, #544073, the poem written in RB's hand. On the back is written in blue pencil the date 1 Oct. 1890, with the names of four students of the class of 1893. The author of the poem is unknown, but quite possibly it was Bennett.

32 RBB Papers, M-3174, #597201, RBB to Borden, 17 April 1918. The letter's history is interesting. It was found in 1961 in Sir Robert Borden's papers by his nephew Henry Borden, who sent it to Beaverbrook (#597200, Henry Borden to Beaverbrook, 29 Dec. 1961).

33 *Dictionary of Canadian Biography* (hereafter DCB), vol. 15, "Jennie Shirreff Eddy"; Gray, *The Calgary Years,* 129–35.

34 RBB Papers, M-3165, #582195, RBB to J-A. Bégin, 23 April 1927; #582209, RBB to L.-A. Taschereau, 3 June 1927.

35 Ibid., M-3164, #561564, RBB to Miss Jane R. McMillan, Toronto, 10 Sept. 1935, personal.

36 The story of RB's inauguration as minister of justice in 1921 is in the *Toronto Mail & Empire,* 26 Mar. 1935, quoting the *Sault Ste Marie Star,* n.d. There is a good account of the 1921 Calgary West election in Ernest Watkins, *R.B. Bennett,* 93–5. Watkins's book owed much to his consultations with Alice Millar, Bennett's secretary, to whom (with three others) his book is dedicated.

37 This is J. Craig Brokovski's summary of Bennett's reaction. Brokovski was interviewed by Watkins in the late 1940s. Brokovski came from Simcoe County, Ontario. He was my mother's first cousin (my mother was a Craig), and we met in Calgary in 1947. Alas, I then knew nothing of his connection with Bennett. See Lukasiewicz, "John Craig Brokovski," 2–11.

38 Watkins, *R.B. Bennett,* 101–2. Re Lady Lougheed, see RBB Papers, #605394, RBB to Dorothy Lougheed Hutchison, 6 Nov. 1935.

39 British Columbia, Dept. of Vital Statistics, death certificate of Alice Elizabeth Millar (1888–1969). Some of the information there recorded is from her Vancouver sister-in-law, Norma Millar. Mildred Bennett's conversation with Alice Millar is reported by Watkins, *R.B. Bennett,* 108. He says that Mildred "always" addressed Alice Millar by her last name. That was probably so in early years, but later in letters it was usually "My dear Alice."

40 Bennett's Canadian income tax returns for 1917–39 are in M-3149. For specific references to 1924, see #556721-730. He was meticulous about

his income tax, even correcting his 1927 return, which he considered
he had underpaid (M-3160, #556849, RBB to AEM, 27 April 1928, from
Ottawa).

41   RBB Papers, M-3160, #575439. The woodlands owned by Eddy's are
     reported on to Bennett by the general manager, C.V. Caesar, 23 Dec. 1926.
     Of the 1,931 square miles, 951 were described as dormant or semi-dormant.

42   Gray, *The Calgary Years,* 230–1, 251–2.

43   *Calgary Herald,* 28 Oct. 1925.

44   The later life of J.T. ("Harry") Shirreff (1866–1926) is an interesting and
     complex story. There were crude allegations that the new Mrs Shirreff
     deliberately plied her husband with whisky (forbidden him by his doc-
     tor), rumours that Bennett scorned. After Harry's death the young widow
     had no current cash to pay death duties to Quebec or even to live on, until
     after the will was probated in late August. Bennett set up the trust fund
     of $250,000 from his own pocket so that she could continue to live at
     Dunara. He also paid the death duties, which were almost as much. She
     later repaid him and was always grateful to him; they remained friends.
     Harry was buried in Fairview Cemetery in Halifax beside his first wife.
     There was a row with Edith Shirreff Richardson over his Halifax tomb-
     stone as well as his will. Mrs Richardson died in California, 30 March
     1930. A nephew, Charles LeBaron Shirreff, surfaced at that time, deli-
     cately suggesting that he should have been remembered. The correspond-
     ence is in M-3163 (vols. 920 and 921 in the UNB collection): #579687, T.P.
     Foran to RBB, 24 Aug. 1926; #579691, RBB to Foran, 30 Aug. 1926, from
     Calgary; #579985, RBB to Mrs Lillian Butcher, Boston n.d. [Dec. 1926]
     from Calgary; Mrs Butcher to RBB, 28 Dec. 1926, from Boston; #579939,
     Ernest Klette to RBB, 3 Dec. 1930, from San Francisco.

45   Maritimers were well up to keeping pace. One example: the schooner
     Doria left Halifax on 17 September 1925, with a cargo of Canadian
     whisky bound for Lima, Peru. She was back in Halifax in four days load-
     ing up a similar cargo for Havana, Cuba. It was obvious where she had
     gone, and where she was going: to the United States.

46   The *locus classicus* of the Byng-King crisis is Eugene Forsey, *The Royal
     Power of Dissolution of Parliament in the British Commonwealth.* Forsey
     was twenty-two in 1926 and watched the crisis unfold from the pub-
     lic gallery in the House of Commons. See his *A Life on the Fringe;* also,
     Roger Graham, *Arthur Meighen,* vol. 2; H. Blair Neatby, *William Lyon
     Mackenzie King,* vol. 2.

47   In the late 1950s Grant Dexter (1896–1961) of the *Winnipeg Free Press*
     was asked by Ernest Watkins about this point: could Bennett have faced

down King's rodomontade about acting ministers? Dexter had observed Bennett in the House of Commons from 1925 to 1936 and believed that Bennett certainly could have (Watkins, *R.B. Bennett*, 123). The story about T.W. Bird is well known, the gloss about his expertise in House of Commons procedure less so. See Roger Graham, *Meighen*, vol. 2, 445–6.

48 Queen's University Archives (hereafter QUA), Grant Dexter Papers, Dexter to J.W. Dafoe, 16 Sept. 1926; LAC, *Eugene Forsey Papers*, vol. 3, Lady Evelyn Byng to Forsey, 12 July [1942?], private.

49 Larry A. Glassford, *Reaction and Reform*, 18, citing QUA, Flavelle Papers, Flavelle to Rufus Pope, 14 Jan. 1927.

50 Neatby, *William Lyon Mackenzie King*, vol, 2, 224–8, has a succinct account of this complex development. Also Gray, *The Calgary Years*, 267–9.

51 Canada, *House of Commons Debates*, 17 Feb. 1927, 403.

52 Ibid., 26 Mar. 1926, 1971–1986; *Senate Debates*, 8 June 1926, 267–82.

53 Canada, *House of Commons Debates*, 18 Feb. 1927, 476, 478; the reference to thrift is in ibid., 26 Mar. 1926, 1975.

54 King's unease over shared cost programs with the provinces is seen in 1929, in the debates over the proposal for an all-Canadian trans-Canada highway. Granting money to the provinces from the federal treasury, King said, "is a thoroughly vicious system" (Canada, *House of Commons Debates*, 21 Feb. 1929, 316). He was then reminded by Bennett and others of his 1927 old age pension system; still he regretted the principle.

55 For the debate on unemployment insurance, see Canada, *House of Commons Debates*, 15 March 1927, 1262; 16 March 1927, 1277.

56 For the Pension Act debate, see ibid., 25 March 1927; Bennett's amendment is 7 April 1927, 2430; amendment defeated, 2438.

57 RBB Papers, M-3160, #575415, C.V. Caesar to RBB, 3 Jan. 1926.

58 Ibid., #575457, gives a list of Eddy's income and profits, presumed to be net for 1923 to 1926: 1923, $81,313; 1925, $210,527; 1924, $282,573; 1926, $119,949. For the telegrams, see M-3161, #575638, RBB to G.R. Millen, 17 May 1927, telg. from Calgary; #575756, RBB to C.V. Caesar, 23 July 1927. There are also two letters with the same date. The second is #575821.

59 RBB Papers, M-3161, #575644, RBB to Victor Drury, 21 May 1927, personal; M-3160, #575416, Ivar Kreuger to RBB, 4 May 1926, cable; M-3161, #575981, Kreuger to RBB, 10 Oct. 1927, telg.; *Ottawa Evening Citizen*, 21 Dec. 1927. The *Citizen* valued the match transaction at $8–9 million.

60 For Mark Irish, see Bliss, *A Canadian Millionaire*, 325.

61 RBB Papers, M-3179, #605438, Mark Irish to RBB, 31 Aug. 1927, enclosed in Irish to RBB, 16 Aug. 1937. The 1927 letter was Irish's own copy, sent to RBB ten years later to remind him of times past. Bennett replied, rather elegantly, that Irish's own life was a full denial of the lazy philosophy he suggested to Bennett in 1927. See ibid., #605439, RBB to Irish, 27 Sept. 1937, from Calgary. It is addressed, "Dear Mark." Bennett's own reference to the leadership is in conversation with Mackenzie King (LAC, King Diaries), 1893–1950, 15 Jan. 1928.

CHAPTER TWO

1 *Canada*, LAC, *Hansard, House of Commons Debates* (hereafter *Commons Debates*), 15 February 1929, 182–5.

2 Ibid., 18 Feb. 1929, 234; Flavelle to David Carnegie, 9 February 1925, quoted in Michael Bliss, *Canadian Millionaire*.

3 The Raddall story is in *The Pied Piper of Dipper Creek and Other Tales*, 330. The most useful book on the history of employment and unemployment is James Struthers, *No Fault of Their Own*. I have used pages 3–43 with great profit.

4 RBB Papers, M-1213, #135826, W.S. Montgomery to RBB, 27 Jan. 1933, from Dalhousie, NB. Bennett scoffed at the rumours. The by-election was held in October.

5 My father told me this story. His perspective is set down in Cyril Waite, "The Corn is Green," 108–13, about his life in small town Ontario in the late 1920s and early 1930s.

6 RBB Papers, M-919, #20565, J.B.M. Baxter to RBB, 1 Feb. 1929, from Saint John; ibid., M-3180, #606555, AEM to J.J. Saucier, 16 Nov. 1933, private and strictly confidential, from Ottawa; P.B. Waite, *The Lives of Dalhousie University*, vol. 2, 34.

7 Larry A. Glassford, *Reaction and Reform*. The best account of the Winnipeg Convention is in Glassford, *Reaction and Reform*, chapt. 2, "Choosing a New Chieftain"; also James H. Gray, *The Calgary Years*, 280–4; Roger Graham, *Meighen*, vol. 2, 491–9; Peter Oliver, *G. Howard Ferguson*, 269–76, 280–6. Ferguson's "corpse" remark is reported in the *Toronto Globe*, 11 Oct. 1927, quoted in Glassford, *Reaction and Reform*, 32. Meighen later claimed, in notes he made for his biographer Roger Graham, that Bennett privately was opposed to Meighen's defending his Hamilton speech before the convention (Graham, *Arthur Meighen*, vol. 3, 498).

8 *Manitoba Free Press*, 11, 12 Oct. 1927.

9 *Montreal Gazette*, 12, 13 Oct. 1927. There is a useful compilation of the Conservative Resolutions in R.M. Dawson, *Constitutional Issues*, 370–7.

10 *Winnipeg Evening Tribune*, 12 Oct. 1927, for the Rotary Club speech; *Manitoba Free Press*, 13 Oct. 1927. Glassford's *Reaction and Reform* has an admirable analysis of the candidates and their backgrounds, 33–4. See also Gray, *The Calgary Years*, 281–5.

11 Thomas Moore (1779–1852) also wrote "The Canadian Boat Song."

12 RBB Papers, M-919, #16888, Macdonnell to RBB, 22 Nov. 1927, from Toronto; *Montreal Daily Star*, 13, 14 Oct. 1927.

13 George Ferguson's account of Bennett and Calgary, in *Manitoba Free Press*, 14 Oct. 1927.

14 RBB Papers, M-919, #17195, Isabella Macdonald Gainsford to RBB, 13 Oct. 1927, from Sturgeon Creek, MB; #17210, Lord Byng to RBB, 14 Oct. 1927, priv. from Thorpe Hall, Essex; #17313, Lady Byng to RBB, 19 Oct. [1927]; M-922, #20297, McRae to RBB [n.d.], "Thought this would please you," enclosing copy of *Picton Gazette*, 3 Nov. 1927. Agnes Macphail's letter is #21812, 18 April 1928. She addressed him as R.B.; he addressed her as Agnes.

15 Ibid., M-919, #16359 Gladys Beaverbrook to RBB, 13 Oct 1927; #19688, RBB to Royal Securities, Montreal [but almost certainly a personal letter to Izaak Walton Killam], 28 Dec. 1927, from Calgary; Anne Chisholm and Michael Davie, *Beaverbrook: A Life*. There is a haunting photograph of Gladys among a series at page 182.

16 RBB Papers, M-919, #16104, Haley Fiske to RBB, 4 Jan. 1928, from New York; #16105, RBB to Fiske, 25 Jan. 1928, from Ottawa.

17 Ibid., M-921, #19491, Senator F.L. Schaffner to Guthrie, 3 Feb. 1927; #18674, Robert A. Raid to RBB, 22 Nov. 1927, confidential, from Toronto.

18 Ibid., M-922, #20340, with neither date nor provenance, unfortunately; #20921, Price to Ferguson, 21 Jan. 1928, private and confidential, addressed to Ferguson at Château Laurier; #20025, Ryckman to RBB, 14 Feb. 1928, private.

19 Ibid., M-921, #19378, Dr. J.E. Bélanger to RBB, 1 Oct. 1927, personal; #19379, RBB to Beach and Baker, Ottawa, 22 Dec. 1927, from Calgary; #19385, A.W. Merriam to J.M. Ross, 23 Dec. 1927, from Ottawa; #19390, J.M. Ross to RBB, 5 Jan. 1928, re the Papineau property.

20 LAC, WLMK Papers, Diary (hereafter King Diaries), 15 Jan. 1928; the story of Bennett being thought by his party too friendly to King was retailed back to King by the governor general, ibid., 3 Feb. 1928.

21 *Commons Debates*, 26 Jan. 1928, 4; 30 Jan. 1928, 13; 13 Mar. 1928, 1244–64. The Tennyson quotation is from "*In Memoriam*," LIV 11.17–20. Bennett was well read in Tennyson.

22 *Commons Debates*, 27 April 1928, 2475. There is an essay to be written on the misconceptions that have arisen about the 1919 passing of Sec. 98 of the Criminal Code. Bennett outlines the history of the 1919 legislation in ibid., 27 April, 2480. It may be useful to append his references here. Meighen introduced Bill #160 on 27 June 1919 (4135); 2nd reading and Committee, 1 July 1919 (4355), 3rd reading, July 2 1919.

On 23 April 1928 (2303) Lapointe had introduced Bill 191 to repeal Sec. 98. Perhaps as a result of the debate, he let Sec. 98 stand and reduced the maximum sentence from ten years to two.

23 Ibid., #2465.

24 The declaration stated that the United Kingdom and its dominions were "autonomous Communities within the British Empire, equal in status, in no way subordinate one to another in any aspect of their domestic or external affairs, though united by a common allegiance to the Crown, and freely associated as members of the British Commonwealth of Nations." See Marshall, "The Balfour Formula," 541–53.

25 *Commons Debates*, 13 April 1927.

26 Ibid., 28 May 1928, 3445–504; Bennett's view of the Balfour Declaration is set out retrospectively in a long letter to Percy Ward of Montreal (RBB Papers, #551116, RBB to Ward, 15 Dec. 1938, from Ottawa).

27 *Commons Debates*, 30 Jan. 1928. For Riel vs. Regina, *Appeal Cases before the House of Lords* X. 678. *Commons Debates*, 28 May 1928, 3445–504. Bennett's speech is at 3475–7. Who the Canadian statesman was Bennett does not say.

28 RBB Papers, M-3174, #596966, Beaverbrook to RBB, 14 Nov. 1927.

29 Chamberlain's account of his private talk with King George V is in University of Birmingham Library, Neville Chamberlain Papers, NC 1/26/431, Chamberlain to Annie, Thurs., 24 July [1930]. The king thought that the whole Balfour Declaration was wrong, that it all ought to be washed out and begun again.

30 *Commons Debates*, 11 June 1928, 4147–61.

31 King Diaries, 29 Sept., 7 Oct. 1928; John Hilliker, *Canada's Department of External Affairs*, vol. 1, 111–13.

32 RBB Papers, M-920, #17404, RBB to R.K. Anderson, 4 May 1928, MP Halton, a circular letter to all Conservative MPs; King Diaries, 23 May 1928.

33 *Commons Debates*, 8 June 1928, 3954–3960.

34 RBB Papers, M-3182, #562780, Borden to RBB, 11 June 1928, from Glens-
    mere, Ottawa; #562781, RBB to Borden, 21 June 1928.

35 Ibid., M-3140, #543943, a third-hand recollection. On 18 May 1948
    Robert Rogers, a researcher at the University of New Brunswick working
    for Lord Beaverbrook on the Bennett Papers, interviewed Mrs R.P. Allen
    in Fredericton. She was the daughter of Mrs Hannah Read, Henrietta
    Bennett's next-door neighbour at Hopewell Cape. Hannah Read reported
    that Mrs Bennett was surprised and disturbed to discover at the age of
    forty-four that she was going to have another child.

36 Reported by the *Ottawa Evening Citizen*, 2 April 1931; Borden's com-
    ment is RBB Papers, M-3174, #597414, Borden to RBB, 13 April 1935, pri-
    vate, addressed "My dear R.B."

37 For Bennett's letter to Beaverbrook, see House of Lords Record Office,
    Beaverbrook Papers, vol. 66, RBB to Max, 24 July 1904, from Calgary. It
    is characteristic of many Bennett letters that the year has to be retrieved
    from the postmark on the envelope. This letter is only partly quoted in
    Beaverbrook, *Friends: Sixty Years of Intimate Personal Relations with
    Richard Bedford Bennett*, 64. Bennett's prediction that Max's new wife
    would find in Max "a true & loving husband" did not, alas, turn out to be
    true. That part of the letter Beaverbrook leaves out. What he does quote is
    usually accurate; omissions are another matter.

38 LAC, MG28, *Progressive Conservative Party Records* IV-2, Bennett file.

39 Two of Bennett's toes had been cut off in some accident that he did not
    mention when he talked to King on 29 July 1930. See King Diaries for
    that date. The source of the information about Peyronié's disease is a
    description by Alice Toner Tompkins, an estranged Fredericton wife, who
    became private secretary to R.B. Hanson, MP, York-Sunbury, 1921–1935,
    1940–1945. She was also Hanson's mistress. How she came to know any-
    thing at all about Bennett sexually is a question. She did not know the
    name of the disease but accurately described its symptoms. I mentioned
    this description to Dr David Wood, my son-in-law, who had seen a case
    of it and identified it at once. Alice Tompkins said her source was Hazel
    Colville; Hazel Colville's daughter, Frances Ballantyne, rejects that possi-
    bility out of hand. Professor Peter Toner of the University of New Bruns-
    wick, Saint John, has given me his aunt's unique information about Ben-
    nett (Dalhousie University Archives [DUA], P.B. Waite Papers, Peter Toner
    to PBW, 27 Jan. 1999; 1 Feb. 1999; 3 Feb. 1999; 8 Sept. 2000). Also ibid.,
    Frances Kemp Ballantyne to PBW, 24 Feb. 1999; 3 Aug. 1999; 19 Nov.
    1999. For Hazel Colville, see chapter 3.

40 *L'Action canadienne-française* 17, 1927, 32.

41 *Toronto Saturday Night*, 30 June 1928, "Lobby and Gallery."

42 J. Murray Beck, *Politics of Nova Scotia*, vol. 2, 110–14.

43 *Halifax Herald*, 27 July 1928.

44 RBB Papers, M-920, #17867, A.W. Merriam to Cantley, 18 April 1929; #17868, Cantley to RBB, 19 April 1929.

45 Hector Charlesworth, *I'm Telling You*, 24; *Calgary Herald*, 18 May 1927, brought to my attention by Professor Donald Smith, University of Calgary.

46 David Ricardo Williams, *Mayor Gerry*, 75–80; RBB Papers, M-3179, #605360, RBB to Daisy (Mrs G.W.) Hartley of Jasper, 12 June 1947. RBB had done legal work for her in Calgary in 1918.

47 RBB Papers, M-922, #21773, R.H. Pooley, leader of Conservative Opposition in BC, to RBB, 1 Feb. 1928; #21795, George Cowan to RBB, 23 Mar. 1928, from Vancouver; #21797, RBB to Cowan, 18 April 1928; #20019, Tolmie to RBB, 28 Oct. 1929, personal and confidential; Robin Fisher, *Duff Pattullo of British Columbia*, 185.

48 RBB Papers, M-922, #19880, RBB to A.E. Ross, MP, Kingston, 12 Dec. 1928, personal; M-923, #21842, Lottie Bowron to RBB, 12 Dec. 1928, from Victoria; #21844, RBB to Lottie Bowron, 13 Dec. 1928, from Victoria.

49 Ibid., RBB's passport M-3153, #563938; his opinion of Der Rosenkavalier, #563227, RBB to AEM, 12 Jan. 1929, from Southampton; the *Vienna Neue Freie Presse*, 25 Dec. 1928, reports the Christmas performance of the Strauss opera. I am grateful to Professor Steven Burns of Dalhousie for checking this reference for me in Vienna. The German lines of the Marschallin: "*Und zwischen mir und dir da fliesst sie [die Zeit] wieder, lautlos, wie eine Sanduhr.*"

50 RBB Papers, M-3143, #549059 n.d., Mme. Adeline Solest was a European divorcée who befriended Mildred Bennett and who may have come to have designs on RB. Eventually she came through Calgary en route to Australia. Her poem raises questions that cannot be answered. What government, or governments, was RBB inveighing against? The reference suggests the three had a box seat at the opera and that RBB in some of the longish German recitatives was not altogether quiet. As for RBB's *affaires de coeur*, Mme Solest's comment remains mysterious.

51 Ibid., M-3153, #563227, RBB to AEM, 12 Jan. 1929, from SS *Majestic* at Southampton. His comment on the Prince of Wales, the future Edward VIII, is in a P.S.

52 King Diaries 2, 4 Oct., 15 Nov. 1928; King's conversation with Borden, ibid., 11 Jan. 1929; *Commons Debates*, 7 Feb. 1929, 2

53 *Commons Debates*, 11 Feb. 1929, 17–29; ibid., 7 June 1928, 4039. RBB's 1928 amendment, that the government's expenditures were "too expensive and extravagant," was voted down 79–33.

54 *Ottawa Citizen*, 20 Mar. 1928, also 3, 10, 16 Apr., 30 May 1928; cited in Frank W. Peers, *The Politics of Canadian Broadcasting*. Peers gives an admirable account of the background, pp. 3–62. The editorial from the *Ottawa Citizen* of 20 March is quoted on page 56 via the *Toronto Daily Star*, 21 March 1928. It is a curious coincidence that the first radio editorial in the *Citizen* appeared two days after the first American broadcast of "Amos 'n' Andy" on Sunday, 18 March 1928.

55 Peers, *Canadian Broadcasting*, 39–40; *Commons Debates*, 6 June 1929, 3341.

56 D'Arcy Marsh, *The Tragedy of Henry Thornton*, 116–17; RBB Papers, M-922, #19874 CB, Naismith to RBB, 4 Dec. 1928; King Diaries, 4 Oct. 1928; King and Joan Patteson that evening read together a hundred pages of Sir Oliver Lodge's *Ether and Reality*.

57 There is a summary of CNR broadcasting in G.R. Stevens, *History of the Canadian National Railways*, 326. Bennett's protest is RBB Papers, M-922, #19933, RBB to W.D. Robb, vice-president, CNR, 28 July 1929, from Calgary. For King's view of the liberal function of national radio, see King Diaries, 10 Oct. 1929.

58 Marsh, *Thornton*, 119–20. The original idea was that the CNR and the CPR would both contribute to the building of the Lord Nelson Hotel in the proportion 2.5: 1, since the CPR only reached Halifax via Saint John, the Digby ferry, and the subsidiary Dominion Atlantic Railway. Sir Edward Beatty raised the ante to exclude the CNR. In any case the CNR needed a new station and preferred a new hotel. See Stevens, *History of the Canadian National Railways*, 339–40. Bennett's comment is in *Commons Debates*, 8 June 1928, 4019.

59 For Bennett's remarks, see *Commons Debates*, 4 June 1929, 3189–96.

60 Ibid., 14 Feb. 1929, 133–8; King Diaries, 14 Feb. 1929.

61 RBB Papers, M-923, #21521, RBB to Mrs Allan Sinclair, 27 May 1929; King Diaries, 11 Mar. 1929.

62 *Commons Debates*, 11 June 1929, 3534–43. Bennett was parodying a King speech of 9 April 1929, 1403–4.

63 RBB Papers, M-922, #16793, RBB to Mrs Edith Birnie, 21 June 1928; #16902, RBB to Col. G.O. Sanders, Calgary, 26 Nov. 1928.

Ibid., #16817, G.P. Graham to RBB, 19 Oct. 1927; #16819, RBB to Graham, 30 June 1928. Bennett explained the long delay in replying as owing to his having put Graham's letter to one side as meriting a hand-written reply, whence it became side-tracked. Senator George Graham (1859–1943) King had appointed to the Senate on 20 Dec. 1926. See RBB Papers, M-3174, #597142, RBB to Borden, 3 Feb. 1930; M-3175, #599645, WLMK to RBB, 3 Oct. 1928, handwritten; #599648, same, 13 Oct. 1929.

64 Ibid., M-922, #20012, RBB to Tolmie, 24 Aug. 1929, personal, from Calgary. There is reference to Tolmie and patronage in Robin Fisher, *Duff Pattullo of British Columbia*, 219. See also RBB Papers, #20019, Tolmie to RBB, 28 Oct. 1929, personal and confidential, from Victoria.

65 RBB Papers, M-923, #21859, W.K. Morrison to RBB, 1 Aug. 1929, addressed to RBB at Rycroft, Gen. A.D. McRae's Vancouver home; #21851, H.H. Stevens to RBB, 21 June 1929, confidential; #21871, W.K. Morrison to RBB, 3 Aug. 1929, based on a clipping from a Vancouver newspaper.

66 Ibid., #21904, RBB to Cy Peck at Nanaimo, 2 Oct. 1929; M-922, #20020, Pooley to RBB, 21 Nov. 1929.

67 Ibid., M-317, #599645, WLMK to RBB, 31 Oct. 1928.

68 Ibid., M-3149, #556970-4, for RBB's income tax returns; M-3152, #562806, RBB to AEM, 12 Dec. 1929, from Ottawa.

69 Ibid., M-3175, #599571, RBB to Jackson Dodds, general manager, Bank of Montreal, Montreal, 31 Dec. 1935, enclosing cheque in full payment. There are several letters on this subject in #599556, some with the local Bentley branch of the Bank of Montreal.

70 Ibid., M-3152, #562694, RBB to AEM, 30 Oct. 1929, from Ottawa.

71 "R.B.'s Little Weaknesses," by Arthur P. Woolacott, *Saturday Night*, 16 Nov. 1929, 3.

72 *Commons Debates*, 24 Feb. 1930, 33; 3 April, 1228.

73 King Diaries, 1 May 1930; *Commons Debates*, 1 May 1930, 1678–80.

74 *Commons Debates*, 6 May 1930, 1831–6.

75 Ibid.; King Diaries, 6 May 1930.

76 Ibid., 2 June 1930; 30 May 1930, 2943.

CHAPTER THREE

1 RBB Papers, #22346, RBB to Harvey Kavaner of Red River Grain Co.,13 May 1930, personal; ibid., #22350, RBB to David Beaubier, 14 May 1930, personal; #19315, RBB to Blondin, 18 May 1930; RB's 1930 itinerary is given in two places, slightly different but complementary: #19258 and #19989. There is no date or provenance on either. For Milner and reporters on the King trains, see #21728, Milner to RBB, 19 May 1930, from Edmonton; #21730 RBB to Milner, 26 May 1930, personal, from Ottawa.

2 Mildred's statement to Mackenzie King was at an Ottawa party to cele-
brate her engagement to Bill Herridge. LAC, King Papers, Diary, 11 April
1931. Her remark chiding her brother is quoted by Bennett himself in a
talk with King (King Diaries, 29 July 1930). RBB Papers, #561352, Peter
McGibbon to RBB, n.d. but ca. 5 April 1931 from Bracebridge, Ont.

3 RBB Papers, #18229, RBB to Rhodes, 23 Jan. 1930, personal, addressed
"My dear Ned"; Grant Dexter, "Young Canada Goes to Washington."
Dexter says Herridge and Bennett first met at Eugene Lafleur's funeral
early in May 1930. This may be incorrect.

4 King Diaries, 9 June 1930. The best account of the 1930 election is in
Larry A. Glassford's *Reaction and Reform*, 72–97. See also J.M. Beck's
Pendulum of Power, 191–205.

5 Glassford, *Reaction and Reform*, 78, citing Dominion Bureau of Statistics
(DBS), Trade of Canada, 1935.

6 *Canadian Annual Review 1929–30*, 97. Much has been made of the verb
"blast." In the draft of the speech prior to the broadcast, Bennett had
struck it out, Herridge re-inserted it, and by the time RB was reading it,
it was too late. "And that phrase, O'Leary," said RB to Grattan O'Leary
five years later, "has not done me any good." The story is reported in QUA,
Grant Dexter Papers, Dexter to Dafoe, 4 Jan. 1935.

7 Public Archives of Nova Scotia (hereafter PANS), Edgar Rhodes Papers,
vol. 627, Rhodes to RBB, 24 June 1930, private and confidential; Bruce
Hutchison, *Mr. Prime Minister*, 242. It is also cited by Glassford, *Reaction
and Reform*, 80. Hutchison was thirty-one years RB's junior. They had
met several times.

8 C.G. Power (1888–1968) was Liberal MP for Quebec South, 1917–55. See
Norman Ward, *A Party Politician*, 264; PANS, Rhodes Papers, vol. 653,
A.D. MacRae to Rhodes, 9 June 1930.

9 RBB Papers, #20108, M.B. Peacock to RBB, 24 July 1930; Ward, *Memoirs
of Chubby Power*, 265.

10 King Diaries, 29 July 1930.

11 Ibid., 7 Aug. 1930.

12 Ibid., 5 Aug. 1930; Roger Graham, *Meighen*, vol. 2, 355–7, vol. 3,
26–8. Webster's letter to Meighen is 18 Jan. 1931; RBB Papers, #14614,
Meighen to RBB, 14 May 1930.

13 Beck, *Politics of Nova Scotia*, vol. 2, 129; PANS, Edgar Rhodes Papers, vol.
653, Rhodes to W.F. Nickle, 1 Feb. 1930; ibid., Rhodes to R.L. Blackburn,
25 Jan. 1930; ibid., RBB to Rhodes, 1 Feb. 1930; King Diaries, 1 Nov.
1930, reporting conversation with Rhodes. He also told King that the Liberal party were lucky to be out of office.

14 Armstrong and Nelles, *Southern Exposure*, 86–7; the best book on Beaverbrook is Chisholm and Davie, *Beaverbrook,* 36–7. RBB Papers, #67265, Cahan to RBB, 7 Aug. 1930, telg. For the Perley sketch, see John English, *Shadow of Heaven*, 162.

15 RBB Papers, #18424, anonymous letter to Senator R.H. Pope, 20 Feb. 1930; Lavergne to RBB, 27 Nov. 1928, quoted in La Terreur, *Les Tribulations des conservateurs au Québec*, 12. LAC, D.G. Creighton Papers, vol. 3, Michel Brunet to Creighton, 11 Aug. 1956.

16 Glassford, *Reaction and Reform*, 66; Rumilly, *Maurice Duplessis et son temps*, vol. 1, 70; Black, *Duplessis*, 32–3.

17 RBB Papers, #22346, RBB to Harvey Kavaner, Red River Grain Co., 13 May 1930, personal.

18 *Saturday Night*, 3 March 1928, has a short piece on H.H. Stevens. Stevens's recollection of Bennett's 1927 remark is from an interview, Stevens with Richard Wilbur, 31 May 1966, quoted in Wilbur's *H.H. Stevens*, 68; RBB Papers, #18049, M.J. Alvanoff to RBB from Vancouver, 17 Dec. 1929; #18230, RBB to Alvanoff, 1 Feb. 1930; #18863-4, Geo. B. Jones to RBB, 18 Dec. 1929, from Apohaqui, N.B.; RBB to Jones, 27 Dec. 1929. Jones was Conservative MP for Royal.

19 On the *Port Hope Times*, see RBB Papers, #20921, W.H. Price to Ferguson, 21 Jan. 1928, private and confidential; #20925, Ryckman to RBB, 14 Feb. 1928; on National Press, Winnipeg, #21112 to #21206; the quote is from #21133, RBB to J.T. Haig, 11 Jan. 1929, personal, from Ottawa.

20 Ward, *Memoirs of Chubby Power*, 265.

21 Notes re the September 1930 *Commons Debates*: on the $20 million, 11 Sept. 1930, 136; on the glass industry, 20 Sept. 1930, 542; on shoes, 22 Sept. 1930; Agnes Macphail, 16 Sept. 1930, 295; on the financial question, RBB Papers, #196060, gives available cash at close of business, Thurs., 2 Sept. 1930; #196068, Sellar to RBB, 6 Sept. 1930, memo of loan maturities, 1930–37; #196105, Minute of Council, 6 Oct. 1930; #196109, Sellar to RBB, 6 Oct. 1930.

22 King Diaries, 29 July; 13, 16 Aug. 1930.

23 Ibid., 14 May 1929.

24 C.P. Stacey, *Canada and the Age of Conflict*, vol. 2, 8–24.

25 King Diaries, 29 July 1930; LAC, MG 30 E148, John R. Read Papers, vol. 10, 13–15.

26 Story, "Canada's Covenant," 43, reporting an interview with John Read, 25 Oct. 1973.

27 RBB Papers, #102237, Anderson to RBB, 28 Aug. 1930, personal and confidential; #192240, RBB to Anderson, 4 Sept. 1930, private and personal;

#102253-5, telegrams to Bracken, Andersen, and Brownlee. *Ottawa Journal*, 24 Sept. 1930, "Bennett at Work"; MacLean, *R.B. Bennett*, 28–9. MacLean was Bennett's secretary for two years, 1932–34. The book was published originally without RB's knowledge. MacLean told RB that three Canadian publishers refused the book because they thought it put Bennett in too favourable a light. MacLean published it at his own expense, and it went through several printings between 1934 and 1935. The radiograms from Ottawa were not about trivia. They were about the appointment of Col. Leo Laflèche to the new Pensions Appeal Court. Laflèche wanted to be assured that his acceptance would not prejudice his being considered for deputy minister of defence. RB assured him it would not. In fact in 1932 Laflèche was appointed to the position. See RBB Papers, #321476, Sir Arthur Currie and Sir P. Lake to RBB via Louisburg radio, 24 Sept. 1930, from Victoria; #321479, RBB to Perley, 25 Sept. 1930 from *Empress of Australia*.

28   RBB Papers, #102039, list of the Canadian delegation. The British government offered to pay Mildred Bennett's hotel bill, #102159, but almost certainly it was paid by her brother.

29   LAC, John R. Read Papers, vol. 10, 17; RBB Papers, #103754, Leo Amery to RBB, 1 Oct. 1930; Alex I. Inglis, *Documents on Canadian External Relations*, vol. 4, 229; Stacey, *Historical Documents*, vol. 5, 483; for Snowden's speech, see Stacey, *Canada and the Age of Conflict*, vol. 2, 138. RB said in 1932, "I went to London [in 1930] with a very definite idea in my mind ... and I believed it would be received exactly as it was received" (*Commons Debates*, 26 April 1932, 2406). *London Times*, 9 October 1930; *London Observer*, 12 Oct. 1930; *London Sunday Times*, 12 Oct. 1930; *London Spectator*, 16 Oct. 1930; *Bristol Times and Mirror*, 10 Oct. 1930. A massive spate of other clippings are collected in RBB Papers, M-4533 (clippings file in no discernible order). RBB Papers, #102840, Herridge to R.H. Coats, 17 Oct. 1930.

30   LAC, John R. Read Papers, 17. Read's Uncle Bedford is the source of RBB's middle name. For RB's praise of Read's appointment, see *Commons Debates*, 20 May 1929, 2666. There is another incident in Calgary, ca. 1913, rather like the one described by Read, when RB was dealing with a cub reporter from the *Calgary Albertan*, a paper he did not like. It is quoted in the *Regina Leader-Post*, 5 July 1947, and in my *The Loner*, 53.

31   *Commons Debates*, 6 May 1930, 1831; *Manchester Guardian*, 24 Nov. 1930, for the cotton parable; 7 Nov. 1930 for RB's reference to the Canadian standard of life.

32   RBB Papers, #102183, Skelton to RBB, 17 Oct. 1930.

33 The figures are presented as typical years from Conservative Party head-quarters to Herridge, 22 Oct. 1930, personal. The *London Morning Post* was particularly strong in support of British millers. See RBB Papers, #102849. The most magisterial survey of the whole subject is Ian H. Drummond, *Imperial Economic Policy*, 145 et seq. See also Stacey, *Canada and the Age of Conflict*, vol. 2, 124–34. RBB Papers, #102186, RBB to Mary Waagen, 18 Oct. 1930. Waagen was the daughter of Sir Joseph Hickson, with whom RB had worked for many years during the war. She was a Conservative party worker in Vancouver, whom RB much respected and listened to. RBB Papers, #19781, RBB to Bessie Gowan Ferguson, 27 April 1928. Miss Ferguson worked for the *Toronto Mail and Empire*. For RB's views on Russian wheat in 1930, see RBB Papers, #488887, RBB to Joseph Lyster at Cabri, Sask., 31 Dec. 1930, from Calgary.

34 Chisholm and Davie, *Beaverbrook*, 297. The authors pick up this very Canadian side to Canadian history and to Beaverbrook. Bennett's back-ground is in my *The Loner*, 6–7. For Bennett on free trade and Canada in 1930, see RBB Papers, #101749, RBB to James F. Macdonald, 22 Nov. 1930, at Linlithgow.

35 Diana Cooper, *Autobiography*, 172; for A.J.P. Taylor and Beaverbrook, see Chisholm and Davie, *Beaverbrook*, 501–5; for a delicious episode of young Max Aitken in Newcastle, N.B., in 1896, see my *The Loner*, 22–3; Beaverbrook, *Friends*, 52–3.

36 Beaverbrook, *Friends*, 54–64.

37 RBB Papers, #138932, Perley to RBB, 2 Nov. 1930, cable; #138935, RBB to Perley, 5 Nov. 1930, cable; #138948, Central Creameries, Victoria, to Perley, 20 Nov. 1930, telg., on the price of Australian butter "away below actual cost of production stop in years of our experience situation has never been more demoralized."

38 RBB Papers, #101124, for *Hell's Angels*; #101457 for the Edgar Wallace play. Wallace (1875–1932) was a popular and hugely prolific British author who moved to California in the early 1930s and died there; RBB Papers, #101553, Prince of Wales dinner, 17 Oct. 1930. Walter Allward (1876–1955) was commissioned in 1921 to build the Vimy Memorial. RBB Papers, #103164, Allward to RBB, 9 Oct. 1930, on Canadian Battle-field Memorials Commission paper, from his Maida Vale studio; #102165, RBB to Allward, 13 Oct. 1930.

39 Stanley (1907–94), "From New Brunswick to Calgary," 245–6; MacLean, *R.B. Bennett*, 20.

40 Aldred, "The Public Career of Major-General Alexander D. McRae," 152–3; Oliver, *G. Howard Ferguson*, 377–80, 392.

41 Great Britain, *House of Commons Debates,* 5s, 1550, 27 Nov. 1930; Thomas's apology is quoted by Ernest Watkins in *R.B. Bennett,* 153; RB's protest is in RBB Papers, #102925, n.d. This is a typed letter, and clearly represents RB's feelings on the subject of "humbug." Quite possibly it was not sent.

42 Wilbur, *H.H. Stevens,* 92–3; RBB Papers, #139002, Stevens to RBB, 25 Dec. 1930, telg., from Port Coquitlam.

43 *Manitoba Free Press,* 31 Dec. 1930; for a luminous, elegant history of the Department of Finance, see Bryce, *Maturing in Hard Times.*

44 RBB Papers, #139008, Tolmie to RBB, 28–29 Dec. 1930, telg. from Regina; #139019, RBB to Tolmie, 30 Dec. 1930, telg.; #139021, RBB to Tolmie, 31 Dec. 1930, telg.; #139095, RBB to Merriam, 2 Jan. 1931, telg., from Calgary; #139558, Tolmie to RBB, 14 Jan. 1931, telg.; #139156, E.J. Mahoney to RBB, 4 July 1931, from Stoney Creek, Ont., telg.; #139162, J.S.H. Matson to RBB, 14 July 1931, from Vancouver; #139170, Tolmie to RBB, 14 July 1931, telg.; RBB to Tolmie, 17 July 1931, telg. The trade agreement between Canada and Australia is noted in #138466.

45 Mackenzie King reports the tensions between Willingdon and Bennett, not without some *Schadenfreude;* King Diaries, 20 Dec. 1930; RB's banquet for Willingdon is reported in ibid., 14 Jan. 1931. RB's trip to Washington is in RBB Papers, #184150. Tentative program, #184151, Hume Wrong to RBB, 24 Jan. 1931; #184187, Hume Wrong to Frank Noyes, President, Associated Press, 5 Feb. 1931, personal; #184194, Wrong to RBB, 21 Feb. 1931, from Toronto; #184226, Noyes to Wrong, 30 Mar. 1931.

46 C.P. Stacey, *Canada and the Age of Conflict,* vol. 2, 146, quoting *New York Times,* 31 Jan., 2, 6 Feb. 1931. For Beauharnois, see the excellent work by T.D. Regehr in *The Beauharnois Scandal.* The engineering background is exceptionally useful (xii, xiii, 6–7, 80).

47 This description of the prime minister's office in the 1930s is taken from the *Ottawa Citizen,* 2 May 1935. Other references: *Ottawa Journal,* 24 Sept. 1930; *Queen's Quarterly,* winter 1931, 173; *Toronto Mail and Empire,* quoted in *Ottawa Journal,* 9 May 1931. See also Bryce, *Maturing in Hard Times,* 74.

48 Bryce, *Maturing in Hard Times,* 74.

49 W.L. White, "The Treasury Board in Canada," 111, cited in Bryce, *Maturing in Hard Times,* 77.

50 *Commons Debates,* 17 March 1931, 57, 60; *Queen's Quarterly,* "The Current Political Scene," 361; for King's observations, *Commons Debates,* 16 March 1931, 46; LAC, John R. Read Papers, vol. 10; King Diaries, 18 Feb. 1931.

51 *Commons Debates,* "wall of despair," 28 April 1931, 1072–7; world conditions, 29 April 1931, 1103; responsibility, 21 April 1931, 785.

52 Ibid., 29 April 1931, 1099–1104.

53 Bryce, *Maturing in Hard Times,* has a valuable table, "Budget Forecasts and Outcomes, 1929–39 to 1939–49," 108–9.

54 *Commons Debates,* 1 June 1931, 2142.

55 Ibid., 16 July, 3855.

56 King Diaries, 1 June 1931; *Commons Debates,* 11 April 1931, 18 Feb. 1931; RBB Papers, #561352; Peter McGibbon to RBB, 6 April 1931, from Bracebridge.

57 *Canadian Magazine* (April 1931). Grant Dexter (1896–1961) wrote the article. He was at the time the Ottawa correspondent for the *Winnipeg Free Press.* His piece describes Herridge as shy and reclusive, reluctant to accept RB's big offer. Other, perhaps later, Ottawa sources refer to him as "wild Bill." Later evidence does suggest his shyness was temporary.

58 *Ottawa Evening Citizen,* 14 April 1931; *Toronto Daily Star,* 14 April 1931; RBB Papers, #561420, Mildred to RBB, n.d.; #561462, Frank Regan to RBB, 15 April 1931 from Ottawa; #561468, S.J. Gauthier to RBB, 16 April 1931, from Montreal; #561470, RBB to Gauthier, 20 April 1931.

59 King Diaries, 24 June 1931; *Commons Debates,* 1 July 1931, 3246.

60 Regehr, *Beauharnois,* 132.

61 Ibid., 3.

62 *Commons Debates,* 22 May 1930, 2418–20; 20 Sept. 1930, 567; re campaign contributions, ibid., 31 July 1931, 4398. RB said in 1932 that he refused to allow acceptance of Beauharnois money (ibid., 11 Feb. 1932, 142). Whitaker, *The Government Party,* 12–13; Regehr, *Beauharnois,* 113–14; RBB Papers, #513295-6, Frank Regan to McRae, 10 July 1931; #513293, McRae to Regan, 11 July 1930. See Regehr, *Beauharnois,* 122–3.

63 *Commons Debates,* 19 May 1931, 1737–44.

64 RBB Papers, #514290-1, Cahan to RBB, 13 July 1931; King Diaries, 12 July 1931.

65 Oliver, *G. Howard Ferguson,* 399.

66 Mackenzie King's well-known "valley of humiliation" speech is in *Commons Debates,* 30 July 1931, 4387.

67 The five-stanza *Saturday Night* poem is quoted by Agnes Macphail, ibid., 4411; for RB's opinion of Sweezey, ibid., 4400; RBB Papers, #518533-6, Sweezey to RBB, 12 Sept. 1931; #513537, RBB to Sweezey, 15 Oct. 1931.

68 These paragraphs are based substantially on Regehr's *Beauharnois,* 146–7.

69 Bennett's remark about the western drought is cited in Stevenson, "Current Events: The Canadian Political Scene," 568–9; Stevenson's comment on the Bennett cabinet, *Queen's Quarterly*, spring 1931, 361; for problems of Regina, see Pitsula, "The Mixed Social Economy of Unemployment Relief in Regina," 100. Liberal objections to the Relief Act were based on "peace, order and good government" in its preamble, which they believed a cunning attempt to give the government draconian power. Bennett's argument was that the clause was there to justify spending money on matters over which the government had no authority. See Ward, *A Party Politician*, 283.

70 Dexter, "The Canadian Political Scene," 745.

CHAPTER FOUR

1 This account of Bennett's Sunday, 20 September 1931, comes from his secretary, Andrew D. MacLean, R.B. *Bennett*, 36–37; the *Montreal Daily Star* has a long editorial appreciation of RB as he retired from office 7 March 1938.

2 Robert B. Bryce, *Maturing in Hard Times*, 125–6.

3 King Diaries, 17 Oct. 1931, 21 Oct. 1932; RBB to Sydney Dobson, 30 Nov. 1946, cited in Duncan McDowall, *Quick to the Frontier*, 260. Dobson was a Cape Bretoner who had started as a junior in Sydney, N.S., in 1900, and was now president. *Grant Dexter Papers*, QUA, Dexter to John W. Dafoe, 6 Oct. 1931; Beaverbrook Papers, vol. 65, RBB to Max, 3 July 1942. For Sun Life, RB's 1928 correspondence with T.B. Macaulay, Sun Life's president: RBB Papers, #15752, RBB to Macaulay, 2 March 1928; #15769, Macaulay to RBB, 14 June 1928; #15771, RBB to Macaulay, 15 June 1928; the 1932 crisis and its solution is mentioned by a relative of George Finlayson, then superintendent of Insurance. See LAC, MG31 D19, Finlayson-Wilbur Correspondence, Jean Finlayson to Wilbur, 28 Feb. [1967]. The Borden correspondence is RBB Papers, #597190, Borden to RBB, 3 Oct. 1932; #597191, RBB to Borden, 7 Oct. 1931.

4 *Ottawa Journal*, 21 Nov. 1931,"The Toll of Public Life"; *Saturday Night*, 28 Nov. 1931.

5 C.S. Tompkins to RBB, mid-April 1931, enclosing memo of Graham Towers, in Bryce, *Maturing in Hard Times*, 131.

6 RBB Papers, #285751, Mark Robertson to RBB, 8 Dec. 1931, from London Life, Edmonton. This letter was enclosed in an envelope marked "Not to be opened by anyone but the Prime Minister." RBB Papers, #285754, RBB to Robertson, 21 Dec. 1931.

7 King Diaries, 23 June 1931; Rhodes's conversation, ibid., 1 Nov. 1930.

8   Webster to Meighen, 18 Jan. 1931, in Graham, *Meighen*, vol. 3, 28. Webster and RB were friends and colleagues, both being on the board of governors of Dalhousie University. See *Winnipeg Free Press*, 4 Feb. 1932.

9   Graham, *Meighen*, vol. 3, 33, 36–7; *Senate Debates*, Feb. 1932.

10 RBB Papers, #s514579-84, RBB to Morris Wilson, general manager of the Royal Bank, 3 Oct. 1931, quoted by T.D. Regehr, *Beauharnois*, 167.

11 Ibid., 171, 184–5.

12 *Commons Debates*, 8 Mar. 1932, 898–900.

13 Ibid., 18 March 1932, 1281–2; Chubby Power has an account of the background and consequences of this incident, in Ward, *A Party Politician*, 288–93. The quip that Power used was not original with him. It was made about British Prime Minister Ramsay MacDonald, in the British House of Commons. It is characteristic of Power's candour that he revealed the source of his quip.

14 Stevens, *History of the Canadian National Railways*, 307–8.

15 Ibid., 309–17.

16 *Commons Debates*, 8 June 1928, 4019, 4039, 4043; ibid., 27 May 1929, 2828–39; RBB Papers, #19933, RBB to W.D. Robb, 22 July 1929, replying to Robb to RBB, 6 July 1929, personal.

17 Marsh, *The Tragedy of Sir Henry Thornton*, 155. Marsh's book is *parti pris* for Thornton, with Marsh's particular animus directed against Manion, minister of railways. Manion's answer is in his *Life Is an Adventure*, 300–2. See also Bliss, *A Canadian Millionaire*, 481.

18 LAC, Robert Manion Papers, vol. 14, Thornton to Manion, 1 Oct. 1930, personal; RBB Papers, #102187, Thornton to [Herridge], 2 Oct. 1930, cable; Perley to RBB, 2 Oct. 1990; #102190, Perley to RBB, 2 Oct. 1930, confid. cable; #102192, RBB to Perley, 2 Oct. 1930, confid. cable. On Thornton's forced resignation, Manion Papers, vol. 4, Manion to RBB, 30 May 1932, personal and private. Marsh, in *Thornton*, 272, says Thornton was given only $50,000.

19 1932, Special Committee on Radio Broadcasting, Minutes of Proceedings & Evidence, 486–7, cited in Peers, *Canadian Broadcasting*, 87.

20 *Commons Debates*, 18 May 1932, 3035–6.

21 There is a comprehensive list of newspapers and which side they supported in Peers, *Canadian Broadcasting*, 77.

22 RB in *Commons Debates*, 6 June 1935, 3347. Re the CRBC, the story in Peers's *Politics of Canadian Broadcasting* is chilling.

23 *Toronto Daily Star*, 31 Dec. 1931, quoting the *New Statesman and Nation*, a poem by J. MacFlecknoe satirizing a Bennett speech on "Bonds of Empire"; for the 1894 conference, Waite, *The Man from Halifax*, 410–11; 1932 references, Hilliker, *Canada's Department of External*

Affairs, vol. 1, 143–5; Drummond, *Imperial Economic Policy 1917–1939*, 170 et seq. There is a useful MA thesis by Kurt Peacock, "The Forgotten Nationalist: R.B. Bennett and the British Empire, 1930–1932."

24   House of Lords Record Office, *Beaverbrook Papers*, vol. 65, Beaverbrook to RBB, 23 Jan. 1932, draft cable; Beaverbrook to RBB, 4 Feb. 1932, cable. A good example of Beaverbrook's pungent exaggeration: that the British remission of the 10 per cent duty was "entirely due to Ferguson's intervention. His influence here is bigger than any High Commissioner of any Dominion at any time."

25   Granatstein, *A Man of Influence*, 41–2; Sir William Clark to Dominions Office, 19 Mar. 1932, cable, in Drummond, *Imperial Economic Policy*, 210. For D.W. Clark, RBB Papers, #203512, Clark to RBB, 15 Oct. 1932, from Queen's. RB wrote to Clark, "When can you come to us? I should like it to be as soon as possible" (#203513, RBB to Clark, 22 Oct. 1932).

26   Drummond, *Imperial Economic Policy*, 192.

27   Ibid., 217; Beaverbrook Papers, vol. 65, Beaverbrook to RB, 6 June 1932.

28   University of Birmingham Archives, *Neville Chamberlain Papers*, NC1/26 #468, Neville Chamberlain to Annie Chamberlain, 22 July 1932, from Ottawa; besides his letters to his wife, Chamberlain recorded the day-to-day events of the conference fairly extensively in his journal, which is cited as NC 2/17. I have not cited the quotations from Chamberlain's diary separately.

29   Walter Runciman set down his talk with Bennett in the Runciman Papers, University of Newcastle-on-Tyne Archives, quoted in Drummond, *Imperial Economic Policy*, 296–9; Runciman's mocking comment when RB was denouncing Russian trade, 27 July, is reported by Thomas Robertson, assistant editor of the *Winnipeg Free Press*, Dafoe Papers, LAC, Roberton to Dafoe, 27 July 1932. It is cited in Kottman's excellent *Reciprocity and the North Atlantic Triangle*, 25.

30   RBB Papers, #548977, H.A. Gwynne to RBB, 11 Aug. 1932, confidential, from the Château Laurier; the J.H. ("Jimmy") Thomas story is quoted by John Stevenson in "The Imperial Economic Conference of 1932," QUA, John A. Stevenson Papers, file # 7.

31   QUA, Grant Dexter Papers, Dexter to Dafoe, 16 Oct. 1932. Dexter went to some trouble to report his interview with Bennett as accurately as possible. He did not take it down in shorthand but, as soon after the interview as he could, made notes of what Bennett had said and then wrote it up for Dafoe.

32   Ibid., Dafoe to Dexter, 19 Oct. 1932. It says much about Dafoe's shrewdness that he claimed, a week after the conference opened, that he

suspected a Bennett-Bruce-Amery conspiracy that, with Beaverbrook, would force the British government to regroup and jettison its Labour members. Dafoe did not write an editorial along those lines but in October 1932 wished he had.

33 *Commons Debates,* 10 Oct. 1932, 32, 47; Cambridge University Library, Stanley Baldwin Papers, f.156, Lascelles to Baldwin, 22 Nov. 1932 from Ottawa. Lascelles added an aphorism, sometimes quoted, that he had heard somewhere, that "R.B. is partially educated but wholly uncivilized." Like most aphorisms, it is a triumph of wit over judgment.

34 *London Economist,* 18 Jan. 1936, cited in Stacey, *Canada and the Age of Conflict,* vol. 2, 145; the article in the *Canadian Magazine,* Oct. 1932, is "Canada Gets Her Share," by E.C. Buchanan; Manion's opinion is from his diary, Manion Papers, vol. 105, 5 Sept. 1932; Meighen, *Unrevised and Unrepented,* 315. Rudyard Kipling (1845–1936) admired Bennett as much or more for his devotion to Canada as for his imperial sentiments, or so a close personal friend of Kipling's reported after Kipling's death on 18 Jan. 1936. See RBB Papers, #549852, J.H. Barry to RBB, 18 Feb. 1936. In 1932 after the Ottawa Conference, Kipling sent RB the stanza from "Our Lady of the Snows," or so Bennett claimed to J.H. Barry; RBB Papers, #549856, RBB to Barry, 22 Feb. 1936, personal.

35 RBB Papers, #597742, Hazel Colville to RBB, 6 Jan. 1930; PBW Papers, Frances Ballantyne to PBW, 3 April 1990; interview, 5 July 1997, at Oakville, Ont. As for other letters from Hazel missing from the Bennett Papers, RB was capable of destroying them himself, from principle, pride, or pique. Alice Millar, long his devoted secretary, was in Fredericton in 1948 and destroyed quantities of what she called "unhistorical" letters in the Bennett Papers. She was perhaps, as Frances Ballantyne suggested, jealous of women in RB's life (Frances's comment on my draft of interview with her, 5 July 1989). For the Chamberlain reference, Birmingham University Library, Chamberlain Papers, NC 2/17, Diary, 23 Aug. 1932; for King's comment, King Diaries, 15 Dec. 1932.

36 McGill University Archives, Hazel Colville Papers, RBB to Hazel Colville, Saturday [27 Aug. 1932], from the Château Laurier, Ottawa. These papers were given to McGill by Hazel Colville's daughter and were brought to my attention by Pamela Miller, Sir William Osler Librarian of the McGill Archives.

37 Sir Edward Kemp (1858–1929) married twice, first in 1879 to Celia Wilson, by whom he had three daughters (Hazel was born in 1889); second, in 1925, to Virginia Copping, a widow, by whom he had another daughter.

38 Hazel Colville Papers, RBB to Hazel Colville, Sunday night [28 Aug. 1932] from the CPR train approaching Fort William.

39 Ibid., RBB to Hazel, Tues., 20 Sept. 1932, from the Château Laurier; inset quotation is RBB to Hazel, Mon., 10 Oct. 1932, from House of Commons. (Monday of Thanksgiving weekend was not at that time a holiday.)

40 Ibid., RBB to Hazel, Mon., 17 Oct. 1932, from Toronto.

41 Ibid., RBB to Hazel, Mon., 31 Oct. 1932, from Ottawa; Tues., 1 Nov. 1932, marked only All Saints' Day. Hazel's letter that so occasioned RB's reaction is missing (along with all her other letters) although he might well have wished to keep it. Against that is his penchant for destroying personal letters, as well as Alice Millar's destructions in 1948 at the University of New Brunswick.

42 King Diaries, 16 Nov. 1932. King has the wrong date, for RB's invitation to Hazel says 17 Nov.; ibid., 25 Nov. 193; LAC, Robert Manion Papers, vol. 105, Diaries, 17 Nov. 1932.

43 King Diaries 8, 15 Dec. 1932. Joan Patteson, a woman of discretion and astute political talent, was married to Godfroy Patteson, who was older, unwell and seemed to be wholly complaisant with what might have appeared to be a cool ménage-à-trois. King would visit Joan Patteson at remarkably late hours for talks and reading English literature to each other. It is not difficult to surmise more, for King was susceptible to women, but of that we have as yet no evidence.

44 RBB Papers, #597744, RBB to editor, *Boston Advertiser*, 21 Oct. 1932, telg.; #597745, J.W. Reardon to RBB, 22 Oct. 1932; #597749, same, 24 Oct. 1932; *Ottawa Journal*, 6 Dec. 1932.

45 Hazel Colville Papers, RB to Hazel, 12 May 1933. The italics in the Wordsworth poem are RB's. Hazel was at this time already abroad.

46 Alice Toner Tompkins's information. She was secretary (and more) to R.B. Hanson (1879–1948), MP for York-Sunbury (1921–35, 1940–45). She knew both Bennett and Hazel Colville. Professor Peter Toner at UNB in Saint John has kindly given me his aunt's information. See DUA, PBW Papers, Peter Toner to PBW, 27 Jan., 1 and 3 Feb. 1999, 8 Sept. 2000. The three sonnets, called "Field of Honor," of which I have quoted the first, are by Sara Henderson Hay, a well-published American poet. They are found in *Good Housekeeping*, vol. 95 (Sept. 1932), 19.

CHAPTER FIVE

1 RBB Papers, #547963, H.A. Gwynne to RBB, 9 Dec. 1932; #549845, Kipling to RBB, 15 Dec. 1932, from Brown's Hotel, London. Kipling asked

that RB not address him as "Mr Kipling" but as "Kipling," as between gentlemen who were acquainted, and so signed himself. Senator Raoul Dandurand, Liberal leader in the Senate, suggested to RBB, 6 Dec. 1932, that while he was overseas he could take up with French officials the commemoration of the fourth centenary of Jacques Cartier's first visit to Canada in 1534, suggesting that perhaps members of the French cabinet might come to Canada for it. See #548957, Dandurand to RBB, 6 Dec. 1932, from Montreal.

2   A succinct and valuable summary of this and other issues surrounding unemployment is Struthers, *No Fault of Their Own*, 75–8. Unemployment figures are in his appendix 2, 416; for Charlotte Whitton's western report, see RBB Papers, #478800-1, #478823 et seq., and in Struthers, 77–8; for her influence on Bennett, see Rooke and Schnell, *No Bleeding Heart*, 87–8.

3   RBB Papers, #487589, Clifford Clark to Rod Finlayson, 7 Jan. 1933, quoting Bracken's letter, 17 Dec. 1932 to Rhodes, and Rhodes's reply. Finlayson was RB's executive assistant.

4   RBB Papers, vol. 813, memo, Finlayson to RBB, ca. Dec. 1932, in Struthers, *No Fault of Their Own*, 80. Struthers (86) blames Bennett for the failure of the Unemployment Conference, that he did not want the unemployment issue on his plate, not then. Given his 1931 promise, he probably had no option. I have taken RB's constitutional position as his standing point, and the turbulence of North American finance as his justification. See *Commons Debates*, 29 April 1931, 1099–1104; LAC, Robert Manion Papers, vol. 18, Manion to his son James, 21 Jan. 1933.

5   Keynes, *Essays in Persuasion*, 168–79; Schlesinger, *The Age of Roosevelt*, vol. 1, *The Crisis of the Old Order*, 474–5; vol. 2, *The Coming of the New Deal*, 5.

6   LAC, Arthur Meighen Papers, vol. 214, #136083. Macdonnell was first vice-president of the Board of Trade; *Toronto Daily Star*, 24 Jan. 1933.

7   *Toronto Daily Star*, 26 Jan. 1933.

8   Ibid., 27 Jan. 1933. Eggleston's column was widely copied by other newspapers. The words of this hymn are by Henry Lyte (1793–1847).

9   Borden's account of the "tramps" at Glensmere is in RBB Papers, #597185, Borden to RBB, 14 Aug. 1931, personal. See also Grayson and Bliss, *The Wretched of Canada*.

10   Coote, *Commons Debates*, 1 Feb. 1933, 1698; RBB, ibid., 3 March 2671, 2676, 2677.

11   RBB Papers, #547275, University of Alberta's *The Gateway*, 13 Oct. 1933.

12 Bennett's speech, *Commons Debates,* 27 March 1933, 3417–3420; King Diaries, 27 March 1933; William Irvine, MP Wetaskiwin, *Commons Debates,* 3439.

13 LAC, Robert Manion Papers, vol. 18, Manion to his son James, 24 April, 2 May 1933; Schlesinger, *The Age of Roosevelt,* vol. 2, 209.

14 McGill University Archives, Hazel Colville Papers. RB wrote two letters to Hazel that day, Friday, 2 June 1933. Neither has a date, except "Friday afternoon" and "Friday later."

15 Ibid., RBB to Hazel Colville, Thursday afternoon [8 July 1933], mailed in London; Schlesinger, *The Age of Roosevelt,* vol. 2, 210.

16 RBB Papers, #121244, Robertson to Skelton, 16 June 1933; Robertson to his father, n.d., both cited in Granatstein, *A Man of Influence,* 45; Morris, *Farewell the Trumpets,* 335.

17 Hazel Colville Papers, RBB to Hazel, 6 July 1933, from London. The most recent and balanced account of the 1933 London Economic Conference is Kottman, *Reciprocity and the North Atlantic Triangle.* Chapter 2, 29–78, deals with the London Economic Conference; see also Schlesinger, *The Age of Roosevelt,* vol. 2, 215–22.

18 Kottman, *Reciprocity and the North Atlantic Triangle,* 69, quoting the *New York Times,* 7 July 1933; he also quotes Bullitt to Roosevelt, 8 July 1933 about possible reciprocity negotiations with Canada.

19 Hazel Colville Papers, RBB to Hazel, 28 July 1933; 17 July 1933: 12 Aug. 1933; his being fat, 8 July 1933; on being left alone, 28 July 1933.

20 Line 6 of the octet in the second sonnet in the series "Field of Honor" by Sara Henderson Hay, *Good Housekeeping,* vol. 95, 1932, 19; for Alice Toner Tompkins, see chapter 4, note 46.

21 Bryce, *Maturing in Hard Times,* 18–19, a solid and essential work; McDowall, *Canada's Royal Bank,* 255.

22 Graham Towers's recollection of the 1932 meeting is in Fullerton, *Graham Towers and His Times,* 37–8; Bryce *Maturing in Hard Times,* 82.

23 McDowall, *Canada's Royal Bank,* 117.

24 Fullerton, *Graham Towers,* 31.

25 RBB Papers, #S436794–436801; Bryce, *Maturing in Hard Times,* 137.

26 For Lord Macmillan's interview with Mackenzie King, see King Diaries, 27 Sept. 1933. For the Bank of Canada, there is an excellent Ph.D. thesis by Linda Grayson, "The Formation of the Bank of Canada, 1913–1938"; RBB Papers, #62872, F.D.L. Smith to RBB, 23 Nov. 1933; #62873, RBB to Smith, 24 Nov. 1933, in Grayson, 238. For Brownlee, see QUA, Franklin Lloyd Foster, "John Edward Brownlee: A Biography," 2 vols., Ph.D. thesis,

Queen's University, 1981. Gray has a more popular account, *Talk to My Lawyer*, 112–33.

27 LAC, Robert Manion Papers, vol. 4, RBB to Manion, 18 Nov. 1933; vol. 105, King Diaries, 1 Sept. 1933; vol. 4, RBB to Manion, 22 Nov. 1933, personal.

28 RBB Papers, #606563, F.D.L. Smith to RBB, 3 Oct. 1933, from Toronto; Manion Papers, vol. 4, RBB to Manion, 22 Nov. 1933, personal.

29 Manion Papers, vol. 84, Notes and Memoranda, 9 Dec. 1933; vol. 15, Manion to James Manion, 23 Aug. 1933; same, 12 Jan. 1934, very confidential.

30 Glassford, *Reaction and Reform,* 134; Manion Papers, vol. 15, Manion to James Manion, 27 Jan. 1934, confidential.

31 Hazel Colville Papers, RBB to Hazel, 23 Dec. 1933, from the train.

32 DUA, PBW Papers, Frances Stephens Ballantyne, interview with PBW, 5 July 1989; Frances Ballantyne to PBW, 16 Aug. 1989.

33 RBB Papers, #486325, RBB to J.B. Carswell of Burlington Steel, 28 Nov. 1933; #486332, RBB to A.C. Pigott of Pigott Construction, Hamilton, 30 Nov. 1933.

34 Ibid., #239072, Stewart to RBB, 12 Jan 1932; #239074, RBB to Stewart, 12 Jan. 1932.

35 C.P. Stacey has a short section on this subject in *Historical Documents of Canada,* vol. 5, 196–9; *Commons Debates,* 14 May 1919, 2395; 12 Feb. 1929, 90; 14 Feb. 1929, 113; *Vancouver News-Herald,* 4 June 1935; *Vancouver Province,* 4 June 1935, has similar sentiments.

36 RBB Papers, #235816, RBB to H. Featherstonehaugh, Toronto, 13 Mar. 1931; #237563, same to same, 12 Feb. 1932; #237204, RBB to Lord Bessborough, governor general, 1 Nov. 1933.

37 *Commons Debates,* 17 May 1933, 5116; 23 May 1933, 5235, 5323; 24 May 1933. The break in the dates was owing to RBB's absence in New Brunswick for the 250th anniversary of the Loyalists' arrival.

38 *Toronto Globe,* 1 Jan. 1934; *Halifax Herald,* 1, 2, and 3 Jan. 1934.

39 RBB Papers, #237631, RBB to James Ray, Lockeport, N.S., 4 Jan. 1934.

40 King Diaries, 4, 5 Jan. 1934; RBB Papers, #237626, Sir Thomas White to RBB, 30 Dec. 1933, personal.

41 LAC, H.H. Stevens Papers, RBB to Stevens, 31 Jan. 1931; in Wilbur, *H.H. Stevens,* 93; DUA, Carleton Stanley Papers, Stanley to W.D. Herridge, 18 Jan. 1932, personal; RBB Papers, vol. 908, RBB to G.F. Pearson, 12 April 1932; Waite, *The Lives of Dalhousie University,* vol. 2, 54–6; RBB Papers, #607612, RBB to Manion, 11 Mar. 1933, personal. On the Workers'

Economic Conference, *Ottawa Citizen*, 7 Aug. 1932, in Crowley, *Agnes MacPhail*, 115.

42   *Toronto Globe*, 16 Jan. 1934, in Wilbur, *H.II. Stevens*, 108–11.

43   Ibid.; Stevens's Jan. 1934 resignation and RB's reaction to it are in a later Bennett letter. See Stevens Papers, RBB to Stevens, 27 Oct. 1934, in *H.H. Stevens*, 116.

44   Cited by Rev. Francis Stevens in letter to R.H. Wilbur, 7 March 1969, in *H.H. Stevens*, 114.

45   *Commons Debates*, 2 Feb. 1934, 188–9.

46   Ibid., 2317, 18 April 1934; 2743, 7 May 1934.

47   King Diaries, 4–9 May 1934.

48   *Commons Debates*, 4 June 1934, 3637–8; Gray, *Winter Years*, 210 (1976).

49   *Commons Debates*, 3638; RBB Papers, #203409, RBB to Clark, 6 March 1934; Bryce, *Maturing in Hard Times*, 162. George Curtis (b. 1908) graduated in law from the University of Saskatchewan in 1927, then went on to Oxford as a Rhodes scholar, taking two degrees there. After his work with the Government of Saskatchewan, he went to Dalhousie University in 1934 as a professor of law. Larry MacKenzie, president of UBC, brought him to Vancouver in 1945. George Curtis sent me this story (DUA, PBW Papers, Curtis to PBW, 14 Feb. 1992 from Vancouver, transcribed in 1984). James Gray (1906–95) expressed this view in many conversations, 1985–1990, when we were weighing whether to do a Bennett biography together.

50   *Commons Debates*, 21 June 1934, 4151, 4168.

51   Ibid., 4238. Glassford, *Reaction and Reform*, 147, says that RB shouted, "Since when has it become the law in Canada ..." across the floor of the Commons.

52   *Commons Debates*, 22 June 1934, 4243–6.

53   RBB Papers, #603752, G.D. Stanley to George Robinson, 7 Aug. 1947, from Calgary.

54   Ibid., #543643, R.K. Finlayson "This Man Bennett," article in Glenbow Archives, 10. In 1935 there was some amelioration, and the banks were given some further compensation. See Fullerton, *Graham Towers*, 63.

55   Ibid., 55–62.

56   English, *Shadow of Heaven*, vol. 1, 170–1; Pearson's musing about faking exhaustion is in Pearson to O.D. Skelton, 24 Mar. 1939, Pearson Papers, vol. 2, cited in Story, "Canada's Covenant," 42. Pearson recalled RB's remark about Skelton in an interview with John Hilliker, 23 Sept. 1970, in *Canada's Department of External Affairs*, vol. 1, 137.

57 *Toronto Globe* , 9 Dec, 1933; RBB to Rev. Richard Roberts, 21 Dec. 1933, confidential, in RBB Papers, vol. 429; Stacey, *Canada and the Age of Conflict*, vol. 2, 159–60.

58 RBB Papers, #136373, RBB to Hanson, 30 Sept. 1933, personal; ibid., #136375, Hanson to RBB, 3 Oct. 1933, personal; #136376, RBB to Hanson, 5 Oct. 1933, personal; #136383, Hanson to Merriam, 16 Dec. 1933; #136385, Merriam to Hanson, 5 Jan. 1934; ibid., #239543, Merriam to Robert C. Matthewson, 30 Sept. 1930.

59 Glassford, *Reaction and Reform* 141, citing MacLean, *R.B. Bennett*, 77, and *Manitoba Free Press*, 6 July 1938.

60 RBB Papers, #586533, RBB to Lt Col. B.F. Parkinson, 14 Feb. 1934, personal; #586534, Norman Smith to RBB, 14 Feb. 1934; #58654, #58658, RBB to Smith, 15 Feb. 1934.

61 RBB Papers, #543831, Robert Rogers interview with George Cloakey, RB's driver, ca. 1947.

62 Ibid., #543719, Brig.-Gen. J.J. Stewart to Alice Millar, 27 Sept. 1947, from Lethbridge.

CHAPTER SIX

1 RBB Papers, #543643, Finlayson MS, 252; the quotation from Molière is act I, scene 1, of *Le Misanthrope*. The translation is mine.

2 *Commons Debates*, 21 Jan. 1935, 60–2.

3 RBB Papers, #543883, Robert Rogers's interview with Capt. Ronald Bennett, 9 July 1950; the Rensselaer Polytechnic address is in RBB Papers, #238962–238974.

4 Acheson, *Morning and Noon*, 178, cited in Donald Story, "Canada's Covenant," 54; RBB Papers, #184696, Herridge to Finlayson, 23 Jan. 1935, private and confidential; on the cabinet, #184753, same, 3 Oct. 1935, private and confidential; on civil service, #184732, same, 5 Aug. 1935, private and confidential; #18504, same, May 1935, private and confidential.

5 Prof Elliott of Harvard, a close Washington friend of Herridge's, told King in 1935 the story of Herridge chuckling as he wrote the New Deal speeches for RB, the irony being that King would never bring in such legislation, not being willing to affront the constitution. See King Diaries, 4 June 1935. For the Ottawa speech, see *Ottawa Citizen*, 15 Dec. 1934; *New York Times*, 15 Dec. 1934; Sir Robert Borden, *Letters to Limbo*, 159–60.

6 Glassford has an admirable summary of Bennett's New deal speeches and
their effects in *Reaction and Reform*, 154–7; see also *Ottawa Journal*, 3
Jan. 1935; Borden, *Letters to Limbo*, 183–5; *Montreal Daily Star*, 9 January 1935. *The Star* was quoted by Ralston in the House of Commons. See
Commons Debates, 26 March 1935, 2119.

7 King Diaries, 15, 16, 18 January 1935; RBB Papers, #185027, Herridge to
RBB, 20 Nov. 1934, private and confidential.

8 King Diaries, 14, 21 Jan. 1935.

9 *Commons Debates*, 17 Jan. 1935, 5; 21 Jan. 1935, 58–62; the 1930 statistics that RB sought are in RBB Papers, #196038–196236, mostly correspondence with Watson Sellar, comptroller of the Treasury, a bundle of
Treasury Board correspondence, e.g., #196564, on what was the available
government cash on 1 Sept. 1930. The letter to Borden is #597317, RBB to
Borden, 5 Oct. 1933, personal.

10 RB could get impatient with academics. MacKay admitted there were
errors, but when he tried to change his article, it was already in print. See
Waite, *The Lives of Dalhousie University*, vol. 2, 54–6.

11 King Diaries, 21 Feb. 1935. Mackenzie King's extensive diaries include
interviews with Bennett, Cahan, and Sir George Perley.

12 Ibid., 6 March 1935.

13 Ibid., 15 March 1935; Manion Papers, vol. 5, Manion to Bruce, 11 Mar.
1935, personal and private; Rhodes Papers, vol. 1199, Rhodes to Borden,
12 March 1935, personal.

14 *Commons Debates*, 15 March 1935, 1745–6; for Cahan on Stevens, see
King Diaries, 15 March 1935.

15 King Diaries, 15 April 1935.

16 Ibid., 18 April 1935.

17 Gordon, *Walter Gordon*, 21. Gordon and his wife were in London at the
time and shared gossip with Pearson. See also English, *Shadow of Heaven*,
vol. 1, 170–1.

18 The report of the Silver Jubilee is Bennett's report to King, King Diaries,
21 May 1935; see also Ziegler, *King Edward VIII*, 231.

19 King Diaries, 5 June 1935.

20 For King's discussion with Bennett, King Diaries, 21 May 1935; with
Cahan, 27 May 1935.

21 Charlesworth, *I'm Telling You*, 171–2. Charlesworth makes the telling
observation about Stevens as promoter. See also *Commons Debates*, 19
June 1935, 3804.

22 *Commons Debates*, 19 June 1935, 3809; King Diaries, 19 June 1935.

Notes to pages 212–20   321

23 Struthers, *No Fault of Their Own*, 96–7; *Commons Debates*, 24 Feb.
    1933, 2449–2463, Wesley Gordon, MP Timiskaming South, Minister of
    Labour.

24 For RB's comment on the camps, *Commons Debates*, 24 June 1935, 3899;
    his useful summary, ibid., 10 Feb. 1936, 42; *Vancouver Province*, 13 May
    1935, quoted in Horn, *The Dirty Thirties*, 335; trekker diary quoted by
    J.S. Woodsworth; see *Commons Debates*, 27 June 1935, 4050.

25 The Macdonald Report is available most conveniently in a compilation of
    documents published in Ronald Liversedge's *Recollections of the On to
    Ottawa Trek*, 125–45. A most useful collection of documents is appended,
    put together by Victor Hoar at the suggestion of Michiel Horn.

26 The best work on this strike and its aftermath is Waiser's *All Hell Can't
    Stop Us*. On committees, 47; Williams, *Mayor Gerry*, 186–97; for the 30
    May meeting, Liversedge, *Recollections*, 83–4.

27 Waiser, *All Hell*, 60–3.

28 Ibid., 68; *Winnipeg Tribune*, 13 June 1935, cited in Waiser, *All Hell*, 74–5.

29 *Commons Debates*, 21 May 1935, 2921.

30 The different elements at play in this complicated situation are well set
    out in Waiser, *All Hell*, 109–16.

31 Ibid., 119.

32 *Commons Debates*, 2 July 1935, 4139.

33 Liversedge, *Recollections*, "The Interview between the Delegation of Strik-
    ers and the Prime Minister and His Cabinet," 194–216. This reference,
    210.

34 *Commons Debates*, 24 June 1935, 3899, for RB's report on his meeting
    with the trekkers.

35 King Diaries, 27 June 1835. I have made minor alterations in the tenses.

36 Evans's remark was probably made at Sudbury on the way back to
    Regina. It is quoted by RB in *Commons Debates*, 2 July 1935, 4124; on
    trekkers moving east from Regina, Waiser, *All Hell*, 146–7; ibid., 165,
    quoting *Regina Leader-Post*, 29 June 1935.

37 LAC, Manion Papers, vol. 14, Webb to Manion, 26 June 1935.

38 *Commons Debates*, 2 July 1935, 4135. RB might well have seen the 1931
    movie *Frankenstein*, with Boris Karloff in the leading role. The original
    novel by Mary Wollstonecroft Shelley was published in 1818.

39 *Commons Debates*, 2 July 1935, 4124; King Diaries, 3 July 1935; for
    Agnes MacPhail, *Commons Debates*, 2 July 1935, 4156. She reported the
    Conservatives' heckling of Woodsworth's speech.

40 King Diaries, 27 June 1935.

41 Ibid., 5 July 1935, 7; for a summary of reasons for the late date, see Glassford, *Reaction and Reform*, 178.

42 Glassford, *Reaction and Reform*, has an excellent analysis of the three
   ideologies within the Conservative Party in 1935: Stevens's, RB's, and
   Cahan's.

43 RBB Papers, #236421, RBB to Roberts, 18 May 1935, personal and most
   confidential.

44 This might seem to be the most arrant piece of gossip, except that I
   have it from a great historian who was at that dinner, George Wilson,
   PHD (Harvard), head of Dalhousie's history department for forty
   years.

45 *Vancouver Province*, 3 June 1935; RBB Papers, #236094; *Winnipeg Tribune*, 3 June 1935, RBB Papers, #236047.

46 RBB Papers, #284172, Leacock to RBB, 18 July 1935.

47 *Calgary Daily Herald* 12[?] Oct. 1935, quoting *St Thomas Times-Journal*
   in RBB Papers, #549797, a group of diverse clippings.

48 The cartoon in the September 1935 issue of *The Canadian* is on the cover
   of the paperback edition of Glassford's *Reaction and Reform*. The cartoonist, however, intentionally or out of ignorance of sailing, has RB
   facing the stern, not the bow.
       Audience estimates are from Glassford, *Reaction and Reform*; for
   Hutchison, see *The Far Side of the Street*, 100–1. Hutchison (1901–92)
   was parliamentary reporter for the *Victoria Times* in 1935.

49 RBB Papers, #284533, F.D.L. Smith to RBB, 9 Sept. 1935; ibid., #284215,
   Leon Ladner to RBB, 6 Oct. 1935, telg.

50 RBB Papers, #184730, Herridge to Finlayson, 3 Aug. 1935, private and
   confidential; #184732, Herridge to Finlayson, 5 Aug. 1935, private and
   confidential. Donald Story has a perceptive section on Herridge in his
   1977 PHD thesis, "Canada's Covenant," 66–70.

51 Extracts of RB's 1935 radio speeches are in Stacey, *Historical Documents
   of Canada*, vol. 5, 110–14. They appeared in the *Montreal Gazette*, 7–16
   Sept. 1935. The private letter is in RBB Papers, #488761, RBB to F.A.
   Reinhardt, Winnipeg, 8 July 1935; the quotation from the first address is
   from the *Halifax Herald*, 7 Oct. 1935; also in RBB Papers, #586082.

52 King Diaries, 5 June 1935; RBB Papers, #184846, Herridge to RBB, 3
   March 1933, private and confidential; Stacey, *Canada and the Age of
   Conflict*, vol. 2, 172.

53 This famous "Riddell incident" has been much discussed. The most con-
   venient references are Stacey, *Canada and the Age of Conflict*, vol. 2,
   179–82; English, *Shadow of Heaven*, 176–80; also Story, "Canada's

Covenant," 309–35. RB's "hornswoggle" verb is in English's quotation; in
Stacey it becomes the less colourful "wriggle." "Hornswoggle" is a verb
that does seem to have a proper Western ring to it.

54 RBB Papers, #549546, RBB to Ferguson, 15 Oct. 1935, cable; #549547,
A.H. Bell to RBB, 15 Oct. 1935, from Ottawa; #549549, RBB to Bell, 19
Oct. 1935.

55 Glassford has an excellent analysis of this election, *Reaction and Reform,*
196–202; see also J. Murray Beck, *Pendulum of Power,* 206–22.

56 One of RB's secretaries, Muriel Black, remarked in her reminiscences
that something he would not tolerate was breach of trust. When a deputy minister was found accepting kickbacks from a successful bidder, RB
fired him by telephone on the spot. See LAC MG 27 III F18, Muriel Black
Papers, "Reminiscences," 6.

57 King Diaries, 15 Oct. 1935. King seems to have had a knack for recalling
conversation. I have assumed he has this one with Bennett roughly right.
In any case it is the only record we have. The diary for that day runs to
nine double-spaced typed pages.

CHAPTER SEVEN

1 King Diaries, 23 Oct. 1935, 22.
2 LAC, Muriel Black Papers, "Reminiscences," 5.
3 RBB Papers, #284012, RBB to Mrs Middleton, 23 Oct. 1935; #549531,
RBB to Mrs H.W. Story, Somerset, England, 9 Nov. 1935; #549553, Louise
Barlow to RBB, 16 Oct. 1935, from Ottawa on Château Laurier paper.
4 RBB Papers, #549540, draft to all defeated Conservative candidates;
#549628, Mrs Gates, Ottawa to RBB, 29 Oct. 1935; #549630, RBB to Mrs
Gates, 4 Nov. 1935, personal. The lines are from "Prometheus Unbound,"
IV, 570.
5 RBB Papers, #549553 Louise Barlow to RBB, 16 Oct. 1935, on Château
Laurier paper; #549680, RBB to Alice Millar (hereafter AEM), 18 Nov.
1935, telg.
6 Gray, *The Calgary Years,* 77–8; RBB Papers, #549692; passenger list, SS
Pennsylvania, Panama Pacific Line; #598796, RBB to Lord Glendyne, 7
Jan. 1936, personal; RBB's view on the "Riddell incident" is in *Commons
Debates,* 10 Feb. 1936, 39–40.
7 RBB Papers, #549977, RBB to Percival Gavagan, 3 Feb. 1936; #549993,
AEM to Gavagan, 14 Feb. 1936, from Calgary.
8 RBB Papers, #549781-3, Howard Turner, Vancouver, to RBB, enclosing Roy Cox's letter in *Maclean's.* Turner and his wife, Phyllis, were

prominent Vancouver Conservatives. RB wrote to Turner, asking after the baby (the future John Turner); the letter quoted is #549783, RBB to Cox, 9 March 1936.

9 *Commons Debates,* 6 Feb. 1936, 5–9; King's crowing, ibid., 10 Feb. 1936, 77.

10 Ibid., 10 Feb. 1936, 29, 35.

11 Ibid., RB quoting Elliott, 61; Wilgress, *Memoirs,* 102–3; Kottman, *Reciprocity and the North Atlantic Triangle,* 110.

12 *Commons Debates,* 10 Feb. 1936, 61–2; In *Canada and the Age of Conflict,* vol. 2, Stacey gives a persuasive argument and the figures, 177.

13 *Commons Debates,* 24 March 1936, 1425–7.

14 Ibid., 14 June 1935, 3608. Blair Neatby, born and educated in Saskatchewan, has a most useful summary of this long story in *William Lyon Mackenzie King,* vol. 3, *The Prism of Unity, 1932–1939,* 104–8, 167–8, 395–8.

15 *Commons Debates,* 24 March 1936, 1462.

16 For Gardiner, see *Commons Debates,* 16 June 1936, 3787; for RB, 23 June 1936, 4136.

17 Ibid., 27 March 1889, 868–9, cited in Waite, *The Man from Halifax,* 240.

18 Thomas, *The Making of a Socialist,* 94–5.

19 RBB Papers, #608760, AEM to George Robinson, [Aug.] 1936.

20 RBB Papers, #509089, Norman MacLeod to RBB, 12 Aug. 1936, telg.; #608770, RBB to Lyons, 11 Aug. 1936, telg.

21 RBB Papers, #609116, Hedstrom to RBB, 29 Aug. 1936, radiogram; #608794, RBB to AEM, 27 Sept. 1936, cable from Sydney, Australia.

22 RBB Papers, #609156, Geoffrey Whiskeard to RBB, 23 Sept. 1936, from Canberra.

23 *Sydney Morning Herald,* 29 Sept. 1936; ibid., editorial, 30 Sept. 1936; RB's Rotary Club speech is summarized in a Canadian Press despatch to Vancouver, 29 Sept. 1936, RBB Papers, #609169.

24 Eric Newby, *The Last Grain Race,* 148.

25 RBB Papers, #608798, RBB to AEM, 7 Oct. 1936, cable; *Melbourne Age,* 16, 17 Oct. 1936.

26 Eric Newby, a new English apprentice aboard the 3,116-ton *Moshulu,* has a vivid account of what it was like in 1938–39. The photographs he took, several from up the masts and out on the yards in bad weather, are stunning. See *The Last Grain Race.*

27 RBB Papers, #609228, to RBB from the Empire Parliamentary Association, 28 Oct. 1936; *Adelaide Chronicle,* 5 Nov. 1936; RBB Papers, #608898, RBB to Sir George Murray, 23 Jan. 1937, from Ottawa.

28 Henry Lawson (1867–1922); many of his ballads are drawn from his six months in the Australian outback in 1892. See Ward, *Penguin Book of Australian Ballads*, 159. The famous Australian song, "Waltzing Matilda," was by Lawson's contemporary, Banjo Patterson (1864–1941).

29 *Perth West Australian*, 3 Nov. 1936.

30 Ibid., 7 Nov. 1936; RBB Papers, #608804, Brooks to AEM, 4 Nov. 1936, from Perth, West Australia.

31 RBB Papers, #609166, Comptroller, Government House, Pretoria to RBB, 3 Nov. 1936, for any night after 26 Nov.

32 Drummond, *Imperial Economic Policy, 1917–1939*, 188, 216, 245.

33 RBB Papers, #608838, AEM to RBB, 3 Dec. 1936, cable; #608839, RBB to AEM, 6 Dec. 1936, cable, from Mafeking. RB said he would reach Ottawa by 25 January, possibly 18 January. He was in Parliament on the 18th.

34 Quoted in the *Michelin Green Guide to Canada*, 111.

35 RBB Papers, #608601 on the *Edinburgh Castle's* sailing and two first-class passengers, RBB and Brooks; #561242, RBB to AEM, 1 Jan. 1937, from *Edinburgh Castle*.

36 RBB Papers, #608878, James Spencer to RBB, 8 Jan. 1937; *Commons Debates*, 18 Jan. 1937, 27; the quotation is from *Othello*, V, ii. I have quoted the Shakespeare; the *Debates* version has only one or two minor differences.

37 King Diaries, 18, 20 January 1937.

38 Ibid., 3 March 1937.

39 *Commons Debates*, 5 April 1937, 2581, for Cahan's speech; 2594 for RBB's; his reference to the 1928 debates is 16 April 1928, 2060; Cahan's recollections are cited in *Commons Debates*, 1 Feb. 1935, 450, and are quoted in Saywell's *The Lawmakers*, 405–6n124. Saywell has a magisterial chapter on this issue, "The New Deal at Court and the End of Appeals," 203–37, an excellent chapter in a remarkable book.

40 *Canadian Bar Review* 15, 397–9, quoted in Saywell, *Lawmakers*, 228.

41 King Diaries, 13 April 1937.

42 Ibid., 8 April 1937.

43 RBB Papers, #563049, RBB to AEM, 8 June 1937, from Bad Nauheim; #563041, RBB to AEM, Sat. [29 May 1937?]; #563051, Mildred to RBB, 13 Aug. [1937], from Mayfair House, New York; #555035, Dr Ems to Dr T.F. Cotton, London, 3 July 1937; #555037, Cotton to RBB, 13 July 1937.

44 RBB Papers, #563051, Mildred to RBB, 13 Aug. [1937], from Mayfair House, New York.

45 RBB Papers, #609705, RBB to George Cruise, 9 Aug. 1937, personal; #609715, RBB to George Challies, an Ontario MLA, 12 Aug. 1937,

personal; #609736, RBB to J. Bartle, Calgary, 14 Aug. 1937, personal; #609734, RBB to B.B. Davis, Brampton, 14 Aug. 1937, personal; #609725, Aubrey Davis to RBB, 9 Aug. 1937, from Newmarket, Ont. There is a useful summary of this episode in Glassford's *Reaction and Reform,* 213–14.

46 Bruce Hutchison's vivid account of this interview is in the *Victoria Times,* "A New Bennett Has Emerged," late July or early August 1937, and also in the RBB Papers, #549798. A less effective and more anodyne version of the same interview is in Hutchison's *The Far Side of the Street,* 101–2; RBB Papers, #563062, AEM to RBB, 10 Sept. 1937, from Ottawa, RBB Papers, #562081, W.D. Herridge to RBB, 24 April 1940.

47 King Diaries, 7 Jan. 1938.

48 Ibid., 27 Jan. 1938; Borden points out King's clever riposte as an example of RB's impulsiveness (Borden, *Letters to Limbo,* 267). The Borden letter is dated 18 Feb. 1936.

49 *Commons Debates,* 28 Jan. 1938, 14

50 RB's position on Canadian federalism is suggested in a brief remark quoted by S.L. Cork, Royal Bank supervisor, Winnipeg, RBB Papers, #610255, Cork to RBB, 17 Mar. 1938; Prang, *N.W. Rowell, Ontario Nationalist,* 488; Waite, *Lives of Dalhousie University,* vol. 2, 55; Rogers comment, *Commons Debates,* 7 Feb. 1938, 208.

51 The official debates record nothing of this incident, nor any speech of Bennett's, yet it is unlikely that King made it up. A possible explanation is that Bennett felt the incident keenly enough to want to expunge it from early proofs of the debates.

52 Glassford, *Reaction and Reform,* 214–15; RBB Papers, #609949, RBB to Charles McCrea, Toronto, 8 Mar. 1935: "Of course I disliked giving up"; #609944, AEM to Willis & Hy O'Connor, 8 Mar. 1938; #609943, Willis & Hy O'Connor to RBB, 7 Mar. 1938, from Government House, Ottawa. Willis O'Connor was private secretary to the governor general.

53 King Diaries, 7 March 1938; *Commons Debates,* 7 March 1938, 1059; RBB Papers, #610025, AEM to George Hoadley, Toronto, 9 Mar. 1938. Hoadley was with the Canadian National Committee for Mental Hygiene. Millar was replying to #610024, Hoadley to Millar, 8 Mar. 1938. Note the speed of despatch and reply of these letters.

54 Ibid., #610374, H.A. Innis to RBB, 7 April 1938, handwritten, from the University of Toronto; #610257, RBB to S.L. Cork, Winnipeg, 25 March 1938.

55 Ibid., #561591, Mildred Herridge to RBB, n.d. [April 1938]. The passage from Ruth is 1:16–17, King James Bible. RB's reaction to Mildred's death is noted in Lord Beaverbrook's *Friends,* 88. For the letters to RB about

Mildred: Lascelles, #561689; Skelton, #561651; Meighen, #561600; Stevens, 561636; Lapointe, #561620; R.S.White, #561710.

56 *Commons Debates,* 24 May 1938, 3194.

57 Stacey, *Canada and the Age of Conflict,* vol. 2, 221; *Commons Debates,* 1 July 1938, 4553.

58 Ibid., 4554.

59 Glassford's *Reaction and Reform,* 222–9, has an excellent account of the background to this 1938 Conservative convention. Meighen's story is in Graham, *Meighen,* vol. 3, 82–3.

60 RBB Papers, #610442, RBB to Edgar, 21 July 1938; Edgar had written, "how unreservedly I have admired your career as a statesman and how warmly I esteem you as a man. No one in public life has your energy, your integrity, or your intellect" (#610441, Edgar to RBB, 5 July 1938, from Lac Brûlé, Quebec).

61 House of Lords Record Office, London, *Beaverbrook Papers,* A/vol.65, Max to RBB, 9 March 1938 (draft); RBB to Max, 5 April 1938; RBB to Max, 19 Nov. 1938, on RMS *Montrose* paper. Beaverbrook quotes much of this letter in *Friends,* 89–90, but omits everything RB says about the House of Lords.

62 Glenbow Foundation, Calgary, Rod Finlayson Tapes, tape 3, conversation reported by John Stevenson.

63 *Beaverbrook Papers* A/vol. 65, RBB to Max, 24 Nov. 1938, from Ottawa. A more extensive version of this letter is printed in Beaverbrook, *Friends,* 90–1.

64 Bennett's January 1939 western itinerary (mostly speeches, presentations, and dinners) was Calgary, 3, 4, 5 Jan.; Edmonton, 6 Jan.; Vancouver, 8 Jan.; Calgary, 11–12 Jan. For Meighen's speech, see his *Unrevised and Unrepented,* 314–21; Glassford gives useful extracts in *Reaction and Reform,* 231–2.

65 Thomas, *The Making of a Socialist,* 96.

66 MacKinnon, *Buffet of True Stories,* 50–1. This reference was brought to my attention by professors Brook Taylor and Ian Robertson.

67 RBB Papers, #553561, RBB to Arthur Beauchesne, clerk of the House of Commons, 28 Jan. 1939, from Halifax; *Halifax Herald,* 30 Jan. 1939; Dalhousie University Archives, PBW Papers, George Curtis to PBW, 30 May 1990.

CHAPTER EIGHT

1 RBB Papers, M-3140, #544073. The author of the poem is unknown but quite possibly it was Bennett.

2   DUA, PBW Papers, James Gray notes, typescript of interview with Frederick Griffin in the *Toronto Star Weekly*, n.d., but probably a Saturday in January 1939.

3   RBB Papers, #551040, RBB to Francis B. Reilly, Regina, 24 Aug. 1938, from Ottawa.

4   RBB Papers, #599521, Sir Samuel Hoare to RBB, 8 Feb. 1939, from 25 Cadogan Square; #599526, Hoare to RBB, 11 Nov. [1939], private and personal.

5   RBB Papers, #563252, RBB to AEM, 1 Nov. 1938, personal; RB's description of renovations at Juniper Hill is in a run of 1939 correspondence with AEM, who was in Ottawa still closing things up; #563283, RBB to AEM, Good Friday 1939; #563300, same, 25 May 1939; #563322, same, 21 June 1939. For invoice, #590874, Lawrence Jones & Co. to RBB, 17 Feb. 1939; see also Lord Beaverbrook, *Friends*, 88–9; RBB Papers, #587196, RBB to Atkinson, 4 Dec. 1938, cable from Calgary; #587197, Atkinson to RBB, 5 Dec. 1939, cable.

6   Ibid., #587496, RBB to Atkinson, 18 June 1940; #587530, same, 28 June 1940; #587558, Atkinson to RBB, 9 July 1940; #587607, Atkinson to AEM, 14 Dec. 1940; #587573 lists a tentative settlement with Greenwood's in May 1940.

7   This account is based on two sources: Alice Millar's statement of 25 July 1939 (#559057) in *Bennett vs. Mansell*, and Lord Beaverbrook's *Friends*, 94–5, Beaverbrook's story includes a Jewish antiques dealer; Alice mentions only that the chair had been seen in another shop; RBB Papers, #559064, Mansell's per A. Capel to Arran Fairfield & Co., 21 Mar. 1940; #559075, RBB to Maurice Arran, 10 April 1940; #559104-6, draft letter of apology.

8   The Massey side is told in Bissell, *The Imperial Canadian*, 150–1. Massey's venom surfaces in a poem from the 1930s. See also Bissell's *The Young Vincent Massey*, 76–7. Bennett's side is touched on in RBB Papers, #592745, RBB to Lord Queensborough, 17 Nov. 1939, and #592756, same, 4 July 1940.

9   For a short history of the Mickleham church, see RBB Papers #592173; #592005, AEM to Langdale-Smith, 16 Dec. 1939; #592081, RBB to Langdale-Smith, 23 Jan. 1940; #592083, Langdale-Smith to RBB, 24 Jan. 1940; #592087, RBB to M.B. Clark, treasurer, Church Council, 6 Feb. 1940.

10   About Guildford Cathedral, #590059, Bishop John Guildford MacMillan to RBB, 24 July 1939; RBB to MacMillan, 26 July 1939; #590070, MacMillan to RBB, 18 Nov. 1940; #590075, same, 8 Oct. 1946.

11   His appointment to the Surrey Bench is in RBB Papers, #610767, R.S.
      Prince to RBB, 1 Feb. 1940; his appointment roster in 1947 is given in
      #572381 and following.

12   RBB Papers, #610973, Lord Lloyd to RBB, 25 June 1939, from Brit-
      ish Council; #610976, J.S. Lewes to RBB, 24 Aug. 1939, with draft itin-
      erary including returning from Cracow by train via Berlin; #610982,
      RBB to Charles Bridge, secretary general, British Council, 14 Nov. 1939;
      #610991, Bridge to RBB, 9 Feb. 1940, with new itinerary; #610995, Lord
      Lloyd to RBB, 1 April 1940. This last letter preceded the German invasion
      of Norway and Denmark by eight days.

13   House of Lords Record Office, Beaverbrook Papers, D393, Beaverbrook
      to Herbert Morrison, 15 June 1940 (copy). Morrison was at this point
      minister of supply. Beaverbrook Papers, Beaverbrook to RBB, 14 July
      1940; same, 3 Aug. 1940.

14   For the Hull adventure, RBB Papers, #592208, Frank Hall of National
      Savings Committee to RBB, 17 May 1940; #592210, RBB to Hall, 18 May
      1940. Reported in the *Hull Daily Mail*, 16 May 1940.

15   For War Weapons Week speeches, RBB Papers, #592214, Hall to RBB, 29
      Oct. 1940; #592216, same, 12 Nov. 1940; #592228, 31 Dec. 1940.

16   For the Birmingham speech, RBB Papers, #559744, RBB to Dick Hanson
      (in Canada), Oct. 1940, copy to R.V. Bennett; #590740-1, Sir Phillip Jou-
      bert, Air Ministry, to RBB, 15 Oct. 1940; RBB to Joubert, 17 Oct. 1940.
      Perhaps one could add here that J.A. Noonan and his wife were guests
      at Juniper Hill for some time. It was RB's way of avoiding being billeted
      with people he did not want. RBB Papers, #599497, RBB to J.L. Hethering-
      ton, 19 Dec. 1940, in Halifax, N.S. Bennett had offered Juniper Hill to the
      government early in the war but it was deemed not suitable.

17   Ibid., #591794, T.A. Macaulay to RBB, 29 Aug. 1940. The Ministry of Air-
      craft Production official, F.C. Wickson, had said, politely but firmly, "I
      rather feel that the official view will be that you will be required to show
      claims under separate contracts" (#591806, enclosed in Macaulay's let-
      ter). The Bennett maxim is noted in a short book by a private secretary,
      Andrew D. MacLean, *R.B. Bennett*, 20.

18   This whole Loewy incident has been given a strange twist owing to
      Beaverbrook's account of it in *Friends*, 104. It leaves out entirely any
      reference to Adolph Lendl or Bette Bertelot (see below). Beaverbrook's
      version is repeated in A.J.P. Taylor's *Beaverbrook*, 422, and quoted
      extensively in Chisholm and Davie, *Beaverbrook: A Life*, 386–7. For
      German-born refugees, see Lafitte *The Internment of Aliens*; on the Isle of
      Man, Chappell, *Island of Barbed Wire*.

19 RBB Papers, #542430, has a short aide-memoire of Lendl's history; #591203 gives Frau Lendl's letter of 6 May 1939, without specific provenance or the German (or Czech?) original; #591213, Lord Rothschild to RBB, 10 Sept. 1940, secret, from War Office; #591217, same, 4 Oct. 1940, secret; #591219, same, 10 Oct. 1940, secret.

20 RBB Papers, #591194, RBB to Beaverbrook, n.d. This is a handwritten letter, and the date is about 29 Oct. 1940; Rothschild to Beaverbrook's private secretary, 11 Nov. 1940, secret.

21 RBB Papers, #590815, RBB to Miss Buxton, 31 March 1944. This correspondence arose because of an *Evening News* report, 17 March 1944, of a Bennett speech made on 16 March at Tottenham, for Salute the Soldiers Week. He was reported as saying of the 60,000 Jewish refugees in Britain, "they were all Germans first." RB replied to Miss Buxton that nothing she said "alters the necessity for the British people taking the utmost care in dealing with enemy aliens."

22 House of Lords Record Office, Beaverbrook Papers, D383. RBB's comments on a memo about magnesium, 15 Jan. 1941; Beaverbrook Papers, RBB to Beaverbrook, 10 April 1941.

23 RBB Papers, #542478, F.D.L. Smith to RBB, 2 Jan. 1942, confidential, quoting Beaverbrook to Smith, 30 Dec. 1941 from Washington. F.D.L. Smith had been managing editor of the *Toronto Mail and Empire* until 1936 when it merged with the *Toronto Globe* to become the *Globe and Mail*. In 1941 Smith was with the Toronto weekly *Saturday Night*.

24 RBB Papers, #551913, Churchill to RBB, 21 May 1941, personal and confidential; RBB to Churchill, 23 May 1941, personal and confidential.

25 RBB Papers, #552036, Brendan Bracken to RBB, 13 June 1941; #552725, signature illegible but after it, "Alias Barb 12/6/41." The Canadian letters: #553440, Mackenzie King to RBB, 12 June 1941, cable; #553400, Massey to RBB, 12 June 1941, telegram; #552494, A.A. Heaps to RBB, 18 June 1941; #552142, M.J. Coldwell to RBB, 12 June 1941; #552494, Isabella "Daisy" Macdonald Gainsford to RBB, 22 June 1941, from St James, Manitoba. Daisy Gainsford (1877–1960) was Sir Hugh John Macdonald's daughter.

26 RBB Papers, #551924, Ede & Ravenscroft to RBB, 17 June 1941; #551948, same, invoice 23 July 1941. Beaverbrook's letter to RB is in #552009. The text of both letters is in *Friends*, 108–11.

27 RBB Papers, #559770, RBB to R.V. Bennett, Friday (marked posted in Canada 11 Aug. 1941).

28 Great Britain, House of Lords, *Debates*, 28 Jan. 1942, cols. 497–510; the later debate is 21 July 1942, cols. 950–1. RB's House of Lords speeches

were edited and published in 2009 by Christopher McCreery and Arthur
Milnes as *The Authentic Voice of Canada*. For RB's maiden speech, see
5–15. D.L. Rogers praised his "statesmanlike and really splendid ora-
tion on a grave Empire problem." See RBB Papers, #593095, Rogers to
RBB, 29 Jan. 1942, from London. Beaverbrook's letter is in RBB Papers,
#597050, Beaverbrook to RBB, 30 Jan. 1942. His later comment suggests
one of his many juxtapositions between Bennett alive and Bennett dead.
Note Beaverbrook's *Friends*, 112: "He [RBB] misjudged the character of
the House and addressed the noblemen like a public meeting instead of a
committee."

29 For the Birmingham and Midland Institute speech, RBB Papers, M-1500,
    #542151, n.d. but probably autumn 1941; for the Sheffield speech,
    ibid., #542580, one of the more comprehensive transcripts; #542235, D.
    Williams to RBB, 21 May 1963, from St Stephen's Club, asking for a copy
    of RB's forthcoming speech. RB's reply, #542236, quoted the poem. Lord
    Elibank's request for RB's support is in #589360, Elibank to RBB, 6 June
    1942, from Walkerburn, Scotland.

30 House of Lords, *Debates*, 1 July 1942, cols. 605-6, 609. Brendan Bracken
    sent a warm note of congratulation for this speech, RBB Papers, #588454,
    Bracken to RBB, 3 July 1942. The March 1944 speech is quoted in
    McCreery and Milnes, *The Authentic Voice of Canada*, 106. RB's New-
    foundland speech of 3 May 1944 is in ibid., 109–16.

31 RBB Papers, #542509, Lady Stella Reading to RBB, 21 Sept. 1939.
    Bennett's offer was subject to the proviso that if the Canadian Red Cross
    should come over to England, they would have prior claim. #543527,
    Muriel Levesey to AEM, 4 Dec. 1939; #542542, AEM to Miss P.Y. Betts, 3
    Feb. 1940; #542543, AEM to Miss Betts, 6 Mar. 1940.

32 RBB Papers, #588816, Jane Carton to RBB, 27 Oct. 1940; #588825, Jane
    Carton to RBB, 2 Dec. 1940. Alice Millar was given the job of check-
    ing out the quotation in Bennett's substantial library. Jan Sobieski III was
    King of Poland (1674–1696). Jane Carton's magnum opus was a book
    of stories, *A Child's Garland* (London: Faber & Faber, 1942), reprinted
    1945.

33 RBB Papers, #588818, Jane Carton to RBB, n.d. but marked "Black Fri-
    day!" The context suggests March 1941.

34 Ibid., #588835, Jane Carton to RBB, 14 April 1941, from Canonbury
    Place N.l; #588837 same, n.d., in pencil on Juniper Hill paper; #588839,
    same, 21 April 1944, from Canonbury Place.

35 Fraser, "Lord Beaverbrook's Fabrications in Politicians and the War,
    147–66. RBB Papers, #563227, RBB to AEM, 12 Jan. 1929, from SS

Majestic to Calgary. This letter had a PS: "[In London] The Prince of Wales asked me to see him & [I] stayed for half an hour a very changed & older man." Edward (1894–1972) was then thirty-five years old and had not yet met Wallis Warfield Simpson. The Vienna *Neue Freie Presse*, 25 Dec. 1928, reports a Christmas performance of *Der Rosenkavalier*, a Viennese custom since 1924. Prior to that the Christmas opera was *Tannhauser*. I am grateful to Professor Steven Burns of Dalhousie's philosophy department for looking up this reference for me in Vienna.

36 RBB Papers, #560062, AEM to R.V. Bennett, 10 July 1947, from Juniper Hill.

37 RBB Papers, #592240, D.M. Malkison, secretary, National Trust, to RBB, 15 Feb. 1939; #592241, same, 15 March 1943, asking for a speech on the present position and future of the National Trust. #588565, RBB to Ralph Wood, 17 July 1941. Juniper Hall is noted in #588610, Minutes of Box Hill Trust, 3 April 1943. Its purchase is reported in the 1944 annual report, in #588636. RB's report as chairman in 1946 is in #588638. "Men of the Trees" is in #591605, H.J. Finlayson, executive secretary to RBB, 27 May 1946, reporting Bennett's unanimous election to their council. Their publication *Trees* in 1947 has a fine obituary of RB (p. 48); also in #591612.

38 RB's 1940 report on his health is RBB Papers, #590079, RBB to Sir Douglas Hacking, of the Conservative and Unionist Central Office, 15 Mar. 1940. Replying to an invitation to speak to the Ladies Carlton Club, RB added, "Frankly I feel more concerned about the British Empire than I ever have and it will require all the effort of the seventy-five million whites therein to maintain its integrity in this crisis of its life." RB seems to have thought of the other races in the British Empire basically as a responsibility.

39 RBB Papers, #562067, RBB to Herridge, 18 Sept. 1939; #562071, Herridge to RBB, 6 Oct. 1939; #562087, same, 19 July 1940.

40 For George and his daughter Joan, see Gray, *The Calgary Years*, 233, 235–7, 240–1; for the 1936 adventure, RBB Papers, #558823, J.H. Menzies, supervisor, Royal Bank of Canada, Calgary, to AEM, 20 Oct. 1936.

41 For RB's opinion of Ronald Jr's proposed marriage, RBB Papers, #559726, RBB to R.V. Bennett, 28 Mar. 1940.

42 RBB Papers, #559836, RBB to R.V. Bennett, Sunday [13 Aug. 1944]; #559844, same, 25 Sept. 1944. For Elva Bennett, #559854, same, 19 Jan. 1945. The *Montreal Gazette*, 20 Jan. 1945, has her obituary.

43 RBB Papers, #559875, RBB to R.V. Bennett, 23 Sept. 1945, from Juniper Hill; #559898, same, 24 Mar. 1946; #559904, same, 5 June 1946; #559907, same, 21 June 1946.

44 RBB Papers, #559923, RBB to R.V. Bennett, 2 Nov. 1946.

45 The photographic portrait in Watkins's *R.B. Bennett* appeared with *The Times* obituary, Sat., 28 June 1947. For Susi Jeans's visit, RBB Papers, #560041, AEM to R.V. Bennett, 7 Feb. 1947. Lady Susi Jeans was the widow of Sir James Jeans (1877–1946), the celebrated astronomer, who had died the previous September. On the maple creams, #560057, AEM to R.V. Bennett, 14 May 1947.

46 RBB Papers, #564423, Mildred Bennett to AEM, n.d., from Château Laurier, but clearly before Mildred was married in 1931; #563617, Hazel Law Sykes to AEM, 30 June 1947; #563480, RBB to F.J. Crawford & Co., Toronto, 15 Mar. 1943; #563481, RBB to R.V. Bennett, 15 Mar. 1943.

47 RBB Papers, #563446, AEM to RBB, 19 June 1947, from off tip of Baja, California; her quotation from *Time* is in #563452, AEM to RBB, n.d. but about 21 June 1947; on RBB's midnight baths, #563445, AEM to RBB, 17 June 1947.

48 RBB Papers, #563511, AEM to RBB, 2 June 1943, from Ottawa, reporting her talk with Garfield Weston; #563652, Rosalind Hayes, daughter of Viscount Finlay, to AEM, 7 July 1947; #563552, Catherine Amery to AEM, 28 June 1947, from 112 Eaton Square; #563859, James S. Duncan to Beaverbrook, 21 Dec. 1959, addressed to La Capponcina. *Friends* was published in 1959; thus it is virtually certain that this letter came to Beaverbrook after it was published.

49 Bennett's diaries are mostly brief notations about appointments. They start in August 1936 and go to the end of 1947: RBB Papers, #570315 to #572391.

50 *Friends*, 118, has a description of that evening; Beaverbrook says RB was "depressed and despondent." That may be true; but reports from other sources near that time would suggest that he was in good spirits. Beaverbrook was writing in 1959 at age eighty, when few were in a position to contradict him. That gave him a power that he thoroughly relished. His method seems to have been: Back up your narrative with sources if you have them; after that, you may have to invent. Jane Carton's account is in RBB Papers, #563619, Janie [Carton] to AEM, Monday, June 30 [1947]. The letter is addressed, "Alice, dear girl," and goes on to say, "There is no real consolation for the loss of a beloved – how can there be?" The word

"beloved" raises a whole roster of speculative questions, especially coming from a woman who knew both RB and Alice well. Like most such questions, it is quite unanswerable and has to be left as a question mark.

51 RBB Papers, #563631 Madge [?] to AEM, 1 July 1947, from the Old Dene, Dorking. "Madge" vigorously protested that RB was not the only one who revered the empire and that his memory should be a rallying point; Morris, *Farewell the Trumpets*, 466.

52 *The Times*, 7 July 1947, published the letter "From a Group of Lord Bennett's Neighbours at Mickleham." Rosalind Hayes read that letter and much approved of it. RBB Papers, #563652, Rosalind Hayes to AEM, 7 July 1947. She spoke of Bennett's "buoyant and loveable personality."

EPILOGUE

1 *Manitoba Free Press*, 6 July 1938, in Glassford, *Reaction and Reform*, 236.

2 RBB Papers, #606073, RBB to J.R. MacNicol, 26 Aug. 1935, private and confidential.

3 CMA *Journal* 29, no. 5 (Nov. 1933): 55. I am indebted to Professor Ross Langley of Dalhousie University Medical School for bringing this to my attention.

4 O'Leary, "Who'll Succeed Bennett?"

5 Interviews with Allan MacLeod, Halifax, 4 Dec. 2000 and 3 Nov. 2008. The needy student was a relative of Dr MacLeod.

6 RBB Papers, #559948, RBB to R.V. Bennett, 3 Aug. 1939, very personal; #559951, R.V. Bennett to RBB, 11 Aug. 1939, cable.

Bibliography

The number references to the R.B. Bennett Papers are discussed in chapter 1, note 2.

ARCHIVAL SOURCES

University of New Brunswick
  R.B. Bennett Papers

Library and Archives Canada
  Progressive Conservative Party Records
  William Lyon Mackenzie King Papers, Diaries, 1893–1950
  Eugene Forsey Papers
  John R. Read Papers
  Findlayson-Wilbur Correspondence
  Robert Manion Papers
  Dafoe Papers
  Arthur Meighen Papers
  H.H. Stevens Papers
  Muriel Black Papers
  Hansard:
    Canada: House of Commons Debates
    Canada: Senate Debates
    United Kingsdom: House of Commons Debates
    United Kingdom: House of Lords Debates

Queen's University Archives (QUA)
  Grant Dexter Papers
  Sir Joseph Flavelle Papers
  John A. Stevenson Papers

Dalhousie University Archives
   P.B. Waite Papers
   Carleton Stanley Papers

McGill University Archives
   Hazel Colville Papers

Public Archives of Nova Scotia
   Edgar Rhodes Papers

New Brunswick Museum
   Alma Russell Papers

Glenbow Foundation, Calgary
   Rod Findlayson Tapes

House of Lords Record Office
   Beaverbrook Papers

University of Birmingham Archives
   Neville Chamberlin Papers

University of Newcastle-on-Tyne Archives
   Runciman Papers

Cambridge University Library
   Stanley Baldwin Papers
Annual Report of Schools of New Brunswick 1889
British Columbia, Department of Vital Statistics
Appeal Cases before the House of Lords
Canadian Annual Review, 1929–1930

                    CANADA, NEWSPAPERS

Calgary Albertan
Calgary Herald
Dalhousie [University]Gazette
Edmonton Bulletin
Halifax Herald
London Free Press
Manitoba Free Press
Montreal Daily Star
Montreal Gazette
Montreal La Presse

Ottawa Citizen
Ottawa Evening Citizen
Ottawa Journal
Port Hope Times
Québec L'Evénément
Regina Leader-Post
Regina Star
Toronto Daily Star
Toronto Globe
Toronto Mail and Empire
Toronto Saturday Night
Toronto Star Weekly
Toronto Evening Telegram
[University of Alberta] The Gateway
Vancouver News-Herald
Vancouver Province
Vancouver Sun
Victoria Times
Winnipeg Evening Tribune
Winnipeg Free Press
Winnipeg Tribune

CANADA, PERIODICALS

L'Action nationale canadienne-française
Alberta History
The Canadian
Canadian Banker
Canadian Bar Review
Canadian Historical Association Journal
Canadian Magazine
Historical Journal
Maclean's
Queen's Quarterly

UNITED KINGDOM, NEWSPAPERS AND PERIODICALS

Bristol Times and Mirror
Country Life
Daily Express

Daily Mail
The Economist
Evening News
Hull Daily Mail
London Morning Post
Manchester Guardian
New Statesman and Nation
The Observer
The Spectator
Sunday Times
The Times

UNITED STATES, NEWSPAPERS AND PERIODICALS

Boston Advertiser
Good Housekeeping
New York Times
Time

AUSTRALIA, NEWSPAPERS AND PERIODICALS

Adelaide Chronicle
Perth West Australian
Sydney Morning Herald

AUSTRIA, NEWSPAPER

Vienna Neue Freie Presse

.PUBLISHED SOURCES

Acheson, Dean. *Morning and Noon: A Memoir*. New York: Houghton Mifflin 1965.

Aitken, Max, Lord Beaverbrook. *Friends: Sixty Years of Intimate Personal Relations with Richard Bedford Bennett*. London: Heinemann 1959.

Aldred, Robert William. "The Public Career of Major-General Alexander D. McRae." Master's thesis, University of Western Ontario, 1970.

Armstrong, Christopher, and H.V. Nelles. *Southern Exposure: Canadian Promoters in Latin America and the Caribbean, 1896–1930*. Toronto: University of Toronto Press 1988.

Beck, J. Murray. *Pendulum of Power: Canada's Federal Elections*. Scarborough: Prentice Hall Canada 1968.

– *Politics of Nova Scotia*. Vol. 2, *1896–1988*. Tantallon: Four East 1988.

Beck, J. Murray, and Claude Bissell. *The Imperial Canadian: Vincent Massey in Office*. Toronto: University of Toronto Press 1986.

Bissell, Claude. *The Young Vincent Massey*. Toronto: University of Toronto Press 1981.

Black, Conrad. *Duplessis*. Toronto: McClelland & Stewart 1977.

Bliss, Michael. *A Canadian Millionaire: The Life and Business Times of Sir Joseph Flavelle, Bart., 1858–1939*. Toronto: University of Toronto Press 1978.

Borden, Robert. *Letters to Limbo*. Edited by Henry Borden. Toronto: University of Toronto Press 1971.

Bryce, James. *The American Commonwealth*. London: Methuen 1888.

Bryce, Robert B. *Maturing in Hard Times: Canada's Department of Finance through the Great Depression*. Kingston and Montreal: McGill-Queen's University Press 1986.

Chappell, Connery. *Island of Barbed Wire*. London: Robert Hale 1984.

Charlesworth, Hector. *I'm Telling You: Being the Further Candid Chronicles of Hector*. Toronto: Macmillan 1937.

Chisholm, Anne, and Michael Davie. *Beaverbrook: A Life*. London: Hutchison 1992.

Cooper, Diana. *Autobiography*. London 1978.

Crowley, Terry. *Agnes MacPhail and the Politics of Equality*. Toronto: Lorimer 1990.

Dawson, R.M. *Constitutional Issues in Canada, 1900–1931*. Toronto: University of Toronto Press 1933.

Dexter, Grant. "Young Canada Goes to Washington." *Canadian Magazine*, April 1931.

– "The Canadian Political Scene." *Queen's Quarterly*, Autumn 1931.

Dictionary of Canadian Biography. University of Toronto/Université Laval, 1966–2005.

Drummond, Ian H. *Imperial Economic Policy 1917–1939: Studies in Expansion and Protection*. Toronto: University of Toronto Press 1974.

English, John. *Shadow of Heaven: The Life of Lester Pearson*. Vol. 1, *1897–1948*. Toronto: Lester & Orpen Dennys 1989.

Fisher, Robin. *Duff Patullo of British Columbia*. Toronto: University of Toronto Press 1991.

Forsey, Eugene. *The Royal Power of Dissolution of Parliament in the British Commonwealth*. Toronto: Oxford University Press 1943.

– *A Life on the Fringe: The Memoirs of Eugene Forsey*. Toronto: Oxford University Press 1990.

Foster, Franklin Lloyd. "John Edward Brownlee: A Biography." 2 vols. PhD thesis, Queen's University, Kingston.

Fraser, Peter. "Lord Beaverbrook's Fabrications in Politicians and the War, 1914–1916." *Historical Journal* 25, no. 1 (1982).

Fullerton, Douglas H. *Graham Towers and His Times: A Biography*. Toronto: McClelland & Stewart 1986.

Glassford, Larry A. *Reaction and Reform: The Politics of the Conservative Party under R.B. Bennett, 1927–1938*. Toronto: University of Toronto Press 1992.

Gordon, Walter L. *Walter Gordon: A Political Memoir*. Toronto: McClelland & Stewart 1977.

Graham, Roger. *Arthur Meighen: A Biography*. Vol. 2: *And Fortune Fled*. Toronto: Clarke, Irwin 1963.

– *Arthur Meighen: A Biography*. Vol. 3: *No Surrender*. Toronto: Clarke, Irwin 1965.

Granatstein, J.L. *A Man of Influence: Norman A. Robertson and Canadian Statecraft, 1929–1968*. Toronto: Deneau 1981.

Gray, James H. *R.B. Bennett: The Calgary Years*. Toronto: University of Toronto Press 1991.

– *Talk to My Lawyer! Great Stories of Southern Alberta Bar and Bench*. Edmonton: Hurtig 1987.

– *The Winter Years*. Toronto: Macmillan 1966.

Grayson, Linda. "The Formation of the Bank of Canada, 1913–1938." PhD thesis, University of Toronto, 1974.

Grayson, L.M., and Michael Bliss. *The Wretched of Canada: Letters to R.B. Bennett, 1930–1935*. Toronto: University of Toronto Press 1971.

Hilliker, John. *Canada's Department of External Affairs*. Vol. 1: *The Early Years, 1909–1946*. Montreal and Kingston: McGill-Queen's University Press 1990.

Horn, Michiel. *The Dirty Thirties: Canadians in the Great Depression*. Toronto: Copp Clark 1972.

Hutchison, Bruce. *Mr. Prime Minister, 1867–1964*. Toronto: Longmans 1964.

– *The Far Side of the Street*. Toronto: Macmillan 1976.

Inglis, Alex I. *Documents on Canadian External Relations*. Vol. 4, 1916–1930. Ottawa 1971.

Jackson, T., ed. *The Works of the Reverend John Wesley*. London 1829.

Keynes, J.M. *Essays in Persuasion*. London: Macmillan 1931.

King, William Lyon Mackenzie. *Industry and Humanity: A Study in the Principles Underlying Industrial Reconstruction*. Boston and New York: Houghton Mifflin 1918.

Knafla, Louis A. "Richard 'Bonfire' Bennett: The Legal Practice of a Prairie Corporate Lawyer, 1898 to 1913." In *Beyond the Law: Lawyers and Business in Canada, 1830 to 1930*, edited by Carol Wilton, 354. Toronto: University of Toronto Press for the Osgoode Society 1990.

Kottman, Richard N. *Reciprocity and the North Atlantic Triangle, 1932–1938*. Ithaca: Cornell University Press 1968.

La Terreur, Marc. *Les Tribulations des Conservateurs au Québec*. Quebec: Les Presses de l'Université Laval 1973.

Lafitte, F. *The Internment of Aliens*. New York: Penguin 1940.

Leacock, Stephen. *Sunshine Sketches of a Little Town*. Bodley Head 1912.

Liversedge, Ronald. *Recollections of the On to Ottawa Trek*. Edited by Victor Hoar. Toronto: McClelland & Stewart 1973.

Lukasiewicz, Krystyna. "John Craig Brokovski: Calgary Lawyer with Polish Roots." *Alberta History* (Summer 2002): 2–11.

MacEwan, Grant. *Eye Opener Bob*. Edmonton: Institute of Applied Art 1957.

MacKinnon, Frank. *A Buffet of True Stories: Politics, Live Wires and Black Sheep*. Calgary: Detselig Enterprises 1999.

MacLean, Andrew D. *R.B. Bennett: Prime Minister of Canada*. Toronto: Excelsior 1934.

Manion, Robert. *Life Is an Adventure*. Toronto: Ryerson 1936.

Mann, Thomas. *Buddenbrooks*. New York: Vintage 1984.

Marsh, D'Arcy. *The Tragedy of Henry Thornton*. Toronto: Macmillan 1935.

Marshall, Peter. "The Balfour Formula and the Evolution of the Commonwealth." *Round Table* 90, no. 361 (September 2001): 541–53.

McCreery, Christopher, and Arthur Milnes, eds. *The Authentic Voice of Canada*. Montreal and Kingston: McGill-Queen's University Press 2009.

McDowall, Duncan. *Quick to the Frontier: Canada's Royal Bank*. Toronto: McClelland & Stewart 1993.

Meighen, Arthur. *Unrevised and Unrepented*. Toronto: Clarke, Irwin 1949.

Michelin Green Guide to Canada. Michelin: Quebec 1982.

Morris, James. *Farewell the Trumpets*. London: Faber and Faber 1978

Neatby, Blair. *William Lyon Mackenzie King*. Vol. 2, *The Lonely Heights, 1924–1932*. Toronto 1963: University of Toronto Press.

– *William Lyon Mackenzie King*. Vol. 3, *The Prism of Unity, 1932–1939*. Toronto: University of Toronto Press 1976.

Newby, Eric. *The Last Grain Race*. London: Secker and Warburg 1956.

O'Leary, Grattan. "Who'll Succeed Bennett?" *Maclean's*, 1 May 1938.

Oliver, Peter *G. Howard Ferguson, Ontario Tory*. Toronto: University of Toronto Press 1977.

Outler, A.C., ed. *The Works of John Wesley*. 4 vols. Nashville: Abingdon Press 1985.

Peers, Frank W.. *The Politics of Canadian Broadcasting, 1920–1951*. Toronto: University of Toronto Press 1969.

Peacock, Kurt. "The Forgotten Nationalist: R.B. Bennett and the British Empire, 1930–1932." Master's thesis, University of New Brunswick, 1998.

Pitsula, James. "The Mixed Social Economy of Unemployment Relief in Regina during the 1930s." *Canadian Historical Association Journal* 15, no. 1 (2004).

Prang, Margaret. *N.W. Rowell: Ontario Nationalist*. Toronto: University of Toronto Press 1975.

Raddall, Thomas. *The Pied Piper of Dipper Creek and Other Tales*. Toronto: McClelland & Stewart 1943.

Rasporich, A.W., and H.C. Classen. *Frontier Calgary*. Calgary: University of Calgary Press 1975.

Regehr, T.D. *The Beauharnois Scandal: A Story of Canadian Entrepreneirship and Politics*. Toronto: University of Toronto Press 1990.

Rooke, P.T., and R.L. Schnell. *No Bleeding Heart: Charlotte Whitton, A Feminist on the Right*. Vancouver: UBC Press 1987.

Rumilly, Robert. *Maurice Duplessis et son temps*. Montreal: Fides 1973.

Saywell, John T. *The Lawmakers: Judicial Power and the Shaping of Canadian Federalism*. Toronto: University of Toronto Press 2002.

Schlesinger, Arthur M., Jr. *The Age of Roosevelt*. Vol. 1, *The Crisis of the Old Order, 1919–1933*. Boston: Houghton Mifflin 1957.

– *The Age of Roosevelt*. Vol. 2, *The Coming of the New Deal, 1933–1935*. Boston: Houghton Mifflin 1959.

Simpson, Jeffrey. *Spoils of Power: The Politics of Patronage*. Toronto: Collins 1988.

Smith, Donald Warren. "The Maritime Years of R.B. Bennett, 1870–1897." Master's thesis, University of New Brunswick, 1965.

Smith, Philip. *The Treasure-Seekers: The Men Who Built Home Oil*. Toronto: Macmillan 1978.

Stacey, C.P. *Historical Documents of Canada*. Vol. 5, *The Arts of War and Peace, 1914–1945*. Toronto: Macmillan 1972.

– *Canada and the Age of Conflict*. Vol. 2, *1921–1948, The Mackenzie King Era*. Toronto: University of Toronto Press 1981.

Stanley, George F.G. "From New Brunswick to Calgary." In *Frontier Calgary*, edited by A.W. Rasporich and H.C. Classen, 245–6. Calgary: McClelland & Stewart West 1975.

Stevens, G.R. *History of the Canadian National Railways*. New York: Macmillan 1973.

Stevenson, J.A. "Current Events: The Canadian Political Scene." *Queen's Quarterly* (Summer 1931).

Story, Donald Clarke. "Canada's Covenant: The Bennett Government, the League of Nations and Collective Security, 1930–1935." PhD thesis, University of Toronto, 1977.

Struthers, James. *No Fault of Their Own: Unemployment and the Canadian Welfare State, 1914–1941*. Toronto: University of Toronto Press 1983.

Taylor, A.J.P. *Beaverbrook*. New York: Simon & Schuster 1972.

Thomas, Lewis H., ed. *The Making of a Socialist: The Recollections of T.C. Douglas*. Edmonton: University of Alberta Press 1982.

Waiser, Bill. *All Hell Can't Stop Us: The On-to-Ottawa Trek and Regina Riot*. Calgary: Fifth House 2003.

Waite, Cyril. "The Corn is Green." *Canadian Banker* 82: 108–13.

Waite, P.B. *The Man from Halifax: Sir John Thompson, Prime Minister*. Toronto: University of Toronto Press 1985.

– *The Loner: Three Sketches of the Personal Life and Ideas of R.B. Bennett, 1870–1947*. Toronto: University of Toronto Press 1992.

– *The Lives of Dalhousie University*. Vol. 2, *1925–1980: The Old College Transformed*. Montreal and Kingston: McGill-Queen's University Press 1998.

Ward, Norman, ed. *A Party Politician: The Memoirs of Chubby Powers*. Toronto: Macmillan 1966.

Ward, Russell. *The Penguin Book of Australian Ballads*. Hammersmith: Penguin 1964.

Watkins, Ernest. *R.B. Bennett: A Biography*. Toronto: Kingswood House 1963.

Whitaker, Reginald. *The Government Party: Organizing and Financing the Liberal Party of Canada, 1930–1958*. Toronto: University of Toronto Press 1977.

White, W.L. "The Treasury Board in Canada." PhD thesis, University of Michigan, 1966.

Whittier, John Greenleaf. *Complete Poetical Works of John Greenleaf Whittier*. Boston: Houghton Mifflin 1894.

Wilbur, Richard. *H.H. Stevens, 1878–1973*. Toronto: University of Toronto Press 1977.

Wilgress, Dana. *Memoirs*. Toronto: Ryerson 1967.

Williams, David Ricardo. *Mayor Gerry: The Remarkable Career of Gerald Grattan McGeer*. Vancouver and Toronto: Douglas & McIntyre 1986.

Wilton, Carol, ed. *Beyond the Law: Lawyers and Business in Canada, 1830 to 1930*. Osgoode Society: University of Toronto Press 1990.

Ziegler, Philip. *King Edward VIII*. London 1990: HarperCollins.

Index